THE GREAT TRADITION AND ITS LEGACY

AUSTRIAN HISTORY, CULTURE, AND SOCIETY
General Editor: Gary B. Cohen, Center for Austrian Studies,
University of Minnesota

THE GREAT TRADITION AND ITS LEGACY

The Evolution of Dramatic and Musical Theater
in Austria and Central Europe

Edited by

Michael Cherlin, Halina Filipowicz,
and
Richard L. Rudolph

Berghahn Books
NEW YORK • OXFORD

First published in 2003 by
Berghahn Books

www.berghahnbooks.com

First paperback edition published in 2004

© 2003, 2004 Michael Cherlin, Halina Filipowicz, and Richard L. Rudolph

Library of Congress Cataloging-in-Publication Data

The great tradition and its legacy : the evolution of dramatic and musical theater in
 Austria and Central Europe / edited by Michael Cherlin, Halina Filipowicz, and
 Richard L. Rudolph.
  p. cm. – (Austrian history, culture, and society ; v. 4)
  Includes bibliographical references and index.
  ISBN 1-57181-173-7 (cl.:alk.paper) — ISBN 1-57181-503-4 (pbk.:alk.paper)
   1. Theater–Austria–History. 2. Musical theater–Austria–History. 3. Theater–
Europe, Central–History. 4. Musical theater–Europe, Central–History.
I. Cherlin, Michael. II. Filipowicz, Halina. III. Rudolph, Richard L., 1935–
IV. Series.

PN2611 .G65 2003
792'.09436—dc21

2002028185

British Library Cataloguing in Publication Data

A catalogue record for this book is available from
the British Library.

Printed in Canada on acid-free paper

The editors of this volume gratefully acknowledge the publishers' permission to reprint the following articles:

Christine Kiebuzinska, "Elfriede Jelinek's *Nora* Project: or, What Happens When Nora Meets the
Capitalists," *Modern Drama* 41, no. 1 (1998): 134–45. © 1998. *Modern Drama.*

Jeanette R. Malkin, "Pulling the Pants Off History: Politics and Postmodernism in Thomas Bernhard's
Eve of Retirement," *Theatre Journal* 47, no. 1 (1995): 105–19. © 1995. Johns Hopkins University Press.

Ernst Wangermann, "'By and By We Shall Have an Enlightened Populace': Moral Optimism and the
Fine Arts in Late-Eighteenth-Century Austria," *Austrian History Yearbook* 30 (1999): 1–15. © 1999.
Center for Austrian Studies, University of Minnesota.

CONTENTS

ILLUSTRATIONS

Table

CHAPTER 13

Examples

CHAPTER 15

Examples

PREFACE

B oth dramatic and musical theater are part of the centuries-old tradition that has made Austria—especially Vienna—and the old Habsburg lands synonymous with high culture in Central Europe. One can still readily see classical works performed today in Vienna, Prague, Budapest, or Kraków. One can also see avant-garde productions that range far and wide in experimentation and in shocking the theater-going public. In fact, as we all know, many of the works seen as classics today created great trauma in audiences upon their first presentation. This book is in part a celebration of the theatrical history of the region, but more specifically, the authors attempt to analyze the inner workings and dynamics of theater from its inception to the present, and at the same time discuss the ever important interplay between society, audience, and the creators of theatrical works. Much of the creative work done in this region, whether in music, dance, or drama, was the basis for further developments in other parts of the world, and thus is significant in general theatrical history. At the same time, much of the work was part and parcel of the social and cultural dynamics of the old monarchy and the twentieth-century Austrian republics. Although the book offers a historical panorama, it does not presume to be historically comprehensive, but rather is designed to give readers fresh insights into multiple aspects of theater in the region, and to discuss in depth the creative process and inner workings of these theatrical productions.

There are many fascinating phenomena associated with theater, as readers of this volume will soon see, but as a social historian, there is one aspect of theater that I would like to stress, which is the importance of theater in public and civil discourse. This is particularly marked in the monarchy and in Austria. In Russia, and in much of Eastern Europe, under the repressive regimes, it was the poet and writer who became the center of political discourse. There was no avenue for free public discussion, so literary journals became the arena of such discussion, both under the czars and the communists. Similarly in the old monarchy and in Austria, the rigidity of a hierarchical and authoritarian society was one of the reasons that experimentation, breaking the boundaries, and protest against authority were manifested in theatrical productions. And as the classical canon came to be embraced by the political and societal authorities, a counterpoint motif in the theater began to develop, in the form of satire, ridicule, and outright attempts to shock the established views at the most fundamental level. This shock value, from Nestroy and Mozart, through the artist Egon Schiele and the Secession, to the modern playwrights Thomas Bernhard, George Tabori and Elfriede Jelinek, all followed this tradition. This dialectic was often played out between the younger and older members of society. It was loved by those opposed to the social status quo, and hated by those who tried to conform to the respectable norms of society, but above all it made theater one of the central loci of social discourse.

In 1989, during one of my sojourns as a visiting professor in Austria, I was suddenly immersed in the great debate over the new play *Heldenplatz* by Thomas Bernhard, which is discussed further in this volume. Bernhard, as usual, drove arrows into the Austrian public, putting his words of rebuke into the mouths of the characters in a play based on a family of Jewish exiles returning to Vienna. The debate about the production of this play, in the bedrock traditional Burgtheater, went on for many months, long before the play actually opened! What fascinated me was the deep and broad nature of the public discussion. On one occasion I went with friends to the home of a wine peasant on the "Weinstrasse" along the Austrian-Slovenian border. There was discussion of the Bernhard play, and one of the daughters of the peasant family lent me a collection of essays and newspaper articles concerning the play—a rather large volume—that had been published even before the play began. The uproar over this production, along with other similar ones through the years, left me with a great appreciation of the vital role played by theater as a means for citizens to come to grips with social and political problems, as well as with questions of public and individual identity. What all this goes to say is that the reader is cordially invited to share in this discussion of theater itself, and also of theater in its broader social meaning.

For the most part, the essays in this book began as presentations at an international symposium on "The Great Tradition: Dramatic and Musical Theater in Austria and Central Europe," on the occasion of the twentieth anniversary of the Center for Austrian Studies at the University of Minnesota in 1997. The original articles have all been rewritten, and others that throw light on the central aspects of this tradition have been added. The book, therefore, comprises essays by scholars who are international in origins and diverse in their interests, methodologies, and conclusions, thus offering the reader a view of the wide variety of approaches currently being used to study dramatic and musical theater, as well as deeper insight into the nature of the great tradition and its continuing evolution.

We are deeply indebted to the Center for Austrian Studies for its assistance in bringing this work to fruition, as we are to the various colleagues who have commented on the work both during and after the symposium, and we are especially grateful to Seulky McInneshin and Arnold Lelis, our assistant editors.

Richard L. Rudolph
Healdsburg, California

CONTRIBUTORS

Eva Badura-Skoda has been professor of music at the University of Wisconsin-Madison and guest professor at the Mozarteum, Boston University, Queens University, McGill University, and the Universität Göttingen. She has published scholarly books and numerous articles in various languages, mainly about performance practice problems and the Viennese classical period composers. In 1986 she was decorated with the Austrian Honorary Cross Literis et Arbitus.

Evan Baker is a researcher, writer, and lecturer in Los Angeles. His research focuses on the history of opera staging, production, and theater architecture. His most recent publication (as coeditor with James Deaville) was *Wagner in Rehearsal, 1875–1876: The Diaries of Richard Fricke* (1998). He is presently writing a history of opera production for Yale University Press.

Hans-Peter Bayerdörfer is professor at the Institute of Theater Research at the Ludwig-Maximilians-University of Munich. Jewish-German theater and literature relationships in Austria and Germany are primary areas of his research interests.

Michael Cherlin is professor of music theory at the School of Music, University of Minnesota. His research focuses on relations between music and text and on the Second Viennese School. Recent papers include "Memory and Rhetorical Trope in Schoenberg's String Trio," published in the *Journal of the American Musicological Society* (fall 1998), and "Motive and Memory in Schoenberg's First String Quartet," included in a festschrift for David Lewin, *Music of My Future: The Schoenberg Quartets and Trio,* published by Harvard University Press (2001).

Sibylle Dahms is associate professor at the Institute of Musicology of the University of Salzburg, where she is also curator of the significant dance collection, Derra de Moroda Dance Archives. Her research focuses on opera and dance history, particularly from the sixteenth to the nineteenth centuries.

Halina Filipowicz is professor of Slavic literatures at the University of Wisconsin-Madison. Her interdisciplinary research spans the intersection of drama, performance, gender, and cultural mythology, with particular emphasis on taboo topics in Polish and Polish-Jewish cultural studies. Her publications include *A Laboratory of Impure Forms: The Plays of Tadeusz Różewicz* (1991; Polish translation, 2000), several special issues, and numerous book chapters and articles. She is currently working on a monograph entitled *Democracy at the Theatre: Drama, Transgression, and Polish Cultural Mythology, 1786–1989.*

Christine Kiebuzinska is professor in the Department of English at Virginia Tech. She is the author of *Revolutionaries in the Theater: Meyerhold, Brecht, and Witkiewicz* (1988) and *Intertextual Loops in Modern Drama* (2001). She has authored numerous articles and reviews on modern drama, including ones on Elfriede Jelinek and Thomas Bernhard, that have appeared in *Modern Drama, Theatre Journal, Comparative Literature,* and *Modern Language Studies.*

Jeanette R. Malkin is senior lecturer at the Department of Theatre Studies, Hebrew University, Jerusalem. She has published widely on contemporary German and American theater, including works on Heiner Müller, Thomas Bernhard, and Sam Shepard. She is currently coediting a book, *Jews and the Emergence of Modern German Theater,* for the Wisconsin University Press. Her most recent book is *Memory-Theater and Postmodern Drama* (University of Michigan Press, 1999).

Michael Patterson is professor of theater in the Department of Performing Arts at De Montfort University, Leicester, England. He has published several books on German-language theater, including a comprehensive bibliography. His book on British political theater, *Strategies of Political Theatre: Post-War British Playwrights,* was published by Cambridge University Press in 2003, and he is now working on *The Oxford Dictionary of Plays.*

Alfred Pfabigan is professor in the Institute of Philosophy at the University of Vienna. He recently published *Thomas Bernhard—Ein österreichisches Weltexperiment* (1999) and *Die Enttäuschung der Moderne* (2000).

Peter Revers is professor of music history at the University of Music and Dramatic Arts in Graz. His research focuses on eighteenth- to twentieth-century music and the reception of Far Eastern music in Europe around 1900. Recently he published *Das Fremde und das Vertraute: Studien zur musiktheoretischen und musikdramatischen Ostasienrezeption* (The Foreign and the Familiar: Studies on the Reception of Far Eastern Music in Music Theory and Music Drama) (1997), and *Mahlers Lieder* (Mahler's Songs) (2000).

Richard L. Rudolph is professor of history, emeritus, of the University of Minnesota and is the former director of the Center for Austrian Studies at that university. He has written on various aspects of the social and economic history of Central and Eastern Europe.

Harold B. Segel is professor emeritus of Slavic and comparative literature at Columbia University. His more recent books include *The Vienna Coffeehouse Wits, 1890–1938* (1993), *Pinocchio's Progeny: Puppets, Marionettes, Automatons and Robots in Modernist and Avant-garde Drama* (1995), *Stranger in Our Midst: Images of the Jew in Polish Literature* (1996), *Egon Erwin Kisch: The Raging Reporter* (1997), *Body Ascendant: Modernism and the Physical Imperative* (1998), *Political Thought in Renaissance Poland* (2003), and *The Columbia Guide to the Literature of Eastern Europe since 1945* (2003).

Ernst Wangermann is professor emeritus of Austrian history in the Institute of History at the University of Salzburg. His research focuses on the Austrian Enlightenment and on enlightened reform and the impact of the French Revolution in the Habsburg Empire. He has coedited *Genie und Alltag* (1994), which explores the social and intellectual context of Mozart's compositions, and contributed an essay on the eighteenth century to *Das Millennium: Essays zu tausend Jahre Österreich* (1996). Most recently, he has contributed the entries on the Austrian Enlightenment and Joseph II to the new *Encyclopedia of the Enlightenment*.

Carl Weber, professor of directing and dramaturgy in the Drama Department at Stanford University, has been a collaborator of Bertolt Brecht and has directed widely in both Europe and North America. He has published numerous essays, and has edited and translated several volumes of writings by Heiner Müller and the anthology *Drama Contemporary: Germany*. His research focuses on German-language drama and performance. Most recently, he was the editor, commentator, and translator for *A Heiner Müller Reader* (2001).

Gretchen Wheelock is associate professor of musicology at the University of Rochester's Eastman School of Music. She is the author of *Haydn's Ingenious Jesting with Art* (1992) and has published essays on issues of gender in Mozart's opera in *Musicology and Difference* (1993) and *Siren Songs: Representations of Gender and Sexuality in Opera* (2000).

DRAMATIC THEATER

INTRODUCTION

Rethinking Drama and Theater in Austria and Central Europe

Halina Filipowicz

Most people, when they think of the performing arts in Austria, remember the Great Tradition: Mozart, Haydn, Mahler. But what of Johann Nepomuk Nestroy, Karl Goldmark, Elfriede Jelinek? What of Thomas Bernhard's "scandalous" plays, which have delighted some critics and terrified others? Can we now come at the Great Tradition differently? It is to redress the balance in creative, interdisciplinary ways and to explore the remarkably innovative achievement of what is known as the Great Tradition that we offer this volume. It brings together new readings of a rich juxtaposition of major and minor works, the relation of these works to cultural, intellectual, and political history, and the questions they raise for problems of critical theory. Though widely divergent in their thematic preoccupations and methodological approaches, the essays do not attempt, of course, to cover fully this broad and diverse area. The spotlight is on Austria, with excursions into Germany and Poland that extend the scope of inquiry, offering new insights into the culture of two of Austria's Others.

The chapters on drama and theater open up a debate that continues throughout the volume and considers these questions among others: what are the ethical gains and shortcomings of a cultural solidarity through the aesthetic? Does a "fetishization" of the aesthetic merely reinforce the status quo? These questions are not new, but they have gained new resonance in literary and cultural studies since the late 1980s.[1] What emerges most persistently from the debate in this volume is a sense that the situation of the performing arts in Austria and Central Europe does not fit snugly into established theoretical frameworks, precisely because of the vexed political questions that hover over the recent history of this region. Here, the artist's obligation to transmute historical chaos to imaginative order has always seemed to be at once more urgent, more fragile, and more burdensome, even stifling, than elsewhere in Europe. In "Theses on the Philosophy of History," Walter Benjamin encapsulates this conundrum through the image of a Klee drawing, *Angelus Novus*: "His face is turned toward the past. Where we perceive a chain of events, he sees only one single catastrophe which keeps piling wreckage upon wreckage and hurls it in front of his feet. The angel would like to stay, awaken the dead, and make whole what has been smashed. But a storm is blowing from Paradise; it has got caught in his wings with such violence that the angel can no longer close them. This storm irresistibly propels him into the future to which his back is turned, while the pile of debris before him grows skyward. This storm is what we call progress."[2] This powerful passage, however, leaves thoroughly and disturbingly open-ended the question about the identity of "we" and about the relation between what "we" see and what "we" want to see. One way to grapple with this issue is to turn to the representational paradoxes of drama and theater.

The essays on drama and theater, chronologically as well as conceptually, straddle two epochs: the Enlightenment and the "new beginning." By the "new beginning" I mean the artistic reforms, liberties, and audacities that, between the late 1880s and the outbreak of World War I, changed European drama and theater almost beyond recognition. That passionate revisionist project was far from articulating a comprehensive and uniform program. Instead, it included realistic, naturalistic, symbolist, and ritualistic strands. If there was one element that the revisionist project had in common, it was a radical shift away from a theater that had been commodified for consumption by "cultured," middle-class audiences. That shift was predicated on a belief—quite far-ranging in its implications—in the autonomous nature of theater or, more precisely, on a belief in the autonomous nature of the *art* of theater. In other words, the thrust of the reformist vision was to insist that theater is a fully independent art form rather than either entertainment or a vehicle for dramatic literature.

Today, in our era of packaged, distant, "cool" culture, the need for live theater as an art form, indeed for any kind of live (and hence "warm") theater, is ever more problematic. And no wonder. In the technophilia world of total absorption by simulacra, where everything has always already been mediated, reproduced, or represented by technologies, live theater seems passé. And yet, paradoxically (unpostmodernistically?), live performance still manages to hold out an irresistible promise of what is often called, archaically, "theater magic." How does live theater produce so strong a mechanism for "magic" recognition? Can the appeal, indeed the mystery, of live theater be seen as originating in its contradictions and aporias rather than in its unequivocal groundedness in the real?

It seems almost a banality to say that live theater is the most communal of all the arts: it depends on public performance and collective viewing. Much of what we like to call the magic of live theater relies on the give-and-take between an individual perspective and an experience shared with others in the same space. It seems almost another banality to declare that live theater can work its magic outside the instrumental capacity of simulation technologies. On bare ground, without any technological advantages, an actor can create a world that is more intense and real than the world most of us know. The craft of acting is laid bare without the attendant "mysteries" of character, sets, costumes, props, and music. Through the magic of performative transformation, this theater degree zero can be the site of revelation but not necessarily of communication—or at least not of communication in any instrumental or functional sense.

It seems still another banality—yet one that we, as participants in the twentieth century's "rampantly visualist culture," or, more precisely, in the twentieth century's surrender to the monocular imagery of the photograph, cinema, and television, can tend to lose sight of—to point out that live theater is differently visual.[3] In the epistemological sense, of course, theater subscribes to a kind of visual absolutism: it tends to represent as though a thing can be known only if it is seen and seen clearly, at times even as if seeing was constitutive of truth. Theater's visualism, however, always carries a subversive propensity, because, unlike the camera, it offers unmediated and decentered vantage points and thus challenges all unitary ambitions.

At first sight, then, it may seem that in theater everything conspires to resist our withdrawal from involvement. However, the characteristic formation of modern theater depends on a silent audience immobilized before the proscenium frame where all the action is (simulated). Removed from participation, from visibility, we "take in" the show from our seats in a darkened auditorium— a throng of strangers disciplined by and into the illusion of community. Contemplating with detachment, with no move to intervene, we watch. "Interest" is the name of a lack of involvement. This epitomizes modern theater itself. And yet it is hard to underestimate the silent gaze, the voyeuristic immobility of the audience. That is, even the silent and passive audience—whether in a proscenium frame theater or in a theater-in-the-round—is always implicated already as a witness. By sharing space and time with performers, the audience is always imagined as contained within, and complicit with, the stage reality it is viewing, or rather, witnessing. To put this in broader terms, a public act of theatrical performance, which is only too available for forms of collective identification, projection, detachment, and, yes, complicity, can be regarded as a fundamental way of seeing the world, of living it.

But the connections between theater and life are yet more complicated, more paradoxical. In Pirandello's famous metadramatic play, *Six Characters in Search of an Author*, the actors, who, within the illusion of the play, would appear to be the most "real" people on stage, begin to seem pale and superficial as the story unfolds. As June Schlueter has observed: "We soon find that the failure of the Actors to record accurately the experience of the Characters lends a validity to the Characters, upsetting our earlier delegation of them to the world of illusion and of the Actors to the world of reality.... The audience must now adjust its thinking to include the possibility that illusion is more real than reality."[4]

This conclusion about the unsettling and often contradictory connections between theater and life, illusion and reality, performance and identity is further complicated by the fact that theatrical enactments create gendered bodies as live public spectacles, rather than merely as actors and characters. The concreteness of the performer's breathing, moving, and sweating body helps to instill an erotic investment in our national romances. In a live performance, exhibitionism and epiphanic revelation are unevenly mixed. A large part of theater's craft and appeal involves constantly altering the link between the visible appearance and the invisible reality of intimate sensation, the most secretive part of the performer's (and the spectator's) body. But live theater is also the most precarious of all the arts. To a notion of a permanent, even timeless work of art, theater opposes a mode of expression that is always provisional and unpredictable. Performance metaphors are thus hard to resist. All performance exploits the incitement of desire, and the pleasures of a darkened theater auditorium are not unlike a form of retarded climax. Actors talk freely of good and bad houses that affect the quality of particular performances. On some nights, a performance comes off; on others, it has the feeling of a museum display.

In short, it goes almost without saying that the representational paradoxes of live theater compel us to pay closer attention to the relation between what "we" see and what "we" want to see and how this "we" is configured. This has some resonant implications for widespread claims about the authority of drama and theater in Central Europe, where the arts generally and the institution of the national theater in particular were of powerful significance to periods of great national upheaval, development, and transformation. Without denying the claims about the authority of Central European drama and theater, the essays gathered here are attentive to the fact that this authority has always worked in unexpected ways, silencing certain voices and spotlighting others. Thus, it is important to move beyond grand synthesizing modes in order to uncover the enormously interesting and constantly shifting networks of relations between different voices and traditions. There is simply no end to that sort of work.

* * * * *

"The magic of the stage captivates the eyes, the ears, the mind and the heart.... It is certain that people are more impressionable and capable of emotion in the public theater than in any other situation. The mind is totally free, and through the removal of all other sensations, ready to receive any impressions.... Moreover, through the mass of spectators, both the eagerness of expectation and any impressions made are greatly enhanced." This tribute to the seductive, indeed hypnotic power of live performance seems to have come out of the counterculture movement of the 1960s. It sounds like a rebuttal to those critics who dismissed avant-garde theater as an elaborate fraud perpetrated on a naive public by long-haired, left-wing subversives. However, this tribute belongs to a very different era. It was published in 1780, during the heyday of Enlightenment optimism. Its author, Benedict Dominic Anton Cremeri, was among those who challenged the enduring legacy of antitheatrical prejudice. Today, when we take the irresistible appeal of live theater for granted or, alternately, think of theater as little more than a pleasurable pastime, it is easy to forget about the social anxiety that often accompanied early modern theater. Those who looked with disdain and hostility at theater felt that it was threatening to culture because it tells lies and hence undercuts our moral sensibility. This is the context in which Ernst Wangermann, in chapter 1, sets up the Enlightenment's revisionist approach to drama and theater. His essay, "'By and By We Shall Have an Enlightened Populace': Moral Optimism and the Fine Arts in Late-Eighteenth-Century Austria," provides an important historical background to the entire volume and particularly to the essays on drama and theater.

Wangermann locates the origins of a renewed legitimization of drama and theater in the moral philosophy of the Enlightenment, specifically in Shaftesbury's concept of moral aesthetics. To its proponents, such as Cremeri, rational insight was not enough. It had to be supplemented by appeals to our senses and emotions. And although theater had earlier been considered morally suspect, it was now seen as uniquely suited for the job. By making powerful affective appeals, theater, according to Shaftesbury's moral aesthetics, was capable of persuading spectators to change their moral and civic conduct. Again, this idea sounds as if it has come out of the counterculture of the 1960s, when theater was often an ethical response to embattled social and political realities. Then, too, theater sought to involve audiences emotionally in order to rouse them to social responsibility and civic action.

This conclusion may be complicated by giving equal attention to the subversive, indeed transgressive, power of live theater. After all, a theatrical performance, which allows—literally, physically, not only figuratively—for multiple vantage points, undermines all homogenizing, if not totalizing, ambitions that would ensure a reformed society or disciplined polity. To put it differently, a performative enactment, by its very anti-monocularism, can subvert authoritarianism and the one unified perspective engineered from "on high."

First, however, it may be useful to consider how the fundamentally optimistic idea of the power of live theater to bring about social and political change resonated in a Central European country that, by the end of the Enlightenment, had lost its statehood. I have in mind Poland, which by 1795 had been partitioned by Austria, Prussia, and Russia. The concept of moral aesthetics, which Wangermann discusses, was eagerly embraced in Poland under foreign rule (1795–1918). For one thing, it authorized the use of the stage as a civic forum for the inculcation of patriotic morality and social solidarity. The tradition of moral aesthetics continues to nurture the arguments of those critics who fall into the grand-sounding rhetoric about Poland as the heart of Europe and defensively proclaim the moral superiority of Polish culture vis-à-vis the materialistic West. For example, in the special issue of *Theatre Journal* on Eastern Europe since the opening of the Iron Curtain in 1989, Elżbieta Baniewicz silently draws on moral aesthetics when she evokes "the tradition that has shaped the unique character of Polish theatre and the special expectations of Polish theatregoers."[5] She traces this tradition back to the Enlightenment, when the Polish national theater was established in Warsaw:

"Founded in 1765 by the last king of Poland,... the first professional, public, and Polish-language theatre fulfilled an important role from the very beginning. It awakened the collective conscience. It spoke out on social and political issues, encouraging people to fight their invaders—Russia, Prussia, and Austria. This role became especially apt after 1795, when Poland was divided among the three invaders and lost its independence for 128 years. During these difficult decades, theatre was the only institution where Polish was used officially. There is, then, probably no other place in the world where theatre has served to preserve national identity as it has in Poland."[6]

While making these sweeping claims, Baniewicz, like many other critics, confines her discussion to canonical works by talismanic figures of Polish culture. She dismisses the popular repertoire outright as simplistic and banal and therefore unworthy of analysis. To avoid a possible misunderstanding, I want to emphasize that the issue here is not whether critics should be harsh or generous toward popular culture, but how the critical establishment exercises its power to promote a normative, monolithic vision of a cultural tradition. Were the acknowledged masterpieces of Polish drama the only plays that participated in the project of constructing national self-image in Poland under foreign occupation? If we accept that major and minor works share cultural authority in varying degrees, then popular plays could be given their due.

By taking just such plays as a case in point, my own chapter, chapter 2, "Taming a Transgressive National Hero: Tadeusz Kościuszko and Nineteenth-Century Polish Drama," examines how the popular repertoire in Poland under foreign rule contributed to the invention of a particular vision of Poland's past in order to shape civic consciousness and national self-perception. The plays that serve as my artifacts feature Tadeusz Kościuszko (1746–1817), arguably the most Polish of Poland's national heroes, upheld as a model of upright character and patriotic passion. My essay, however, focuses on Kościuszko's transgression of cultural norms, which regulated the Polish discourse of national self-image.

In foregrounding Kościuszko's transgression, my reading of the popular plays about Kościuszko takes stock of some of the blind spots in Poles' construction of their history. My analysis reveals right-wing, propagandistic texts within mainstream Polish drama and questions the dominant assumption that political theater is always left-wing. But this is half the story. Arguing that Kościuszko's transgression could never be completely silenced or evaded, I uncover the plays' double-voicing and examine their "ungrammaticalities"—the ambivalence, the contradictions, and the suppressed alternatives inscribed within a seemingly coherent, essentialist construction of Kościuszko as a performer of immaculate Polishness. In more general terms, then, the topic of my study is the paradoxical, self-contradictory process by which a culture grapples with transgressive difference.

The double-voicing of some of the Kościuszko dramas can be productively juxtaposed with the ventriloquism of Johann Nepomuk Nestroy's plays. Nestroy took a certain illicit pleasure in making the most of the fact that theater is an unsettling game of reality and unreality, an art of illusion practiced to perfection. Carl Weber's chapter, "Nestroy and His Naughty Children: A Plebeian Tradition in the Austrian Theater," deepens our understanding of Nestroy's art and of his legacy, which lives on in the plays of Wolfgang Bauer, Peter Handke, Elfriede Jelinek, Werner Schwab, Marlene Streeruwitz, Peter Turrini, and others. At the same time, the essay can be read as a response to Wangermann's essay in that it highlights Nestroy's work as a crucial corrective to the moral aesthetics of Shaftesbury and his followers.

In presuming the power of live theater, moral aesthetics depended on an unproblematic communication between actors and audiences—an idea that was steeped in cognitive utopianism. As Wangermann has observed, it was believed that "when truth was mediated and conceived as beauty,… people, enraptured and carried away by the beauty, [would] act on this truth and practice virtue." Nestroy put this utopianism into question. While Enlightenment reformers such as Joseph von Sonnenfels sought to clean up popular entertainment and turn it into an effective instrument of moral education, specifically censuring "the smutty double entendres and antics of the traditional *alt-wiener Volkskomödie*" (as Wangermann reminds us in his essay), Nestroy's art as actor and playwright relied precisely (so to speak) on double entendres, slips of tongue, and mispronunciation. He confronted his contemporaries with their imperfections, including their language. As Weber points out, in chapter 3, Nestroy's plays "reveal language as a most unreliable, treacherous, and inconsistent tool of communication.… Nestroy's plots are often triggered or twisted by a misreading of language, while the gesture of characters is delineated by their linguistic idiosyncrasies."

At the most obvious level, Nestroy's plays were a preposterous challenge to bourgeois respectability. In typical Nestroyan ventriloquism, they provocatively enacted the idiom of mainstream culture in order to mock the sham of that culture. But, as Weber argues, the real challenge Nestroy presents to his audiences—then and now—is in his uncomfortable reminders that the transparency of language and therefore an unproblematic communication can never be assumed. In Nestroy's theater, language takes center stage, always calling attention to its own slipperiness and insufficiency. His characters are trapped in an insidious linguistic system where language continues to pull the rug out from beneath them.

Nestroy's plays were making way for a different kind of drama and theater— the drama and theater that are attentive to the unreliability of language and to the epistemological limits of a theatrical enactment as verbal communication. Chapter 4, Harold B. Segel's "Pantomime, Dance, *Sprachskepsis*, and Physical Culture in German and Austrian Modernism," picks up where Weber's essay has left off. What interests Segel are the cultural, social, and political circumstances in which stage action for the first time began in earnest to override speech. Segel contextualizes the popularity of wordless performance, such as dance and pantomime, at the turn of the twentieth century within the modernist cult of physicality and within what may seem to be a misguided, illusory opposition between "fallen," "artificial" verbal language and untainted, "natural" body language. In short, theater (and its audience) had to learn, as it were, to speak differently.

Chapter 5, Michael Patterson's "Populism versus Elitism in Max Reinhardt's Austrian Productions of the 1920s," takes a different approach to the dissatisfaction with the existing theater. He reminds us that a search for a new theater had to do not only with aesthetics, but also with social and political dynamics. Artists sought to restore theater to the social and cultic significance it had enjoyed in ancient Greece and in the Middle Ages, or, to put this in more general terms, they attempted to meet a social need for a new sense of community that would help unite a disintegrating Europe. For example, the particular success of Reinhardt's production of *Jedermann* was to speak at once to multiple audiences, highbrow as well as middlebrow, and to argue to those audiences for a mode of civic identity that includes rather than excludes, that creates rather than denies community.

Patterson's chapter can be read as yet another response to Wangermann's essay in that it raises important questions about what it means to make populist theater. Patterson argues that the line between cultic theater and indoctrination is very thin; hence he cautions against the seductive appeal of populist theater: "A well-intentioned, but nationalistically colored search for a true theater of and for the people to some extent anticipates the blind devotion cultivated by the Nazis." In this context, it is necessary to point out that Segel, in his essay, links the preoccupation, even obsession, with physicality to nationalistic and militaristic ideologies emerging in Central Europe—in Slavic lands as well as in Germany—at the turn of the century. Ultimately, then, Segel's and Patterson's essays concern the possibilities, limits, and dangers of performance inside theater and out. We thus return to the basic questions that resonate with particular force in discussions of performance and performativity in Central European societies suspicious of their manifold Others. What exactly does live theater do? When does it empower audiences to become critical thinkers? When does it numb their sensibilities? Who are the spectators and who are the actors anyway?

* * * * *

With the chapters by Christine Kiebuzinska, Hans-Peter Bayerdörfer, Alfred Pfabigan, and Jeanette R. Malkin, the discussion moves on to explore the work of the writers who are among Austria's most flagrant and relentless disturbers of the national peace: Elfriede Jelinek, George Tabori, and Thomas Bernhard. They have been said to abuse Austrian audiences with their confrontational, scandalous plays. However, the four essays suggest that their struggle with social amnesia and with the hypocrisies, euphemisms, and taboos of postwar culture is long-standing and deep, rather than merely scandalizing.

Kiebuzinska, in chapter 6, "Elfriede Jelinek's *Nora* Project; or, What Happens When Nora Meets the Capitalists," elaborates on Weber's point that Jelinek is one of Nestroy's "naughty children." Her close reading of *Was geschah, nachdem Nora ihren Mann verlassen hatte oder Stützen der Gesellschaften* (What happened after

Nora left her husband and met the pillars of societies) (1979) examines Jelinek's verbal tactics. In setting up an intertextual echo chamber where bits and pieces of contemporary discourse and excerpts from Ibsen's *A Doll's House* and *The Pillars of Society* jostle each other, Jelinek's main focus, argues Kiebuzinska, "is not on the characters who are ... mere self-conscious fictions, but on the nature of discourse as she probes language and its ability to reformulate, reiterate, and translate the already spoken." To put this in broader terms, Jelinek offers a theatrical experience in which multiple temporal codings are conflated in a typical postmodern ploy: the past is freed of its "historicity" and made contemporary.

Ostensibly, then, Jelinek's *Nora* project unmasks the persistence of patriarchal practices that devalue the nonmale Other. However, Jelinek does not stop at interrogating a complicated relationship between victim and victimizer, but reveals hidden tensions and contradictions between middle-class and working-class women, which undermine a naive notion of antipatriarchal sisterhood. It is easy to blame Jelinek for bolstering some of the worst gender stereotypes that pander to social prejudice: aren't women always petty and quarrelsome? As Kiebuzinska suggests, though, Jelinek's play makes clear that glorifying the gender transgression of a middle-class woman such as Nora may serve only to obscure the very complex nature of social structures that mediate gender and power. Thus, reading for gender is necessary but not sufficient. Jelinek's play invites a reading that would take into account the cultural vulnerabilities of both gender and class.

The chapters by Bayerdörfer, Pfabigan, and Malkin turn to the work of Tabori and Bernhard. In discussing their plays on Austria's willing part in Nazism, in the destruction of Austrian Jews, and in the repression of its past, these essays join the current critical debate on Holocaust representability. The Holocaust is not simply an event of the past and not simply history. It has left a legacy that continues to affect our thinking about what art can and cannot do politically and epistemologically. Furthermore, no other event in modern history has confronted artists and audiences with the kind of crisis in representation that the Holocaust has: deeply felt skepticism about, even a distressing loss of faith in, the ability of art to represent the real. As Lawrence L. Langer puts it, "How should art—how *can* art—represent the inexpressibly inhuman suffering of the victims, without doing an injustice to that suffering?"[7] Aesthetics seems to be at odds with historical accuracy. But what is the accurate historical record of the Holocaust? For scholars such as Robert Skloot, claims to referentiality and authenticity ignore the complexities of language and representation. "Does history," asks Skloot, "lie in the details of train schedules and the caloric count of the ghetto diet? Or is it the shape of the Holocaust experience, brimming with atrocity and unexplainable mystery?"[8] Our knowledge and understanding of facts, moreover, depend on their representation—by participants, by witnesses, and ultimately by historians. We do not know facts per se but only facts mediated by representation.[9]

Representing the trauma of the Holocaust on stage is fraught with additional problems that are different from those presented by literature, film, or visual arts, because live theater has an immediacy that the other forms lack.[10] From the point of view of the audience, the temptation is particularly strong to approach theatrical enactments as human documents rather than as a performance filled with artifice. But this is precisely the problem. No other representation of the Holocaust raises the troublesome issue of aestheticized violence more persistently, more poignantly, than the theatrical one. Putting the Holocaust on theatrical display always runs—indeed courts—the risk of transforming violence into a conventionalized object of aesthetic contemplation, horror into voyeuristic pleasure. In broader terms, the theatrical representation of the Holocaust can be seen as opening—in all its ethical ambiguity—the question of the relations between disinterested contemplation, aesthetic pleasure, and complicity.

On the one hand, then, there is something ethically disturbing about representing the Holocaust in live performance: it may seem fraudulent or frivolous to make a spectacle of unspeakable suffering.[11] On the other hand, if the trauma of the Holocaust constitutes something like an ultimate limit, a void in the midst of representation where words fail to do justice to suffering, then theater, which can "show" silence, is uniquely qualified to give "voice" to the experience that, in a very real sense, cannot be put into words. As Heiner Müller has observed, "the basic thing in theatre is silence. Theatre can work without words, but it can not work without silence."[12] Thus, while the corporeality of theater may weigh a Holocaust play down and eventually lock its epistemological potential in the minute details of quotidian reality, there is also the possibility that in performative enactments one can say "in things" what cannot be said in words. Moreover, theater, by its very nature, makes the most of the fact that we tend to imagine the past in terms of the present. In theatrical enactments, everything happens here and now, within a physical and temporal realm we share with actors and characters. While the other art forms allow a stable distance between then and now, and hence a greater possibility for emotional detachment, theater turns the past into a palpable part of the present, of the here and now in which we live.

Bayerdörfer, in chapter 7, "George Tabori's Return to the Danube, 1987–1999" calls our attention to the paradoxes of Tabori's innovation in modern theater, particularly in representing the Holocaust on stage. Tabori is well aware that the lessons drawn from the Holocaust tend to be trivial or banal. He wants to represent a tainted history without deflecting its impact through mawkish sympathy and didactic anachronisms. He refuses to balance the concerns of the present against a "useful" past from which we can learn. Therefore he chooses what I would call tugs-of-war between reality and imagination, fact and fiction, art and nonart, now and then, observer and observed. His objective lies beyond these binaries, but he only gets beyond them by going through them. What he seems to strive for is, above all, a solidarity between self and other through sensual experience, a solidarity that comes about not through moralistic melodrama or sentimental pity but through a recognition that "it is impossible to confront the past without sensing it again in one's skin, nose, tongue, buttocks, legs, and stomach."[13]

Bayerdörfer contextualizes his discussion of Tabori's plays within a comparative framework that includes Bernhard's *Heldenplatz* (1988). Pfabigan, in chapter 8, "Thomas Bernhard's *Heldenplatz:* Artists and Societies beyond the Scandal," offers a close reading of the most provocative of Bernhard's works, one that caused an enormous scandal even before it opened.[14] Located at the center of historic Vienna, the Heldenplatz, or Hero's Square, embodies, as many have noted, much of Austria's history. In March 1938, hundreds of thousands of cheering Austrians gathered at the Heldenplatz to welcome Hitler and applaud his triumphant speech announcing the Anschluß. In Bernhard's play, which premiered at Vienna's famous Burgtheater on the fiftieth anniversary of the Anschluß, the Heldenplatz metonymically stands for Austria itself. Central to Pfabigan's analysis of the play is the process of Othering Austria by the characters; that is, a dysfunctional family decides that they are healthy and that "Austria" is the reason for their anguish. "Austria" is a blank outline onto which they project anxieties that go back many years. In other words, "Austria" becomes the scapegoat for whatever they need to reject in themselves. They use this particular construction of Austria in the same way scapegoats have always been used: to foreclose self-knowledge, to displace blame onto the Other, and thus, ultimately, to feel better about themselves.

It is always important to ask the basic question: what is so scandalous about Bernhard's plays? Pfabigan's reading tends to depoliticize *Heldenplatz* by turning it into a psychological parable that has hit a particularly sensitive nerve in contemporary Austria. His answer frames the author and the work as the source of the scandal. Malkin's answer, in chapter 9, "Pulling the Pants Off History: Politics and Postmodernism in Thomas Bernhard's *Eve of Retirement*," complicates this interpretive possibility by proposing to consider the experience of the passive, voyeuristic spectator: "Bernhard's plays may begin on the stage, but they always end in the audience."

First, however, Malkin unravels the political, social, and cultural contexts that underline the modernist-postmodernist tension operating in *Vor dem Ruhestand* (Eve of retirement) (1979). It is, of course, a cliché of literary studies that Marcel Proust's arabesquelike use of involuntary memory marked a modernist turning point in the aesthetic expectations of Romanticism while also foreshadowing the further step taken by postmodernism.[15] This further step is evident in Bernhard's use of ironic double-voicing or split discourse in order to parody, in Malkin's words, "the shared, official 'memory' of a Nazi past through image and icon, while … forbidding forgetfulness by giving voice to 'hidden' taboos, to 'unspoken' (yet still active) national texts, by confronting the audience with the conflated facts, memories, taboos, and emotions of a still present past." As Malkin shows, then, the postmodernist poetics of memory is far from being a conversation solely among literary texts. Its mimetic referentiality is just as strong, indeed crucial, for the production of meaning in *Eve of Retirement*. In the end, the play seeks to deny us an easy, unequivocally linear reading of a remembered past, to confuse us with versions and duplications, gaps and fragmentations, involuntary associations and—most important—screen memories. To miss this aspect of Bernhard's play is to go after the screen memories, which, like all screen memories, are designed to attract attention and to divert it from the censored traumas they disguise. It is up to us to resist the temptation of the screen and to go after the memories painfully hiding beyond the grave.

The problematic position of history in the postmodernist project is at the heart of any discussion of the phenomenon,[16] and Malkin is attentive to the postmodernist "equal weighing of such seeming contraries as the self-reflexive and the historically grounded, the inward direction of form and the outward direction of politics."[17] To expand the scope of inquiry and to offer a comparative perspective, one could point out numerous parallels between Bernhard and Tadeusz Różewicz, arguably one of the hidden masters of Polish Jewish culture in the latter half of the twentieth century, and specifically between *Heldenplatz* and *Pułapka* (The trap) (1982).[18]

Briefly, the context. For Polish audiences, as for Austrian audiences, the most "loaded" subject is Jews. Poles acted ambiguously during the Holocaust—some saving Jews, others helping Hitler murder them, the majority simply standing by. Poles' complicity in the Holocaust—what Jan Błoński has called "shared responsibility through failure to act"[19]—was, for over fifty years, blurred and obfuscated, ignored, or denied. This suggests a reason why, as Błoński has observed, "there are so few literary works that treat the theme of the attitude of Polish society to the Jewish Holocaust. It is not only because literature is rendered speechless in the face of genocide. The theme is too hot to handle; writers have felt that they come into conflict with their readers' sensibilities."[20]

Both Bernhard and Różewicz share a pitiless intervention into the repressions of the national past. Both have been purposefully insensitive, indeed insulting, to their audiences: Austrians and Poles who are determined not to see themselves as anything other than Hitler's first victims.[21] Like Bernhard, Różewicz depends, in his confrontational plays such as *The Trap*, on calculated theatrical self-reflexivity to break the taboos that haunt his society's perceptions of history. For example, he implicates the applauding audience in the ironic ending of *The Trap* in a way that anticipates the closing scene of *Heldenplatz*. I would fully extend to *The Trap* what Malkin has said of Bernhard's *Eve of Retirement* and *Heldenplatz* and Handke's *Publikumsbeschimpfung* (Insulting the audience) (1966). These plays change "the audience into 'actors,' challenging them to react, to defend themselves, perhaps to reject the power position implicit in the hold of the stage (in the theater or the political arena) over the passive viewer." In short, plays such as *The Trap* and *Heldenplatz* turn our gaze as audience members back on ourselves. These plays, along with many other works discussed in this volume, make us less innocent in our contemplation, our voyeuristic pleasure, our interest.

Notes

1. See especially Wayne Booth, *The Company We Keep: An Ethics of Fiction* (Chicago: University of Chicago Press, 1988); Rey Chow, *Ethics after Idealism: Theory, Culture, Ethnicity, Reading* (Bloomington: Indiana University Press, 1998); J. Hillis Miller, *The Ethics of Reading: Kant, de Man, Eliot, Trollope, James, and Benjamin* (New York: Columbia University Press, 1987); Martha Nussbaum, *Love's Knowledge: Essays on Philosophy and Literature* (New York: Oxford University Press, 1990); and Martha Nussbaum, *Poetic Justice: The Literary Imagination and Public Life* (Boston: Beacon Press, 1995).

2. Walter Benjamin, "Theses on the Philosophy of History," in *Illuminations*, trans. Harry Zohn (New York: Schocken, 1969), 257–58.

3. Walter Ong, *The Presence of the Word: Some Prolegomena for Cultural and Religious History* (New Haven, Conn.: Yale University Press, 1967), 63; see also 10.

4. June Schlueter, *Metafictional Characters in Modern Drama* (New York: Columbia University Press, 1979), 24.

5. Elżbieta Baniewicz, "Theatre's Lean Years in Free Poland," trans. Joanna Dutkiewicz, *Theatre Journal* 48, no. 4 (1996): 466.

6. Ibid.

7. Lawrence L. Langer, *The Holocaust and the Literary Imagination* (New Haven, Conn.: Yale University Press, 1975), 1. This debate is too rich and complex to be fully represented here. For a useful overview of the rapidly growing critical discourse on this topic, see, for example, Sara R. Horowitz, "Introduction: The Idea of Fiction," in *Voicing the Void: Muteness and Memory in Holocaust Fiction* (Albany: State University of New York Press, 1997), 1–32.

8. Robert Skloot, review of *Stages of Annihilation: Theatrical Representations of the Holocaust*, by Edward R. Isser, *Shofar: An Interdisciplinary Journal of Jewish Studies* 17, no. 4 (1999): 141.

9. For this argument in the context of literary representations of the Holocaust, see, for example, James E. Young, *Writing and Rewriting the Holocaust: Narrative and the Consequences of Interpretation* (Bloomington: Indiana University Press, 1990).

10. See Robert Skloot, *The Darkness We Carry: The Drama of the Holocaust* (Madison: University of Wisconsin Press, 1988), xiv, and Robert Skloot, introduction to *The Theatre of the Holocaust: Four Plays*, ed. Skloot (Madison: University of Wisconsin Press, 1982), 16.

11. On this issue, see Vivian M. Patraka, *Spectacular Suffering: Theatre, Fascism, and the Holocaust* (Bloomington: Indiana University Press, 1999).

12. Arthur Holmberg, "A Conversation with Robert Wilson and Heiner Müller," *Modern Drama* 31, no. 3 (1988): 458.

13. George Tabori, *Unterammergau oder Die guten Deutschen* (Frankfurt am Main: Suhrkamp, 1981), 202.

14. The most comprehensive sourcebook documenting the reception of *Heldenplatz* has been compiled by the Burgtheater. See *Heldenplatz: Eine Dokumentation* (Vienna: Burgtheater, 1989). For a discussion in English of the reception of *Heldenplatz*, see Christine Kiebuzinska, "The Scandal Maker: Thomas Bernhard and the Reception of *Heldenplatz*," *Modern Drama* 38, no. 3 (1995): 378–88.

15. For an overview of the idea of the postmodern in literature, see Hans Bertens, *The Idea of the Postmodern: A History* (New York: Routledge, 1995), esp. 4–7. As Bertens points out, confusion about the term "postmodernism" abounds at least in part because over the past three decades it has had different meanings in different artistic fields and at different conceptual levels (3–18).

16. See Linda Hutcheon, *A Poetics of Postmodernism: History, Theory, Fiction* (New York: Routledge, 1988).

17. Joseph Natoli and Linda Hutcheon, "Reading a Postmodern Reader," in *A Postmodern Reader*, ed. Natoli and Hutcheon (Ithaca, N.Y.: Cornell University Press, 1993), xi.

18. For an English translation, see Tadeusz Różewicz, *The Trap*, trans. Adam Czerniawski (Amsterdam: Harwood, 1997).

19. Jan Błoński, "The Poor Poles Look at the Ghetto," in *Four Decades of Polish Essays*, ed. Jan Kott (Evanston, Ill.: Northwestern University Press, 1990), 234.

20. Ibid., 231.

21. This determination is still very strong in Polish society, and it is no doubt responsible for certain blind spots in Poles' construction of their history, as the stormy reception of Jan Tomasz Gross's *Neighbors: The Destruction of the Jewish Community in Jedwabne, Poland (Sąsiedzi: Historia zagłady żydowskiego miasteczka*, 2000; English trans. 2001) has made it clear. The predominant response to his book has been one of defensiveness, sharp polemic, or denunciation rather than an open and thoughtful debate.

Part One

THE ENLIGHTENMENT AND THE "NEW BEGINNING"

Chapter 1

"BY AND BY WE SHALL HAVE AN ENLIGHTENED POPULACE"

Moral Optimism and the Fine Arts in Late-Eighteenth-Century Austria

Ernst Wangermann

I have chosen as my theme that aspect of the Enlightenment mentality which has long seemed to me its most attractive side—its optimism concerning the prospects of the moral and material improvement of humankind. Insofar as this optimism was associated with a particular notion of the role that the fine arts could play in improving human and social relationships, my contribution might be considered a kind of Auftakt or overture to the discussion of musical and dramatic theater in Austria in the following chapters. The theme is a large one, and I shall confine myself to some basic aspects. I shall try to trace the source of the association of moral philosophy with the fine arts, to identify the paths by which the idea of this association reached Austria in the course of the eighteenth century, and finally to highlight some of its practical manifestations in the field of education, the theater, and music.

Much Enlightenment thought has its roots in the upheavals and developments in seventeenth-century England. It is in England that we first find the new ideas about God, the universe, and humankind that gradually achieved ascendancy on the Continent in the course of the eighteenth century. The new ideas were articulated in the main by the natural philosophers (the intellectuals whom we would now refer to as scientists) and by theologians who studied and interpreted their works and discoveries. Together, the English natural philosophers and theologians presented a new conception of nature, a nature governed by laws accessible to the human mind and exemplifying a harmonious order, which could not but dazzle the human imagination and fill all those coming under its spell with awe and admiration for its Creator. The laws of nature and its harmonious order came to be regarded as a kind of second revelation of God, which supplemented and in some ways modified the revelation derived in the past by Christian theologians from Holy Scripture.[1]

The vision of a perfect order of nature was widely popularized in England about the turn of the seventeenth and eighteenth centuries. The chief popularizers were the theologians chosen to deliver the annual lectures that Robert Boyle had endowed with the aim of countering what he believed to be a growing trend toward irreligion and materialism. The Christian gloss that they gave to the new world picture gave rise to the term *physico-theology*—a term actually chosen by one of the Boyle lecturers as the title of his work.[2] This vision quickly spread beyond England to the Continent and transformed people's conception not only of the exalted sphere of Newtonian physics, but of all parts of God's universe, down to the humblest. In the course of preparing the material for this essay, I came across the work of a Protestant minister in Nordhausen entitled *Insecto-Theologia.* The subtitle indicates clearly the line of argument attempted by the author—"a rational attempt to show how the careful observation of the insects, normally little regarded, can lead mankind to a knowledge and adoration of the power, wisdom, goodness, and justice of God."[3]

The order and harmony now perceived in the universe and in the whole of nature—in Newton's firmament, in Robert Boyle's atomic matter, or even among the lowly insects—was of course assumed to extend also to humankind and society. From this assumption, some conclusions could be drawn that changed profoundly people's perception of themselves and of their place and role in this world. The absence of order and harmony actually experienced, for instance through the hardships deriving from social inequality or through the misfortunes resulting from oppression and war, would no longer have to be perceived, as hitherto it largely had been, as the *unavoidable* consequence of the fall of man and hereditary sin. It could now be perceived as the *avoidable* consequence of humankind's insufficient understanding of the rules of conduct deducible from the natural order and the laws underlying it. Hence it was now possible to expect that a fuller understanding of this order and these laws would result in a more satisfactory ordering of human and social relationships. The prospect of such rational improvement made it possible to think of a world in which men and women, so far from accepting suffering as trials imposed on them by the inscrutable will of God to prepare them for eternal life, would, on the contrary, expect to find bliss and happiness (*Glückseligkeit*) as the favored children of a most benevolent father.[4]

This prospect and vision, which it has become fashionable to dismiss wholesale as Enlightened utopianism,[5] provided in the eighteenth century a strong incentive to offer men and women guidance and instruction concerning the attitudes and rules of conduct most conducive to their earthly happiness. The "moralists," as they were sometimes called, saw it as their task to give moral education a wholly new direction. While the preachers of all confessions had hitherto emphasized the paramount need of the avoidance or forgiveness of sin, so that fallen man could inherit eternal life after death, the Enlightened moralists emphasized positive conduct, industrious productive activity promoting the common good, through which men and women could serve God and at the same time find happiness in this world, thus enjoying on earth a foretaste of heavenly bliss.[6]

* * * * *

The link between this moral philosophy and the fine arts is to be found in the thought of the English Neoplatonists, and above all in the writings of Anthony Ashley Cooper, third earl of Shaftesbury. The Neoplatonists made the inclusion of humankind in the harmonious order of nature, which was at odds with the hitherto prevailing notion of man's corruption in consequence of the Fall, credible, and in the course of time even widely convincing, by postulating an innate "moral sense," which, if nurtured and encouraged in men and women, would produce a tendency to conduct conforming to the welfare of the species, that is, to virtuous conduct.[7] The moral philosopher could, of course, contribute to this nurture and encouragement of the moral sense by rational argument supported by empirical verification. According to Shaftesbury and his followers, however (and this is the crucial point), rational understanding alone, the mere insight that moral and virtuous conduct in the long run brings more individual satisfaction and happiness than inconsiderate selfishness, was *insufficient* to motivate people actually to follow the path of virtue. If people were to be motivated to follow the path of virtue, it was necessary to *supplement* rational insight by a corresponding inclination of the sentiment and the emotions; and this inclination could be effected, it was believed, by conveying to people's imagination a sense of the harmonious order of nature in its ravishing beauty. With people's imagination thus stirred, the harmonious order of nature might become for them an irresistible example on which to model their conduct. If people could conceive of themselves as an integral part of the harmonious order of nature, its magic would begin to work on them, and they would find in themselves the strength of will required for virtuous conduct conforming to this order. To use the terms found so often in the contemporary aesthetic literature, only when truth was mediated and conceived as beauty would people, enraptured and carried away by the beauty, act on this truth and practice virtue. In this way, Shaftesbury and his followers arrived at the unity of truth, beauty, and virtue (*das Wahre, Schöne und Gute*), which was to become something of a cliché in the discourse of Enlightenment aesthetics and still strikes a chord in us today.[8]

Shaftesbury's "moral aesthetics," as I shall call the notion of this unity, was a challenge, a challenge above all to the practitioners of the fine arts. It was a challenge to the Muses, to which the Muse of poetry was the first to rise. James Thomson saturated his *Seasons* with Shaftesburyian perspectives, which he clearly spelled out at the start in the preface to the first part to be published, *Winter* (1726): "I know no subject more elevating, more amusing, more ready to awake the poetical enthusiasm, the philosophic reflection and the moral sentiment, than the works of Nature."[9] John Gilbert Cooper, in his preface to the *Power of Harmony*, made the same point using more explicitly Shaftesburyian terms: "This then is the design of the poem, to show that a constant attention to what is perfect and beautiful in nature will by degrees harmonize the soul to a responsive regularity and sympathetic order."[10] Shaftesbury's ideas, and the poetry inspired by them, soon crossed the Channel. The *Seasons* were translated into German by Barthold Heinrich Brockes in Hamburg, while Shaftesbury's first German translator, Johann Joachim Spalding, proclaimed himself carried away by the beauty and perfection of nature and irresistibly tempted to model his conduct on its inspiring example: "With the profoundest pleasure I lose myself in the contemplation of this universal beauty, of which I try to be a part such as will not disfigure it."[11]

A decisive role in disseminating Shaftesbury's moral aesthetics in the German-speaking world was played by Moses Mendelssohn. His first publication, the *Philosophische Gespräche*, was directly modeled on Shaftesbury's *Moralists*. Though Mendelssohn warned artists against the temptation of merely duplicating the role of the preacher and squeezing a sermon into an artistic mold, he gave Shaftesbury's thesis—that motivation to virtuous conduct could not come from mere rational insight into the course of action required by moral obligation, but required also the emotional sensation aroused by the perception of harmony and beauty—its classic formulation in the German language:

> Reason and the power of imagination, mind and heart, must combine to motivate us to action. When rational argument is supported by beauty and grace, the power of imagination is easily prompted to agreement. Reason strives after perfection, and pleasant sensation is the temptation of the imagination. This is the basis of the relevance of the fine arts to moral philosophy. Rational arguments convince our reason of the excellence of virtue; the fine arts secure the concurrence of our power of imagination. The former prompt us to pay virtue our respect, the latter make it attractive. The former show us the (virtuous) path to happiness, and the latter line it with flowers.[12]

The work that contains this remarkable passage was an essay that won the prize of the Berlin Royal Academy in 1763 on the strength of the casting vote of the chairman of the philosophical class, Johann Georg Sulzer.[13] At that time Sulzer, a native of Switzerland, was already working on his fundamental work on aesthetics, the *Allgemeine Theorie der schönen Künste*. In the keynote entry "Schöne Künste," first published in 1771, we find the following passage: "The artist will make men do all that is necessary for their happiness with a gentle and amiable compulsion. We must therefore regard the fine arts as the necessary assistants of the wisdom that is concerned with the welfare of mankind. Wisdom knows everything about what men ought to be. It shows them the path to perfection. But it cannot give them the strength to take that often arduous path. The fine arts make it smooth and line it with flowers, which, by their delightful scent, irresistibly entice the wanderer to continue on his way."[14]

A comparison of these two passages leaves no doubt that Sulzer derived his fundamental aesthetic position from Mendelssohn's essay. My main concern, however, is not with the question of originality. I am concerned, rather, with the practical conclusions widely drawn from this position by contemporaries, after Mendelssohn and Sulzer had succeeded in popularizing the position by their remarkable formulation of it. These conclusions may be briefly summarized as follows.

First, given the relevance of the fine arts to the welfare of society and the happiness of the individual, governments were urged to vigorously promote the fine arts and accord artists a status commensurate with the importance of their function. In the 1760s and 1770s, the years in which the works from which I have quoted were published, writers in Britain, France, and the Habsburg Empire urged legislators to take appropriate action, invoking examples from ancient Greece and republican Rome, where, it was argued, the importance of the arts in furthering morality, public spirit, and patriotism had been appreciated.[15]

Second, writers on aesthetics accorded priority to music combined with poetry, because, with regard to the moral potential of the fine arts, they considered this to be the art form most suited to achieve the required emotional impact. The most important reflection of this order of priorities in musical development was the rise in popularity of the concert oratorio, above all in the form given to it by Handel in the oratorios composed for English texts, in which, significantly, the choruses are much more prominent than in the earlier Italian oratorio. The sources we have on audience reaction do indeed confirm that eighteenth-century audiences were more deeply moved by Handelian choruses than by anything they had heard before.[16] I do not consider it a coincidence that Handel moved in the circles of the English Shaftesburyians and that these were his most consistent supporters.[17] Nor do I consider it a coincidence that, outside Britain, the city in which one could hear Handel's oratorios most frequently performed after his death was Berlin, where Mendelssohn and Sulzer had launched their persuasive version of Shaftesbury's moral aesthetics.

So much for the provenance and general dissemination of moral aesthetics. Let us now turn to its introduction and influence in Austria in the latter half of the eighteenth century.

* * * * *

A number of memoranda were submitted to Maria Theresa in or about the year 1770, urging her to encourage the arts, to commission monuments recording worthy deeds for later generations, and thus to follow the example of antiquity.[18] These proposals were endorsed by the chancellor of state, Prince Wenzel Anton Kaunitz, who reinforced the arguments of the memorialists by pointing out that economic advantages could also be expected from a systematic encouragement of the arts. Maria Theresa was persuaded, and she provided funds for the refoundation of the

Academy of Fine Arts (Akademie der Bildenden Künste) under Kaunitz's protectorship in 1772, for the endowment of two Rome scholarships every year for promising young artistic talents (one of the first Rome scholars was Friedrich Heinrich Füger), and for the embellishment of the park of Schönbrunn Palace with statuary symbolizing not the military power of the Habsburgs, but sober social and republican virtues.[19]

The agitation for governmental support for the "regular" and morally unexceptionable (*gesittete*) German drama and against the smutty double entendres and antics of the traditional *alt-wiener Volkskomödie* has been frequently dealt with in the literature. Robert Kann has written about it perceptively in *A Study in Austrian Intellectual History*.[20] It is associated above all with Joseph von Sonnenfels, to whom the central section of the *Study* is devoted. In his textbook on the science of government, Sonnenfels wrote: "Like a gifted architect, who can place the decorative elements in his building in such a way that they contribute to the building's stability, the legislator must know how to use popular entertainments as an effective means of moral education."[21] Though Sonnenfels wanted to be regarded as the lone pioneer who finally in 1770 secured the decision to ban improvisation, lewdness, and antics from the Viennese stage, it is worth recalling other writers who fought in the same cause, as Hilde Haider-Pregler has done.[22] I should here like to recall one of these others not mentioned by her, one who exemplifies very well the heady optimism that the notions of moral aesthetics seemed to stimulate and from whose writings the words quoted in the title of this lecture are taken—Benedict Dominic Anton Cremeri. He began his career as a strolling player and had read some of Mendelssohn's and Sulzer's aesthetic works. At the time of publishing his pamphlet on the theater in 1780, he held a modest post in the provincial administration of Upper Austria. Joseph II's theatrical reforms of the 1770s had aroused his enthusiasm and stimulated his optimism. In this mood he was convinced that the dramatic theater was uniquely suited to stir the emotions and open the way to moral improvement: "The magic of the stage captivates the eyes, the ears, the mind and the heart…. It is certain that people are more impressionable and capable of emotion in the public theater than in any other situation. The mind is totally free, and through the removal of all other sensations, ready to receive any impressions,… is eagerly waiting for them, looking forward to them. Moreover, through the mass of spectators, both the eagerness of expectation and any impressions made are greatly enhanced."[23]

Though proclaiming himself proud to be a subject of Joseph II, Cremeri ventured to submit proposals for further theatrical reforms, notably for improvements in the education and status of actors. If the extent of governmental support for the theater and respect for its practitioners that he proposed were to become reality, he confidently predicted that "by and by we should be able to boast of having an enlightened populace" (*durch dieß werden wir uns nach und nach auch eines aufgeklärten Pöbels rühmen können*).[24]

An important convert to Shaftesburyian moral aesthetics as formulated by Moses Mendelssohn and Johann Georg Sulzer was Gottfried van Swieten. As imperial ambassador to the court of Frederick II from 1770 to 1777, he had become acquainted with Sulzer, though he had apparently avoided Mendelssohn.[25] He had frequented the amateur concerts organized by Princess Amalia and her circle, where regular performances of Handel's choruses and oratorios could be heard. He returned to Vienna in 1777 with a passion for Handel and copies of some of his oratorio scores. Soon the first performances of Handelian choruses and oratorios took place in Vienna, at van Swieten's instigation, it is reasonable to suppose. To provide a regular financial basis for oratorio performances, van Swieten recruited the wealthy and music-loving nobility in Vienna to the Gesellschaft der assoziirten Cavaliere.[26] In the 1780s, this society commissioned Mozart to adapt the Handel oratorios selected for performance to suit Viennese taste and conditions, and it was later to commission from Haydn his "Handelian" oratorios, *The Creation* and *The Seasons.*

In 1781 Joseph II appointed van Swieten to the presidency of the Commission on Education and Censorship. In this capacity he did his utmost to promote the moral aesthetics he had come across in Berlin and to apply it in practice. He put the works of Shaftesbury and Sulzer on the list of books that every university library had to hold.[27] In 1783 he revised the syllabus for the philosophical studies that all students had to take prior to going on to theology, law, or medicine, making aesthetics and fine arts obligatory subjects for all students. Joseph II then had to be persuaded of the need for a chair in these subjects at all universities— not an easy task.[28] During his ten-year presidency, van Swieten was able to make two appointments to these chairs: in Freiburg he appointed Johann Georg Jacobi, and in Prague, Gottlieb August Meißner. Both were Protestant writers in whose works moral-aesthetic concerns are of fundamental importance. From the letter in which van Swieten outlined to Jacobi what he expected from him, we can see clearly what his concerns were in making these appointments: "If you proceed in parallel with the teacher of philosophy, and get your students to rediscover in classical literature what they have heard from him; if by your presentation of classical literature you can persuade your students of what he has tried to convince them of, and thus to make the truths he has imposed on them attractive to them, then your work will be properly integrated with the rest of their studies."[29] If we recall the passages I have quoted earlier from Mendelssohn and Sulzer, we can see that Jacobi's task was to line the arduous path of virtue pointed out by the philosophy teacher with the delightfully scented flowers of classical literature, in order to entice the students irresistibly to follow this path.

While van Swieten was working on his new philosophy syllabus, he was also collaborating with Otto Heinrich von Gemmingen, author of *Der Deutsche Hausvater*, in publishing a journal, *Der Weltmann*, which addressed itself explicitly to an aristocratic readership. The message this journal carried to its readers was analogous to that which van Swieten was trying to convey to the students: if a young nobleman seriously occupied himself with aesthetics and the fine arts, he would soon come to regret his dissolute ways, return to the virtues of his noble ancestors, improve his estates, and promote the welfare of his subjects instead of ruthlessly exploiting them; in short, he would come to realize that he was a citizen (*Staats-bürger*) before being a member of this or that estate.[30] The journal frequently brought intelligent commentaries on current theatrical productions and urged its readers to visit the theater in order to watch the performance from beginning to end, and not as a part of the day's social round for a man of fashion.

Among the many criticisms of van Swieten's philosophy syllabus that were submitted to Joseph II toward the end of his reign was, as we might expect, that of excessive accumulation of compulsory subjects and overburdening the students with learning material. This was said to result in superficiality and useless speculation.[31] In defending his syllabus against these charges, van Swieten, in his *Präsidialvortrag* of 15 August 1791, invoked the arguments of his mentor Sulzer with great passion and conviction, but at such length that it would be tiring for the reader if I were to quote from his *Vortrag* verbatim.[32] The decision by then lay with Joseph's successor, Leopold II. He not only sided with the critics, but dismissed Gottfried van Swieten from the presidency of the education commission in December 1791. Leopold's reasons for taking this step were largely political, but one immediate result was that fine arts and aesthetics were demoted to optional subjects in the philosophy syllabus. Van Swieten's leading critic among his ministerial colleagues was Karl Anton von Martini. Though an enlightened reformer in legal matters, Martini was a traditionalist in his opinions on moral education: religion and moral philosophy were, in his opinion, more reliable means of encouraging virtue in the students than aesthetics and the arts.[33]

Paradoxically, van Swieten's crusade for moral aesthetics reached its climax *after* his political eclipse. Among the students who had studied philosophy according to van Swieten's syllabus was Heinrich Joseph von Collin. As dramatist and poet, Collin tried to apply the tenets of the moral aesthetics he had learned at the university. His early dramas were derived from moral stories of Gottlieb August Meißner. His first tragedy on the grand scale, *Regulus*, initially performed in 1802, was dedicated to van Swieten. He instructed his publisher to print in every copy the dedication to "the creator of Austrian education, Gottfried van Swieten" (*an den Schöpfer der österreichischen Studien*).[34] Though the reaction of the public was mixed, those who were still holding fast to their Enlightenment perspective recognized the moral-aesthetic aspirations of the young dramatist. Gabriele Baumberg, for instance, welcomed the drama as signaling the renewal of the great dramatic tradition. Collin, she wrote, "elevates his fellow citizens to himself."[35]

At the time of van Swieten's dismissal from the presidency of the education commission, Joseph Haydn was on his first visit to England. He returned for a second visit in 1795. Van Swieten urged him not to miss the annual Handel Commemoration Concert. From Haydn's London notebooks we can see that he was duly impressed by it, and that he was even more impressed by a choral concert given by a massed choir of orphans in Saint Paul's Cathedral. Nothing in his life, Haydn recorded, had ever moved him so deeply.[36] He returned to Vienna with a text for an oratorio that was said to have been intended for Handel. It contained the story of the creation based on passages from Genesis and Milton's *Paradise Lost*. Van Swieten undertook to translate and adapt it for Haydn. His adaptation transformed the text into an undiluted expression of the moral optimism that van Swieten had promoted in his educational reforms and that, since his administration of the schools and universities, was leaving its mark even on the teaching of theology. Joseph Anton Gall, a secular priest whom van Swieten had put in charge of the schools, had written the following in a schoolbook on religion that he entitled *Liebreiche Anstalten und Ordnung Gottes die Menschen gut und glückselig zu machen* (God's loving arrangements and order to make men virtuous and happy):

Let us look at the earth and see how God has made it into a beautiful and well-appointed dwelling; how the sun lights it up and warms it; how the air, the fertile rains, the springs, brooks, and rivers cool and moisten it; how the plants in infinite variety, beauty, and fertility grow out of the earth. These conditions make it possible for countless creatures to live on land, in the water, and in the air. They find food and, as we can see, they enjoy their existence. But we human beings have good reason to take special delight in our existence, since, of all living creatures on earth, we enjoy most of the good things. For this was God's chief purpose with us human beings, to make us his noblest creatures on earth and to make us exceedingly happy. God is our most benevolent father.[37]

If we were looking for a brief summary of van Swieten's text, I do not think we could do better than to take this passage of Joseph Anton Gall. It is not surprising that students who were learning theology based on the conception of God and God's chief purpose, as formulated by Gall, experienced growing difficulties with the doctrine of original sin and the disastrous consequences of the fall of man. Having promoted a line in the teaching of theology that raised doubts about the doctrine of original sin in the minds of several generations of students,[38] van Swieten adapted the oratorio text of *The Creation* for Haydn in such a way that the theme of the Fall and Redemption, which is so fundamental to the creation story in Genesis, was altogether eliminated from it. Haydn was able to enter fully into the spirit of van Swieten's text,[39] which called forth his most intense piety and inspired him to perhaps his greatest music. The music and the poetry combine powerfully to impress on us that with the coming of light the forces of darkness were banished forever; that with the creation of Adam and Eve, God had created the noblest creatures inhabiting the fruitful earth; and that, enraptured by the beauty and marvels of the earth, the couple were well set on the way to a life of exceeding happiness, a foretaste of eternal bliss.[40] To maximize the impression of the work on the audience, the text was distributed free of charge on the occasion of the first public performance.[41]

* * * * *

The vision of unclouded earthly happiness and harmony may seem to us today absurdly utopian. But at the very time of the making of *The Creation*, Rudolf

Zacharias Becker demonstrated its feasibility in his best-selling *Not- und Hilfs-büchlein für Bauersleut*. In this remarkably practical "utopia," he described the evolution of a village from poverty and backwardness to happy, forward-looking prosperity. The transition is achieved by a combination of applying reason, learning from experience, and exercising moral goodwill.[42] It is one of the sad ironies of history that van Swieten's and Haydn's *Creation* and Becker's *Not- und Hilfs-büchlein* appeared at a time of increasingly embittered warfare, the time of the Revolutionary and Napoleonic wars. The astonishing enthusiasm aroused by Haydn's *Creation* throughout Europe, across all frontiers and battle lines, did not prevent the war, briefly suspended in 1802, from breaking out again in 1803. The story is told of an officer in the French army, which occupied Vienna in 1809, calling on the aged composer and singing to him the aria he most treasured—"Mit Würd und Hoheit angetan." A few days later, he died a senseless death in the battle of Aspern.

I do not want to conclude on a note of sad irony. "O Freunde, nicht diese Töne! Sondern laßt uns angenehmere anstimmen, und freudenvollere." (Friends! Not such [martial] sounds! Let us strike up more pleasant and more joyous ones.)[43] An account of the theme of moral optimism and the fine arts in the late eighteenth century cannot be satisfactorily concluded without some reference to Beethoven and Schiller. In the 1780s, Schiller was one of the foremost champions of what I have called in this essay moral aesthetics. In a work of 1784, significantly entitled "The Stage Considered as a Moral Institution," he wrote: "Humanity and toleration are becoming the dominant spirit of our time; their rays have penetrated as far as the courts of law, and further—into the heart of our princes. And how much of this has been the work of our theaters? Was it not our theaters that acquainted human beings with one another, and revealed the secrets of their springs of action?"[44] The young Beethoven was an avid reader of Schiller and frequently quoted from him when asked to write something into the *Stammbuch* of a friend. On one of these occasions, he wrote down a quotation from Schiller's *Don Carlos*:

Die Wahrheit ist vorhanden für den Weisen,
Die Schönheit für ein fühlend Herz. Sie beide
Gehören für einander.
[Truth exists for the philosopher,
beauty for a feeling heart. They belong
to one another.][45]

Another author who has been shown to have profoundly influenced Beethoven was Christian Sturm, with his *Reflections on the Works of God in Nature*. This is one of the many works illustrating the deep and long-lasting influence of Shaftesbury in the German-speaking world, as we can see from the following passage that Beethoven excerpted in one of his notebooks: "One can rightly describe nature as a school of the heart, because it teaches us unmistakably what our duties are toward God, as well as toward ourselves and our fellow human beings."[46]

Clearly, Beethoven identified with, and wanted to work within, the tradition of moral aesthetics. The dedication of his First Symphony to Gottfried van Swieten is further evidence of this identification. Beethoven's setting of six moral poems by Christian Fürchtegott Gellert in 1803 and the slightly later Pastoral Symphony are rooted in this tradition as firmly as Haydn's *Creation* and *The Seasons.*

There is some evidence that Beethoven was planning to set to music Schiller's "Ode an die Freude" (Ode to joy) soon after its first publication in 1786, in the heyday of Enlightenment optimism. The Habsburg censorship, tightened during the 1790s so that all Schiller's writings were banned, must have put an end to this plan. But evidently it was not altogether forgotten. That Beethoven returned to Schiller's ode and its optimistic vision after the poet himself had abandoned it, after the personal despair of his deafness, after the *Battle* Symphony of 1813, after all that provoked the mystical and Romantic reaction in so many of his contemporaries—that deserves our attention! In the *Choral* Symphony, Beethoven reaffirmed his faith in God as a most benevolent father, renewed—I quote Maynard Solomon—"the search for the Elysium,... for fraternal and familial harmony,... [and] for a just and enlightened social order," and created "the most universal paradigm of fraternity in world culture."[47] He restated the theme of enlightened moral optimism in a form adequate to the nineteenth century. I conclude with the expression of the hope that the disasters and disappointments we have gone through since then will not preclude the theme from being restated adequately and persuasively for our own time.

Notes

1. For a fuller development of these points, see chapter 5 of Margaret C. Jacob, *The Newtonians and the English Revolution, 1689–1720* (Ithaca, N.Y.: Cornell University Press, 1976).
2. William Derham, *Physico-Theology; or, A Demonstration of the Being and Attributes of God from the Works of Creation* (London, 1713).
3. The title page of this work is worth citing in full in the original German: "Friedrich Christian Lessers, In der Kayserl. Freyen Reichsstadt Nordhausen an der Kirche am Frauenberge *Pastoris,* und des Waysenhauses *Administratoris,* wie auch der Kayserl. *Leop. Carol. Acad. Nat. Curiosor.* Mitgliedes, *Insecto-Theologia, Oder: Vernunft- und Schriftmäsiger Versuch, wie ein Mensch durch aufmerksame Betrachtung derer sonst wenig geachteten Insecten zu lebendiger Erkenntnis und Bewunderung der Allmacht, Weisheit, der Güte und Gerechtigkeit des grosen Gottes gelangen könne.* Dritte vermehrte Auflage. Leipzig, in der Großischen Handlung, 1758."
4. For the "Puritan" revolutionary roots of the orientation toward happiness in this world, see Christopher Hill, *Some Intellectual Consequences of the English Revolution* (Madison: University of Wisconsin Press, 1980), 88.
5. See Rolf Grimminger's subheading "Die Utopie der vernünftigen Praxis" in his otherwise good introduction to *Hansers Sozialgeschichte der deutschen Literatur,* 2nd ed., vol. 3, ed. Rolf Grimminger (Munich: Hanser, 1980), 16.

6. Roy Porter summarizes this position well, though he stresses self-interest rather too much, in "The Enlightenment in England," in *The Enlightenment in National Context*, ed. Roy Porter and Mikulás Teich (Cambridge: Cambridge University Press, 1981), 8–11.

7. The literature on the third earl of Shaftesbury is growing rapidly. For the notion of a moral sense inherent in human nature in conformity with universal harmony, see Basil Willey, *The English Moralists* (London: Chatto and Windus, 1964), 223ff., and John K. Sheriff, *The Good-Natured Man: The Evolution of a Moral Ideal, 1660–1800* (University, Ala.: University of Alabama Press, 1982), 6–10.

8. Anthony Ashley Cooper, third earl of Shaftesbury, *The Moralists*, in *Shaftesbury: Standard Edition, Complete Works, Selected Letters, and Posthumous Writings*, ed. Wolfram Benda et al., vol. 2, pt. 1 (Stuttgart-Bad Canstatt: Frommann-Holzboog, 1987). In *The Moralists* Shaftesbury himself tried, through the words of Theocles, to mediate truth as beauty. This literary form, in which the beauty of nature and the harmony of the universe are invoked to induce a moral response, was often imitated and is known as a "rhapsody."

9. James Thomson, *Poetical Works*, ed. J. Logie Robertson (London: Oxford University Press, 1908), 240–41.

10. John Gilbert Cooper, "The Power of Harmony: The Design," in *The Works of the English Poets*, vol. 15, ed. A. Chalmers (London, 1810), 519.

11. Johann Joachim Spalding, *Die Bestimmung des Menschen*, rev. ed. (Leipzig, 1768), 40.

12. Moses Mendelssohn, "Abhandlung über die Evidenz in metaphysischen Wissenschaften," in *Gesammelte Schriften—Jubiläumsausgabe*, ed. Alexander Altmann, with the collaboration of H. Bar-Dayan, E. Engel, S. Lauer, and L. Strauss, vol. 2 (Stuttgart-Bad Canstatt: Frommann-Holzboog, 1972), 326–27.

13. Alexander Altmann, *Moses Mendelssohn: A Biographical Study* (London: Routledge and Kegan Paul, 1973), 116.

14. Johann Georg Sulzer, *Allgemeine Theorie der schönen Künste*, 2nd ed., pt. 3 (Leipzig, 1792–94), 77–78. All translations are those of the author unless otherwise stated.

15. This "campaign" has, so far as I know, not been the subject of systematic study on a comparative basis. For the Habsburg Empire, see the memoranda submitted to Maria Theresa on this question in *Österreichisches Staatsarchiv, Abt. Allgemeines Verwaltungsarchiv, Studienhofkommission* (bis 1791), Fasz. 61; hereafter cited as Studienhofkommission (bis 1791*).

16. A notable example is the reaction of the poet Johann Heinrich Voss to the Hamburg performance of Handel's *Messiah* in Klopstock's German translation: Johann Heinrich Voss to Ernestine Boie, Jan. 5, 1776, in *Briefe von J. H. Voss nebst erläuternden Beilagen*, vol. 1, ed. Alexander Voss (Halberstadt, 1829), 295ff.

17. For a fuller development of this point, see Ernst Wangermann, "Revolution in Music—Music in Revolution," in *Revolution in History*, ed. Roy Porter and Mikulás Teich (Cambridge: Cambridge University Press, 1986), 230ff.

18. See note 15 above.

19. Ernst Wangermann, "Maria Theresa: A Reforming Monarchy," in *The Courts of Europe: Politics, Patronage, and Royalty, 1400–1800*, ed. Arthur G. Dickens (London: Thames and Hudson, 1977), 288, 293, 302–3.

20. Robert Kann, *A Study in Austrian Intellectual History: Late Baroque to Romanticism* (London: Thames and Hudson, 1960), 208–24.

21. Quoted by Hilde Haider-Pregler, "Entwicklungen im Wiener Theater zur Zeit Maria Theresias," in *Österreich im Europa der Aufklärung: Internationals Symposion in Wien 20.–23. Oktober 1980*, vol. 2, ed. Richard Plaschka et al. (Vienna: Verlag der österreichischen Akademie der Wissenschaften, 1985), 702.

22. Hilde Haider-Pregler, *Des sittlichen Bürgers Abendschule* (Vienna, 1980), 329–47.

23. Benedict Dominic Anton Cremeri, *Eine Bille an Joseph II: Aus der Herzkammer eines ehrlichen Mannes* (Frankfurt and Leipzig, 1780), quoted here from the recent reprint in *Maske und Kothurn* 37 (1991): 109–31, here 118.

24 Ibid., 131.

25. See Moses Mendelssohn to Herz Homberg, Berlin, 1 July 1782, in *Gesammelte Schriften—Jubiläumsausgabe*, vol. 13 (Stuttgart-Bad Canstatt, 1977), 67. Mendelssohn asserts in this letter that van Swieten studiously avoided meeting him and his fellow Jews during his stay in Berlin. I find this paradoxical, and can only assume that he did this for the sake of his official task of keeping on good terms with Frederick II, whose antipathy to Mendelssohn and the Jews was notorious.

26. Andreas Holschneider, "Die Judas-Macchabäus-Bearbeitung der österreichischen National-bibliothek," in *Mozart-Jahrbuch*, 1960/61, 180.

27. Studienhofkommission (bis 1791) (see note 15 above), Fasz. 14, Konv. Bibliotheken, 118 ex 1785.

28. Ernst Wangermann, *Aufklärung und staatsbürgerliche Erziehung. Gottfried van Swieten als Reformator des österreichischen Unterrichtswesens 1781–1791* (Vienna: Verlag für Geschichte u. Politik, 1978), 68–72.

29. Gottfried van Swieten to Johann Georg Jacobi, Vienna, 17 August 1785, Österreichische Nationalbibliothek, Handschriftensammlung, Cod. 9717, fol. 538.

30. See the relevant quotations from *Der Weltmann* in Ernst Wangermann, "Gesellschaftliche und moralische Anliegen der österreichischen Aufklärung," in *Europa im Zeitalter Mozarts*, Schriftenreihe der österreichischen Gesellschaft zur Erforschung des 18. Jahrhunderts 5, ed. Moritz Csáky and Walter Pass (Vienna: Böhlau, 1995), 266–67.

31. Wangermann, *Aufklärung und staatsbürgerliche Erziehung*, 95–99.

32. I have quoted the most important passages in ibid., 105ff.

33. See his observations on van Swietens *Vortrag* of 15 August 1791, in Studienhofkommission (bis 1791), Fasz. 25, Konv. Prag *in genere*, 143 ex 1791: "… am wenigsten aber möchte ich mir schmeicheln, durch Ästhetik die Menschen zur Erfüllung ihrer Pflicht geneigter zu machen. Ich dächte hierzu wären Religion und Sittenlehre weit zuverlässigere Mittel."

34. Collin to Unger, 17 March 1802, in *Heinrich Joseph von Collin und sein Kreis: Briefe und Aktenstücke*, ed. Max Lederer, Archiv für Österreichische Geschichte 109/1 (Vienna, 1921), 36.

35. Gabriele von Baumberg to unknown recipient, 26 November 1802, in ibid., 125.

36. Karl Geiringer, in collaboration with Irene Geiringer, *Haydn: A Creative Life in Music*, 3rd ed., rev. and enl. (Berkeley and Los Angeles: University of California Press, 1982), 114.

37. Joseph Anton Gall, *Liebreiche Anstalten …* (Vienna, 1787), 18–19.

38. In Wangermann, *Aufklärung und staatsbürgerliche Erziehung*, 89, 94–95, I refer to some evidence of these doubts based on a number of investigations of theology students suspected of unorthodoxy in the late 1780s, in the course of which these students repeatedly acknowledged having these doubts.

39. See Joseph Haydn to Karl Ockl, Eisenstadt, 24 July 1801, in *Joseph Haydn: Gesammelte Briefe und Aufzeichnungen*, ed. Denes Bartha (Kassel: Bärenreiter, 1965), 373–74.

40. The best analysis of van Swietens text is Martin Stern, "Haydns 'Schöpfung.' Geist und Herkunft des van Swietenschen Librettos," in *Haydn-Studien* (Cologne) 1, no. 3 (1966): 121–98, here 176ff.; and Herbert Zeman, "Das Textbuch Gottfried van Swietens zu Joseph Haydns 'Die Schöpfung,'" in *Die Österreichische Literatur: Ihr Profil an der Wende vom 18. Zum 19. Jahrhundert (1750–1830)*, ed. Herbert Zeman (Graz: Akademische Verlagsanstalt, 1979), 404–25.

41. Zeman, *Die Österreichische Literatur*, 404, with reference to the account in Joseph Richter's *Eipeldauerbriefe*.

42. Rudolf Zacharias Becker, *Noth- und Hilfsbüchlein für Bauersleute, oder lehrreiche Freude- und Trauergeschichten* (Gotha, 1788). See Wolfgang Ruppert, "Volksaufklärung im späten 18. Jahrhundert," in *Hansers Sozialgeschichte* (see note 5), 344ff.

43. These are the words written by Beethoven himself to serve as a preface to Schiller's *Ode to Joy* in his setting of the ode in the last movement of the Choral Symphony.

44. Quoted from *Schillers Werke: Bibliothek Deutscher Klassiker*, vol. 1 (Berlin and Weimar: Aufbau Verlag, 1974), 244.

45. Maynard Solomon, "Beethoven and Schiller," in *Beethoven Essays* (Cambridge, Mass.: Harvard University Press, 1988), 207.

46. Quoted in Anton Schindler, *Biographie von Ludwig van Beethoven*, vol. 1 (Münster, 1860), 152. On Sturm's influence on Beethoven's religious ideas and the latter's conformity to the main tenets of Reform Catholicism, see Arnold Schmitz, "Beethovens Religiosität," in *Bericht über den I. musikwissenschaftlichen Kongreß der deutschen Musikgesellschaft in Leipzig* (Leipzig: Breitkopf and Härtel, 1926), 274–79.

47. Solomon, "Beethoven and Schiller," 214–15; Maynard Solomon, "The Ninth Symphony," in *Beethoven Essays*, 30.

Chapter 2

TAMING A TRANSGRESSIVE NATIONAL HERO
Tadeusz Kościuszko and Nineteenth-Century Polish Drama

Halina Filipowicz

My starting point is a deceptively simple query. What happens when transgressors of cultural norms, which camouflage class and gender inequalities, prove themselves worthy of admission to a pantheon of national heroes? The cult of national heroes, of course, has been indispensable in promoting national unity and pride. Instilling the people with properly national characteristics, modeled after national heroes, has been a central preoccupation for educators, artists, and scholars. Transgressive candidates for national heroes make this task harder but not impossible. Hence it is necessary to rephrase the question. How does the admission of transgressors to a patriotic canon work in a national community under foreign occupation? Who or what gets passed on, passed down, passed across? Who or what gets passed over? In short, how does cultural memory work? Examining these questions will help to interpret a culture and what it is most willing and even anxious to sacrifice.

Tadeusz Kościuszko (1746–1817) is not ordinarily seen as a transgressor of cultural norms.[1] In fact, to regard "the incredibly decent Kościuszko" as a transgressor borders on sacrilege.[2] In the Polish contribution to the Herderian tradition of *Volksgeist* and *Nationalcharakter*, he is Polishness embodied. Americans have "American exceptionalism." Germans have "*der deutsche Sonderweg*." Poles and Polish Americans have Kościuszko.[3] Kościuszko, if his biographers are to be believed, was an exceptionally Polish Pole, a man positively overflowing with stock Polish attributes: love of freedom, courage in adversity, passionate, selfless generosity, and especially "that most engaging quality of his nation, what we may term the Polish sweetness."[4] He has been regarded as the leading symbol of the

Polish nation, the bearer of a democratic mandate, the inspiration for domestic change and (through his participation in the American Revolution) international commitment. His enduring presence in Polish and Polish-American cultures is the most persuasive evidence that he has been a particularly stable locus for national self-image and cultural allegiance.

Kościuszko's popularity is not surprising. In Kościuszko, Polish culture has found a world-class hero. The familiar story tells of a man of modest background and unimpressive presence who rose to international stardom. First, he made a name for himself in the American Revolution. Then, in March 1794, he assumed the command of a Polish insurrection against Russian occupation and catalyzed the nation's will to resist. In April, he scored a spectacular victory over the Russian troops at Racławice; during the summer, he led a successful defense of Warsaw against the Prussian siege. When Russians captured Kościuszko in October, the insurrection came to a sudden stop as if it was his charisma that kept it going. Released from a Russian prison after the death of Catherine the Great two years later, he spent the rest of his life as a political exile in Western Europe. Revolutionary France granted him honorary citizenship. Poets such as Byron, Coleridge, and Keats celebrated him as a great hero.

Kościuszko's credentials are impeccable. What, then, constitutes his transgression? As a preface to the Polish National Symbolic, as it relates to imagining Kościuszko, it is helpful to reiterate a historical context.[5] The axis of the Kościuszko story is one of the more tantalizing puzzles of European history: the partitioning of the Polish-Lithuanian Commonwealth by Austria, Prussia, and Russia in the eighteenth century. Polish history, so to speak, was organized with a dramatic sense: first the glory of Poland's dynastic union with Lithuania, then reversal, the destruction of hopes, and the tragic fall, just as the modernizers of the state embarked on an ambitious program of reforms. The final victory of the reformers was the cherished though short-lived Constitution of 3 May 1791. Four years later the Commonwealth was erased from the map of Europe.

The subsequent movement for the liberation and political unification of the state made it necessary to enlist the help of women and peasants. Thus it was a fortuitous coincidence, one might say, that the historical moment that saw the collapse of the Commonwealth produced two national heroes who transgressed the traditional boundaries of class and gender. They were Kościuszko, a gentry-born champion of peasant rights, and Emilia Plater (1806–31), an aristocratic woman turned soldier who distinguished herself in the anti-Russian uprising of 1830. The careers of these threshold-crossing, boundary-violating, shape-shifting figures may be said to symbolize the emergence of a new, democratic Poland.[6]

Kościuszko became a type of thinker unique to the late Enlightenment: a radical *philosophe*, one of a small group of left-wing or left-leaning *Aufklärer* who sought to turn the liberty of reason to libertarian political ends. (In the eighteenth century, the term *philosophe* had a double meaning: a thinker and a social reformer.) A passionate opponent to slavery, he was preoccupied with issues that still resonate politically: individual rights, material and cultural inequalities, social justice. During the insurrection of 1794, he faced a conundrum that R. R. Palmer astutely sums up: "For Kościuszko, the problem was to maintain maximum unity among Poles, to give the mass of the people something to fight for. He believed from the beginning that this meant the abolition of serfdom. But abolition of serfdom would offend many estate-owners, whose courage, military experience, and dedication to independence were also needed. If 'unity' included the lower classes, the upper class would become disunited. If independence could be obtained only by revolution, some would lose interest in independence."[7] In the Połaniec Proclamation of 7 May 1794, Kościuszko did abolish serfdom to the extent that he declared serfs free. He also reduced the number of days that peasants were required to work without pay on landlords' estates, and he exempted from labor service those peasants who enlisted in his army. He organized peasant battalions armed with scythes at the time when peasants were seen as raw, undisciplined, cowardly men, unfit for knightly enterprise. In other words, he sanctioned the incursion of the loathsome Other into the exclusionary ethos of patriotic heroism.[8] His idea of a citizen army, or, in more general terms, his effort to democratize patriotic heroism, was the first step toward the civic empowerment of the Other.

Today we can stand back a bit and ask: can a grant of partial rights to peasants, appeals to their ambivalent patriotism, and generalized expressions of national solidarity stand in for a sense of citizenship and participatory democracy? Kościuszko's once offensive radicalism may now appear a disturbing conservatism. It was not always like this. In the years after the French Revolution, he was rumored to be a dangerous radical, a revolutionary propagandist, indeed a "Jacobin." In the course of his posthumous career, his radical image was softened but not forgotten. As Adam Asnyk pointed out in a satirical poem, "Nowa szkoła historyczna" (A new school of history), in 1890 conservatives saw Kościuszko as a rabble-rouser, "a madman who instigated a revolt of the proletariat."[9]

This nervousness was not simply a matter of response to a national hero who was hard to take. Compounded with that factor, at least for a time, was real fear lest a national insurrection get out of hand and turn into revolutionary terror. Briefly, the context. In 1846, the Polish gentry launched an uprising in Kraków, with an appeal in the name of independence to the Austrian-occupied province of Galicia. The Habsburg government issued a counterappeal to the peasants of the province, urging loyalty to the emperor and resistance to the Polish gentry. Polish peasants preferred to cast their lot with the Habsburg dynasty. Their response was unexpectedly ferocious. Led by Jakub Szela (1787–ca. 1862), they rose against the Polish gentry, killing hundreds of estate owners in the region around Kraków and Tarnów. The massacre darkened the image of the Polish peasant for a long time to come. Those unforgettable scenes showed the appalling ease with which past resentments and current tensions could be tapped, and thus they put into question the fundamental element of the Kościuszko myth: patriotic solidarity across class lines.

Szela has cast a long shadow on the Kościuszko myth—a shadow that we have yet to see fully. He is like a photographic negative, reflecting what is excluded from other, more heroic or exemplary characterizations of Poles. In the years after the trauma of 1846, Kościuszko's mythmakers were in a difficult bind: how to educate and mobilize peasants for the cause of Poland's independence without endorsing the idea of a social revolution? What most authors anxiously guarded against was the issue of the rigid stratification of Polish society. In a society that had long been obsessed from top to bottom with class, the storybook heroism of Kościuszko and his peasant soldiers offered, paradoxically, a convenient alternative to specifying the dynamics of class antagonism that drove the murderous violence of 1846. Social and religious conservatives sought to corral Kościuszko as an ideological soul mate—a champion of national unity who never harbored revolutionary inclinations. Though Kościuszko's religious views were always close to agnosticism, Catholic commentators in particular sought to make him over as a sentimental coreligionist. In short, Kościuszko served as an all-purpose ideological epoxy, fixing disparate and often unpredictable orders of meaning within a seemingly coherent framework of Polishness.

It was only after World War II that the dominant construction of Kościuszko began to lean toward the left. He was now upheld as a protosocialist—a likely recruit to the left-wing movement if not the Communist Party. But the official, Communist-sponsored conception failed to displace the earlier, popular image of "the incredibly decent Kościuszko." He survived, and with very little wear and tear. As soon as the Communist system collapsed in 1989, he was pressed into service again: the restoration of a fully democratic Poland was celebrated with a revival of Władysław Ludwik Anczyc's 1880 blockbuster, *Kościuszko pod Racławicami* (Kościuszko at Racławice).[10] In retrospect, the staging of Anczyc's play was arguably the first sign that what emerged from the nonviolent revolution of 1989 was a highly traditional culture, rooted in conservative ideology and religious fundamentalism.

Kościuszko's grant of partial rights to peasants to secure their participation in the 1794 insurrection is the more familiar aspect of his transgression. But there is more to Kościuszko's transgression than meets the eye. One of the key elements of the narratives of his life is his romance with Ludwika Sosnowska, the daughter of a wealthy and ambitious nobleman. In the eyes of Józef Sosnowski, Kościuszko, a poor and unknown officer, was not a viable suitor. Sosnowski rebuffed Kościuszko's marriage proposal and arranged for Ludwika to marry Prince Józef Lubomirski. According to some vague accounts, Kościuszko and Sosnowska planned to elope. Details are sketchy; hence it is impossible to determine whether they are gossip or fact. More interesting, however, is the reaction of Kościuszko's biographers. They rush in to explain, exonerate, and idealize.[11] This insistence that Kościuszko could never have contemplated a socially forbidden act such as elopement suggests a deeper need than biographical accuracy.

One might speculate that Kościuszko's sexuality complicated the sealing off of private vulnerabilities from public virtues that is so necessary a part of the normal program of heroism and thus left his contradictions unprotected. Clearly, his biographers have found it necessary to allow the national hero only "respectable" sexuality, sublimating his unhappy love and forbidden desire into an inspiration for his patriotic project. At the same time, the emphasis on his enduring love of a woman exorcises a sexual subtext that shadows his image as a national hero who never married: the possibility that he could do without women. Even his most devoted biographers note that he was seen as an "effeminate" figure, soft and emotional. The Sosnowska story at once removes the imputation of Kościuszko's gender bending and reasserts his heterosexuality. He is safely returned to his all-male world where he substitutes the love of country for would-be pleasures of the flesh.

It is a truism that transgressive heroes must be tamed before they can be celebrated. It is fascinating to examine the ways in which Kościuszko has been tossed around by his contemporaries and posterity, adjusted, simplified, corrected, sanitized, popularized, helped out by happy endings, bowdlerized, appropriated by this elite group, reinterpreted by that faction, and fully understood by few. But even if Kościuszko's mythmakers were biased and self-serving, shouldn't they be allowed to take their inevitable (yet often illuminating) wrong turns? This is precisely the point of my study. My essay is not an attempt to reevaluate the Kościuszko myth. Rather, at the center of my chapter is a fascination, or perhaps obsession, on the part of Polish and Polish-American cultures with a transgressive hero, a fascination that has not faded over time. I am interested less in the man underneath the elaborate constructions of cultural mythology than in the constructions themselves, or in the ways Kościuszko has been repeatedly reformulated, often in paradoxical terms, in answer to different ideological needs. A fresh look at these constructions becomes vital to a better understanding not only of what happened long ago but also where we stand today. In more general terms, then, the topic of my study is the ambivalent, self-contradictory process by which a culture shelters naive illusions of acceptance of (transgressive) difference that nevertheless translate into discriminatory or repressive social practices.

* * * * *

While it is certainly true that Kościuszko lives on in the flourishing world of Kościuszko scholarship, it remains equally true that Kościuszko has had an even richer life beyond scholarship. An obvious place to begin exploring popular constructions of Kościuszko would be among plays.[12] The discussion could be expanded, *mutatis mutandis*, to other forms of cultural practice—to the torrent of Kościuszko-inspired poems, songs, drawings, paintings, and pamphlets that often assumed a quality of manic kitsch. Nonetheless, drama offers what the other forms lack. If poetry is the "purest" form of literary art, drama is the most "impure," "contaminated" as it is by its performative aspects. This, one could argue, makes drama and theater uniquely qualified to regulate collective memory. After all, a theater performance can make the past come alive as a palpable part of the present. At the same time, performative enactments create gendered bodies as live public spectacles, thus helping to instill an erotic investment in our patriotic romances. In Poland under foreign rule (1795–1918), the performative dynamics of live theater were often bound up with issues of Polish identification and continuity. Theater, professional as well as amateur, became one of the most important cultural forces at work, simultaneously reflecting, consolidating, and shaping communal loyalties and norms.

It would be exciting to discover a whole set of unfamiliar masterpieces among the Kościuszko plays, but they have so far proved resistant to such classifications. Specifically, nineteenth-century Polish plays about Kościuszko belong to popular culture. From today's perspective, it is embarrassing that several of these works should be vastly more successful than the great masterpieces of Polish canonical authors, which were often regarded as box-office death. To be sure, the popular repertoire requires some stretch of historical imagination for its significance to be grasped. But this repertoire can hardly be dismissed. The omission of popular plays from serious consideration in Polish studies is shortsighted because, whatever we may think of their art and their politics, these plays were an important force in the formation of the Polish National Symbolic. As cases in point, I selected Konstanty Majeranowski's *Pierwsza miłość Kościuszki* (Kościuszko's first love) (1820), Józef Ignacy Kraszewski's *Równy wojewodzie* (On a par with the governor) (1866), and Bogusława Mańkowska's *Tadeusz Kościuszko, czyli cztery chwile życia tego bohatera* (Tadeusz Kościuszko; or, four moments in the life of the hero) (1880).[13] Anczyc's *Kościuszko at Racławice*, the most widely performed Polish play in pre-1918 Polish theater, rounds out this list. I propose to examine several overlapping issues. How did drama and theater in Poland under foreign rule participate in the process of forging Kościuszko into a national myth, which not only survived into this century but rose to an even higher standing because of a collective need for such a figure or, rather, for the self-flattering national image he has come to represent? How did drama and theater exorcise Kościuszko's transgression? Did his transgressive body unbend at least some of the reflexes of national self-fashioning?

The credit for being the first Polish play to feature Kościuszko belongs to Majeranowski's *Kościuszko's First Love*. The premiere of this play in 1820 in Kraków coincided with the first manifestations of Polish Romanticism—Adam Mickiewicz's early poetry. However, *Kościuszko's First Love* seems far removed from the sweeping anti-establishment rhetoric of Mickiewicz's Romantic manifesto, "Oda do młodości" (Ode to youth) (1820). In fact, *Kościuszko's First Love* and its sequel, *Kościuszko nad Sekwaną* (Kościuszko on the Seine) (1821), pay a glowing tribute to Tsar Alexander I, who was instrumental in establishing the Kingdom of Poland as a result of the settlements of the Congress of Vienna in 1815. This tribute in itself is not surprising.[14] It seems odd, though, that Majeranowski needed Kościuszko, who had fought against Russia, to legitimize a paean to a Russian tsar. Did Majeranowski rewrite the story of Kościuszko to appropriate him for the Russophile orientation in Poland?

Kraszewski's *On a Par with the Governor* was the first Kościuszko play since Majeranowski's *Kościuszko on the Seine*. It opened less than two years after the bloody defeat of the insurrection of 1863 against Russia. Together with Mańkowska's *Tadeusz Kościuszko* and Anczyc's *Kościuszko at Racławice*, it belongs to the post-1864 period known as positivism. The cause of a free Poland seemed dead; further resistance appeared futile. At what many consider the most vulnerable moment in nineteenth-century Polish history, positivist thinkers and writers strategically unfurled a banner of grassroots reforms and hard work. They sought to work within the confines of a repressive political system in order to advance economic and social progress and thus to ensure national survival and cultural self-assertion. The responsibility of the arts was to aid this project. How do the Kościuszko plays of Kraszewski, Mańkowska, and Anczyc fit into the utilitarianism governing the arts in post-1864 Poland?

* * * * *

Majeranowski's *Kościuszko's First Love* seems to cancel Kościuszko's transgression, political as well as sexual. The year is 1776. The simple, melodramatic plot follows a romanticized interpretation of Kościuszko's decision to join the American Revolution. Kościuszko, a young officer of minor gentry, is in love with Julia, daughter of the Count.[15] He cannot marry her so he becomes a freedom fighter. So far, so routine. But what of the elopement? Kościuszko is too much a man of honor to contemplate such a transgressive act. It is a treacherous Polish king who bears the blame for misrepresenting Kościuszko as a transgressor of sexual norms. The king concocts an intrigue that convinces the Count that Kościuszko and Julia plan to run off. The enraged Count orders Kościuszko imprisoned for life. The scheme fails, and Kościuszko embarks for America. Just before his departure, he plunges into a prophetic monologue. Kościuszko the prophet is an original touch. He predicts a heroic struggle of the national community to save Poland and acknowledges the patriotic valor of peasant soldiers. He caps his monologue with a puzzling homage to Tsar Alexander I, "the angel of the North," who will restore the Polish state.[16]

The anti-aristocratic thrust of *Kościuszko's First Love* is obvious. The play seizes Kościuszko's personal predicament to expose Poland's internal weakness, which makes the country vulnerable to foreign invasion. Anarchy reigns supreme if it is possible for an aristocrat to imprison a man deemed undesirable as his daughter's suitor. The unlawful attack on Kościuszko mounted by the Count with the king's approval becomes a metonymy of the lawlessness of the Polish ruling class, which has undermined the stability of the state. The play puts on trial the political and social system of the prepartition gentry republic. Is Kościuszko's paean to the good Russian tsar, then, the flip side of the play's criticism of the bad Polish aristocracy? I will return to this issue.

We the audience may well expect to see Kościuszko as an ambitious young officer who wants to make his mark on history. Beginning with the opening scene, however, we *see* a neurotic nebbish. At the same time, we *hear* characters who are convinced that he would be the one to lead Poland to its future glories. The contrast between the public Kościuszko whom the characters envision and the private Kościuszko whom we see is so striking that we may wonder whether we have the same man in mind. To become a maker of history one needs immense self-confidence, assertiveness, perseverance, immodesty, and competitiveness—qualities that this Kościuszko clearly lacks. To make things worse, the play seems to offer no clue as to how this distraught lover will be transformed into a public figure of heroic proportions. What are we to make of the play's jump cuts and double focus?

While Kościuszko lacks agency, Julia's authority is unquestionable. Hers is the stable and assured voice that projects "unfeminine" rationality, strength, and determination. She confesses her love to Kościuszko. She initiates a conversation about their future. She reprimands him for his weaknesses. In other words, Julia is "masculinized," Kościuszko is "feminized."[17] At this point, it is necessary to ask, somewhat naively: what has attracted Julia to Kościuszko? The play draws on the romantic concept of love that is made in heaven and therefore cannot be undone by earthly circumstance. This concept is modified by Julia's conviction that their love is not merely a union of hearts but also, and more importantly, a union made under the auspices of "suffering humanity."[18] She fell in love with Kościuszko when she saw him burst into tears at the sight of an old and homeless serf whom he then saved from destitution. Kościuszko as a Good Samaritan is another original touch in this play. *Kościuszko's First Love*, one might conclude, does not insist that famous historical figures must be more than ordinarily human. Without denying this interpretation, I submit that we might expand our understanding of Majeranowski's play by considering the following argument. There is, curiously, something very wifely about Kościuszko's affective responsiveness. Such excessive feeling may be at fault, but it is nonetheless valorized as a sign of the finest masculinity. The play stakes a claim that the proper heroes are those who can outwoman women, so to speak. That is, they must claim their place in the world through acts of compassion and charity rather than will to power.[19] In recoding the terms of heroism, the play challenges the traditional manly ideal central to the militarist ethos.

It is still a bumpy plot. Kościuszko's American sojourn clearly poses a problem in the play. Poland needs him, yet he abandons it. According to one of the most frequently recycled clichés about Kościuszko, it was the humiliation he suffered in the Sosnowski household that drove him out of Poland. Here, Kościuszko initially insists that it does not become a man of honor to flee. The Count's henchmen are hunting him down to kill him, but he is resolved to wait for his death at their hands. However, Trzembosz, the chief administrator of the Count's estate, revokes his pledge of obedience to the Count and drives out the troops that have arrived to arrest Kościuszko. Trzembosz explains to Kościuszko that he has disobeyed the Count for two interrelated reasons: in the name of "man's sacred rights," that is, human rights, and on behalf of a besieged Poland that only

Kościuszko can save.[20] Kościuszko is shocked and outraged—not by the Count's scheme, but by Trzembosz's refusal to carry it out. Trzembosz has reneged on his obligation to his master, Kościuszko points out. To Kościuszko, civil disobedience cannot be reconciled with the rule of law.

In the key textual moment of the play, Trzembosz proves that it can. He argues that every person has a God-assigned duty to perform. Servants' duty is to obey their masters; masters' duty, to protect those who serve them. When the masters renounce their obligation, the servants must take action to protect their own rights. Is Trzembosz suggesting that Poland is on the brink of a social revolution? Not necessarily. One of the complicating issues in *Kościuszko's First Love* lies in the convergence of Polish patriotism and Russophile enthusiasm. How was it possible for Polish audiences to reconcile the play's pro-Russian, loyalist stance with the cultural memory of Kościuszko, who led an anti-Russian insurrection? We will never know for sure, but Trzembosz's monologue suggests a possible answer. His argument can be read allegorically as a warning to the Russian tsar should he fail to respect the agreement that bound him and his Polish subjects as a result of the Vienna settlements of 1815. Thus, *Kościuszko's First Love* may be said to anticipate the moral economy of plays written and performed during the uprising of 1830. In Stanisław Bratkowski's *Akademik warszawski* (The Warsaw student) (1831), for example, characters lament the proliferation of lawlessness in the Kingdom of Poland. Tsar Alexander I has granted Poles a constitution only to turn it into "a plaything of despotism."[21] Since the tsar has broken his legal contract with the Poles, the characters argue, they are justified to rise against Russia in order to restore the rule of law. *Kościuszko's First Love* turns slyly, wryly subversive. Ultimately, it is Trzembosz who has the last word, while Kościuszko is a hero in training. Kościuszko has compassion, charity, and a gift of prophecy. What he needs, and what he gets, is an introductory lesson in civil disobedience and popular protest. Thus, Majeranowski's seemingly simple play poses questions that are still the stuff of political discourse.[22] What is the role of popular protest in the consolidation of an emerging democracy? Is it a threat or a godsend?

* * * * *

It is difficult to imagine a play that would draw on the cult of Kościuszko while evading the specific circumstances of his role in Polish history. But Kraszewski's *On a Par with the Governor*, which inaugurates the post-1864 series of the Kościuszko plays, does just that. We see Kościuszko suspended between his American career and his Polish stardom. After his return from America in 1784, he is in charge of reforming and strengthening the Polish army. He appears on stage only briefly, to provide a character reference for the aristocratic playboy Bronisław, who has enlisted in the military to make up for his reckless ways. Under Kościuszko's watchful eye, Bronisław is socialized into acceptable morality.

Kraszewski's Kościuszko is a self-made man of democratic convictions who has steadfastly relied only on his talent and hard work to advance his career. This

Kościuszko, then, seems well qualified to challenge the inherited social order in the future. Indeed, his transgressive potential can be found in the textual rifts that suggest harsh criticism of the political and social system of the old Polish republic. For example, Kościuszko still chafes at the thought of the humiliation he has suffered at the hands of his aristocratic superiors. To test his transgressive potential, it is necessary to examine the implications of his costume.

On his uniform of a cavalry officer, Kościuszko wears a medal of the American Cincinatus Society. That is, he is a Cincinatus-like patriot destined to take up arms against foreign invaders but longing for a simple life away from the political limelight. This is the model that Bronisław, the reformed aristocrat, puts into practice. He serves the republic in crisis. By the play's end, he has been wounded in battle, the Polish army has suffered a defeat, and a Russian ambassador in Warsaw assumes control over Poland's future. In the closing lines, Bronisław announces that he will settle with his wife-to-be in "the countryside, where one can find peace and quiet, away from the world and the people."[23] The final scene, which shows Bronisław coming to terms with the world in an atmosphere of contented domesticity, does not fit into the rest of the play very satisfactorily—unless we keep in mind that this is precisely the model that Kościuszko has authorized. To put it differently, the cult of Kościuszko is translated into a cult of domesticity and simple pleasures of rural life.

This rural ideal was central to the ideology of social conservatism that continued to pervade Polish culture in the nineteenth century. For example, in Anczyc's *Kościuszko at Racławice*, the most successful play about Kościuszko, four acts out of five are set in the countryside near Kraków, featuring an intimate, accessible rural nation, a "little" Poland, so to speak. There is also the possibility that the domesticating efforts of Kraszewski's play echo the positivists' depoliticizing admonitions. The idea of an independent Poland seems so uncertain that it cannot be eagerly anticipated or fully imagined; therefore it is necessary to think small.

By the 1880s, as the phenomenal popularity of Henryk Sienkiewicz's historical novels makes clear, a collectively held history became a therapeutic ritual that enabled Poles under foreign rule to escape from current events. It was a history that had been domesticated and petrified; it concealed no mysteries. In 1880, two new plays about Kościuszko became available: Mańkowska's *Tadeusz Kościuszko* and Anczyc's *Kościuszko at Racławice*. How do they approach Kościuszko's story? Do they also celebrate the past as a closed, non-negotiable fragment of Polish culture? And what of Kościuszko's transgression?

Mańkowska's *Tadeusz Kościuszko* reenacts the familiar scene: Ludwika Sosnowska's father rebuffs Kościuszko as her suitor and insists that she marry Prince Lubomirski. As the action unfolds, Ludwika follows—literally—Kościuszko's career. She is a witness to his patriotic oath sworn in Kraków and to his triumph at Racławice. In the epilogue, she visits him in Switzerland, bringing her two sons with her. The play ends on an uplifting note, as Ludwika's sons pay a tribute to

Kościuszko, their spiritual mentor, and pledge to continue his patriotic project. Thus, the play comes full circle: Ludwika's sons draw inspiration from the man whom she has inspired.

Here, as in Majeranowski's *Kościuszko's First Love*, Kościuszko's future greatness shines through the episodes of his early life. Moreover, both plays sexualize Kościuszko's career: his stardom is an imperfect compensation for his unhappy love and forbidden desire. Mańkowska, however, departs in two important ways from the formula codified by Majeranowski's play. First, she reverses the characterizations of Ludwika and Kościuszko. Here, it is Ludwika who is the wilting lover. Granted, Mańkowska gives Ludwika a particular form of female power—sexual allure that generates Kościuszko's potential for greatness. Yet Ludwika's female agency is simultaneously circumscribed. She lacks the strength to oppose her father's will. Kościuszko, on the other hand, resolutely draws together the "feminine" world of emotion and the "masculine" spirit of military and heroic ambition under the banner of patriotic passion. Second, Mańkowska introduces the transgressive trauma of elopement, recoded here as abduction. Kościuszko urges Ludwika to run off with him, but she evades his pleas. Averting her gaze, she admits to her inability to resist both her father and her emotions. Finally, she nearly faints, withdrawing into a state of canceled agency. It is at this moment that Kościuszko takes her away. The abduction is promptly discovered, and Ludwika is returned to her father.

What arguments does Kościuszko use to convince Ludwika to elope with him? Her love, he says, will empower him to lead an insurrection that will liberate Poland. Simply put, the future of Poland depends on Ludwika's willingness to be party to a sexual transgression. Yet matters are not so simple. Kościuszko's intention to marry Ludwika seems to detransgress his attempted transgression of sexual norms. He is a man of probity, after all. Moreover, his attempted transgression appears to have a patriotic sanction: he needs Ludwika's love to carry out his patriotic project. But this is precisely the problem. Kościuszko seeks to reconcile a conflict between private desire and patriotic obligation. That is, he wants to marry both Ludwika and Poland. This indeed is a transgressive act. By the premises of Polish cultural mythology, the project of Poland's liberation requires undivided attention and thus cancels marriage and procreation. Polish patriots are allowed only one legitimate desire: desire for Poland.

The problem is compounded by the fact that Kościuszko's attempted transgression of sexual norms threatens to disrupt the traditional social boundaries and power relationships. He wants to marry outside his social sphere; therefore, he urges Ludwika to defy parental authority. In a striking move, the play minimizes our support for the transgressive Kościuszko by refusing to present Ludwika's father as an unequivocally negative character. Sosnowski, though headstrong and impulsive, is a patriot who has defended Poland against foreign invaders. The handsome prince, who contends for Ludwika's hand, is also spared a negative characterization. We see him moments after he has saved Sosnowski's life during a hunting accident.

With the transgressive Kościuszko thrown out of the Sosnowski house, traditional sexual and gender norms prevail. Ludwika marries the man of her father's choice and becomes an exemplary Polish mother who keeps patriotic tradition alive at home and passes it on to her children. When she hears of an impending insurrection, she follows Kościuszko like a guardian angel. In Kraków, she stands to the side while he swears a patriotic oath. At Racławice, she performs the traditionally sanctioned role of a nurse. She meets the social expectations for gender-appropriate behavior whereby women can exist only at the symbolic peripheries as men's inspirations, helpmates, or rewards.

Yet I cannot leave this interpretation without asking why Mańkowska includes Ludwika in the Kraków and Racławice scenes at all. Why not simply omit her, when to do otherwise was to court danger? After all, the play's premise is that, roughly speaking, intimate relations are important. If I were to take this premise to its logical conclusion, I would have to say that the insurrection of 1794 failed because Ludwika did not dare to transgress the norms of sexual morality.

But there is more to Ludwika's story. For all its support of the dominant presumptions of patriarchal culture, the play never shows Ludwika at her husband's home, tending the flame of domesticity. The married Ludwika is always on the road. To follow Kościuszko to Kraków and Racławice, in other words, she has escaped the bonds of marital possession and family obligation. This is a fascinating reversal of the plot of Kraszewski's play in which the cult of Kościuszko leads Bronisław to choose domestic sanctuary over the public realm. Here, the cult of Kościuszko dedomesticates Ludwika. In authorizing a breach of female duty, it introduces noise into the patriarchal script.

Granted, the play provides a justification for Ludwika's mobility. Ludwika, her maid explains, carries a secret message from General Karol Kniaziewicz to Kościuszko. But this perfunctory justification is no justification. When Ludwika meets Kościuszko in Kraków, she presents him with a laurel twig and a patriotic donation, but not with the letter. Kościuszko's sexual transgression has succeeded after all. Although the elopement has failed, the transgressive intensity of forbidden desire is the key through which Ludwika's subversive potential is unlocked. Unable to resist the pull of Kościuszko's charisma, she has abandoned the domestic realm. Kościuszko the lover has empowered the wavering, wilting Ludwika. Does Kościuszko the leader empower peasants?

* * * * *

Having examined the transgressive process of female empowerment in Mańkowska's *Tadeusz Kościuszko*, I want to turn to the negotiations of class in Mańkowska's play as well as in Anczyc's *Kościuszko at Racławice*.

In contrast to Mańkowska's Tadeusz Kościuszko, Kościuszko in Anczyc's play hovers on the outskirts of the plot, never fully integrated into it. Moreover, there is no Ludwika here. Anczyc is interested solely in Kościuszko's public career. Both plays, however, hinge on a key point of agreement. Taking a therapeutic approach to the wounds of Polish history, Mańkowska and Anczyc cancel the defeat at Maciejowice, which marked the end of the Kościuszko insurrection, and highlight the victory at Racławice. Armed only with scythes, a novice battalion of peasants seized Russian cannons and decided the outcome of the battle. Polish cultural mythology has capitalized on that bold charge with a vengeance, as if to make up for the earlier notion of the cowardly peasant. This mythology has attributed the Racławice victory solely to the daring of the peasant soldiers. Moreover, it has turned a minor battle into one of the most glorious moments of Polish history, a memorable show of national unity in the struggle for an independent Poland. Mańkowska and Anczyc draw on the Racławice myth, but they are well aware that the empowerment of the peasants could be a double-edged sword. Hence the Kościuszko insurrection becomes a consuming project: getting along with it, exorcising it, taming it, or affirming it.

Once again Mańkowska's play inserts some unexpected twists into a well-known story. With the exception of the first act, Kościuszko always wears a peasant coat, while the historical Kościuszko only put on a peasant coat after winning the battle of Racławice. According to a widely accepted interpretation, his cross-class transvestism was a tribute to the heroism of his peasant troops and a celebration of a newly forged link of patriotic solidarity. In Mańkowska's play, however, Kościuszko has dressed across class lines since the Polish-Russian war of 1792. Even in his Swiss exile, he wears a jacket that resembles a Polish peasant coat. Clearly, this Kościuszko seeks a common denominator with the people: he changes his attire so that he can become one with the peasants even before and then after the insurrection of 1794. It is easy to think of him as a sort of rustic hero who has assumed both a peasant dress and peasant identity. But what does his "peasantness" signify?

One could invoke here cultural constructions that ground national identity in space. According to a traditional trope, peasants are closest to the native soil and therefore closest to "the national soul." Thus, the "peasantness" of Mańkowska's Kościuszko signifies his native deep-rootedness, which is silently accepted as being crucial to reading his "immaculate Polishness" properly. However, this very "peasantness"—the construction of Kościuszko as a champion of an essentialist Polishness preserved by the simple folk—would set him dangerously apart from the other classes. How does the play deal with this problem? In the scene of the patriotic oath-taking in Kraków, the peasants have no voice of their own. In pledging their support for Kościuszko, they merely follow a script prepared by upper-class men. The issue of peasants' labor service on landlords' estates is never raised. The play makes it very explicit that these pious, submissive peasants pose no threat to the social order. Seen in this context, Kościuszko's peasant coat gives evidence of his allegiance with the peasants, which then instigates a search for what lies beneath. And, inevitably, what lies beneath is a moral goodness that can be claimed as common property in a nation economically divided.

But why does Kościuszko administer the patriotic oath under King Jan Sobieski's banner? After all, Sobieski has not been associated with the plight of

Polish peasants. In the epilogue, Sobieski is present through the sword with which he won the battle of Vienna in 1683. In 1798, after the capture of Loretto in Italy, Polish troops affiliated with Napoleon's army found Sobieski's sword and presented it to Kościuszko, having declared that only Kościuszko was worthy of it. Mańkowska seizes this historical fact to frame the play's epilogue. On the one hand, Kościuszko presses Sobieski's victorious sword to his chest, his head tilted up to the heavens. On the other hand, Ludwika's sons, who have come to visit Kościuszko, kiss Kościuszko's own swords as if they were holy relics. Thus, the two young men not only pay homage to Kościuszko, but also are initiated symbolically into a patriotic brotherhood. In this configuration of swords, Kościuszko becomes an intermediary between the past and the future. He is an heir to the tradition of Polish military glory, emblematized by Sobieski, as well as a patron saint of a future victory eagerly anticipated by Ludwika's sons. This idea brings the play to a halt for a ponderous, if hopeful, moment. Accordingly, the stage lights create the effect of the rising sun. Message received, we can leave the theater.

But where does this leave the Polish peasants? While the two young aristocrats are empowered by Kościuszko's swords, the peasant soldiers' initiation into the patriotic enterprise took place, we will remember, under Sobieski's banner. But why Sobieski? What are the implications of the connection that the play seeks to establish between Sobieski and the peasants who fought under Kościuszko's command? Sobieski's sword, which Kościuszko hugs in the epilogue, is the weapon that defeated the Turkish army in the battle of Vienna and thus saved Europe from non-Christian rule. Moreover, the sword was Sobieski's votive offering to the Virgin Mary of Loretto. Within this frame of reference, Sobieski is seen primarily as a deliverer of Christendom. Hence, Kościuszko's liberationist project is recoded as a holy war against Russian and German "heretics."[24] By the premises of the play, Kościuszko's peasant troops fought for the "true" faith, Catholicism.[25] Clearly, the play makes extraordinary maneuvers to reconcile the conflicting demands of national independence and social hierarchy. Ultimately, the play legitimizes the peasants' participation in the insurrection by displacing their— and Kościuszko's—potentially transgressive energy onto religious Others, thereby masking social anxieties and antagonisms in Poland under foreign rule.

* * * * *

In contrast to Mańkowska's play, Anczyc's *Kościuszko at Racławice* openly acknowledges Kościuszko's transgression of class boundaries. While it is a truism of Polish studies that Anczyc claims Kościuszko as an advocate of the solidaristic unification of all classes, I will argue that the play is much more ambivalent.[26]

Unlike many other Kościuszko dramas, *Kościuszko at Racławice* has the dramatic pace and rhythm that come only from a belief in the significance of human action. The play begins on 24 March 1794 with Kościuszko's arrival in Kraków and his patriotic oath. From the second act on, the action takes place exclusively in the countryside, building up toward the peasant soldiers' famous charge at

Racławice, the victory over the Russians, and Kościuszko's induction of the peasant Bartosz Głowacki to the ranks of the nobility in recognition of his battlefield heroism.[27] Once the Russian troops are driven out, the traditional, paternalistic social order is restored with the peasants' explicit endorsement and approval. It is tempting to conclude that the peasants in *Kościuszko at Racławice* have performed the act that, in Polish cultural mythology, peasants exist to accomplish: defeating the enemy, then getting out of the way.

But the issue is more complicated, more paradoxical. Early in the play the peasants as well as the noblemen are unmoved by Kościuszko's call to arms. The peasants do not want to be involved in what they perceive as a gentry war. The gentry are skeptical of anti-Russian resistance and hostile to a mobilization of the masses. There is a divide between classes that seems impossible to bridge. Moreover, the play admits the possibility that the insurrection is indeed an act of revolutionary terror. To many of the characters Kościuszko is a dangerous radical sowing division and destabilizing the social order. As the Squire says, "Kościuszko begins his insurrection by inciting peasants against their masters."[28] In a bold rhetorical move, Anczyc does not take for granted an audience of like-minded spectators who agree about what the bad things in Poland are—foreign invasion, absence of widespread patriotic commitment—and who even agree about why they are bad. Instead of silencing critical voices, instead of glossing over dissent, his play confronts conflicting interests and disagreement head-on, even though it is designed for a broad audience. This is arguably the most striking aspect of Anczyc's play, one that has gone unnoticed in critical studies.

For the first time in a Kościuszko play, moreover, peasants are allowed to speak their own text. What they say goes against the solidaristic code of the Kościuszko myth: they are unwilling to join the uprising because they do not care about the gentry's patriotic project. At this point, the play bravely introduces a new economy of the patriotic gift. Polish patriotic drama has traditionally enshrined sacrifice for homeland, be it blood or domestic happiness. Here, the focus is on the opposite process, that is, the economy of the gift from the insurrection's leader to the people. Kościuszko's announcements of the gift frame the play's action. In the first act, he authorizes a temporary exemption from labor duties for those peasants who enlist in his army. In the fifth act, he declares Głowacki a nobleman. The premise of the play can be summed up as follows: it is not beside the point to ask what the insurrection can do for you.

No other nineteenth-century play about Kościuszko mentions the suspension of peasants' labor duties. Anczyc's break with this tradition is so radical that it may overshadow a significant detail: Kościuszko's gift fails to move the peasants. Even his invocation of a religious precedent for the insurrection does not persuade them.[29] The double motivator, economic as well as religious, simply does not work. In the third act, therefore, we see a different approach to the mobilization of the peasants. They gather up their heroic resolve in response to an inspiring battle song by a village bard.[30] The song testifies to the power of art to turn indifferent masses into eager freedom fighters. Before, the peasants were skeptical about Kościuszko's offer; now they enthusiastically respond to Gło-wacki's call to arms. The problem is that a peasant leader inciting other peasants to armed combat is an explosive idea that could make post-1846 audiences uneasy. The earlier version of *Kościuszko at Racławice*, completed in 1870, skirted the issue.[31] How does the revised text handle this problem?

The spatial configuration of the third act is helpful. We see a smithy and a linden tree in the front, and a village church in the back. Built on a slight elevation, the church presides over the patriotic mobilization in the village. The peasant recruits march under a banner featuring the patrons of Poland (the Black Madonna and Saint Stanisław) and proceed to the church to attend mass. In other words, the empowerment of the peasants is sanctioned by the Catholic Church as a temporary expedience arising out of dire national circumstances.

But the threat of a social revolution keeps rising from the dead. It is hard to resist a conclusion that the play's obsessive references to the French Revolution symbolize the unspeakable: the massacre of the Polish gentry during the peasant uprising of 1846. In the fourth act, at the vulnerable moment of pre-battle nervousness, two radical members of Kraków's city council seek to win the peasant recruits to their side:

> Dzianotty: Before, the gentry let Poland perish; now, peasants and townspeople will liberate Poland....
>
> Sztummer: We can do without the gentry. We must follow the example of the French. Long live the people![32]

Dzianotty and Sztummer propose to better Kościuszko's offer to the peasants. He has promised them a temporary reduction of labor service; Dzianotty and Sztummer announce a land reform after Poland is liberated. Predictably, this enrages the landowners who have enlisted in Kościuszko's army. The newly forged national unity is on the brink of collapse; the anti-Russian insurrection threatens to spill into a civil war.

In the play's key monologue, Głowacki rejects Dzianotty and Sztummer's revolutionary overtures: "This is not France. We're not after the land of our landlords because that would go against the tenth commandment.... If we stand united—gentry, peasants, townspeople—Poland will be free."[33] Głowacki's repulsion for revolutionary propaganda appears attractive because it makes room for the recognition of Polish difference. In other words, the class threat is buried under the cultural threat posed by foreign models, and the cultural threat is used to highlight the superiority of the so-called Polish national character over the aggressive, treacherous, and materialistic identity of the rest of Europe, East (Russia) or West (France).

Anczyc's play ends with a solidaristic tableau that could have been entitled "This is not France" (to borrow Głowacki's line). The gentry, the peasants, and the townspeople are placed strategically in front of a cross and a gentry manor. Thus, the play closes with the evocation of a national community as a hierarchical, extended, and inclusive family, albeit a family with a difference. Earlier, the family was represented as querulous and ineffectual. Now, in order to create a new Poland, it is necessary to gather peasants and nonpeasants in a collective identity precisely through the act of not quarreling over that identity. What is most remarkable about this play is that it has managed, against all odds, to amass significant levels of cultural capital that was still viable in 1989. The play does so by its skill both in producing an illusion of a pluralist culture and in reactivating a sense of Poland as a pure nation resistant to "the Parisian plague."[34]

* * * * *

Anczyc had the last word on Kościuszko in the nineteenth century. He took the "suspicious" idea of an "alliance with the masses" and reworked it into a winning formula for the patriotic discourse that was determined to detransgress Kościuszko's transgression.[35] Is this all?

An initial reading of the nineteenth-century plays about Kościuszko may conclude that they sidestepped the thorny issue of transgression. Trying to make some sense of the complicated tangle of foreign oppression, poverty, and social inequalities, those plays reduced the experiences of the past and the present to patriotic fantasies, which were then offered up for public consumption. The terms of those fantasies were attractive precisely because they were presented as a simple opposition of good and bad, self and other, deserving and undeserving. However, the mixed messages and awkward ambivalences in the Kościuszko plays discussed here indicate that already in the nineteenth century Kościuszko was able to evade even the most dedicated of his tamers.

In this study, I have considered the Kościuszko plays both inside and outside the system of Polish nationalism. Just like other types of nationalism, Polish nationalism suppresses certain memories and concerns, while emphasizing others. The repressed memories and concerns, however, do not disappear. They can be heard, for example, in the alternative voices in Majeranowski's *Kościuszko's First Love* and Mańkowska's *Tadeusz Kościuszko*. In ironic or paradoxical twists, these voices cut the vicious circles of Polish cultural mythology with the sharp blade of censored traumas and taboos. The Kościuszko plays, then, can be seen as an attempt by some of the characters (perhaps against the authors' better judgment) to claim equal weight for alternative voices that challenge the hierarchies of status, gender, and authority.

Notes

1. Kościuszko has become the object of a flourishing academic industry. In the past decade alone, there were several full-length works on him and plenty of articles. For accounts in English of his military career and political thought, see, respectively, James S. Pula, *Thaddeus Kościuszko: The Purest Son of Liberty* (New York: Hippocrene Books, 1999), and Andrzej Walicki, *The Enlightenment and the Birth of Modern Nationhood: Polish Political Thought from Noble Republicanism to Tadeusz Kościuszko*, trans. Emma Harris (Notre Dame, Ind.: University of Notre Dame Press, 1989). For a useful overview in English of the revolutionary implications of the 1794 uprising led by Kościuszko, see R. R. Palmer, *The Age of the Democratic Revolution: A Political History of Europe and America, 1760–1800*, vol. 2 (Princeton, N.J.: Princeton University Press, 1964), 146–56, and Jerzy Kowecki, "The Kościuszko Insurrection: Continuation and Radicalization of Change," trans. Jerzy Kołodziej and Mary Helen Ayres, in *Constitution and Reform in Eighteenth-Century Poland*, ed. Samuel Fiszman (Bloomington: Indiana University Press, 1997), 497–518.
2. James R. Thompson, review of *Thaddeus Kościuszko: The Purest Son of Liberty*, by James S. Pula, *The Sarmatian Review* 20, no. 1 (2000): 680.
3. For a recent example of incorporating Kościuszko into the notion of "Polish exceptionalism," see Thompson's review of Pula's *Thaddeus Kościuszko*.
4. Monica M. Gardner, *Kościuszko: A Biography* (London: Allen and Unwin, 1920), 111.
5. For the concept of the National Symbolic, I am indebted to Lauren Berlant, *The Anatomy of National Fantasy: Hawthorne, Utopia, and Everyday Life* (Chicago: University of Chicago Press, 1991). This concept combines the core notion of Jacques Lacan's theory—that identity is conferred through language—with Benedict Anderson's idea that discursive practices constitute the imagined community of a nation. The National Symbolic, then, is a field of discursive practices such as myths and rituals that provide "an alphabet for a collective consciousness or national subjectivity" and thus transform individuals into "subjects of a collectively held history" (20).
6. I discuss Plater's gender transgression in my article, "The Daughters of Emilia Plater," in *Engendering Slavic Literatures*, ed. Pamela Chester and Sibelan Forrester (Bloomington: Indiana University Press, 1996), 34–58.
7. Palmer, *The Age of the Democratic Revolution*, 148. As Palmer also points out, Polish historians have been "divided by the same issues, some preferring to see in the movement of 1794 little more than a national uprising against foreigners, while others find in it, in addition, an attempt to deal with class antagonisms, including serfdom, in Poland" (148).
8. In this context, I should add that Kościuszko encouraged Jewish participation in the uprising of 1794 and welcomed Colonel Berek Joselewicz's Jewish regiment into his troops. See, for example, Reuben Ainsztein, *Jewish Resistance in Nazi-Occupied Eastern Europe, with a Historical Survey of the Jew as Fighter and Soldier in the Diaspora* (New York: Barnes and Noble, 1974), 112–14.
9. Adam Asnyk, *Poezje* (Warsaw: Państwowy Instytut Wydawniczy, 1974), 635. All unattributed translations from Polish are mine.
10. The production, directed by Bogdan Augustyniak, opened on 24 June 1989 at the Stefan Żeromski Theater in Kielce.
11. See, for example, Tadeusz Korzon, *Kościuszko: Życiorys z dokumentów wysnuty* (Kraków: Muzeum Narodowe w Rapperswylu, 1894), 102.
12. Studies of the Kościuszko myth give only perfunctory attention to drama and theater, even though surveys of the Kościuszko plays are available in Wiktor Hahn, *Kościuszko w polskiej poezji dramatycznej* (Poznań: Księgarnia św. Wojciecha, 1918), and Dobrochna Ratajczakowa, *Obrazy narodowe w dramacie i teatrze* (Wrocław: Wiedza o Kulturze, 1994).
13. Dates refer to the first production, except for Mańkowska's play, for which I give the publication date since the premiere was delayed until the centenary of Kościuszko's death in 1917.

14. In the period immediately after 1815, conciliatory sentiments toward Russia were quite common among Poles. On the one hand, their hopes in Napoleon had just been painfully crushed; on the other hand, Alexander I seemed to offer sound guarantees for an autonomous Polish state. Swept by a wave of Russophile enthusiasm, many Poles were willing to reconcile themselves to Russian rule. On this issue, see, for example, Adam Galos, "Tradycje Naczelnika powstania Kościuszkowskiego i Racławic w XIX w.," in *Panorama Racławicka: Materiały z sesji popularnonaukowej Wrocław 1984*, ed. Krystyn Matwijowski (Wrocław: Dolnośląskie Towarzystwo Społeczno-Kulturalne, 1987), 17–35.

15. In elevating Ludwika to the rank of countess, Majeranowski makes the difference in social status more difficult for the lovers to negotiate.

16. Konstanty Majeranowski, *Pierwsza miłość Kościuszki* (Kraków, 1820), 25.

17. Thus, the play makes an important point: gender is not class-neutral. Julia's social status as a countess empowers her to take the initiative.

18. Majeranowski, *Pierwsza miłość Kościuszki*, 7.

19. In *Kościuszko on the Seine*, Majeranowski takes this idea one step further and juxtaposes Kościuszko and Napoleon. Whereas Napoleon's will to power has shifted the boundaries of virtue and vice, Kościuszko performs a symbolic act of cultural healing to restore these boundaries. Paradoxically, then, the restoration of ethical boundaries necessitates a destabilization of gender boundaries.

20. Majeranowski, *Pierwsza miłość Kościuszki*, 20.

21. Stanisław Bratkowski, *Akademik warszawski* (Warsaw, [1831?]), 13.

22. See, for example, Grzegorz Ekiert and Jan Kubik, *Rebellious Civil Society: Popular Protest and Democratic Consolidation in Poland, 1989–1993* (Ann Arbor: University of Michigan Press, 1999). For a different interpretation of *Kościuszko's First Love*, see Piotr Mitzner, "Epoka Majeranowskiego," *Pamiętnik Teatralny* 39, nos. 3–4 (1990): 337–58, and Ratajczakowa, *Obrazy narodowe w dramacie i teatrze*, 180–82.

23. Józef Ignacy Kraszewski, *Równy wojewodzie* (Poznań, 1868), 158.

24. Bogusława Mańkowska, *Tadeusz Kościuszko, czyli cztery chwile życia tego bohatera* (Poznań, 1880), 41.

25. Ibid.

26. See, for example, Dobrochna Ratajczakowa, "*Kościuszko pod Racławicami* Anczyca—arcydzieło patriotycznej sceny popularnej," in *Kościuszko—powstanie 1794 r.—tradycja: Materiały z sesji naukowej w 200-lecie powstania kościuszkowskiego 15–16 kwietnia 1994 r.*, ed. Jerzy Kowecki (Warsaw: Biblioteka Narodowa, 1997), 285–304.

27. There is no historical evidence to confirm that Kościuszko did indeed declare Głowacki a nobleman. Rather, he granted the peasant hero, whose real name was Wojciech Bartosz, a new surname (Głowacki) and an officer's commission. See Jan Lubicz-Pachoński, *Wojciech Bartosz Głowacki: Chłopski bohater spod Racławic i Szczekocin* (Warsaw: Państwowe Wydawnictwo Naukowe, 1987), 71–78.

28. Władysław Ludwik Anczyc, *Kościuszko pod Racławicami*, in *Życie i pisma*, vol. 3, ed. Marian Szyjkowski (Kraków, 1908), 231.

29. In his speech in Kraków, Anczyc's Kościuszko invokes a successful defense of the shrine of the Black Madonna in Częstochowa against the Swedish siege in 1655 as a model for the insurrection of 1794.

30. The bard's narrative is an extended quotation from Teofil Lenartowicz's epic poem, "Bitwa racławicka" (The battle of Racławice) (1859).

31. For a comparison of both versions, see Piotr Mitzner, "*Kościuszki pod Racławicami* droga na scenę," in *Dramat i teatr pozytywistyczny*, ed. Dobrochna Ratajczakowa (Wrocław: Wiedza o Kulturze, 1992), 103–4.

32. Anczyc, *Kościuszko pod Racławicami*, 243–44.

33. Ibid., 244.

34 Ibid., 162.

35. Tadeusz Żeleński, *Pisma*, vol. 25, ed. Henryk Markiewicz (Warsaw: Państwowy Instytut Wydawniczy, 1968), 199.

Chapter 3

NESTROY AND HIS NAUGHTY CHILDREN

A Plebian Tradition in the Austrian Theater

Carl Weber

When explaining, in 1955, that plays are to be written not merely "for" the stage but "with the stage," Friedrich Dürrenmatt ranked the farces of the Austrian nineteenth-century actor-playwright Johann Nepomuk Nestroy alongside the comedies of Aristophanes as models of such a writing "with the stage."[1]

Nestroy's contemporary, Friedrich Count Schwarzenberg, noted in 1844 that "in Nestroy there lives a truly Shakespearean spirit, humor, and wit."[2] And in 1912 the eminent Austrian writer and critic Karl Kraus claimed that Nestroy "is the first German satirist in whose work language itself reflects on the things [that constitute human life]."[3] Outside the German-language theater, however, Nestroy is barely known. The reasons are many; the most obvious one is the difficulty of transposing his Austrian idiom into another tongue and finding equivalents for the complex constructs of speech he has culled from the various patterns of language as spoken in early-nineteenth-century Vienna.[4] One of his farces, *Einen Jux will er sich Machen* (He is looking for a lark) (1842), has been adapted by Thornton Wilder in two different versions, *The Merchant of Yonkers* (1938) and *The Matchmaker* (1954), which in turn were adapted for the book of the musical *Hello, Dolly!* (1964). Later the same play became the source for Tom Stoppard's comedy *On the Razzle* (1981). But, to my knowledge at least, this text remains the only one of Nestroy's that succeeded—and succeeded phenomenally, indeed—when transposed to the English-language stage, if in drastically adapted versions. In fact, both Wilder's and Stoppard's adaptations were eventually played with great success in translation on the German stage. What Wilder and Stoppard did with Nestroy's text mirrors his own practice of taking extant plays and novels and using their plots as the basis for his own inimitable pieces. Herein, too, he showed a truly Shakespearean spirit, one might say.

At the time of his death, in 1862, he enjoyed an enormous popularity in Vienna; his funeral became a spectacular event attended by many thousands who represented an audience spanning all classes of Viennese society.[5] It is no exaggeration to claim that no other writer portrayed and commented on Austrian life between the Vienna Congress of 1815 and the Austro-Prussian war of 1866 as poignantly and entertainingly as Nestroy did in his more than eighty texts for the stage. His plays encompassed a broad spectrum of forms, from the "magic play" of popular Viennese tradition to farce, vaudeville, pantomime, folk comedy, and literary parody.

Born in 1801, the son of a Vienna lawyer, Nestroy attended two of the most enlightened Viennese secondary schools and then began to study law. Already at seventeen he performed as an amateur opera singer. After a first professional engagement in Vienna, he spent several years, mainly as a singer, with theaters in Amsterdam, Brno, Bratislava, and Graz, while his quickly recognized talent led to an increasing number of acting parts. By the end of the 1820s, he had begun to write satirical "magic farces" and so-called quodlibets with leading parts for himself, which included songs in which he commented on the events and mores of the age.

In 1831, he returned to Vienna for good, as leading actor and playwright-in-residence at the Theater an der Wien. There, and later at the Theater in der Leopoldstadt, he became an immensely popular comedian and author who knew very well how to please his audience. Yet he never ceased to probe their tolerance, confronting his fellow Viennese with their follies, hypocrisy, and greed and their penchant for smaller and larger cruelties. Many of his best texts had scant success due to their aggressive critique of contemporary life, while critics kept complaining about Nestroy-the-actor's merciless portrayal of Austrians from all levels of society. Except for the brief period between the March revolution of 1848 and its brutal suppression in October of the same year, Nestroy had to present every one of his stage texts to the censor; there were several he never submitted, knowing full well a performance would not be permitted. Others had to be changed according to the censors' edicts, or Nestroy decided to shelve them. He was, however, famous for his gift for extemporizing and in this way inserted subversive content into his performance. His ad-libbing resulted in the cancellation of one of his contracts and once even led to a brief prison sentence.[6]

According to contemporary sources, Nestroy possessed an inimitable talent for suggesting hidden meaning through facial expression and physical gesture that would turn a completely innocuous line into a subversive comment on social and political issues of the day. He appears to have achieved this, for instance, by ways of emphasizing specific words and thus exploiting their associative potential, be it through inflections conveying a double entendre, a mispronunciation that would alter a word's meaning, a seemingly unintended slip of the tongue, or the many other mimetic strategies available to an accomplished stage performer.[7]

Nestroy must have been, in the truest sense of Brecht's term, a gestic actor. The gestus of his characters is usually implied by their idiosyncratic idiom, as, for example, in *Der Färber und sein Zwillingsbruder* (The dyer and his twin brother) (1840). In other texts, as in *Kampl* (1852), Nestroy prescribed it meticulously in director's notes. Through his use of gestic language as well as the actor's performing body, the writing and staging of his texts provided a hard-hitting analysis of the conduct he observed among his Viennese fellow citizens.

A concept of drama comparable to the one Nestroy developed has reappeared in a particularly forceful manner in the work of several Austrian playwrights in the late twentieth century. The Nestroy scholar Franz H. Mautner has pointed out that two members of the Graz circle of writers who emerged as important playwrights in the late 1960s, Peter Handke and Wolfgang Bauer, revived in their work Nestroy's unmasking of the constructedness of language and the ways human thinking and behavior are manipulated by language.[8] I propose that an emulation of Nestroy's art is also distinctly traceable in the texts of Elfriede Jelinek, Werner Schwab, Marlene Streeruwitz, and Peter Turrini as well—all Austrian authors who have made their mark in the German-language theater in the past thirty years. I need to point out, however, that by "emulation" I do not imply that these writers have been sharing a project that "follows in Nestroy's footsteps." Those authors are, in fact, as different in their views of the world and the theater as could be and may even profoundly disagree with each other's agendas. Nevertheless, they do have aspects in common, in their respective dramaturgy and approach to language as well as in their aggressive portrayal of the contemporary Austrian, that echo those of Nestroy's theater. If they are children of the Nestroy tradition, they are rather the "naughty" ones who toy with it in a refreshingly irreverent manner.

* * * * *

Nestroy created a body of work, as author and performer, that displayed many features that were later claimed to be an achievement of modern drama in the early and middle twentieth century, and that even anticipated much of what strikes us today as distinctly postmodern in contemporary theater. The ways in which he constructed his texts, scrutinized, manipulated, and critiqued language and the ways in which he performed as an actor (as far as we can assess the latter from the obviously subjective reviews of his acting)—all these aspects of his work set him apart from his contemporaries.

Nestroy's dramaturgy does not appear to have followed a particularly planned or preconceived path; it often changed from play to play. At times it seemed to move toward a specific goal—like, for instance, the "genuine" Viennese folk play many of his critics kept demanding from him—but it would then take another unexpected turn. Many such turns appear to have been guided by the "unseen hand" of the market. Nestroy worked within a theater culture that was strictly commercial and he had a keen instinct for changes in the public's taste and in theatrical fashion. He did not uncritically respond to those fashions and frequently satirized or parodied them, notably with respect to the work of Hebbel and Wagner, along with other authors, such as Karl von Holtei, who are by now forgotten. Yet while he certainly utilized dramatic genres or topics according to their prospective box-office potential, the mutations he constructed still managed to convey certain political and social convictions, namely his disgust with the disintegration and corruption of human relationships in an emerging capitalist economy, his early embrace of democratic ideas and later disappointment and even scorn for the utopian promises of the failed revolution that shook 1848 Europe. The Berlin writer and satirist Kurt Tucholsky (1890–1935) once remarked: "The satirist is a deeply hurt idealist: He wants the world to be good but it is bad, and so he keeps flinging himself against everything that makes it bad." He might have spoken about Nestroy, who increasingly expressed his disenchantment with a society that under the cloak of "moral" conventions had discarded all values and was ruled by unbridled self-interest. Of course, his critics accused him of embracing cynicism and obscenity.[9] The works of the contemporary authors I call Nestroy's "children" are particularly concerned with comparable features of their own Austria, where they witness an ever-increasing duplicity and shallowness that are pervading all levels of society and invalidate every kind of human relationship.

When we look at the many different sources he adapted for his plays, be they stage works or forms of literary narrative, we discover that Nestroy took every imaginable liberty with the structures inherent in their respective genres. The linear narrative is disrupted, often without the slightest pretext, to allow for direct addresses to the audience that comment on contemporary Austrian society and its follies. These inserts were usually the high point of the performance for Nestroy's audience. They started with a song of many verses in ballad fashion, with a catchy refrain easy to remember and quote, which was followed by an extended monologue. Sometimes the monologue came first and culminated in song. Neither the action nor the character that Nestroy was performing often justified these inserts. He stepped out of his role and added his comment as author-actor. In nearly all of his plays he wrote a role for himself, and frequently also one for Wenzel Scholz, who was to become his partner for twenty-five years. Their characters usually performed set pieces of song and monologue, though the roles they played were often hardly central to the plot. Nestroy was tall and gaunt, Scholz short and fat; Nestroy often played a negative character, Scholz usually a well-meaning but not very bright person. They made a classic pair of comics, such as was later to become a staple in movies.[10]

But in other ways, too, Nestroy liked to interrupt the progress of the narrative, with brief sketchlike scenes by characters more or less irrelevant to the plot, for example, with slapstick interludes, silent pantomimes, and so forth. In the later years of his career, after the failed 1848 revolution, his plots often became so convoluted and multilayered that they were hardly more than a pretext to unfold scenes that satirized Austrian life, alternating with parodic interludes and other forms of comment on, or caricature of, contemporary society and the theater this society cherished. An analogous strategy is particularly evident in Jelinek's *Burgtheater* (1982), a scathing portrayal of the Austrian aptitude to gratify whoever has political power, be it Hitler or the postwar regime under Allied control. Jelinek even called the play a "Farce with Songs," as Nestroy had labeled many of his texts.

The self-referentiality in performance, the subversion of theatrical illusion after it had been created, combined with great care for the specific scenic detail, and the breaking of the fourth wall not merely by way of asides but by engaging the audience in direct conversation, even something akin to a dialogue—all these aspects of Nestroy's work were rediscovered, one might say, by the modern theater during the first half of the twentieth century. Mautner has shown that Brecht, Ödön von Horvath, and Dürrenmatt, among others, employed many of the distancing, epic, or absurd techniques that Nestroy had mastered with such consummate skill. Martin Esslin has claimed that Nestroy anticipated the theater of the absurd with his brilliant use of "linguistic absurdity" and his mockery of the serious drama of his time.[11]

There is one aspect of Nestroy's theater that sets it completely apart from that of his contemporaries, namely the function of language on stage. His plays reveal language as a most unreliable, treacherous, and inconsistent tool of communication. Often, speeches do not say what they are supposed to mean or do not mean what they appear to say. Language, as spoken by Nestroy's characters, usually operates on at least four levels, though the characters themselves rarely recognize this. They tend to misunderstand or misread each other's verbal statements and respond in a most inappropriate manner, depending on their station in the Austrian social hierarchy, primarily one of middle- or working-class status. They speak a jargon concocted from what was labeled "High German," from the language of business, bureaucracy, and the judiciary in the Habsburg Empire, from the pseudopoetic German that dominated the contemporary stage, and, mainly, from a vernacular Viennese that is riddled with Czech, Italian, Hungarian, French, and Yiddish expressions. The confusion of idioms is most pronounced among the members of the newly rich class of "speculators" or "capitalists," as Nestroy often calls them in his lists of characters. These characters try to skate elegantly on the thin ice of language but they keep breaking through and lapse into broad vernacular that gives away their carefully camouflaged social background and the hollowness of their pretensions. Nestroy's plots are often triggered or twisted by a misreading of language, while the gestus of characters is delineated by their linguistic idiosyncrasies.

Nestroy's ear for and brilliant command of the sounds and rhythms of the spoken word were, along with his mimetic virtuosity, frequently applauded by critics and colleagues, but also attacked for his "cynical" use of them.[12] His sensitivity to the sounds of speech is also evident in the skill with which he used phonetic spelling to specify idiomatic language. In voluminous notebooks, he collected terms and phrases he had heard or read in order to use or paraphrase them in his plays, and there is hardly a parallel to his verbal and syntactical adventurousness among the authors of his time—nor elsewhere in German-language drama. The living spoken language as a manipulating and manipulated agent of human inter-action was at the core of Nestroy's theater. His contemporary successors often make this function, or rather, the nonfunctioning of language as a means of human agency a striking feature of their texts, however different they may be in other respects.

In a comparable vein, Nestroy toyed with the visual language of theatrical con-ventions. From his earliest magic farces to the late plays (which he still labeled farces although several critics considered them to be folk comedies),[13] to his last text, *Häuptling Abendwind* (Chieftain Evening Breeze) (1862)—a remarkable precursor of the mid-twentieth-century theater of the absurd—Nestroy scrupu-lously prescribed in his stage directions the theatrical images, groupings of char-acters, sets, and so forth, that often satirized in hilarious fashion the prevailing conventions of the contemporary stage. He also experimented with a complex visual interweaving of plots by staging them on two or even four simultaneous sets, as in *Zu ebener Erde und im ersten Stock* (At ground level and on the second floor) (1835) and *Das Haus der Temperamente* (The house of humors) (1837); experiments rarely pursued by others in his own time or even in modernist and postmodern performance.

All his plays close with a "happy ending," brought about in such an abrupt manner and so contrived in its visual configuration of characters and scenic accoutrements that it subtly or openly mocked the preferred sentiments of his Viennese audience. In fact, the facetious ways in which he resolved his convo-luted fables actually reaffirm what the plays were telling us all along: namely, that the world is a site of unpredictable chaos ruled by accident—an inscrutable and heartless "fate" he liked to invoke in monologue and song—and that life is driven by the human follies of greed, envy, lust, vanity, and worse. His was a position diametrically opposed to the utopian ideas the Austrian Enlightenment had pro-moted in the late eighteenth century, when even the Emperor Joseph II regarded the theater as an instrument to educate and better an ignorant populace. Nestroy confronted that same populace with their darkest desires and exposed the ways in which they camouflaged them with their pathetic sentimentality. He was hardly trying to "better" his audience. Instead, he showed them their stupid or shabby behavior, made them laugh at themselves, and left it up to them to make of it whatever they liked.

* * * * *

It is Nestroy's perception of human endeavors and the way in which he presented them on stage that made me think of several Austrian playwrights as his "naughty children." They observe the lifestyles, ambitions, and pursuits of their contem-poraries with comparable mischievous mirth and gleefully expose the dark urges that propel them. Their plays amount to a harsh portrayal of contemporary

Homo Austriacus, a picture even more radical than was Nestroy's, informed as it is by the profound distrust of any ideology that the experience of twentieth-century history has taught their authors—again not unlike Nestroy, who viewed the ideologies of his time, whether liberal or conservative, with acute skepticism.

Nestroy anticipated much of what became prevailing thought in the twentieth century. He contemplated, for instance, an understanding of language that Freud would later elaborate after observing the ways his patients were using and misusing language. Nestroy also perceived that language steers our thinking and our perception of the world, as another Viennese, Ludwig Wittgenstein, explained it later and as Handke has shown us in his plays. And there was no one who revealed like Nestroy, in his parodies of Friedrich Hebbel and Wagner, that there lurks something sinister, cruel, and dangerous beneath the surface of much "high" German art and language, though his hilarious mockery of those holy cows had the Viennese audience in stitches.

I first heard the echoes of Nestroy in the ways in which language is employed and critiqued in the works of Elfriede Jelinek, Werner Schwab, Marlene Streeruwitz, and Peter Turrini. They share his joy of game-playing with language and his keen ear for the treachery of jargon, which reveals as much as it tries to hide the trivial and cruel urges that propel people whose speech and thoughts are conditioned by the popular media, their daily fodder. As different as Jelinek's *Raststätte, oder Sie Machens Alle* (Roadside inn, or, they all are doing it) (1994) is from Schwab's *Volksvernichtung, oder Meine Leber ist sinnlos* (Extermination of the people; or, my liver has no purpose) (1992), or Streeruwitz's *Elysian Park* (1993) is from Turrini's *Schlacht um Wien* (Battle for Vienna) (1995), in all of these plays language, in its syntax and meaning, is manipulated or distorted to a lesser or larger degree. Vernacular turns of phrase and occasional phonetic spelling are employed, and all these speech games serve to reveal the characters' underlying, often dark, motives, their confused state of ignorance, but most of all the constructedness of language that conditions their thinking and behavior. These texts often strive for a verbal wit similar to that of Nestroy, they employ and parody their characters' class-derived lingo, and offer other reminders of Nestroy's satire. Many of their characters, like those of Nestroy's, might be described as "prisoners of language," that is, of the particular jargon their social station and culture has coerced them to use.[14]

Yet it is not only the problematizing of language that constitutes a link between Nestroy's theater and that of his late-twentieth-century children. The dramaturgy, which demonstrates such a skillful command of, as well as disrespect for the rules prescribed by the contemporary dramatic genres is certainly comparable. Contemporary Viennese authors freely experiment with linear narrative and share Nestroy's penchant for shorter or longer digressions and for the appearance of odd characters who have no particular bearing on the plot but serve to comment on the play's topic—or any other subject that the author so desires. Streeruwitz's *New York, New York* (1993), Schwab's *ESKALATION ordinär* (Escalation vulgar) (1994), and Turrini's *Battle for Vienna* offer particularly striking examples. While some of the contemporary plays may deconstruct the text in more radical ways than Nestroy did, when looking at contemporary theater practice, where deconstructed narrative and language have been at home for a long while, and comparing it with that of Nestroy's time, we discover that he was quite as radical as the contemporary authors dare to be. The same may be said about the ways theatrical conventions are used in contemporary Austrian drama, though the new plays are less adventurous in the use of the imagery or parody of prevailing theatrical fashions—with some notable exceptions, as, for instance, Jelinek's *Totenauberg* (Totenauberg/Death/Valley/Summit) (1992) and Streeruwitz's *New York, New York*. They do, however, frequently parody or use as a point of reference the performative modes of television, that dominant matrix of perception and language in contemporary society.

* * * * *

Nestroy's texts approximated a project comparable to that of his contemporaries, Balzac in France and Dickens in England: namely, a *comedie humaine* of urban and rural Austria under Habsburg rule, from the Vienna Congress to the Treaty of Prague, which ended Austria's hegemony in Central Europe—even if, as far as we know, he hardly harbored such an ambition.[15] Nestroy's heirs in the contemporary Austrian theater share his cold, hard gaze when viewing the society and the theater of their age. It is a gaze akin to that of an anthropologist—a very biased one, to be sure—who observes the habits and beliefs of a tribe from a carefully maintained distance that reveals more than any close proximity, which might invite identification, would ever permit.

Nestroy knew his Viennese inside out and had no illusions about them. Our contemporary authors are the same. Their plays have, of course, many features in common with those of other present-day German-language dramatists, yet there is a specific Austrian, or rather, Viennese, sensibility that sets them apart—just as Nestroy's plays were of a different breed in the German nineteenth-century theater. There are unique traits that have been shared by many writers who work in and for Vienna (Arthur Schnitzler, Karl Kraus, and Jura Soyfer come to mind among others, but to discuss their work would go far beyond the topic of this essay.)

What is it that made the ear of Viennese writers so keen for the slightest perturbations of language, its undercurrents, the disparity of pretense and meaning, the sounds and rhythms of the spoken word and the melody of dialect and specific idioms? Nestroy grew up and spent nearly all of his life in the capital of an empire where, in addition to Viennese German, at least ten other languages were spoken, some of them by substantial segments of the populace. The language in Nestroy's plays is riddled with idioms of non-German origin. The rapidly developing urban society of early-nineteenth-century Vienna, a city that doubled its population within Nestroy's lifetime, was unique for its multi-ethnicity, which set it apart from other large urban centers in the German countries, such as Berlin, Hamburg, or Frankfurt.[16] Vienna was the first truly multicultural city in early modern Europe, when industrialization began to dissolve the old forms of communal and individual life. It stands to reason that living in this Babel of tongues could not but sharpen the ear and the mind for the complexities of spoken language and their ethnic and social roots. Habsburg Vienna's rapidly changing urban life and its multi-ethnic culture may explain why only a Viennese actor and author, who not merely wrote but also spoke his texts, could anticipate in his work a critique of language that was not fully developed and formulated until nearly a century had passed since his death. On the other hand, he drew on the ancient tradition of Austria's popular theater, a truly "plebeian tradition," to use a term the critic Hans Mayer once coined. In that respect, Nestroy was not unlike his Parisian contemporary, Eugene Labiche, whose plays evolved from a comparable tradition. Yet Nestroy, far more than Labiche, pushed this tradition toward a sophisticated, critical aggressiveness that would be appropriated again by Austrian authors during the last decades of the twentieth century.

Vienna is still situated at the crossroads of European culture and tradition, and it was particularly so as the capital of a neutral country during the years of the Cold War. Nestroy's contemporary "children" grew up in this hub of crisscrossing influences from East and West. There was hardly a place more suitable to sharpen ears and minds for the pitfalls that competing ideologies and their languages and cultures were creating. At the very end of the nineteenth century, the Viennese playwright and critic Hermann Bahr argued that Nestroy was a new type of man "who had nothing of the past in him.... He sees a quite new breed of humans moving in quite antiquated forms; that appears funny to him."[17] Bahr's assertion could well be applied to the characters we encounter in the theater of Nestroy's "children" at the end of the twentieth century.

Nestroy and his successors constitute, in form and spirit, a distinctly Austrian tradition that has no parallel in the German-language theater.[18] A trenchant analysis and comparison of selected works by Nestroy and his "naughty children," based on close readings and informed by recent findings in performance theory, would reveal many more intriguing aspects of this rich and remarkably fertile tradition. This essay could only try to circumscribe the field that might be explored by such an investigation.

Notes

1. Friedrich Dürrenmatt, *Plays and Essays: The German Library*, vol. 89 (New York: Continuum, 1982), 242.
2. Franz H. Mautner, *Nestroy* (Heidelberg: Stiehm, 1974), 23.
3. Karl Kraus, "Nestroy und die Nachwelt: Zum 50. Todestage," *Die Fackel* 349–50 (Vienna, 1912), 12.
4. Martin Esslin, for one, stated that "most of Nestroy's dialogue is untranslatable." Martin Esslin, *The Theatre of the Absurd* (London: Eyre and Spottiswoode, 1962), 241.
5. The *London Times* reported from Vienna, 10 June 1862, that "between 40,000 and 50,000 persons were assembled in the streets through which the coffin containing the mortal remains of the Austrian Aristophanes were carried." Quoted in W. E. Yates, *Nestroy and the Critics* (Columbia, S.C.: Camden House, 1994), 1. The number of mourners is the more impressive when one considers that the population of Vienna in the early 1860s was about 600,000. W. E. Yates, *Nestroy, Satire, and Parody in Viennese Popular Comedy* (Cambridge: Cambridge University Press, 1972), 68.
6. Yates, *Nestroy, Satire, and Parody*, 149–50.
7. A. Silberstein, *Oesterreichische Zeitung* (1861), 46. As quoted in R. Harrison and K. Wilson, *Three Viennese Comedies by J. N. Nestroy* (Columbia, S.C.: Camden House, 1986), 2.
8. Mautner, *Nestroy*, 24, 73, 158, 210, 366, 368, 371–72.
9. Discussed by Yates, *Nestroy and the Critics*, 12–23.
10. One cannot but think here of performers such as Laurel and Hardy, the early Danish film comics Pat and Patachon, and even the Marx brothers, whose performance style appears to share traits with Nestroy's acting, as far as we can infer from critical assessments of his style.
11. Esslin, *Theatre of the Absurd*, 241.
12. Discussed by Yates, *Nestroy and the Critics*, 3–5.
13. Ibid., 11, 17, 21.
14. I owe the term "prisoners of language" to Peter Hoyng, "Austrian: Petit and Haute Bourgeoisie as Obsessive Prisoners of Language: A Comparative Study of Werner Schwab's *Die Praesidentinnen* and Thomas Bernhardt's *Ritter, Dene, Voss*" (paper presented at the Great Traditions Conference sponsored by the Center for Austrian Studies, Minneapolis, Minn., 1997).
15. Two of Nestroy's contemporary critics, August Frankl and Moritz G. Saphir, compared him to Dickens. See Yates, *Nestroy and the Critics*, 4–5. Later criticism has suggested that Balzac was an influence on Nestroy. Ibid., 22.
16. Between 1830 and the late 1860s, Vienna's population had grown from just under 320,000 to more than 600,000. Yates, *Nestroy, Satire, and Parody*, 68.
17. Hermann Bahr, *Wiener Theater (1892–1898)* (Berlin: Fischer, 1899), 463.
18. I would like to add a brief note about a contemporary American playwright who, probably with little if any knowledge of Nestroy's work, exhibits in his texts a quasi-Nestroyan sensibility, with comparable preferences in dramatic structure, the treatment of language, and even an ironic use of spirits from the realm of angels and magic, like Nestroy's in his "magic farces." I am talking of Tony Kushner, of course, who in *Angels in America, The Illusion, Slavs, The Heavenly Theater*, and other plays, employs many of the techniques we find in Nestroy's theater. Kushner is acutely aware of his Jewish heritage and its dialectics in thought and language. Nestroy's theater displays comparable dialectical features that set it apart from the work of his contemporaries. He may have been quite open to the modes of thinking and behavior that the influx of Jewish citizens was inserting into Viennese culture, even if some of his texts, at least on their surface, appear to correspond to a growing Austrian antisemitism, which eventually led to the horrendous excesses of the next century. Many of his characters were members of the emerging class of "capitalists" and "speculators." In a society that barred Jews from most professions and careers, apart from trading and money lending, they were naturally very much present in this group. Nestroy frequently made use, and also fun, of their speech patterns, an idiom that fused German with Yiddish in its syntax and vocabulary. For a discussion of Nestroy and antisemitism, see Yates, *Nestroy and the Critics*, 67–68.

Chapter 4

PANTOMIME, DANCE, *SPRACHSKEPSIS*, AND PHYSICAL CULTURE IN GERMAN AND AUSTRIAN MODERNISM

Harold B. Segel

The Russian writer Mikhail Kuzmin was an active participant in Saint Petersburg's lively cabaret life in the early years of the twentieth century. Besides songs and dramatic skits, he also wrote pantomime. One of his pantomimes, *Dukhov den v Toledo* (All Souls' Day in Toledo), was staged apparently only once, on 23 March 1915, at the Moscow Kamerny Theater under the direction of Aleksandr Tairov. The pantomime had in fact been commissioned by Tairov so that the season in which it was performed would have at least one pantomime, given the contemporary interest in nonverbal drama. As Tairov himself declared: "Not wishing to be left that year … without a work in pantomime, we found ourselves in a very difficult position since *all the literature on pantomime belongs to German authors and composers.*… We then turned to Russian authors, and M. A. Kuzmin showed an interest in our proposal and wrote the pantomime *All Souls' Day in Toledo*. This work is the first effort by a Russian writer in the sphere of pantomime."[1]

Tairov's recognition of German supremacy in the field of pantomime, however flattering, needs qualification. In comparison with the English and the French, the German-speaking world, at least until the turn of the century, had in fact been pantomime poor. What made Tairov regard German-language pantomime so highly was the enthusiasm for the genre among German and Austrian modernist writers. No slouch when it came to knowledge of Western drama and theater, Tairov shared with Vsevolod Meyerhold a particular interest in the German stage. Meyerhold, after all, had translated and staged a few of Arthur Schnitzler's smaller plays. Tairov himself had staged Schnitzler's pantomime *Der Schleier der Pierrette* (The Veil of Pierrette) for the 1913/14 season of Konstantin Mardzhanov's Free Theater. We may not be able to document Tairov's familiarity specifically, say, with Frank Wedekind's four "Tanzpantomimen" of the 1890s—*Die Flöhe oder der Schmerzenstanz* (The Flea, or, The Dance of Pain), *Der Mückenprinz* (The Prince of Gnats); *Bethel,* and the most impressive of the group, *Die Kaiserin von Neufundland* (The Empress of Newfoundland). But Tairov undoubtedly knew Schnitzler's other pantomime, *Die Verwandlung des Pierrot* (The Transformation of Pierrot), and might well have known at least Hugo von Hofmannsthal's *Amor und Psyche* or *Das fremde Mädchen* (The Strange Girl), or both. Both works premiered in Berlin's Theater in der Königgrätzer Strasse in September 1911 and were published later that year under the title *Grete Wiesenthal in "Amor und Psyche" und "Das fremde Mädchen": Szenen von Hugo von Hofmannsthal.* The Grete Wiesenthal of the title was, of course, the celebrated Viennese dancer who had much to do with Hofmannsthal's interest in pantomime and had herself lectured on pantomime on two occasions.[2] Since *The Strange Girl* was also made into a film in Stockholm in May 1913 and had its premiere in the Berlin Cinés-Theater in September of that year, the work could easily have come to Tairov's attention.

But even if we begrudge the Russian director any knowledge of the contributions to pantomime of Wedekind, Schnitzler, Hofmannsthal, Hermann Bahr, Richard Beer-Hofmann, Carl Einstein, and others, there was still a solid reason for his willingness to believe that German authors held a patent on the genre of pantomime at the time. That was Max Reinhardt's spectacular premiere production of *Das Mirakel* (The Miracle) in London in 1911, or the slightly less heralded production of *Sumurun* in 1910, in which Grete Wiesenthal played a lead role. Both works were also staged in the United States to considerable acclaim, adding further luster to the German reputation in nonverbal theater.

Despite its lack of significant antecedents, German-language pantomime had indeed reached an unprecedented level at the turn of the century. More important than the number of pantomimes written was the stature of the writers who experimented with the genre. At least from the early eighteenth century on, pantomime existed on the level of popular entertainment, entertainment for the fairground and later the music hall. And like similar entertainment, it began to attract the attention of serious artists in the late nineteenth century, nowhere more so, it would seem, than in Germany and Austria. However, this attention cannot be attributed solely or principally to the contemporary enthusiasm of so-called high art for popular and folk culture. Wedekind is a case in point. Of his four pantomimes, certainly the best—and the one most reflective of his ideas on Eros and Thanatos—is *The Empress of Newfoundland.* It is also directly linked to the circus and music hall.[3] The lead male figure in the work is the weightlifter Eugen Holthoff, who was modeled either on a weightlifter Wedekind had seen in performance or on the well-known strongman of the time, Eugen Sandow, whose reputation spanned both sides of the Atlantic. Now if we compare Wedekind's second most striking pantomime, *The Prince of Gnats*, a work steeped in sexual and other violence, any at best tenuous links with a circus or similar milieu are superseded by far firmer bonds with the contemporary modernist preoccupation with physicality. This preoccupation, which grew into an obsession, I believe, in the German-speaking world, forms the appropriate analytical context not just for *The Prince of Gnats*, but indeed for turn-of-the-century German and Austrian pantomime in general. With Wedekind, the point is driven home in no uncertain terms by the original publication of *The Prince of Gnats* as an integral part of one of Wedekind's strangest pieces, *Mine-Haha oder Über die körperliche Erziehung der jungen Mädchen* (Mine-Haha; or, On the Physical Education of Young Girls). But more about both works shortly.

Pantomime, as we know, does not necessarily have to incorporate dance scenes. But an outstanding feature of turn-of-the-century pantomime, particularly in the German context, is the extent to which it did incorporate dance. Wedekind's pantomimes are all designated "Tanzpantomimen," suggesting a rhythmically elevated form of pantomime in which dance predominates. Most of Hofmannsthal's more numerous pantomimes are similarly identified as "Tanz-pantomimen," and Carl Einstein's *Nuronihar* of 1913 was inspired by his admiration for the Polish dancer Stasia Napierkowska, a fact reflected in the prominence of dance in the work. The dance element in Schnitzler's *Veil of Pierrette* is also anything but negligible.

Why this embrace of dance by pantomime? In the same period that major writers were experimenting with pantomime, the phenomenon we know as modern dance was electrifying audiences in Europe and America, but mostly in Europe where the classical ballet tradition was obviously stronger and more resistant to change. That the earliest reformers of traditional dance were American women—Loie Fuller, Isadora Duncan, and Ruth St. Denis—should come as no surprise in view of the American lack of tradition and the vigor of the women's movement at the turn of the century. But social conservatism was still strong enough in the United States to compel its pioneers of modern dance to make their reputations initially, and mostly, in Europe. All three dancers were lionized by the European artistic and intellectual elite, and, in the case of St. Denis, three of her greatest admirers were the debonair and enterprising Count Harry Kessel, Gerhart Hauptmann, and above all Hofmannsthal, who, besides planning pantomimes and other works for St. Denis to perform in, also made her the subject of one of his best essays, "Die unvergleiche Tänzerin" (The Incomparable Dancer).

Before long, that is by the early years of this century, the Europeans had their own exponents of modern dance, but, significantly, primarily in the German-speaking world—Grete Wiesenthal, for example, in Austria, both as a solo dancer and in performance with her sisters Berta and Elsa, and the formidable Marie Wiegmann, who became best known in this country under the Anglicized name of Mary Wigman. It was Wigman, working especially with her most important teacher, Rudolf von Laban, who became most closely associated with "expressive dance" (*Ausdrucktanz*), which has to be acknowledged as the most important German contribution to dance in this century.[4]

The common denominator in the new fascination with modern dance and pantomime, and in the interaction of dance and pantomime, is what I regard as the modernist cult of physicality. But dance and pantomime share another important feature besides movement, one that also caught the fancy of modernist artists—the absence of speech, or, more precisely, the absence of spoken speech, since the body, after all, does represent an autonomous system of communication.

* * * * *

If we take into consideration the new semantic weighting of gesture at the expense of dialogue in the drama of the period, a rather convincing case can be made for a calculated movement from the verbal to the nonverbal. This subversion of the traditional role of spoken speech in drama may indeed have begun with Maeterlinck in the spirit of Symbolist stylization. However, it was carried further by Chekhov, Hauptmann, Hofmannsthal, Gertrude Stein, and of course others. The enhanced role of gesture in modernist drama was paralleled by the breakdown of traditional dramatic speech, as in Stein in a more extreme form, and I mention Stein in this context because she lived in Europe at the time, close to the vortex of modernist change, and wrote most of her early revolutionary "plays" there.

The great impact of dance on pantomime was felt as well in drama, reinforcing the shift from the verbal to the nonverbal. This took the form principally of an ever greater accommodation of dance scenes, sometimes of an improvised nature, such as Nora's tarantella in Ibsen's *Doll's House*, the folk dance in Strindberg's *Miss Julie*, or the dance of Salomé in Oscar Wilde's play of the same name. The ubiquity, and on occasion centrality, of dance in modernist drama is easily documented. It embraced dramatic writers as divergent, say, as Yeats, Hauptmann, and the Pole Stanisław Wyspiański. In the case of Hauptmann, I am thinking specifically of *Und Pippa tanzt!* (Dance on, Pippa!), in which dance is equated with the life force and Eros and Thanatos meet again in the grotesque relationship between Pippa and Hahn. That the dance craze of the early twentieth century had developed so far as to lend itself to mockery is evident in Georg Kaiser's play *Europa* of 1915, which spoofs the whole modernist dance phenomenon while at the same time vigorously espousing the modernist cult of the physical. Dismissing dance as effete, Kaiser's play, which undoubtedly reflects the impact of World War I, appeals for virility, strength, and the hard discipline of warriors.

Notwithstanding Kaiser's views, dance continued to exert a tremendous impact on the arts, and not just pantomime and drama. Fiction also responded accordingly, as we can see, for example, in one of Alfred Döblin's best short stories, "Die Tänzerin und der Leib" (The Dancer and the Body), in which the tormented and ultimately fatal relationship between a young dancer and her body is used to explore the place of the artist in the creative process.

Concurrent with, and I believe underlying, the rise of pantomime, modern dance, and the subversion of spoken dialogue in the drama was the exceptional interest at the time in physical culture. This expressed itself not only in the pursuit of gymnastics, physique building, and wellness in general, but more importantly in the expansion of existing physical culture associations or organizations and the establishment of new ones. I have in mind above all the German Turnverein and the Czech Sokol, which were national movements far more than they were athletic organizations. It may be true that Friedrich Ludwig Jahn's Turnverein dates back to the early years of the nineteenth century and arose in direct response to the wars with the French. Nevertheless, the movement reached its apogee in the late nineteenth and early twentieth centuries and became inextricably linked with German nationalism and militarism. This was not surprising in light of the reception of Jahn's *Deutsches Volkstum* and the emphasis on *Kriegsübungen* (military exercises) in his *Die Deutsche Turnkunst zur Einrichtung der Turnplätze* (The Art of German Gymnastics and the Establishment of Athletic Grounds, 1816).

The Czech Sokol organization was established in the 1860s as a way of promoting the Czech national spirit and the Czech language which for a few centuries had been subject to intense Germanization. Modeled on the German Turnverein and founded, in fact, by Bohemianized ethnic Germans, the Sokol was at its strongest in the late nineteenth century and the early decades of the twentieth. It was indeed during this time that the movement spread to other Slavic lands—Poland, Yugoslavia, Bulgaria, and even Russia. Besides its vigorous espousal of the Czech language and Czech national pride, the Sokol eventually acquired an undeniable nationalistic character. The more anti-German the Sokol organization became, the more it encouraged antisemitic feeling, an expression of popular resentment against the majority of Czech Jews who traditionally favored the use of German over Czech and identified with German culture, regarding the Czech as provincial.

The pervasiveness of the modernist enthusiasm for physical culture shows up in sometimes odd ways. Earlier, I mentioned Wedekind's pantomime *The Prince of Gnats* and the unusual circumstance of its publication. Unlike his other pantomimes, *The Prince of Gnats* is actually embedded in another text of quite different character, *Mine-Haha; or, On the Physical Education of Young Girls*. This is a prose commentary on the physical education of young women in the form of a putative memoir by an elderly former schoolteacher who committed suicide. In a familiar authorial fiction, Wedekind claims that the memoir found its way into his hands and that he merely edited it for publication. *Mine-Haha* was originally intended to serve as the introduction to a projected novel to be called *Hidalla oder Das Leben einer Schneiderin* (Hidalla; or, The Life of a Seamstress). Both it and the introduction were to form in turn part of a major work on a new sexual culture to which the title "Die grosse Liebe" (The Great Love) is usually assigned. Typical for his time in this respect, Wedekind was attracted to contemporary ideas on physical education, particularly the physical education of girls. The more he reflected on the subject, the more he became convinced that through physical education young women would develop a healthier attitude toward their bodies and a more natural awareness of their own sexuality. This is the subject essentially of *Mine-Haha*, but the work also seems to strike a cautionary note regarding excessive concern with the physical.

The memoir comprises the recollections of the years its author spent as a very young girl in a communal institution devoted to physical culture together with other young girls and boys. Apparently taken away from their parents at an early age, the children are kept in prisonlike conditions where their education is limited to the development of physical beauty and the mastery of one's own body. Dance and music are major components of the "curriculum"; intellectual culture has no place in it. At first the boys and girls train together, but from the age of about seven the sexes are separated. From that point on the narrative concerns itself only with the training of the girls. The atmosphere of the institution is cold and sterile; dress is uniform; and conversation, even at meals, is kept to a minimum. The girls are denied any worldly knowledge, including sexual; they are forbidden ever to get into bed with one another; and they are prevented from forming any lasting friendships. At a certain stage in their development, the most attractive and talented girls are chosen to perform in a theater located on the grounds of the institution. The productions are held for adult audiences and in this way bring income to the institution. The work the narrator is asked to perform in is the pantomime called *The Prince of Gnats*. It is in this way that Wedekind has woven his pantomime into the narrative of *Mine-Haha*. The isolation and worldly ignorance in which the girls are brought up extends to their participation in the theatricals. They have little understanding of the plays they perform in and so cannot fathom the sometimes boisterous reactions of the spectators. *The Prince of Gnats* exemplifies this. The pantomime is shot through with lust and brutality, but the girls acting in it show little awareness of its contents.

The modernist cult of physicality underlay not only the tremendous spread of gymnastic and other physical culture activities, but also the great new public enthusiasm for sports. To a great extent, sports came of age at the turn of the century, a fact symbolized by the rebirth of the Olympic games in 1896 under the leadership of Baron Pierre de Coubertin. Before long, sports became as worthy a subject of art as dance had become in the painting of Degas. Literature also kept pace; the German Kasimir Edschmid and the Frenchman Henry de Montherlant epitomize, I believe, the modernist literary embrace of sports. Both writers, incidentally, are remarkably similar in their erotically charged enthusiasm for sleek female athletes, as a comparison of Montherlant's *Le songe* (The Dream, 1922) and Edschmid's *Sport um Gagaly* (The Contest for Gagaly, 1928) easily demonstrates. On the popular level, the responsive chord struck in the German-speaking world by the contemporary sports mania is manifest in the appearance of such once popular books as Bernhard Leitner's *Wie wurde ich stark?* (How did I Become Strong? 1897), Theodor Siebert's *Katechismus der Athletik* (Catechism of Athletics, 1898) and *Der Kraftsport* (Weightlifting,

1907), Albert Stolz's *Mannesschönheit* (Manly Beauty, 1912), and Ferdinand Hüppe's *Hygiene der Körperübungen* (Gymnastics Hygiene, 1910). Also working to promote the new European enthusiasm for physical culture and sports was the experience of war, both good and bad. It was the humiliation at the hands of the French in the time of Napoleon that gave rise to "Vater" Jahn's Turnverein movement. The poor performance of the English troops in the Boer War led not long after to Lord Baden-Powell's creation of the Boy Scouts, which, despite claims to the contrary, was motivated as much by imperialism and colonialism as the Turnverein was by nationalism. If the French defeat in the Franco-Prussian war of 1870/71 stirred the French to an appreciation of the need for a national program of physical culture, German military success followed by economic success prompted Fritz Winther in his *Körperbildung als Kunst und Pflicht* (Physical Education as Art and Duty, 1919) to admonish his countrymen that they could not afford to rest on their laurels to the neglect of their physical well-being and the continued cultivation of bodily strength. So spoiled had the Germans become by success, and so bleak the outlook, that Winther expresses grave concerns even about their racial health and his fear of eventual "racial suicide" ("Rassenselbstmord"). In order to prevent it, the good professor advocates physical education as the foundation of a sound culture of the body. It is, he declares, a "dictate of our time—the well-being of the individual demands it no less energetically than the future of the race."[5]

Although Winther's preoccupation with racial hygiene owes much to Jahn's nationalism, *Physical Education as Art and Duty* also reflects the cultural climate of the turn of the century. Winther is no less concerned with the physical education of the female than he is with that of the male; his views on women's dress, for example, follow the enlightened thought of his day, echoing the prescriptions of such bohemian apostles of proper nutrition and liberated dress as Peter Altenberg and Karl Wilhelm Diefenbach. Most important, Winther accords dance an exceptionally prominent role in physical education and training and exhibits an impressive knowledge of leading contemporary dancers, mentioning not only such well-known figures as Isadora Duncan, Ruth St. Denis, and Else Wiesenthal, but also Sent Mahesa, Ellen Tels, Clotilde von Derp, Rita Sacchetto, and Gertrud Leistikow.

The defeat of Germany and Austria-Hungary in World War I seemed the fulfillment of Winther's warnings and prompted new calls for national physical regeneration. After the defeat of the Central Powers, the undeniable nationalism of the German physical culture movement acquired an additional, more menacing, dimension, that of intensifying racism. This was the common thread running through the works of such writers as the vehemently antiChristian Willibald Hentschel, the pathologically antisemitic Viennese Adolf Lantz (or, as he preferred to be called, Jörg Lanz von Liebenfels), and the apostle of nudity, Richard Ungewitter, who opined that it was in a state of nudity that the best mate could be found and that the circumcised Jewish male could immediately be exposed.

* * * * *

It would be tempting in a way to lay prime responsibility for the modernist cult of physicality on late-nineteenth- and early-twentieth-century philosophical trends, beginning ideally with "Von den Verächten des Leibes" (On the Detractors of the Body) in the first part of Nietzsche's *Zarathustra*. Chronology, however, negates the possibility. But whether shaped by the same forces or in a position to aid and abet them, contemporary philosophical thought, as emanating primarily but not exclusively from Germany and Austria, by and large accorded with the new emphasis on the physical at the expense of the intellectual. In the eleventh aphorism of *Menschliches, Allzumenschliches* (Human, All-too-Human), Nietzsche voices with his customary clarity the central tenet of the language skepticism that looms so large in German and Austrian thought of the period. In his opening statement, he acknowledges the importance of language for culture: "The meaning of language for the development of culture lies in the fact that in it man juxtaposed to the one world a world of his own, a place which he thought so sturdy that from it he could turn the rest of the world upside down and make himself lord over it." Believing that in language he had knowledge of the world, man acquired "that pride by which he has raised himself above the animals." But, Nietzsche declares, man ultimately deluded himself into thinking that not only was he giving things labels, he was expressing the highest knowledge of things with words. Man lived for a long time with this self-delusion; however, in his own time, Nietzsche says, "it is dawning on men that in their belief in language they have propagated a monstrous error."[6]

The Prague German writer Fritz Mauthner went much further than Nietzsche in his denunciation of language, above all in his weighty three-volume *Beiträge zu einer Kritik der Sprache* (Commentaries to a Critique of Language, 1901, 1902).[7] Some of his basic ideas occur in the context of a put-down of Nietzsche's views. "Nietzsche might have produced a more forceful critique of language," Mauthner writes, "had he not concerned himself so one-sidedly with moral concepts, and had his own splendid power of speech not seduced him into wanting to be both thinker and verbal artist at one and the same time. His mistrust of language is boundless, but only insofar as it is not *his own* language."[8]

While acknowledging Nietzsche's "hatred for language" (*Hass gegen die Sprache*) and "even his disdain for himself as a wordmaker," Mauthner consistently takes issue with Nietzsche over his presumed unwillingness to reject language as an epistemological tool, having limited himself, as Mauthner sees it, just to the repudiation of language as an instrument for the expression of mood (*Stimmung*). Agreeing with Nietzsche that language is splendid material for verbal art, Mauthner establishes the irreconcilable difference between himself and Nietzsche by rejecting language as "a miserable tool for knowledge." In setting forth his own views, Mauthner maintained that language (or speech) cannot convey the content of thought. To verbalize destroys the uniqueness of that which is thought. Experience can also not be translated into words. Reality can only be lived. "Only through action do we understand the world of reality," he declared. With Mauthner, we are not far removed from Wittgenstein's conviction, as expressed in the preface and at the conclusion of the *Tractatus*, that "what we cannot speak about we must pass over in silence." In other words, unless the limits of language as the expressions of thoughts are understood, philosophy will continue to pose problems it should have no need to pose. As we know so well from the *Tractatus* and his other writings, Wittgenstein's concern with language shaped not only his ideas but the very form in which they were presented—spare, stripped to essentials conceptually and verbally, uncompromising in its almost painfully rigorous self-discipline.

No discussion of turn-of-the-century philosophy, however synoptic, and its compatibility with modernist physicality would be complete without mention of Henri Bergson. What brought the Frenchman the great fame he enjoyed in his day was the broad appeal of his views to the developing modernist outlook. That reputation hinged largely on a single book, *L'Evolution créatrice* (Creative Evolution), which first saw the light of day in 1907. Less concerned with language as such than were his Austrian and German counterparts, Bergson shared the growing disdain for the intellect, shifting the emphasis instead from intellect to instinct, from intelligence to intuition, and from the conscious to the unconscious. Raising high the standard of spontaneity, he seemed to issue a clarion call to all those chafing beneath the yoke of tradition and convention. The élan vital, insofar as it was understood, was perceived as an embrace of creativity, of creative freedom, of liberation from fixity. One can easily appreciate the extent to which Bergson's widely disseminated views lent further weight to the new program of physical culture, action, and direct involvement in life.

The cultivation of pantomime by German and Austrian modernists, with which this essay began, was in a sense the tip of an iceberg. When we go beneath the surface, we find a remarkable contemporary enthusiasm for physical culture, coupled with growing disdain for intellectual culture. This pursuit of the physical was virtually universal in Europe at the time. But it acquired a resonance, and an intensity, in the German-speaking world that it did not elsewhere. We can see this in the experimentation with pantomime of German and Austrian writers, in the achievement in modern dance of such figures as Grete Wiesenthal and Mary Wigman, and in the nature of the gymnastics and sports movement. The disillusionment with language—and culture—that lay at the heart of the *Sprachskepsis* of turn-of-the-century German-language thought obviously heightened the appeal of the nonverbal and physical, as we know well from the case of Hofmannsthal. But *Sprachskepsis* was as much a condition of the new cult of physicality as a contributing factor to it. In order to discover the root causes of the obsession with physicality, certain manifestations of which I have tried to sketch here in a limited way, we would have to examine yet again the social, political, and cultural institutions of Wilhelminian Germany and Habsburg Austria.

Notes

1. Quoted by A. G. Timofeev, "M. Kuzmin," *Teatr IV* (Oakland, Calif.: Berkeley Slavic Specialties, 1994), 398.

2. Perhaps the best introduction to Grete Wiesenthal and her career in dance is the exhibition catalog *Die neue Körpersprache: Grete Wiesenthal und ihr Tanz*, ed. Reingard Witzmann (Vienna: Eigenverlag der Museen der Stadt Wien, 1986). For a short but good article on Wiesenthal in English, see "Vanguard of the Liberated Waltz," *Austria Kultur* 5, no. 6 (November/December 1995): 16–17.

3. For the texts of Wedekind's writings on the circus and music hall, see "Zirkusgedanken" (153–62), "Im Zirkus" (163–69), and "Middlesex Musikhall: Ein Fragment aus meinem Londoner Tagebuch" (188–90) in Frank Wedekind, *Prosa: Erzählungen, Aufsätze, Selbstzeugnisse, Briefe*, ed. Manfred Hahn (Berlin and Weimar: Aufbau, 1969). "Zirkusgedanken," about performances of the Circus Herzog, was first published in the *Neue Zürcher Zeitung* on 29 and 30 June 1887. "Im Zirkus" also deals with performances of the Circus Herzog, which Wedekind took in while in Zurich. The piece was first published in the *Neue Zürcher Zeitung* in two parts, on 2 and 5 August 1888. The music hall piece was first published under the title "Fragment aus meinem Londoner Tagebuch" in Julius Schaumberger's periodical *Mephisto*, 28 November 1896.

4. For an excellent study of Mary Wigman in English, see Susan Manning, *Ecstasy and the Demon: Feminism and Nationalism in the Dances of Mary Wigman* (Berkeley and Los Angeles: University of California Press, 1993). For a good collection of Mary Wigman's own writings on dance, see Walter Sorell, ed. and trans., *The Mary Wigman Book: Her Writings Edited and Translated* (Middletown, Conn.: Wesleyan University Press, 1975). A good introduction to Laban's contributions to the development of modern dance is Samuel Thornton, *Laban's Theory of Movement: A New Perspective* (Boston: Plays, 1971).

5. Fritz Winther, *Körperbildung als Kunst und Pflicht* (Munich: Delphin, n.d.), 8.

6. Friedrich Nietzsche, *Menschliches, Allzumenschliches: Ein Buch für freie Geister* (Stuttgart: Kröner, 1964), 22, 23. All translations are those of the author unless otherwise stated.

7. For critical assessments of Mauthner's critique of language, see especially Gershon Weiler, *Mauthner's Critique of Language* (Cambridge: Cambridge University Press, 1970); Katherine Arens, *Functionalism and Fin de Siècle: Fritz Mauthner's Critique of Language* (New York: Lang, 1984); Elizabeth Bredeck, *Metaphors of Knowledge: Language and Thought in Mauthner's Critique* (Detroit, Mich.: Wayne State University Press, 1992); and Martin Kurzreiter, *Sprachkritik als Ideologiekritik bei Fritz Mauthner* (Frankfurt am Main: Lang, 1993). There is also interesting material in Linda Ben-Zvi, "Samuel Beckett, Fritz Mauthner, and the Limits of Language," *PMLA* 95, no. 2 (March 1980): 183–200. For a brief survey of the language issue in turn-of-the-century Austrian philosophical thought, see William M. Johnston, *The Austrian Mind: An Intellectual and Social History, 1848–1938* (Berkeley and Los Angeles: University of California Press, 1971; first paperback printing, 1983), 176–99.

8. Fritz Mauthner, "Nietzsche und Sprachkritik," in *Beiträge zu einer Kritik der Sprache*, vol. 1 (*Zur Sprache und zur Psychologie*), 2nd ed. (Stuttgart and Berlin: Cotta, 1906; 1st ed., 1901), 366.

Chapter 5

POPULISM VERSUS ELITISM IN MAX REINHARDT'S AUSTRIAN PRODUCTIONS OF THE 1920S

Michael Patterson

Berlin, 1910. The Kammerspiele of the Deutsches Theater is performing a small-cast production by Max Reinhardt, a revival of Ibsen's *Ghosts*, with which the Kammerspiele had opened four years previously, using a striking set design by Edvard Munch. The auditorium, itself not much larger than the stage, seats 346. Tickets cost twenty marks each, about the amount a female manual laborer could hope to earn in two weeks, or the equivalent of two hundred eggs, one hundred liters of milk, or ten kilos of mutton. So the audience comprises the cultural elite of Berlin, attired in furs, jewels, and dinner jackets. A few weeks later in the German capital, the Zirkus Schumann has dispensed with its high wire and performing lions to play host to Reinhardt's production of *King Oedipus*. The vast circular auditorium seats thousands, the cast numbers hundreds, and the cheapest tickets can be bought for fifty pfennigs, one-hundredth the price at the Kammerspiele, or the cost of two hundred grams of butter.

On the one hand, Reinhardt, high priest of "a temple for the elect"[1]; on the other, Reinhardt, grand showman to the masses, later to be appointed director of the Berlin Volksbühne, intending to help the theater "once more to become a social factor."[2] Intimacy versus spectacle; the whisper versus the shout; elitism versus populism: contradictions that formed essential elements of the rich personality that was Max Reinhardt, arguably the most versatile practitioner of the art of theater in the twentieth century. Thus he says to his biographer Gusti Adler: "Since I've been in the theater I've been haunted and finally obsessed by a certain idea: to bring together actors and audience—squeezed together as tight as possible."[3] Yet, one page later in the same biography, he admits: "The so-called 'good' public is in reality the worst. Dull sophisticates. Inattentive, blasé, used to being the center of attention themselves.... Only the gallery is worth anything."[4]

Reinhardt was not alone in his aspiration to make his theater a truly popular medium again. In the early years of the twentieth century, progressive theater practitioners repeatedly expressed a profound dissatisfaction with the state of the theater of the day. There were the court theaters, notably the Königliches Schauspielhaus in Berlin and the Burgtheater in Vienna. Here innovation was impossible, and a diet of expensively dressed classics and historical dramas was served, in accordance with Kaiser Wilhelm II's injunction not to perform contemporary realist plays in his theater, because one does not "plant potatoes in a vineyard."[5] Then there were the municipal and commercial theaters of the major cities and towns, significantly often under the jurisdiction of the *Gewerbepolizei* (police administration concerned with trading) and so regarded as businesses rather than cultural institutions. Predictably, therefore, these theaters tended to satisfy the conventional taste of the urban bourgeoisie. The only recent models of innovation had been Wagner's search for the *Gesamtkunstwerk* (the total work of art), coupled with the founding of the Festspielhaus in Bayreuth, and Otto Brahms's championing of naturalist theater and the creation of the Freie Bühne in Berlin. But the Festspielhaus had opened in 1876, the Freie Bühne in 1889, and neither had yet succeeded in initiating the cultural renewal that was so longed for by young German-speaking intellectuals of the 1900s.

When they looked for past models of great periods of theater, that of ancient Greece, the Middle Ages, the Spanish Golden Age, or Shakespeare, one thing appeared common to all of them: such theater was popular, offering a cultural experience to the whole community, reinforced in the case of the first three by a common religious belief that bound the audience together. The desire to renew the theater became therefore not only an aesthetic striving but also a search for a spiritual reawakening: for a theater that would be founded on a newly integrated society, for a theater that might indeed help in the creation of this new sense of community. This is the essentially utopian vision inspired by Nietzsche's image of Dionysian fellowship in *Die Geburt der Tragödie* (The Birth of Tragedy) and is reflected in works such as Georg Fuchs's *Die Schaubühne der Zukunft* (The Theatre of the Future, 1905) and *Die Revolution des Theaters* (Revolution in the Theatre, 1909): "This movement which is now considered revolutionary, is merely the renascence of a sound inheritance after a period of chaos which was at variance with our best traditions."[6]

But where was this "renascence" to come from? One possibility was to embrace existing popular culture. In pursuit of this, some theater practitioners, not without a certain sentimental condescension, embraced the *variété* (the vaudeville), a form that was lively, skillful, theatrically rich, founded on a close rapport with the audience, and evidently popular with the "ordinary public." As Fuchs rather sneeringly put it: "vaudeville offers unlimited scope to physical perfection and finds worthy recruits amongst the very dregs of the proletariat."[7] The vigor and fun of the *variété* offered the desired populist dimension, and indeed its format had been adopted by the cabaret, as in Reinhardt's own *Schall und Rauch* (Sound and Smoke). But, with the best will in the world, the *variété*, with its tawdry urban image, could hardly form the source of a communal spiritual renewal.

A more compelling alternative was offered by rural folk-theater. Here Fuchs found the hope for a possible renewal. On New Year's Day 1905 he was an enthusiastic member of the audience (or should one say congregation?) at the revival, after a three-hundred-year interval, of a Passion play in a small Bavarian town: "The atmosphere was hushed, as in a church … everything that was universal and essential became significant … there was harmony throughout that was a joy to see … everything that was done was developed according to the ways and customs of the land."[8] Perhaps in the simple staging by peasants of a medieval piece could the way forward be found.

Vienna, 1920. Reinhardt has left Berlin. There are many reasons why the acknowledged king of the Berlin theater has abdicated. Postwar Berlin is no longer very congenial. There has been fighting in the streets, the new directions in theater seem to be leading into the unshaded emotionalism and schematic characterization of Expressionism or into the megaphone dramaturgy of the new political theater. The growing Berlin film industry seems to be threatening the very future of live theater. And besides, Reinhardt is an Austrian and is returning home.

Already in 1917 there had been proposals to invite him to direct at the Burgtheater, but these had come to nothing because of petty squabbles in the administration. However, in the late summer of 1918, Reinhardt met Leopold Freiherr von Andrian, who had just been appointed as *Generalintendant* of the Court Theaters in Vienna. The two men clearly established a strong rapport, and the thrust of their discussions can be gleaned from a letter from Reinhardt, dated September 1918. Significantly, Reinhardt argued for a widely accessible theater, firmly rooted in rural Austria: "Especially at this time it has become clear that theater is not a luxury for a small upper class but an indispensable spiritual food for the public at large." To this end he supported the building in Salzburg of a festival hall that would give to Austria the blend of quasi-religious devotion and theatrical spectacle enjoyed at Bayreuth and Oberammergau. In an unashamedly nationalistic reference, he speaks of the ideal site for this *Festspielhaus*: "a site on the slope of the hill of Maria Plain, which looks across the border to Bavaria like an emblem of Austria."[9]

The collapse of the Austro-Hungarian Monarchy and the resultant administrative upheavals put an end to Andrian's and Reinhardt's plans. However, Hugo von Hofmannsthal, whom Reinhardt almost a decade previously had encouraged to do an adaptation of the medieval morality play *Everyman*,[10] now proved instrumental in securing Reinhardt's future in Austria, and was rewarded by having his *Jedermann* staged regularly as the centerpiece of the annual Salzburg Festival. This not only seemed like a realization of Fuchs's vision for the renewal of theater; it was a highly appropriate collaboration, since, like Reinhardt, Hofmannsthal had experienced the tension between elitism and populism, between the intensity of his early lyric poetry, as the young "Loris," and the search for a more public voice through the theater.

In the autumn of 1919 Reinhardt had gone to Salzburg to begin work on Max Mell's adaptation of the *Halleiner Weihnachtsspiel* (the Hallein *Christmas Play*), to be performed over Christmas in the Franciscan church there, but desperate food shortages forced rehearsals to end. So it was not until the summer of 1920 that Reinhardt began to realize his plans for a popular festival theater by staging the Austrian premiere of Hofmannsthal's *Jedermann* on the Domplatz in Salzburg. The simple atmospheric setting on the splendid steps of the Salzburg Cathedral assured much greater success than that enjoyed by the Berlin premiere of *Jedermann* in December 1911, staged like *Oedipus* in the Zirkus Schumann. As Franz Hadamowsky commented: "Under Reinhardt's direction ... the play has lost its theatrical character and has become an institution of higher spirituality."[11]

The spiritual quality of the production was not a little helped by the weather. Bernhard Paumgartner, director of the Mozarteum, who sat watching the performance beside Reinhardt, reported: "In the western sky a storm threatened. Suddenly however, when Moissi as Everyman recited the Lord's Prayer, the sun broke through the clouds, casting a gentle evening light. The cupola and towers at the front of the cathedral shone in a transfiguring glow. For the first time a flock of doves flew upward. A deep sense of awe settled on us all. Reinhardt himself was so overcome that he was hardly able to speak."[12] Hofmannsthal himself spoke of the awe-inspiring quality of the event: "The cries uttered by invisible spirits to warn Everyman of his approaching death sounded ... from all the church-towers of the city, as twilight deepened about the five thousand spectators. One of these criers had been placed in the highest tower of a medieval castle, built far above the city, and his voice sounded, weird and ghostly, about five seconds after the others, just as the first rays of the rising moon fell cold and strange from the high heavens on the hearts of the audience."[13]

Something of Reinhardt's longing to restore the theater to the social and cultic significance it had enjoyed in ancient Greece and in the Middle Ages seemed to have been achieved. Already in 1911, Reinhardt, in terms reminiscent of Fuchs, had spoken of his vision: "The audience of the great folk-theater of the future will enter the theater like a place of worship."[14] Or, as he expressed it in the 1920s: "The fundamental idea was: to let the theater become a festival again, as it was in ancient times and in the Middle Ages under the leadership of the Church, while in the great city it is in most cases rather entertainment and amusement."[15] Even Reinhardt's major spectacles had in Berlin been only a part of the capital's entertainment; here in Salzburg, so the story goes, ordinary life came to a halt, while the fortunes of Everyman captured the attention of the whole community: "Traffic is completely stopped, and the whole city listens and watches breathlessly."[16]

The acting style was also geared to a simple storytelling tradition. In his published dissertation on Reinhardt's staging of *Jedermann*, Stefan Janson speaks of "stylization like the woodcuts of the late Middle Ages.... The stiff marionette-like gestures are repeatedly emphasized in the notes in the margins of the prompt-book."[17] The tone was set by the playing of the Prologue, described by Rein-hardt's promptbook as "immobile, abrupt, curt, peasant-like."[18] And of Werner Krauss's performance as the Devil, Hadamowksy reports, "He played a gross, stu-pid Devil, one from an old fairytale."[19]

One of the more significant changes made to Hofmannsthal's text was the increase of ten guests in the banquet scene to twenty. This, together with a band of musicians and servants, not only enhanced the spectacular quality of the scene, but also allowed Reinhardt to involve local amateurs in the production. Thus, "a peas-ant player from Reichenhall played the Peasant; a citizen of Salzburg, Curiosity."[20]

Had Reinhardt then fulfilled his ambition of creating a truly popular theater in his homeland, one that would help to unite a disintegrating Europe in a new sense of community, and one that would restore the cultic significance of per-formance to its place in earlier civilizations? Before answering this question, let us pursue the career of that other Reinhardt: Reinhardt the aesthetician, Reinhardt the Viennese cultural leader, Reinhardt the elitist.

* * * * *

After his failed attempt in 1917 to be accepted into the inner circles of the Burgtheater management, Reinhardt looked elsewhere, first staging a number of productions in the Redoutensaal of the Hofburg in Vienna in 1922, causing fur-ther resentment within the Viennese theatrical establishment by being the recip-ient of generous state subsidies for the conversion of the former ballroom into a theater space. His major contribution to theater in the capital, however, came when he took over the Theater in der Josefstadt in 1923.

This fine old theater, a "gem of Austrian baroque architecture,"[21] which had opened in 1788, had established a long tradition of providing popular theatrical fare away from the center of Vienna. The most recent director, Josef Jarno, who had held the post since 1899, had managed to infiltrate into the program of triv-ial farces, especially French imports, more serious work, including Arthur Schnitzler, Ibsen, Shaw, and even Strindberg (who was performed by Jarno when no other Viennese theater would touch him). However, as Joseph Gregor la-mented, not only was the theater hopelessly antiquated—"needless to say, it lacks any electrical or hydraulic equipment"—but it had also lacked a sense of direc-tion—"what this theater possessed was a brilliantly glittering variety of achieve-ments and at the same time a tragic destiny that dragged it down without rendering it ignoble.... What was lacking in this theater was an inner sense of direction,... a style."[22]

Gregor hoped that, under the new management, the Josefstädter Theater would discover a new role. He argued that with the end of German Empire ("This art was of course very strongly anchored in the stylistic concepts of the imperialist age"), there was now no place for mass spectacles: "Now the theater is about to swing back to the opposite, to turn from the theater of the masses to that of the finest dialogue, which will not, however, be the luxury of individuals as in the Kammerspiele, but, as in the Josefstädter Theater, the boon of a stage that was once a people's theater."[23]

Reinhardt's own program was more modest. He declared that his intention was merely "to perform theater with good actors in a suitable building." He was full of respectful admiration for the old building: "The acoustics are wonderful. For me it is like an old violin or a priceless vase."[24] After its full refurbishment, Reinhardt attracted some of the finest German-speaking actors to his new theater, which had a capacity just over twice that of the Kammerspiele, and he soon established it as the leading theater of Austria.

His program was full, serious, and ambitious. It opened with Goldoni's *The Servant of Two Masters* on 1 April 1924. The same month saw productions of Schiller's *Kabale und Liebe* (Intrigue and Love) and, two years after its premiere in Munich, Hofmannsthal's *Der Schwierige* (The Difficult Man). May brought two classical productions, Calderón's *La dama duende* (The Phantom Lady) and Shakespeare's *The Merchant of Venice*. The only lightweight piece was a French play, *Aimée* (Beloved), clearly chosen as a vehicle for Helene Thimig, who appeared in the title role, and the play was not directed by Reinhardt. The summer continued to include classics by Dostoyevsky, Strindberg, and Gogol, as well as one serious contemporary piece, Eugene O'Neill's *Anna Christie*, again none of them directed by Reinhardt. During the autumn and winter months, apart from a revival of Max Mell's *Apostelspiel* (Apostle Play), there were no significant premieres until *A Midsummer Night's Dream* opened in February 1925. There followed Schnitzler's *Anatol*, Shakespeare's *King Lear*, Galsworthy's *Loyalties*, and, in May, Werfel's *Juarez and Maximilian*. For the rest the diet was becoming increasingly trivial, and the high tone of the initial program was engaged in a process of what we would now call "dumbing down."

Production styles were also unadventurous. Photographs in Hans Böhm's *Die Wiener Reinhardt-Bühne im Lichtbild*, which proudly declares that the pictures were taken during the actual performance, reveal conventionally realistic sets and costumes, apart from a fairly outlandish striped design by Oskar Strnad for the costumes in *King Lear*. To judge by these images, the revolution in scenic design that characterized much of the theater of the first quarter of the century, exemplified by the work of Appia, Craig, Roller, and the Expressionists, might simply have never happened. It is noteworthy, too, that none of the texts selected for performance could be considered avant-garde—no Expressionist writers, no Sternheim, no Pirandello, definitely no political theater or *Zeitstücke* dealing with topical social issues. Whatever Reinhardt's attempt to create a renascence in theater, it certainly was not going to lie in his embrace of modernism.

No doubt the good citizens of Vienna did not desire anything very innovative and challenging, and experimental work might well have been inappropriate, but one wonders whether Reinhardt's confession, in a conversation with Manfred Georg in 1932, did not refer to his experience at the Theater in der Josefstadt: "I once made a big mistake. I sat my audience in armchairs that were too comfortable. In armchairs the audience wants to be entertained. On wooden benches they get involved."[25]

Meanwhile, on the wooden benches, the ostensibly populist theater was thriving. *Jedermann* was staged again in the summer of 1921. The following year, a new piece by Hofmannsthal, based on Calderón, *Das Salzburger große Welttheater* (The Salzburg Great World Theater), was performed in the Kollegienkirche. The climax of this piece presents the figure of the Beggar, threatening the figures of power that surround him. In Hofmannsthal's own words: "The Beggar raises his ax against everything that opposes him.... King, Rich Man, Peasant (who over here represents the conservatism of the secure, small propertyholder) ... the edifice of an ordered society that has lasted a thousand years."[26] However, this act of rebellion soon fails, and after a Road-to-Damascus-like conversion, the Beggar drops his ax and resolves to withdraw to the woods to live out his life as a hermit. As in Reinhardt's much-traveled production of Vollmoeller's *Das Mirakel* (The Miracle), where the nun, chastened by her experience of normal life, returns obediently to her convent, the solution here is profoundly Catholic and conservative. And indeed, Reinhardt regarded the Beggar's initial stance as characteristic of the Communists: "The beggar [is] deeply affected by communistic ideas, which are carried ad absurdum."[27]

Reinhardt's intentions were never political, but a public act of performance cannot avoid containing a political meaning, even if it merely reinforces the attitudes of the audience. By allying themselves to a conservative and acquiescent political philosophy, an attempt, amid the chaos of postwar Europe, to preserve "the edifice of an ordered society that has lasted a thousand years," Reinhardt and Hofmannsthal may have been populist in the sense that they reflected the thinking of a Catholic Austrian rural populace. In the wider context of developments across the Continent, they were swimming against the tide of the popular movements of fascism, socialism, and communism.

Nor were the Salzburg productions populist in the sense that they were born of the community, as in Oberammergau. True, local amateurs did participate in minor roles or as extras, and two versions of the piece were later toured by amateurs, one in dialect, the other performed by local children. But the major speaking parts of Reinhardt's production were taken by the top German-speaking actors of the day: Alexander Moissi, Johanna Terwin, Helene Thimig, Hedwig Bleibtreu, Heinrich George, Werner Krauss and Wilhelm Dieterle. Moreover, despite the strong lines of the production, Reinhardt was not prepared to sacrifice the subtleties of fine acting. As Janson records of Reinhardt's promptbook: "It is significant how detailed is the laying down of a particular coloring of mood required by a passage of text."[28]

Moreover, the vast open-air public performance area of the Cathedral Square, which he chose for *Jederman*, was an effort less to make the piece accessible to the ordinary citizens of Salzburg than to enjoy the advantages of a large-scale arena that lent freedom to and exploited the strengths of his actors. As he had said in an interview a decade previously: "Those works of theater, in which decorative detail is forced into the background, once again afford the actor the yearned for opportunity of standing in the middle of the audience, free from the illusions of set design."[29]

The fact is that despite the initial impetus behind the Salzburg Festival productions, Reinhardt was not performing in a populist style or catering for a mass audience. He was here, merely on a larger scale, exploring the aesthetics of the theater and playing to a wider elite. As Janson admits, "The performances did not take place before the 'people,' but before an audience of the international elite, among whom there were many who regarded it as a social duty to have attended a performance."[30]

* * * * *

Reinhardt's hope to restore a sacral quality to theater, one to which audiences would respond in harmonious ecstasy, remained a dream, as it did with the utopian visions of Georg Fuchs, Edward Gordon Craig, Antonin Artaud, and many others. How could it be otherwise in the complex, sophisticated, and individualistic societies of the twentieth century? How indeed could a secular Jew such as Reinhardt identify wholly with the Catholic world of *Everyman* or of Calderón and find here a source of renewal? It would soon become clear that Dionysian ecstasy could not be achieved by theater, however excellently it was performed, but only by appealing to the lowest common denominator in the national psyche. So it was left to that other Austrian showman, Adolf Hitler, to generate a sense of self-surrendering passion in his audiences. It is sobering to reflect that a well-intentioned but nationalistically colored search for a true theater of and for the people to some extent anticipated the blind devotion cultivated by the Nazis. Ominously, the Passion play so praised by Fuchs happened to take place in the town of Dachau,[31] and Reinhardt's "Theater of the Five Thousand," in which "a human ring of thousands ... opens the soul of the people once more to the drama,"[32] was utterly overshadowed just over a decade later by the vast Nazi Party rally at Nuremberg.

One must not imply, however, that Reinhardt, or indeed Fuchs, was instrumental in furthering fascist barbarism. On the contrary, a utopian vision may operate as a progressive force in social thinking. As Mark Fortier argues in *Theory/Theatre*: "As an alternative to questioning or subverting the status quo, cultural forms can also take on a utopian or romance function, presenting a vision of a different social order preferable to our own. As a public space, theatre functions as what the anthropologist Victor Turner calls the liminoid, a place set apart for the process of transformation."[33]

In that "liminoid," Reinhardt devoted his life to creating beauty as he envisioned it and to discovering truth as he understood it. If that beauty and that truth could be communicated best in the intimacy of a small auditorium, as with Ibsen's *Ghosts*, then Reinhardt functioned as an elitist; if, as with *Jedermann*, a vast public arena was more suited, then he could claim to be a populist.

As Hofmannsthal summed it up: "What fascinates him is the solution of any given problem."[34]

Thus, despite occasional pronouncements about the importance of creating theater for the masses, Reinhardt was neither a political nor a social reformer, was neither committed to an agenda of reinventing the nature of the theatrical experience (as was Artaud, for example) nor determined to experiment in isolation free from the pressures of commerce and popular culture (as was, for instance, Jerzy Grotowski). Max Reinhardt was wholly dedicated to the theater, and it was the needs of the theater that he constantly sought to fulfill rather than some political program. As he said in his piece, "On the Living Theatre," written for Oliver Sayler's volume: "It would be a theory as barbaric as it is incompatible with the principles of theatrical art to measure with the same yard stick, to press into the same mold, the wonderful wealth of the world's literature. The mere suggestion of such an attempt is a typical example of pedantic scholasticism. There is no one form of theatre which is the only true artistic form. Let good actors today play in a barn or in a theatre, tomorrow at an inn or inside a church, or, in the Devil's name, even on an expressionistic stage: if the place corresponds with the play, something wonderful will be the outcome."[35]

Reinhart's emphasis then is neither on populism nor elitism, but only on good actors and good theater, on creating a space and an audience appropriate to the dramatic material. And if one were to compare Reinhardt's achievement with that of the other German theatrical giant of our century, Bertolt Brecht, then one has to recognize an ironical twist to their careers: Brecht, the great champion of the masses, forced into exile and having to work in elitist fashion with a select band of supporters; while Reinhardt, having rejected Goebbels's offer of becoming an "honorary Aryan," ends up in the United States working in the most populist medium of the day, Hollywood movies.

Notes

1. Interview with Max Reinhardt by unidentified writer in *Theaterrundschau* 1352 (1911): 11; quoted in *Max Reinhardt: Ich bin nichts als Theatermann*, ed. Hugo Fetting (Berlin: Henschelverlag, 1989), 446.
2. *Das litterarische Echo* 13 (1910/11); quoted in *Max Reinhardt*, ed. Fetting, 447.
3. Gusti Adler, *Max Reinhardt* (Salzburg: Festungsverlag, 1964), 42.
4. Ibid., 43.
5. *Vossische Zeitung* (Berlin), 15 June 1913.
6. Georg Fuchs, *Revolution in the Theatre*, condensed and adapted by Constance Connor Kuhn (Ithaca: Cornell University Press, 1959), 175.
7. Ibid., 146.
8. Ibid., 29.
9. Franz Hadamowsky, *Reinhardt und Salzburg* (Salzburg: Residenzverlag, 1963), 21.

10. "Der Gedanke, die Circusidee gerade auf das Mysterium auszunutzen, liegt so nahe, daß uns jeden Tag irgend jemand zuvorkommen kann." Arthur Kahane (writing on Reinhardt's behalf) to Hofmannsthal, 29 November 1910; quoted from Hugo von Hofmannsthal, Jedermann. *Das Spiel vom Sterben des Reichen Mannes und Max Reinhardts Inszenierungen. Texte, Dokumente, Bilder*, ed. Edda Leisler and Gisela Prossnitz (Frankfurt am Main: Suhrkamp, 1973), 176.

11. Hadamowsky, *Reinhardt*, 33.

12. Ibid., 37.

13. Hugo von Hofmannsthal, "Reinhardt as an International Force," trans. Sidney Howard, in *Max Reinhardt and His Theatre*, ed. Oliver M. Sayler (New York: Brentano, 1924), 25–26.

14. Interview in *Theaterrundschau* 1352 (1911): 11; quoted in *Max Reinhardt*, ed. Fetting, 448.

15. "In Search of a Living Theatre," trans. Lucie R. Sayler, in *Max Reinhardt*, ed. Sayler, 189.

16. Ibid., 190.

17. Stefan Janson, *Hugo von Hofmannsthals* Jedermann *in der Regiebearbeitung durch Max Reinhardt* (Frankfurt am Main: Lang, 1978), 16.

18. Ibid., 12.

19. Hadamowsky, *Reinhardt*, 36.

20. Quoted in *Max Reinhardt*, ed. Sayler, 192.

21. Ibid., 160.

22. Joseph Gregor, *Das Theater in der Wiener Josefstadt* (Vienna: Wiener Drucke, 1924), 54.

23. Ibid., 62.

24. *Neue Freie Presse* (Vienna), 24 March 1924; quoted in *Max Reinhardt*, ed. Fetting, 262.

25. Quoted in *Max Reinhardt*, ed. Fetting, 473.

26. Hugo von Hofmannsthal, "Dritter Brief aus Wien," *Aufzeichnungen* (Frankfurt am Main: Suhrkamp, 1959), 297.

27. Quoted in *Max Reinhardt*, ed. Sayler, 191–92.

28. Janson, *Hugo von Hofmannsthals* Jedermann, 11.

29. *Das litterarische Echo* 13 (1910/11); quoted in *Max Reinhardt*, ed. Fetting, 446.

30. Janson, *Hugo von Hofmannsthals* Jedermann, 65–66.

31. I am indebted to Nigel Ward for pointing this out in his unpublished Ph.D. dissertation, "The Development in European Drama of a Theoretical Framework by Which Directors Approach a Text and Translate It to Performance" (University of Warwick, 1999), 26.

32. Robert Breuer, "The Dramatic Value of Space and the Masses," in *Max Reinhardt*, ed. Sayler, 26.

33. Mark Fortier, *Theory/Theatre: An Introduction* (London: Routledge, 1997), 114.

34. Hofmannsthal, "Reinhardt," quoted in *Max Reinhardt*, ed. Sayler, 26.

35. "In Search of a Living Theatre," in *Max Reinhardt*, ed., Sayler, 64. All translations, except those taken from Oliver M. Sayler's *Max Reinhardt and His Theatre* and from Constance Connor Kuhn's edition of Georg Fuchs's *Revolution in the Theatre*, are those of the author unless otherwise stated.

Part Two

POST-HOLOCAUST
AND POSTMODERN THEATER

ELFRIEDE JELINEK'S *NORA* PROJECT; OR, WHAT HAPPENS WHEN NORA MEETS THE CAPITALISTS

Christine Kiebuzinska

The distinguishing feature of the work of the contemporary Austrian writer Elfriede Jelinek is the unmasking of the illusion perpetuated by misreadings of canonical texts. In her play *Was geschah, nachdem Nora ihren Mann verlassen hatte oder Stützen der Gesellschaften* (What Happened after Nora Left Her Husband and Met the Pillars of Societies), written in 1979 as a reflection upon the centennial of Henrik Ibsen's *A Doll's House,* Jelinek superimposes a strong materialist feminist reading on a range of contemporary issues: the demythologization of canonical texts that adhere to the fictions of everyday life, the continuity of patriarchal structures in capitalist market economies, and the limitations of utopian individualism in feminist myths.[1] Jelinek recognizes that a critique of Ibsen's classic simultaneously necessitates a demystification of the modes of representation, which are most successful in the dissemination of ideologies. In her deconstruction of Ibsen's *A Doll's House,* Jelinek transposes the action of the play to reveal "what happened after Nora left her husband and met the pillars of societies."[2]

Ibsen's *A Doll's House* is continually present in *Nora,* particularly in Jelinek's deconstruction of its idealistic implications, the heroic strength of the heroine, and the utopian hopes for equality in the partnership of the married couple. In Jelinek's version, however, the psychological depth of the characters has disappeared, and illusions about gender equality are undermined by her parody of the clichés that continue to surround the reception of Ibsen's play. Throughout Ibsen's play, we see Torvald carefully creating the terms and appropriate postures of his fictive world out of moral maxims on debt, responsibility, the telling of lies, the aesthetic differences between knitting and embroidery, and even on eating macaroons. Nora in turn has become an accomplished actress in sustaining her fiction of youthfulness and irresponsibility by acting out the prettifying, self-deluding fiction of innocence for the eight years of their marriage. When the "wonderful" does not happen, Nora and Torvald's fictions collapse and they are left, as in theater, with only the appearance of a marriage.[3] Nora discards her dancing girl costume and assumes the adult costume essential to her new recreation of self as an uncompromising and strong-minded heroine capable of taking on all society. It is in this somewhat frayed adult "costume" from the last scene of *A Doll's House* that Nora wanders into Jelinek's script looking for a self-fulfilling job in a factory in order to test her quest for self-realization.

In Jelinek's play, Nora's "redefinition" occurs in the time-space of the Germany of the 1920s, as it is undergoing economic collapse following the economic crash and hyperinflation, ultimately leading to the rise of Hitler's National Socialism. Simultaneously Jelinek also projects the action into the time-space of the 1970s, a time-space that represents the accelerated economic development in West Germany as well as the emergence of Germany's feminist movement. Jelinek sets the play into these time-spaces in order to demonstrate the ideological continuities between National Socialism and the contemporary German *Wirtschaftswunder*, or economic miracle, brought about through market deregulations and highly sophisticated takeover maneuvers, behind which the unseen power of the multinational corporations conspires to overcome political and legal constraints. In her play, Jelinek reveals the mechanism of "the linguistic cover-up of what a capitalist knows and thinks, but doesn't express publicly,"[4] and this was why Jelinek wrote her *Nora* "as a kind of *Wirtschaftskrimi* [business crime novel]."[5]

Since the very title of Jelinek's play refers to both Ibsen's *A Doll's House* and *The Pillars of Society*, it might be fruitful to examine how Ibsen's texts function as pretexts to *Nora*. *A Doll's House* provides the entire ensemble of characters with the exception of Dr. Rank; from *The Pillars of Society* Jelinek borrows the motive of land speculation, for the source of Konsul Weygang's characterization in *Nora* as a speculator, capitalist and profiteer is not difficult to recognize in the figure of Konsul Bernick from Ibsen's play.[6] At the same time, Jelinek playfully changes the "pillars of society" to "pillars of societies," the plural suggesting a dispersal of power structures in the form of multinational banks and corporations. Jelinek also replaces the railroad project, so symbolic of nineteenth-century capitalist expansion, with the much more deadly enterprise of an atomic power plant on the site of a profit-losing cotton mill. Ultimately, Jelinek's reliance on the ethical dilemma rather than the actual characters or situations of *The Pillars of Society* invests contemporary issues with archetypal attributes that bring the continuities of the cultural past into play.

Jelinek's declaration that "plays by women should not deal with emotions"[7] provides a means of interpreting her Nora, for the play serves as an example of her critique of the subjective fictions perpetuated by the many interpretations of Ibsen's drama about Nora's quest for self-realization. In Jelinek's play, however,

Nora's search for meaning takes place within a context wherein the highly individualized mechanism of patriarchal capitalism, so evident in *The Pillars of Society*, absorbs Nora's striving for selfhood to its own purposes. Jelinek eliminates the subtextual depth of Ibsen's characterizations by flattening out characters to mere surfaces in order to show how Nora's aspirations for selfhood must be tested in the reality of the cutthroat jungle marketplace of corporate takeovers, diversions of funds, and the corruption of all traces of moral order.

According to Jelinek, in a society dominated by crude materialism and the predatory pursuit of success, personal self-realization is the ultimate fiction. In re-imagining Nora as an innocent who wanders into the text of *The Pillars of Society*, Jelinek reveals that Nora's conditioning as consumer of her own myth is perfected to the point where individual identity is indistinguishable from societal role. Thus any attempt on Nora's part to change her life by slamming shut the door to the "doll's house" is sabotaged from the outset because it is conceptualized from within the power framework Nora tries to escape, refracted in Jelinek's version in the many "societies" she encounters as she proceeds from mill-worker to a capitalist's mistress and back to the entrapment of the "doll's house."

Jelinek's method depends on the deconstruction of Ibsen's plays by means of a collage that juxtaposes quotations from Ibsen's canonical texts with "ready-mades" from popular scandal sheets, advertisements, television talk shows, soap operas, and popular film. She accomplishes this by means of selecting, transposing, and dispersing fragments from Ibsen's texts and mixing them up with contemporary clichés about individualism and self-realization from contemporary sources. Ultimately, *Nora* reflects Jelinek's experimentation with an intertextual collage of "ready-mades" or "quotations" from Ibsen, Hitler, Mussolini, Wedekind, women's magazines, pulp fiction, and market analysis, as well as quotations from her own interviews and critical articles in which she comments on the limitations of liberal feminism. Though these elements coexist in a single textual space, the relation of these discourses with each other is often in conflict. At the same time, Jelinek's play self-consciously "rewrites" already scripted texts in order to display how ideological myths are perpetuated from Ibsen's time until the present, with the two worldviews coexisting in the "repetition" of archetypes.

The intention of Jelinek's distorted mimicry of Ibsen's pretexts is to foreground and estrange aspects of the original's style and message, while ensuring that the origins of the new imitation are still recognizable. Michael Newman mentions that the success of Jelinek's eclecticism and mixing up of codes depends on the intertext being recognized: "[P]arody is not just an internal relation between the work and its model, but is necessarily pragmatic, in that it assumes the audience will 'get' the reference, and appreciate the double coding."[8]

In foregrounding her explicit references to Ibsen's two classics, Jelinek depends on the audience's knowledge of both *A Doll's House* and *The Pillars of Society*, as well as a familiarity with the ideological debates surrounding contemporary feminism, capitalist market economies, and residues of fascist myths in contemporary politics. However, the fragments from Ibsen and contemporary media are frequently decontextualized, and characters seem to quote from Ibsen's text as second-rate performers rather than as characters. Ultimately, the assembly-line language that the characters have appropriated from Ibsen saps them of their strength to think through and to articulate their situation. As a result, Jelinek's characters occupy a distinctly postmodern space, what Rosalind Krauss calls a "paraliterary space ... of debate, quotation, partisanship, betrayal, reconciliation; but ... not the space of unity, coherence, or resolution that we think of as constituting the work of art."[9]

Quotations from both of Ibsen's texts are marked as if from a *chambre d'échos*, for even before the spectator views the play, the title alone signals that this is a sequel, or "what happens next." Similarly, the first line sets up the identifying relationship to Ibsen's text, "I'm Nora, the same as in the play by Ibsen."[10] The intertextual relationship is thus based on the use of self-reflexive references, as later we are reminded of the relationship to the original when Weygang identifies Nora as "the central character with the same name as in Ibsen" (20). Jelinek calls attention to the fact that her play is a parody of Ibsen, when, for example, Helmer condescendingly acknowledges to Krogstad that Frau Linde is now his housekeeper, "We all know from the theater that you had once loved this woman, the one now in the kitchen" (47). The self-reflexive quotations function to alert the spectator to watch for the follies in the original.

Jelinek transforms Nora by focusing entirely on the surfaces of Ibsen's character. For her, Nora becomes a performing squirrel whose qualifications for the marketplace include the dancing of the tarantella and performing gymnastic exercises such as splits, backbends, and leaps to show her "flexibility." Various references to flying and jumping animals, such as "my little lark" or "my squirrel," are exaggerated. At the same time, allusions to Nora's willful little-girl impudence and obstinacy become parodies of Ibsen's Nora as she threatens to stamp her "little foot" and thump her "little fist" if she does not get her way (30). In this manner, actions are not so much "performed" as "announced" to reveal Nora's unconscious appropriation of her familiar role of the performing squirrel and the chirping lark. Similarly, the other characters from *A Doll's House* are presented as one-track speech machines. For example, Anne Marie quotes automatically her cloyingly sentimental platitudes on motherhood, Frau Linde enacts her one-track spiel on care and devotion, and Torvald flatly pronounces his robotic clichés on fiscal and moral responsibility. Ultimately, these quotations reveal that the characters are merely acting out a previously scripted life text, for it is important to remember that for Jelinek her characters "exist only in language, and as long as they speak, they are present; when they don't speak, they disappear."[11]

In Jelinek's version, Nora epitomizes the exploitation of woman as a sexual object, changing hands several times during the course of the action. Nora collaborates in this process, for she uses her sexuality, both subtly by making herself attractive to Weygang and overtly to wheedle information from Torvald. In order to shatter the conventional connotations of love and marriage, Jelinek confuses these with money and economics by having the former talked about in a style or jargon that would normally be used for the latter, and vice versa: "When one speaks of love, it should be presented completely in an objective manner, and when the conversation turns to economics the tone should be quite sentimental and sensual."[12] Jelinek explains that anyone who at this time believes that it is still possible to present characters who act as individuals is strongly mistaken: "Instead, one can only present characters as zombies, or as holders of constructed ideology or significance, but not as fully developed individuals with joy or sorrow and all that garbage; that is gone, once and for all time."[13]

Nora also presents the contradictions between bourgeois and working-class women's emancipation, and for this purpose Jelinek introduces Eva and the other women workers in the mill factory as the only truly new characters. In particular, Eva serves as Jelinek's skeptical mouthpiece, who in her radicalism, as Ute Nyssen comments, has strong affinities to Ulrike Meinhof.[14] Through Eva, Jelinek condemns Nora's romantic notions of individualism, particularly when the price for Nora's self-realization comes at the cost of the other working women's continuous exploitation, for Eva is the only one to understand that the sudden prettification of their workplace with curtains, flower boxes, a library, and even a children's crèche does not represent improvement but is instead a "cheap" cover-up for the unemployment that threatens to result once the factory changes hands.

Jelinek parodies the language of the contemporary women's movement from the play's first lines as Nora explains that she has left the comforts of her middle-class home so that she can develop herself from "object to subject" in the workplace (7). Thus, Nora's "search for self" (9) clashes with the personnel manager's cynical observation that it is the task of employers to "promote and protect" the "full development" of the personality of their employees (7). While Nora's middle-class assumption is that emancipation comes through self-realization in work, for the mill-factory working women their "productive labor" in the factory is a necessary evil. The scenes in the factory illustrate not only Nora's naïveté but also her insensitivity to the plight of the other women workers, and Jelinek foregrounds this in the slight changes of vocabulary that separate the working women's language and Nora's vocabulary of the 1970s women's liberation. As she tries to explain her abandonment of a husband, children, and the comforts of her middle-class home to Eva and the other female workers, it becomes evident that Nora's language, as the only medium of defining herself, is also what distances her from the other women, who cannot understand her pursuit of her self-determination as "*Lebensaufgabe*" (life's work), since for them the dehumanizing routine of clock-punching, piecework, and quality control has more to do with "*Leben aufgeben*" (to surrender life). While Nora promotes her complexity in referring to her *Verteilung* (inner split) of personal desires, Eva and the others fear *Zerteilung* (dismemberment) by the machines. And while Nora attempts to convince them that marriage and children represent the "falsehood" that prevents women from exploring their innate destiny, Eva counters that for her and the other factory workers, "the machine is the false part" (10).

Through these linguistic juxtapositions Jelinek illustrates that Nora's clichés drawn from the vocabulary of liberal feminism are nothing more than middle-class self-indulgences in the face of the working women's painful struggle with "self-alienation" and "self-estrangement" from love in marriage, the rearing of children, and comforts of home. The hypocrisy of Nora's middle-class values in the factory surfaces, when within moments, she recognizes that she has met the best that can be attained in Weygang and adopts the exaggerated discourse of sentimental love from pulp fiction. Ultimately, Jelinek's characterization of Nora represents her settling of accounts with the liberal and radical feminism of the 1970s, and she focuses on the images of the Nora figure that exhibit the contradictions between Nora's quest for self-realization and such helpless dependent feminine expressions as "I frighten more easily than you do, since feelings are more feminine" (20). Nora's feminism, insofar as Nora understands it, is perverted into a deteriorated myth of the essential difference between the nature of man and woman.

Thus the whole repertoire of Nora's observations about the "essential feminine" (24) is drawn from social Darwinism or biological determinism (23), and the theories from the turn of the century as well as the feminist theories of the 1970s ultimately appear as unhistoricized and unpoliticized reified myths, subsumed equally to the purposes of the radical left as well as the reactionary right, to terrorists or fascists. Therefore it is with extreme awareness of irony that Jelinek has Nora announce that she refuses to be "a sexual parasite" (52). Familiar quotations from Freud, Hitler, and Mussolini on the woman's role are juxtaposed with equally recognizable phrases such as "the history of women until recently was the history of their murder" (51) from the radical feminist movement. In defending her use of these ready-mades, Jelinek explains that as an author she can present her meaning in her own words. However, she writes that "most things have been said so frequently that it's unnecessary to create something that has already been said elsewhere much better." Her main focus is not on the characters, who are, as Jelinek explains, mere self-conscious fictions, but on the nature of discourse, as she probes language and its ability to reformulate, reiterate, and translate the already spoken.[15]

Nora easily confuses phrases generated by the women's movement—for example, "pornography kills women" (18)—with those from the pulp fiction clichés on love. As a result, when later in the play she is turned into an S&M quotation from pornography, she does not recognize her situation. Similarly she is reduced to a stereotype of a femme fatale, (32) femme fragile (33), Wedekind's Lulu (40), or a flapper (57). Nor can she recognize misogynistic stereotypes when her new lover Weygang and his friends quote Freud or imitate Wittgenstein: "A woman is that which does not speak and about what one cannot speak." "Precisely. This Freud says that first one has to experience what it means to be castrated before one can begin to speak" (24). Indeed, Nora illustrates this point of view when she says: "My husband wanted me to be at home and closed up, since the wife should not look to the sides, but primarily into herself or her husband" (7). What Jelinek shows is that Nora fails to develop a critical distance on her marriage with Torvald and instead appropriates the language of the 1970s feminists on the woman's role in marriage. In other words, one stereotype supplants another.

Thus feminist discourse does not liberate Nora but instead makes her a collaborator in the perpetuation of misogynistic stereotypes concerning the feminine. She uses Freud on "penis envy" to explain the inferior creative output of women as readily as her references to "women's solidarity," which she interprets by the fact that "women by nature have a stronger bond to each other" (13). Solidarity is thus made into another myth that collapses in her confrontation with the manager's secretary, a scene that illustrates that class and status are in opposition to notions of solidarity:

> *Nora*: Are you not also a woman …?
> *Secretary*: Of course, isn't that obvious?
> *Nora*: Why don't you then look like a woman, I mean cheerful? Why do you look so joyless?
> *Secretary*: When one's a private secretary to the manager one doesn't need to keep a grin on one's face all the time, particularly since one's personal life circumstances aren't necessarily pretty.
> *Nora*: Don't you feel some solidarity with me?
> *Secretary*: At the most we have in common similar pain in childbirth…. Although I suspect that I'll feel these pains more strongly than you. (15)

The painful juxtapositions of Nora's rhetoric to the working women's reality are balanced with highly comical effects as Nora tries out her rhetoric of liberal feminism when moving into the milieu of the "pillars of societies." Nora's movement into that world has to do with her "artistic" talents, which are soon put to good use by the personnel manager of the factory in which she now works to provide "classy" entertainment in the form of two choral arrangements for mixed voices and a short but "cultured" tarantella dance interlude for distinguished visiting dignitaries, among whom is Konsul Weygang. Weygang and the other dignitaries are interested in buying the profit-losing factory for their project of building an atomic works at the site. Indeed it is obvious that Jelinek's Nora has absorbed exceedingly well Torvald's guidance of her "talent" to please him as the spectator in their private theater in *A Doll's House*. She reminds herself, in Jelinek's version, "to repeat the movements once more, as my husband taught me, sensually, but not too sensually" (18). Despite this, she throws in acrobatic tricks and makes a backbend, thereby "deforming" her body. The manager of the factory takes up Torvald's former paternalistic position and scolds Nora for dancing so "tempestuously," for she might "hurt herself" and hence not be able to fulfill her piecework quota. Weygang, however, is attracted by her grand leaps, twists, and backbends. For the manager, Nora's movements appear "uneconomical," but for Weygang, Nora's body interprets the capitalistic rhetoric of "risk-taking" capitalism, and her painful acrobatic exhibition serves as an ideal model of "flexibility" as she explains that "my husband wanted me to be sensual but not too sensual" (18).

To set off Nora's desirability on the market, Weygang foregrounds his total devotion and overwhelming desire for "my Nora my sunshine and my precious possession." However, though he is quite taken with his new possession, he shows that he is also interested in her exchange value before it turns into a loss: "What is significant about women is that they present easily damaged goods, quality before quantity" (26). The progress of the not-so-subtle buying and selling of Nora occurs when he tempts the Minister, who would also like to possess her, for "she could also be my sunshine as easily":

> *Weygang:* She not only has a face and body, but also a considerable general education.
> *Minister:* You're a good businessman, Fritz, one has to give you credit for that, you know how to sell.
> *Weygang:* Yes, I love her and am totally committed to her.
> *Minister:* I too could love her. (26)

The Minister is excited by the description of Nora's market qualities of incomparable skin, body, and charm, and Weygang entices him further by mentioning that her most significant asset is her childlike innocence, which borders on perversion, almost exactly like Wedekind's Lulu, for, like Lulu, Nora has no discernible moral standards. Since for Weygang Nora's sexuality is an abstract commodity, it can be traded in a manner similar to contracts for "futures" in the financial markets. Though Weygang puts the finishing touches to his deal with the Minister by proclaiming that he will live faithfully with Nora into old age, "like Philemon and Baucis," he soon qualifies this sentimental allusion by letting the Minister know that once his passion wanes, Nora will become available for the Minister's pleasure:

> *Weygang:* In general, that's been my experience, the greatest passion lasts only a short while. If you wait, until my passion has played itself out, you can take her.
> *Minister:* Done.
> *Weygang:* The loss of Nora will cut my heart with knives.
> *Minister:* You shouldn't give her away for nothing. The administrations of three countries are tearing themselves to pieces over the deal, and I have the key to it.
> *Weygang:* It's a deal. Let's say in three weeks. (27)

Jelinek provides several perspectives from which to view Nora's body, for Weygang sees it as both a source for the regeneration of new energy and simultaneously as an expensive investment. Nora, too, views her body as objectified goods or capital: "I've always taken care of my body" (19). In fact, Nora's body provides an access to further riches, and both Weygang and Nora acknowledge that a business transaction has taken place as Weygang watches her perform the tarantella: "Don't I have the right to see my newest most expensive *property?*" asks Weygang, and Nora replies, "But hopefully you also own many more expensive *properties*" (19). By showing the similarity of the language of market economies and love, the semantic romantic language of "you are precious to me" is thus subjected to examination. Thus love becomes a cover-up for the fact that the financially potent Weygang is going to help Nora in her climb up the social ladder. When Nora leaves the factory on Weygang's arm, Eva observes that behind their manifested love lies the "shadow of speculation" (22). In this manner Nora becomes property for the second time.

To enhance her own investment in her body, Nora's acrobatic exercises become a means of marking her market value as a woman. However, with increasing age and decreasing attractiveness, her exercises become less pliable, less graceful, and show her off to a disadvantage. Weygang cold-bloodedly evaluates his investment and its diminishing returns: her aging body with its drooping buttocks, flabby arms, and orange-like cellulose skin (55–56). In his scrutiny of Nora's body Weygang borrows the discourse of the cosmetics industry, with its attention to skin texture, the flabbiness of thighs and upper arms, and disgusting-looking skin. When Nora's body is no longer of any use for Weygang, he accepts it as a market loss. In reflecting on the difference between capital and Nora's body, Weygang comes to the conclusion that unlike the spreading of a woman's body, "capital never decreases in attractiveness when there's more of it," for "it's greatest attraction is that quite simply there's more" (26, 28).

Many of the quotations from *A Doll's House* are distributed subversively to Nora and Weygang, particularly the discourse on frugality and financial solidity. The quotation from Ibsen, "What's the name of the bird that eats up money?" (46) when it is placed in the context of a major speculation by Weygang, no longer represents Torvald's lecture on the bourgeois family ideal of fiscal responsibility. Instead, in the new context, the quotation functions as an expression of "exchange," for Nora cannot just "eat up money" without paying for her keep. Weygang the capitalist can make more money out of money without producing anything. But Nora must literally give of herself; "otherwise buying and selling, trade and exchange come to a standstill" (30).

In Weygang's interests and the interests of capitalism, Nora is completely dispossessed of her voice to make decisions about her body. Assuming her voice, Weygang speaks out both his and her part (32), and Nora remains standing benumbed (33). Weygang shows how well he knows Ibsen's *A Doll's House* by appealing to her to become his "partner" instead of his "little lark." And Nora has nothing with which to resist him but her whole repertoire of arabesques, backbends, and splits. "Often," Weygang explains, "cruelty is a sign of love," as he convinces her in her own voice to seduce Torvald, for the entire enterprise depends on her: "Your big bear would jump around and do all kinds of funny pranks," he promises, disguised by her voice. He patiently explains that the situation at the factory resembles precisely that of Ibsen's *The Pillars of Society*, since, in order for the "railroad" to be built for "the good of mankind," one must have information that will make it possible, for the construction of the "railroad" would make it possible to build "new, bright, and friendly apartments for the workers," which he will name the "Nora-Weygang Blocks." "Oh, beloved, of course," he concludes in her voice, "for now I belong to you entirely and truly" (29–33).

Despite Nora's illusions about the power of her love over Weygang, Weygang is the embodiment of absolute power that determines her sinking value in the sinking of her ass and drooping breasts. When initially Weygang invests in Nora, he offers his financial acceptability, and Nora in exchange offers her body. When later Nora attempts once more to create an even exchange by expressing her interest in his financial deals by agreeing to play the S&M dominatrix to get information out of Torvald, she does not understand that the exchange is uneven, and that Weygang looks on her body as a subject perceiving an object, or the owner his property. It is a relationship in which Weygang has complete control over his goods; he can throw them away, sell them, conduct transactions and exchange, or whatever he chooses: "That's what one does with property, my little lark" (33).

Even as a dominatrix, Nora's role is only an appearance, for, as Jelinek explains, fashion subjugates women particularly insidiously by means of that role. The costume of a dominatrix is sadomasochistic, for the black leather and metal on naked flesh are imposed by the desire of men who must subjugate women even as they receive pleasure from the exchange. The reason, according to Jelinek, that the current fascination with the costume of the dominatrix has become so strong is that men must break the resistance of women with renewed brutality. The dominatrix in her thigh-high leather boots must ultimately be brought to her knees. And men who seek out a dominatrix are overwhelmingly those in power positions, for they seek chastisement in torture chambers as a means of arousing their renewed feelings of innocence in the marketplace. However, business as usual is transacted, and Nora is not among the competitors (48). It is Weygang's power that "whips" Torvald into obedience; Nora is simply his whip. And even the words she uses to assault Torvald are not hers, for she is merely "reproducing" the relationship already established in *A Doll's House*.

The sentences that Jelinek puts into Nora's mouth to accompany the lashes of the whip appear in Ibsen's play as affectionate endearments, such as "Is that my little squirrel that's chattering?" Thus, Jelinek's Nora holds Torvald to the same level of significance as he held her in Ibsen. She pokes fun at the ideal of his prudence and frugality. He can sell the factory grounds to Weygang "so that he won't have to borrow in the future" (46). Jelinek takes these passages, distorts them, and pits them one against the other in order to show that these familiar discourses are the producers of myths of power relationships easily reproducible even by the powerless.

Despite her transitory participation on the side of power in the games that Weygang had initiated, all Nora has to do in order to defend herself against patriarchal power is the pulling together of clichés on "true love," the kind that is revealed in expressions such as "Your look pierces me like lightning" (19). Jelinek's dialogue debases each sentimentalized emotional moment, moving by turns from playfulness to mockery and on to a total undermining of all myths of love. Jelinek parodies the patter of the romance novels in which falling in love is made part of the process of social rise that ultimately culminates in marriage. But instead of "happiness," Jelinek makes visible the calculations that are part of the process, the addition and subtraction of market value. Since Nora's market value has fallen, Weygang pensions her off by giving her a choice of typical spheres of female entrepreneurship: a stationery store or a fabric store.

Using her skills as a composer of texts, Jelinek brings the spectators back to the doll house "idyll" and Nora's new/old marriage with Torvald. Another reversal has occurred, for it is now Nora who works all day at the fabric store, while Torvald, having lost his job at the bank, does the accounts, and as he pores over the daily receipts, he lectures Nora that the first stage of capitalist enterprise necessitates above all "the accumulation of capital" (60). All vestiges of middle-class manners and decorum have disappeared from the once genteel Helmer home as Torvald commands Nora "to shut [her] mouth," and Nora, in turn, screams at the returning children, "Shut your traps, you wretched brats. Can't you hear that your father wants to listen to the business news?" (61). The only trace of her women's liberation is her complaint that Torvald "left her sexually unsatisfied last night" (60).

The evening news on the blaring radio reveals that the cotton mill and the adjoining housing projects have mysteriously gone up in flames during the previous night. It is further reported that the fate of the mill is presently unknown, though Consul Weygang, as chairman of the corporation with controlling interest in the mill, has given assurances that a speedy reconstruction is being considered in order "not to endanger the situation of the workers" (62). As Torvald speculates that most likely it was "the Jews that had ignited the fire," the news broadcast fades into a spirited march evoking the memory of early German fascism. Torvald's expression of delight, "I love to hear this music," ends the play. With the audible lingering strains of the "quoted" march, Jelinek illustrates how the mechanism of the historical process has been set into motion by re-enactment of the past.

Notes

1. Elfriede Jelinek, "Was geschah, nachdem Nora Ihren Mann verlassen hatte oder Stützen der Gesellschaften," in *Theaterstücke* (Cologne: Prometh Verlag, 1984), 7–78.
2. Quotations from German texts are given in translation. This and all subsequent translations from the German are mine.
3. Henrik Ibsen, *A Doll's House*, in *Six Plays by Henrik Ibsen*, trans. Eva Le Gallienne (New York: Modern Library, 1951), 79.
4. Elfriede Jelinek, "Ich schlage sozusagen mit der Axt drein," *Theaterzeitschrift* 7 (1984): 14.
5. Elfriede Jelinek, "Gespräch mit Elfriede Jelinek," interview by Riki Winter, *Dossier über Elfriede Jelinek*, ed. Kurt Bartsch and Günther A. Hofler (Graz: Droschl, 1992), 15.
6. Henrik Ibsen, *Pillars of Society*, in *Henrik Ibsen: Four Plays*, trans. Michael Meyer (London: Methuen, 1990).
7. Elfriede Jelinek, quoted in Brigitte Landes, "Kunst aus Kakanien: Über Elfriede Jelinek," *Theater heute* 27, no. 1 (1968): 7.
8. Michael Newman, "Revisiting Modernism, Representing Postmodernism," in *Postmodernism*, ed. Lisa Appignanesi (London: Institute of Contemporary Arts, 1986), 48; quoted in Allyson Fiddler, "There Goes That Word Again; or, Elfriede Jelinek and Postmodernism," in *Elfriede Jelinek: Framed by Language*, ed. Jorun B. Johns and Katherine Arens (Riverside, Calif.: Ariadne Press, 1994), 135.

9. Rosalind Krauss, "Poststructuralism and the 'Paraliterary,'" *October* 13 (1980): 37.

10. Jelinek, "Was geschah," 8; hereafter cited in the text.

11. Elfriede Jelinek, "Wir leben auf einem Berg von Leichen und Schmerz," interview by Peter von Becker, *Theater heute* 33, no. 9 (1992): 4.

12. Allyson Fiddler, *Reviewing Reality: An Introduction to Elfriede Jelinek* (Oxford: Berg, 1994), 80; quoting Elfriede Jelinek as quoted in Stefan Makk, "Ein politisches Stück übers Kapital," *Kleine Zeitung*, 6 October 1979.

13. Yvonne Spielmann, "Ein unerhortes Sprachlabor: Feministische Aspekte im Werk von Elfriede Jelinek," in *Dossier über Elfriede Jelinek*, 36; quoting Jelinek in *Blauer Streusand*, ed. Barbara Alms (Frankfurt am Main: Suhrkamp, 1987), 41.

14. Ute Nyssen, "Afterword to Jelinek," *Theaterstücke* (Cologne, 1984), 155. Ulrike Meinhof was a member of the Baader-Meinhof group (1970s) that used terrorist attacks in their political struggle against what they feared was the return of fascism masking itself as capitalist expansion. Arrested in 1976, Meinhof was found murdered in her prison cell and became a martyr of the movement.

15. Jelinek, "Ich schalge sozusagen," 15.

Chapter 7

GEORGE TABORI'S RETURN TO THE DANUBE, 1987–1999

Hans-Peter Bayerdörfer

Wiener Blut and *Wiener Schnitzel*

George Tabori loves to declare himself the oldest living "royal-imperial Austro-Hungarian playwright."[1] It took him several decades to return—at least temporarily—to the proper place for a writer of this traditional distinction: in 1968/69 he returned to Europe, first to Germany, then in the 1980s to Austria and to Vienna, and finally to the Burgtheater. As is well known, Tabori is fond of puns, calembours, and clichés in general, so it is hardly surprising that he seems to be fond of Vienna clichés in particular, choosing titles such as *Wiener Blut* and *Wiener Schnitzel* for his writings.

Of course, as used by Tabori, such clichés are highly ironic, their meaning oscillating between triviality and the dialectical meaning. As we know from the first scene of the *Ballad of the Wiener Schnitzel*, the legendary dish, together with the Viennese waltz, Emperor Francis Joseph, and Arthur Schnitzler's "süßes Mädl," symbolizes the irrevocable obsolescence of the Austro-Hungarian Empire, "the mighty empire that covered Europe from Triest to Lemberg like a Schnitzel,"[2] but also the never-ending nostalgia, the longing for turn-of-the-century Vienna and its unique atmosphere. This cliché, however, has still further implications. Morgenstern, the protagonist of the *Ballad*, and specialist in traditional and "nouvelle" cuisine, gives a highly emotional account of the decline of table habits and dining culture in Vienna from the past to the present fast-food schnitzel era. Yet, some aspects included in this historical image of Vienna have apparently neither declined nor substantially changed. Toward the end of the opening scene of the play, when Morgenstern has denied the distinction of a (Kronawitter Guide) star to Hermann's Restaurant in downtown Vienna, he is abused by the owner: "Give him a schnitzel! Stuff it down the Jewish pig's throat!"[3] An appallingly antisemitic act whose actual and symbolic brutality becomes all the more obvious, given that, although the original Vienna schnitzel is made of veal and so, in principle, is kosher, in modern fast-food places, one never knows. In Tabori's writings, Jewish dietary laws represent cultural and ethical values, symbolizing the difference between "essen und fressen" (dining and eating), not only in the trivial semantic sense, but also with reference to fundamental standards in cultural history. The opposite of such dining rules is ultimately cannibalism. In the concentration camp setting of *The Cannibals* (1968/69), those rules mark a borderline between human and inhuman behavior, the dividing line between the persecuted and the persecutors, prisoners and Nazis.

Of course, the question arises—in the case of Morgenstern or Tabori—as to what motivates immigration to countries such as Germany and Austria and a city such as Vienna, where hidden anti-Jewish attitudes come to the surface in everyday trivial situations such as the one presented in this play. One of Tabori's unpublished texts from the years of the Vienna Kreis theater, a stage sketch with the title *Wiener Blut*, deals with the problem of "returning to the Danube":

> Sind Sie der Tabori?
> Glaube schon.
> Es kann doch nicht wahr sein,
> was die Tratschtanten und Onkel murmeln,
> daß Sie nach Wien wandern.
> Doch.
> Sind Sie wahnsinnig geworden?
> Klinisch oder politisch?
> Beides.
>
> [Are you that guy Tabori?
> I think so.
> But it can't be true,
> what the general gossip says,
> that you are about to re-emigrate to Vienna.
> It is true.
> Are you crazy?
> In a clinical or political sense?
> Both.][4]

Tabori's fanatically anti-Vienna antagonist in this sketch seems to closely resemble Thomas Bernhard.[5] The crucial point of the dialogue, however, is the problem of antisemitism and the possible reaction to it through theater. To Bernhard's alter ego it seems to be obvious, "that they [the Viennese] are not the first victims of the Nazis, but quite the reverse. Did you know that every third Viennese hates the Jews?"[6]

But theater, as the Vienna hater continues, is absolutely not the place to come to terms with this situation, and certainly not the Burgtheater, which for hundreds of years has been a "coproduction between the Jesuits and Disneyland."[7] In such a system a Jewish re-immigrant playwright could hardly play more than the role of an alibi Jew, comparable to that of Leonard Bernstein in a different cultural area.[8] Nevertheless, the sketch ends with a partly resigned, partly ironic plea to return:

Ja, dös is halt Wien.

[Yeah, I can't help it, it's Vienna][9]

This final answer is simply another cliché, giving little explanation but echoing instead the title cliché of *Wiener Blut*. Therefore, it seems to be necessary in this investigation to move away from the strictly biographical sketch that merely outlines the problem, and to proceed to a close consideration of the roles and functions which Tabori has taken in his live appearances in public theaters, whenever he took over a role on stage himself. By these appearances, the playwright suggests a close personal attachment to roles in which—in an almost emblematic way—central aspects of Jewish religious and cultural tradition are incorporated.

Return and Re-immigration

Tabori does not show up on stage often, but whenever he does, it is amazing how much effort he makes to appear in the guise of the one who returns. In the 1983 production of his play *Jubilee* in Bochum, commemorating the fiftieth anniversary of Hitler's coming to power in 1933, he presented a cast of dead and live persons assembled in a churchyard and communicating with one another. Dead victims of Nazi terrorism and young German antisemites engage in controversial arguments and violent action, referring to past and present antisemitism. The sequence of events culminates and ends in the return of the dead father, who, like Cornelius Tabori, has perished in Auschwitz. In Bochum, the role of this father image, who entitles his son Arnold to perform the traditional Sabbath ritual of breaking bread by giving him a loaf he has brought from the concentration camp, was played by Tabori himself.[10]

In Vienna, too, several years later, the playwright took special care to model his own stage image as an actor. His first appearance was in the role of the God-Father alias the Jewish kosher cook Lobkovits of *Mein Kampf*, a rather bizarre counterimage to the Divine, as it is usually imagined or symbolized. In contrast to that, the presentation of the divine voice by Tabori himself in *Goldberg Variations*, acoustically from on high, was quite in accordance with religious standards. Besides these "heavenly" roles, it is worth considering that his intriguing and fascinating presentation of the young Romeo in the Shakespeare collage *Lovers and Maniacs*[11] was balanced by the presentation of a hardly less provocative Shylock.[12] Finally, in 1991, in *Babylon Blues*, Tabori appeared as a stagehand, walking onto the stage through the production, seemingly at random. But at the end the stagehand turns into Beckett's Krapp, who leaves the stage and moves into the proscenium. In her review after the opening night, Sibylle Fritsch reported: "At the end, the Budapest-born Tabori delightfully eats a banana, while—according to the motto 'two emigrants meet at the Burg'—he encounters David Hirsch, another Vienna re-immigrant actor, and the two start communicating in the Hungarian language!"[13]

It is obvious that different motives underlie Tabori's self-presentation on stage. The image he creates has to do with the Shoah and post-Holocaust antisemitism, with the image of the fathers who perished and are nevertheless a psychological problem for the sons, the fathers who represent the place and the tradition of their origin, including the notion of the Divine, inherent in that tradition. Last but not least, the image of the returning one has to do with acting in the most fundamental and the most actual sense. Through the permanent present tense of the stage and its audience in the theatrical event, the actor is able to mediate between the present time, the voices of the past, and the languages of origin.

In this context, the appearance of Tabori as a stagehand, in front of the curtain with David Hirsch, may be reminiscent of Tabori's metaphor of the catacombs and the cathedrals, by which he tried to explain his own notion of the style of making theater. There is also a temptation to interpret this in a biographical way, with reference to the life of an exiled playwright who—starting from the catacomb fringe stages—makes his way back to the highbrow theatrical culture from which he was expelled in his youth, finally becoming an honorary member of the cathedral-like Burgtheater. This biographical reading, however, misses the point of the metaphor, by which the actual and provocative appeal of fringe-type experimental theater is contrasted with German and Austrian traditional repertory theaters, in which cultural heritage and national representation are an integral part or sometimes a dominating feature, to the detriment of stage aesthetics. If this is true in the general sense, it refers particularly to the Burgtheater, which was burdened with national and ideological claims for long periods, or had to function on a compensatory level.

Tabori's self-image on stage as the returning one, as well as the catacomb and cathedral comparison, has to be understood against the background of theater history, because it encompasses a specific response to postwar developments in Germany and Austria. The apparently culminating step of his career, his ascension to the Burgtheater, could probably not have happened earlier, for it is closely motivated by and related to the actual development of this stage in the preceding decade, seen from an Austrian standpoint as well as from an outside position in central Europe, especially in German-speaking countries.

Actor and Prophet

The starting point of Tabori's European career as a playwright and stage director is marked by the crisis of the German theater of the 1960s, namely by the end of documentary and political theater. Whatever Tabori's personal motives may have been, his experience with *The Cannibals* on the New York stage in 1968, which fell short of acclaim, and the unexpected but unequivocal success in Berlin in 1969, demonstrated that his methods of dramaturgical construction and his emphasis in structuring the problems were more likely to succeed in the countries of the victimizers than in countries where the problem of the past was not that much at stake in public debate.[14] Certainly, Tabori's dedication to the idea of founding an actors' studio-type theater for "recherches théâtrales," in analogy to Peter Brook or Lee Strasberg, was strong, and so was his fascination with the psychology of Shakespearean roles that develop the identity of love and hatred, desire and cruelty, and so on. Yet Tabori's initial success was due to his ability to stand in the breach that the end of documentary and political theater had left with regard to the German Nazi past and the Holocaust. His own approach was provocative on various thematic levels. On the one hand, he tried to stimulate the imagination to identify with the life, feelings, and behavior of concentration camp inmates on the point of death. The shocking theme of cannibalism in the concentration camps is worked out thoroughly and in detail, yet at the same time the fundamental religious and ethical questions at stake are discussed from different points of view. On another level Tabori broke postwar Germany's taboo preventing a presentation of Jewish characters as dubious, ambivalent people in a moral and individual sense. Only an author of Jewish descent could dare to develop a strategy of Holocaust presentation along these lines, instead of aiming at documentary objectivity—which by that time had been seriously questioned as a stage device in public debate—or idealizing Jewish victims on the stage.

Tabori's dramatic presentation of cannibalism was possible because of two assumptions. First of all, the piece is presented as a memory play of the surviving sons, trying to imagine the fate of the fathers and their personal and ethical reaction to the cannibalistic temptation, on the one hand, and the dehumanizing pressures of the Nazi camp authorities, on the other. Because of the different levels of action, the play demands virtuoso role-playing and role-breaking, which go beyond the devices of Brechtian and pre-Brechtian alienation dramaturgy.[15] Second, the leading character of the play, the uncle, a father figure as imagined by the sons, is dignified by prophetic, that is to say, traditional, Jewish religious texts. Their vast intertextual outreach into Jewish tradition creates a highly intellectualized horizon with respect to the history of religion and ethics.

The playwright's introductory remarks about the sources of the play, allegedly the testimonies of the survivors, can be understood as an ironic attempt to distance himself from documentary realism and its ideological claims. In the English version, this ironic relationship to the documentary is even stronger, since, in one of the last scenes, "uncle's son" refers to a handwritten note, which was "miraculously found" on "uncle's/father's" corpse when the Soviet liberating troops invaded the camp and which was afterwards forwarded to him in New York.[16] It is evident that the author is not interested in documentary and historical realism but seeks a new level of problematization. Beyond its manifold levels of action, the novel approach of his "memory play" aims to create a metalevel on which the religious and theatrical discourses merge, alternately symbolizing one another.[17] In this way Tabori laid the foundations for a new Shoah discourse on the stage, which explicitly addresses itself to spectators of the second and third postwar generations.

Tabori's new procedure mirrors the fact that there are no fully adequate methods of narration and stage presentation when the problem of remembering the Holocaust is to be foregrounded. By developing a stage technique that combined traditional Jewish content and modern alienation acting, he initiated a new theatrical style. The imagination, not the documentation, of the Holocaust became the basic device, which rejected generalized documentary objectivity and attempts at ideological explanation in favor of the spectators' desire to identify imaginatively on an individual level.[18]

Apart from his new approach to the problem of presenting the German and European past on the stage, there are more reasons for Tabori's return to Europe and his settling in Germany. Many impulses came from the theaters in those years, because at the end of the 1960s many theater directors came to be fundamentally open toward new experimental techniques and fringe-inspired stage activities. So, in many respects, Tabori owed his coming to terms as a director and playwright in Germany and Austria to his relationship with the leading post-1968 directors of the so-called Regietheater, such as Boleslaw Barlog in Berlin, Kurt Hübner in Bremen, Dieter Dorn in Munich, and Claus Peymann in Bochum. Such directors allowed him the possibility of either long-term experimental activity on catacomb-type stages, attached to the main houses of the theaters, or gave him the opportunity to stage productions that transcended the in-group attractiveness of his Theater-Laboratory efforts.[19] Of course, from the very beginning, Tabori shared with those directors a fundamentally critical attitude toward German and Austrian political and social development. His inclination toward provocation and challenge was completely in harmony with, for example, Peymann's theater politics in Bochum and later in Vienna, when he tried to transform and reshape the prestigious stages of the Burg according to the maxims of the new "Regietheater" of the 1970s.

Hitler on Stage: "Memory Plays" in Vienna

Certain political and cultural changes can be regarded as the conditions that made the temporary return to the Danube possible. The definite change of political climate in the era of Chancellor Kreisky, 1970–82, made its mark on theatrical culture. The impact of documentary theater and the controversies it generated reached Vienna mainly through productions of the 1970s at the Volkstheater. During the following decade, a reconsideration of the first Austrian republic resulted in a re-evaluation of the theater of the interwar period, such as the plays of Jura Soyfer and his fellow left-wing writers, among others. The critical attention focused on the role of Austrian culture and theater during the Nazi years was highlighted on stage by Thomas Bernhard and with particularly provocative effect by Elfriede Jelinek's play *Burgtheater* (1982), in which the Nazi cooperation of prominent actors of the 1940s and the 1950s was exposed on the stage in quite an aggressive way. The new era at the Burgtheater during Claus Peymann's directorship marked the climax of these trends, expressed strongly through Peymann's cooperation with Bernhard and also with Tabori. Additionally, the Burgtheater stages regained a leading position in the development of Regietheater, which—despite a strong and not wholly unjustified opposition in Vienna itself—resulted in a renewed artistic competition between the Viennese and the German, especially the Berlin, theaters, a rivalry that had exercised a stimulating and creative effect in many earlier periods of Austrian-German theater history. Tabori's Viennese period was marked by his dual approach to the catacomb and the cathedral-type stage. It began, on the one hand, with his intention to found an actors' studio type, the Theater im Kreis, and to stage productions in alternative places, outside conventional theaters.[20] On the other hand, there seems to have been a collaborative agreement of sorts between Tabori and Peymann from the very beginning;[21] but, mainly because of political circumstances, things did not turn out as planned.[22] The Waldheim affair had radicalized the problems of reconsidering the past—by stimulating new discussion centering on the relationship between Austrians and Nazi Germany, on Austrian collaboration and identification during the Anschluß, and, last but not least, on the threatening symptoms of Neo-Nazism in contemporary Austria and Germany. In fact, during the first-night performance on 30 April 1987, when Tabori staged *Mein Kampf* at the Burg-affiliated Akademie Theater, the following day's May Day celebrations were being prepared by the political establishment. On that occasion, the leading Austrian parties, including the Social Democrats and even the Communists—despite being motivated by different reasons and political aims—all proclaimed their support of Waldheim in declarations of public loyalty.[23] Of course, this remarkable coincidence was not accidental. "In his very first attempt," Sigrid Löffler commented several months later, "Tabori has hit the political nerve of his [Viennese] audience. His theater responded to Waldheim's Austria in a direct and embarrassingly precise way, at any rate more so and more aggressively than on the other side, in Peymann's Burg."[24]

The theatrical constellation to which the critic refers, and which is grounded in the political one, is the double appearance of Adolf Hitler in Brecht's *Arturo Ui*, directed by Alfred Kirchner in the Burgtheater, and in the Akademie theater in *Mein Kampf*, the production that laid the foundation of Tabori's standing as a playwright and director in the capital. Looking back on these two productions, Tabori's way of bringing Hitler to the stage is obviously more provocative than the Brechtian approach, despite the sophisticated production by Kirchner. Brecht's parable play of his exile years, despite its Marxist ideological grounding, can be modified to accommodate a view of history in which Austria appears to be the historical victim of Hitler's rise to power, and which largely ignores the problem of whether or not the Anschluß of 1938 met with the approval of a significant percentage of the Austrian people. In Tabori's *Mein Kampf*, this historical question is not directly discussed, either. But the play's tripartite historical construction is provocative to the Austrian mentality and is directly addressed to Vienna. The young Hitler is situated in exactly that fin-de-siècle setting that usually provides the backdrop to the nostalgic idea of the Viennese and Austrian cliché. In Tabori's farce, this epoch is characterized by the confrontation between liberal Jewish mentality and ethics and racist thinking in the monarchy, represented by the emancipated intellectual Shlomo Herzl and the petit bourgeois outback Austrian Adolf Hitler. In terms of mentality and ideology, the old Austro-Hungarian Empire at the turn of the century is directly linked to the Nazi era as a whole, and to the Anschluß years in particular. So Tabori's morality play, in which God and Death are impersonated on stage, explicitly includes Austria in the course of history that leads to the Holocaust. In this respect, the play offers a challenging contribution to the actual debate on the Waldheim crisis, stimulating historical insights and suggesting a new view of bygone Vienna and Austria that contrasts with the convenient but treacherous clichés. As in Germany in 1969, Tabori's play presents a new perspective for facing one's own past and a strong incentive to reflect on the problems of why neofascism and renewed antisemitic tendencies are coming to the fore in contemporary Austrian society.

It is obvious, however, that the direct political confrontations of the summer of 1987 caused Tabori to rethink his theatrical program. Already in July, he had reformulated the original program of the Kreis stage, with its demanding repertory considerations, by adding the new topical and political dimension. It is marked by the plea for direct involvement in contemporary Austrian political, social, and psychological reality: "I want to react to what is going on in Austria now," as the playwright and director put it.[25] His theatrical productions in the following years evidenced this decision.

Heldenplatz and *Masada*

In the next year, 1988, another jubilee was to be "celebrated." Among other events, the fiftieth anniversary of the Anschluß was marked by the unveiling of Alfred Hrdlicka's Holocaust Memorial in Vienna, to which Tabori alluded not only in his sketch *Wiener Blut*, but later on also in the *Ballad*. That year, 1988, saw a certain rivalry between the catacomb and the cathedral stage commitment of the playwrights, resulting in a situation that almost gained emblematic significance, when Tabori and Bernhard obtained complementary roles. The notorious Austria-hater Bernhard had announced his play commemorating the past, *Heldenplatz*, to be staged at the Burgtheater, and rumors about its offensive turn against contemporary Austria, its population, and its institutions had spread in Vienna and, through a press campaign, had stirred up emotions. In any case, the production attracted more attention from the Austrian public as this highly emotional debate took place *before* the opening night. The controversy, both on the political and on the theatrical level, resulted in a scandal that centered on the Burgtheater as the nation's most important cultural institution. After the premiere in November 1988, however, the excitement calmed down and gave way to ever an increasing appreciation of the play.

The play itself reproduced, in a remarkable way, one of the basic motives of Tabori's *Jubilee*, the hallucinatory and traumatic memories of survivors who cannot get rid of the sound of the masses' cheering, in this case of the Viennese crowd's frantic welcoming of Hitler on the Heldenplatz in front of the Hofburg in 1938. The Jewish survivors who have returned from exile in Britain cannot readjust to life in Vienna because the old mentality is still recognizable under the surface of the new post-Nazi Austria. Bernhard's play and Tabori's sketch *Wiener Blut* provide the same diagnosis of the contemporary Austrian mentality.

While *Heldenplatz* was staged in a thoroughly realistic and psychologically subtle way, the problem of remembering and rethinking Nazism and the Holocaust is realized quite differently in Tabori's contribution, the *Masada* performance, written for the memorial season at the Steirische Herbst in Graz in October 1988 and later produced on the Kreis stage in Vienna. In comparison with Bernhard's play, it widens the historical perspective from the Jewish point of view. The history of the persecution of the Jews is represented by the historical span of the almost two thousand years between Masada and Auschwitz. This is visually symbolized on the stage by a model of the Masada fortress, placed in a desertlike landscape, which is surrounded by barbed wire and contains remains and symbols of Nazi concentration camps. The history is hidden under the surface of the desert, but it can be revealed, as with each step the ground itself gives acoustic signals. The *Masada* performance is realized as a scenic sequence in which meditation is permanently stimulated by visual and acoustic events before the text, taken from Flavius Josephus's *Antiquitates Judaicae*, is recited. As in *The Cannibals*, Tabori debates the different modes of reviewing history by putting the historian himself and an unknown survivor victim into polarized positions. On the one hand, we see the assimilated Jew Josephus, whose objective, documentary approach to the annihilation of the Jewish community cannot hide the central motive of self-justification, because he has, after the initial participation in the uprising, joined the Roman side. On the other hand, we witness the helplessness of the Masada woman who is hardly able to articulate her shocking experiences, thus indicating that she does not come to terms with a feeling of guilt because of having survived. The playwright lends her the voice of poetry. The focal point of her role is the declamation of one of Paul Celan's mourning poems about the Shoah, from the volume *Die Niemandsrose*.[26]

The two "environments," *Heldenplatz* and *Masada*, are much closer than the historical and regional differences seem to indicate. But whereas Bernhard's perspective is that of the notorious anti-Austrian insider, Tabori's is that of the outsider, one who from the standpoint of Jewish history faces the same post-Shoah problems: Jewish survival in a non-Jewish German-Austrian postwar society.

The function of Tabori's theater in Vienna in 1987/88 is analogous to that in Berlin in 1969 and in the Federal Republic in 1983. With new theatrical means, he establishes a new mode of discourse about the Nazi past, the Holocaust trauma, and the problems of survival and of the revival of cryptic or overtly Nazi attitudes.

During the following years, Tabori proceeded on both theatrical levels, that of the Burg-/Akademie-theaters as well as that of the Kreis Theater, staging Shoah-related plays, such as *Schuldig geboren* by Peter Sichrovsky, Viktor Ullmann's *Der Tod dankt ab,* and the first Austrian performance of *The Cannibals,* directed by Erich Fried. On the other side, he presented his new play, a Jewish Western: *Weisman und Rotgesicht.*[27] With this play, originally planned for the Rabenhof Werkstatt of the Josephstädter Theater, he definitively moved to the Burgtheater and the Akademie stage, a highly debatable move that included a much lamented breach of contract by Tabori himself. With this step, he had definitively installed himself in the "cathedral," investing far more energy in working with the Burgtheater actors of proven ability and aesthetic achievements, to the detriment of the collective and therapeutic ideals that had been part of the actors' studio and the Kreis program. Tabori had made a choice within the range of his theatrical inclinations. He had accepted the public position of a highly acclaimed re-immigrant playwright and director who apparently was no longer concerned with the possible alibi aspect of his position. Within the Burgtheater programs he shared his interest in Shakespeare as well as in contemporary critical drama with Peymann and, additionally, concentrated on the problems of Jewish identity in post-Shoah Europe. The morality play pattern of *Mein Kampf* was reformulated in the mystery play *Goldberg Variations,* Tabori's greatest success in the 1990s, and once again in *The Ballad of the Wiener Schnitzel.*

Hiob-Job in Vienna

Up to now, the *Ballad* may be regarded as another dramatic attempt at "returning" to Vienna, reworking many basic aspects of the earlier plays. On a visual level, the local Viennese perspective is reformulated, with the scene in the window frame representing the votive church instead of the Heldenplatz monument. The motive of being permanently traumatized by the voices of the Nazi crowd is taken up again from *Jubilee* and *Heldenplatz* and surpassed by the paranoia of the protagonist Morgenstern, in whose mind the traumatic experiences of the persecution of 1938 and the following years reappear. Once again, the humiliation of Jews having to clean Vienna sidewalks with toothbrushes, commemorated in Alfred Hrdlicka's memorial sculpture, is remembered. Outwardly, Morgenstern seems to be completely assimilated into modern everyday Viennese life, but his inward state of mind gives the impression that he is ill. Wherever he goes, he is eager to find traits of antisemitism, and, in an almost maniacal way, he succeeds. Yet his illness is less psychotic than historical, beyond all traditional therapeutic endeavors, as he "suffers from the well-known syndrome of Hebrew paranoia."[28] Torn between feelings of belonging and alienation, he has the frightening experience of being deprived of his state of "acculturation" and acceptance and of being transformed into the old-type Eastern European Jew, according to antisemitic stereotypes. After he has been subjected to the measures of the devilish hairdresser, he has to act out a nightmare scene in front of the mirror when he chases his Eastern European alter ego through the streets of Vienna, denying him shelter and home.[29]

Already in the preceding scene, the intertextual level of the play has been extended to Shakespeare's *Merchant of Venice*, when Morgenstern alludes to Shylock and his famous monologue-type passage: "Hath not a Jew eyes? Hath not a Jew hands, organs, dimensions, senses, affections, passions?—fed with the same food, hurt with the same weapons, subject to the same diseases, healed by the same means, warmed and cooled by the same winter and summer as a Christian is?"[30] To a certain extent, Tabori re-introduces his own earlier catacomb-stage attempts with Shakespeare's play in his Munich *Shylock Improvisations*, in which the classic play was transformed into a post-Shoah version.[31] The actual significance of the Shylock quotes in the *Ballad*, however, is intertheatrical, for Morgenstern was played by Gert Voss, who, in this role, celebrated his own return to Vienna and the Burgtheater after having spent some time with Peter Zadek at the Schiffbauerdamm Theater in Berlin.[32] Furthermore, by quoting Shylock, Voss returned to the role that he had formerly played in Zadek's *Merchant* production at the Burgtheater in 1988, a production in which Voss and Zadek had completely and systematically avoided the slightest hint of the clichés of the Eastern European Jew, whereas Antonio, the merchant, played by Ignaz Kirchner, was much more reminiscent of a traditionally Jewish stockbroker or businessman. In the trial scene this switching of images had resulted in the complete confusion of Portia, who even addressed Antonio as Shylock.[33] The schism that Portia experiences outwardly remains alive in its internalized version, as becomes obvious in the final act at Belmont when no happy ending can be achieved.

In the *Ballad*, the same confusion is taken to its extreme, where it appears to be manifested as paranoia. The way out, as shown in the play, is an additional model of identification, introduced on the scenic level of a dream. Morgenstern is involved in a dialogue with Bildad, a biblical figure who forces him into the biblical identity of Job. The seemingly psychotic split is not simply healed, but appears on an archetypal level, for Job is the one who is restored to everything of which he has been deprived, in a sense surviving his own annihilation. At the same time he is the one who alternately accepts and defies divine authority. At the end of the dream Morgenstern is asked by Bildad: "Are you Job?" And he answers: "Who is not Job?"[34]

The result of this dream encounter is certainly not a harmonious identity, but rather the acceptance of the split. Morgenstern's identity has been shaped by the experience of his incomprehensible survival, confronted with the shocking fate of millions of his fellow Jews and the insight that he will live on as the self-conscious alien, everywhere and forever. With this in mind, he takes his own responsibility for the present and returns to his place of origin, not in terms of locality but of ancestry, like Arnold in *Jubilee*. Morgenstern/Job finds himself situated in the graveyard, between the dead and the living in the heart of Vienna. Now he is ready to enjoy a Wiener schnitzel, but before eating it himself, he offers it to the dead,[35] thus performing the final ritual of *Jubilee* once again.

Epilogue

There are many achievements of Tabori as a playwright and stage director that have not been explored in detail in this essay. Periods of his work, such as the years in Bremen, and many productions have not been taken into consideration. Analysis has been more or less restricted to one strand of development, derived from the topic and the historical impact of his first production on a German stage. Pursuing this strand, it is obvious that the high points of Tabori's career on German and Austrian stages have come whenever previous methods of presenting the discourse of the German and Austrian past on stage have led to a dead end. Given that in both countries the problem of "embezzled history," as Chancellor Vranitzky put it, has to do with the revival of neorightist movements, new responses from the stage were required. Tabori served these needs without returning to the agitating patterns of the 1960s ideological and political theater.[36] Almost twenty years after his debut on the European and German stage, with his Austrian debut he contributed analogously to the founding of a new era of Viennese theater. In 1988, the year of the fiftieth anniversary of the Nazi takeover, when the role of Austria in the Nazi period was again passionately discussed and reconsidered and when contemporary neorightist movements were raising anxiety, he established his position as a Viennese playwright and director.

From this point of view, Tabori may be seen to have followed the steps of many prominent post-1945 re-immigrant writers and theater artists who took responsibility and initiative in postwar German-language theater, and still do. Others could hardly match the strong impact of authenticity of such re-immigrant voices. Once again, Tabori confirms the unique role they have played in reshaping post-Shoah theater, by insisting over and over again that theater in Germany and Austria, in order to be authentic, has to present and contemplate the Shoah as its historical background, not in a historicist sense, but in terms of continuing impact on the present intellectual climate. Tabori has taken this challenge from the catacomb stages to the "cathedral" of Austrian theater and has thus contributed not only to the regional profile of Viennese theaters, but also to its national and central European standing.

Projecting this contribution onto an even wider historical horizon, Tabori's working period in Vienna and his position in the city's theater underline the degree to which the development of German-language theater is indebted to the fundamental creative contributions of artists and writers of Jewish descent, from the time of Mendelssohn and Sonnenfels on. In reaching the symbolic level of Job,[37] the returning protagonist, Morgenstern, and the returning royal-imperial Austro-Hungarian playwright bear the stigma of annihilation. As in the preceding periods, Tabori's Viennese period was dedicated to the German-language stage, where the obligation of remembering the unimaginable, the Shoah and its traumatic impact on the following generations, remains a task that can never be finalized. For some time, Vienna seemed to be the final destination of Tabori's theatrical career. However, it was not final, either in terms of stage art or in the biographical sense of homecoming. In January 2000, Tabori's Berlin period began with the premiere of his *Die Brecht-Akte*.

Notes

1. An example is an interview that Tabori gave at a holiday resort, referring to his place of birth in Budapest, 1914, after he had started writing his autobiography. *Tiroler Tageszeitung*, 20 September 1997.

2. "… die unwiderrufliche Antiquiertheit der Donaumonarchie," das "mächtige Reich, das Europa überzog, von Triest bis Lemberg wie ein Schnitzel." *Theater heute* 5 (1996): 48. The English translations of the quotations given in this essay are not authorized by the playwright and are for the purpose of this essay only. The German text of *Die Ballade vom Wiener Schnitzel* is quoted from *Theater heute* 5 (1996): 46–52; other plays, from the two-volume edition *Theaterstücke* (Frankfurt am Main: Fischer Tb 12301/2, 1994). I want to express my gratitude to Peg Katritzky and Christopher Balme for their kind assistance in translating this text.

3. "Gebt ihm ein Schnitzel! Stopft es dem Saujud in den Schlund!" *Theater heute* 5 (1996): 48.

4. This text is cited in Barbara Maria Schierl, "*Tabori-Theater,*" *Shakespeare und Wien/Theater als Therapie: Theater als Lebensform./Zur Rezeption der Wiener Theaterarbeit des George Tabori von 1986 bis 1990: Eine Dokumentation* (Vienna: Diplomarbeit, 1991), 53–55. I am most grateful to Barbara Schierl and also to Mrs. R. Weid, the librarian of the Institut für Theater-, Film- und Fernsehwissenschaft, Vienna University, who kindly brought this thesis to my attention and sent me numerous Austrian and Viennese Tabori reviews from the press collection of the institute.

5. The name of this writer is explicitly mentioned.

6. "… daß sie [die Wiener] nicht die ersten Opfer der Nazis waren, sondern andersrum. Wissen Sie, daß jeder dritte Wiener die Juden haßt?" Schierl, "*Tabori-Theater,*" 45. With this remark, Tabori is quoting himself from an interview that he gave during the Vienna production of *Mein Kampf*, published in the *Programmbuch*, no. 17 (6 May 1987), Burgtheater, Akademie-Bühne, Vienna, 117–30.

7. Schierl, "*Tabori-Theater,*" 54.

8. "… der liebenswürdigste Alibijude seit der große Lenny nicht mehr so rumhopsen kann." Schierl, "*Tabori-Theater,*" 55.

9. *Wiener Blut*, Schierl, "*Tabori-Theater.*"

10. George Tabori, *Theaterstücke*, vol. 2: 86.

11. The Austrian production was called *Verliebte und Verrückte* and was released in 1989.

12. According to Hilde Haider-Pregler's review (*Wiener Zeitung*, 16 March 1989), Tabori played "an outwardly calm Shylock …, whose only remaining means of communication was hate. 'I pray you, give me leave to go from hence; I am not well,' the humiliated Shylock says before

sinking to the ground and then rising again as Romeo ... [einen äußerlich ruhigen Shylock ..., dem als einzige Verständigungsmöglichkeit nur Haß übrigbleibt. 'Ich bitte Euch, erlaubt mir wegzugehen, mir ist nicht gut', sagt der Gedemütigte, ehe er zusammensinkt und sich danach als Romeo wieder erhebt]."

13. Sibylle Fritsch, "Vom Scheitern Gottes," in *Die Deutsche Bühne* (1991): 8.

14. At that time, by far the main topic of public debate in the United States was the involvement of the political and military power in the Vietnam war and the struggle against its continuation.

15. The most obvious techniques go beyond Brecht toward Pirandello, or the multiplying of play levels (play within a play within a play ...) and the use of the apparently complete breakdown of the technical and the communication system which—for a considerable span of time—leaves the audience without orientation.

16. *The Cannibals*, in *The Theater of the Holocaust: Four Plays*, ed. Robert Skloot (Madison: University of Wisconsin Press, 1982), 253. The differences between the English and the German versions of the New York and Berlin productions of the play still have to be investigated and evaluated with regard to the contribution of Erich Fried, who coproduced them with Tabori.

17. See Sibylle Peters, "Die Verwandlung der Schrift in Spiel: George Tabori's Metaphysik des Theaters: Die Goldberg-Variationen." In *Theater gegen das Vergessen: Bühnenarbeit und Drama bei George Tabori*, ed. Hans-Peter Bayerdörfer and Jörg Schönert (Tübingen: Niemeyer, 1997), 270–82, especially 274.

18. In terms of the history of theater and reception, Tabori's individualizing approach was to a certain extent confirmed by the impact of the movie *Holocaust* almost ten years later, the nationwide reception of the film, and the ensuing lengthy debate. Despite the movie's many shortcomings and simplifications (particularly in comparison with Tabori's subtle dramaturgy), the public response demonstrated the importance of offering the average spectator the opportunity to identify with individual characters, as a step toward being motivated to face the full implications of the Holocaust. Later on, the reception of Claude Lanzman's "Shoah-production" would not have been possible without the public attention attracted by the Holocaust movie of 1979. Subsequently, *Schindler's List*, though on a remarkably higher aesthetic level, continues along the line of the individualizing approaches.

19. A detailed survey of "Taboris Bremer Theater Labor" has been published by Anat Feinberg, with the subtitle "Projekte—Erfahrungen—Resultate," in *Theater gegen das Vergessen*, ed. Hans-Peter Bayerdörfer and Jörg Schönert (Tübingen: Niemeyer, 1997), 98–122. The Vienna Kreis project is documented by B. M. Schierl, "*Tabori-Theater.*" Unfortunately, in this context it is not possible to do justice to the wide spectrum of Tabori's experimental theater projects, which range from Shakespeare to Beckett and Euripides to Kafka, to name just a few.

20. With regard to the Shoah topics, however, continuity was achieved. It is the double suffering of European Jewry, "in the pain of the victims" and "in the embarrassment of the survivors." Sigrid Löffler, "Taboris Träume," *Theater heute* 12 (1988): 5–8.

21. In a letter of 12 January 1990, Peymann informs Tabori both of his decision not to direct a production for the Kreis Theater after all, with a reminiscence: "I have always regarded our idea of cooperation between the Kreis and Burg theaters as the start of something very promising, but not as a fitting conclusion to your theatrical experimentation in Vienna, which unfortunately came to an end far too soon." He continues: "I am looking forward with immense pleasure to your next production for us in the coming season.... Whatever you suggest will be welcome." Quoted by Schierl, "*Tabori-Theater,*" 67, from the Kreis theater archives. ("Ich habe unsere Idee immer als Beginn einer Zusammenarbeit von Kreis und Burg als schöne Perspektive gesehen, aber nicht als Schlußpunkt Deines in Wien leider beendeten und viel zu früh abgebrochenen Experiments.... Ich freue mich schon heute wie ein König auf Deine nächste Inszenierung in der kommenden Saison bei uns.... Du bist für alles willkommen.")

22. Tabori's activity in Austria had started with the failed Salzburg production of 1987, in which his attempt to present Franz Schmidt's oratorium *Das Buch mit den sieben Siegeln* in the Collegienkirche, Salzburg, had caused such a scandal with the church and the city that the production

was canceled. Apparently, even the enfant terrible Tabori needed the direct protection or cooperation of the authorities of theatrical life in order to succeed with such high-profile productions. This turned out to be possible in Vienna, rather than in the traditional climate of the Salzburg Festival atmosphere.

23. The reasons were different: "on the one hand, patriotism, on the other, the declaration of the 'big brother' Soviet Union (*glasnost* and *perestroika* notwithstanding), that Zionism and American imperialism were greater enemies than a forgetful Austrian." ("die einen aus Staatsraison, die anderen, weil der große sowjetische Bruder [*glasnost* hin *perestroika* her] angeordnet hat, daß Zionisten und amerikanischer Imperialismus größere Feinde sind als ein vergeßlicher Österreicher.") Concerning the overheated atmosphere of Waldheim's Vienna, Thomas Rothschild comments: "One is constantly confronted with blatant fascist attitudes," and, he adds, "The thoughts of the average German are probably not too different, although the level of inhibition about speaking out in public is higher." ("Überall begegnet man einer ungefilterten faschistischen Gesinnung ... in den Köpfen deutscher Kleinbürger sieht es wohl nicht viel anders aus. Nur: die Schamgrenze bei öffentlichen Äußerungen liegt höher.") Thomas Rothschild, "Hitler in Wien," *Die Deutsche Bühne* 7 (1987): 28–30.

24. "George Tabori hat den politischen Nerv seines Publikums auf Anhieb getroffen. In seinem Theater wird auf Waldheim-Österreich prompt und peinlich genau reagiert. Genauer und schärfer jedenfalls als drüben in Peymanns Burg." Sigrid Löffler, "Die Gegenwart der Vergangenheit. Das KZ-*Stück Die Kannibalen* und die Fall-Szenen *Schuldig geboren* als Saisonauftakt in George Taboris Wiener 'Kreis'-Theater," *Theater heute* 11 (1987): 25.

25. "Ich möchte darauf reagieren, was jetzt in Österreich passiert." Löffler, "Taboris Träume," 24.

26. "Es war Erde in ihnen und sie gruben," in *Die Niemandsrose* (Frankfurt am Main: Fischer, 1963), 9.

27. The English translation by Jack Zipes, *Weisman and Redface,* was presented as the world premiere English-language production at the Frank Theater in Minneapolis, during the Great Traditions symposium.

28. "Die Ballade vom Wiener Schnitzler," *Theater heute* 5 (1996): 46–52, 49.

29. Ibid., 51.

30. *The Merchant of Venice,* 3.1; *Die Ballade vom Wiener Schnitzel,* 51.

31. "Ich wollte meine Tochter läge tot zu meinen Füßen und hätte die Juwelen in den Ohren" (I would my daughter were dead at my feet, and the jewels in her ear!). *Improvisationen über Shakespeares Shylock: Dokumentation einer Theaterarbeit,* ed. Andrea Welker and Tina Berger (Munich: Kammerspiele, 1974).

32. Heinz Sichrovsky, "Heimgekehrt: Voss in einem tiefschwarzen Auschwitz-Drama," *News* (Vienna) 13 (1996): 140ff.

33. The production had also been presented in Berlin.

34. *Theater heute* 5 (1996): 52.

35. Ibid.

36. The chancellor's saying, "veruntreute Geschichte," is quoted by Michael Merschmeier in his report on the Viennese theatrical scene "Wien nach der Wende," *Theater heute* 11 (1987): 6.

37. A series of essays on Jewish writers and German literature in the twentieth century was edited by Gunter E. Grimm and Hans Peter Bayerdörfer under the main title *Im Zeichen Hiobs* (Königstein: Athenäum, 1985). This title was inspired by German-Jewish writers who, in the years after the Shoah, referred to the biblical figure Job. The first of these were Nelly Sachs in her poems *Sternverdunkelung* (1949) and Margarete Susman in *Das Buch Hiob und das Schicksal des jüdischen Volkes* (1945).

Chapter 8

THOMAS BERNHARD'S *HELDENPLATZ*

Artists and Societies beyond the Scandal

Alfred Pfabigan

When talking about *Heldenplatz*, one cannot deny that Thomas Bernhard's insults against Austria on stage produced the biggest theater scandal in the history of the second republic.[1] But if we concentrate our exclusive attention on the scandal, we give the play an unequivocal nature that it does not have, and we do not give justice to the intellectual work *(Geistesarbeit)* of the author.

What we call a scandal was a phenomenon that accompanied Bernhard's work for decades.[2] He was often accused of provoking scandals to get attention and ensure the success of his work.[3] Although this is an insinuation, Bernhard, a master of press manipulation who knew the rules of "mass-media society," was not as innocent of these scandals as he claimed. At least for *Holzfällen*[4] and *Heldenplatz*, public reactions were foreseeable, and Bernhard instrumentalized the scandal. In both cases, he used the medium of the scandal to extend his work beyond the limits of the book or the play: the reaction of the "victim" in *Holzfällen*, the composer Gerhard Lampersberg, and the indignant outcry of Austria's political and journalistic elite against *Heldenplatz* are a part of the play and confirm the statements of the characters; public reception and its subject melted to one inseparable unit, to a total comedy, in which all of Austria was involved. The provocativeness of the play, which was first performed in the Burgtheater in November 1988, seems to continue even today.

Bernhard's insults against Austria made headlines before the first performance of the play and aroused the collective need for self-protection. Provoked citizens felt mobilized to defend the threatened country, politicians intervened, and the time had come for braggarts and know-it-alls. Strange letters to the editors were published; their authors articulated sadistic fantasies against the sick poet.[5] On the other hand, Bernhard found many defenders who identified with his insults against Austria. I remember the students of my institute papering the walls with quotations criticizing the "hostility toward the spirit" *(Geistfeindlichkeit)* of our university. In this polarized parody of a political discussion, with its "either/or," there was no space for a differentiated position. One can be sad about the reactionary positions, which were articulated in the reception of the play, but on the whole the entire scandal was a gigantic misunderstanding and—as we will see—as such quite funny.

One word about Bernhard's personal relationship to "scandals" beyond their role as instruments of literary expression: studying Bernhard's behavior one gets the impression, that—despite his self-critical comments—he enjoyed the excitement (he called it "Erregungen"). It seems that he used the scandals as an accepted tool for the disposal of aggressive energies and as an important sign of unbroken life, compensating for his deadly disease: despite his weakness, he was still able to provoke the country's powerful figures into reacting. In all his controversies, Bernhard knew what hurt, and especially in the case of Austria it seems he had sadistic feelings legitimized as a justified "revenge."

Bernhard, a master of ambivalence and ambiguity, could claim innocence on a certain point. In the play, he uses two distinctive strategies of distancing himself from his characters and their view of the world. First, when seen from the perspective of his entire oeuvre Bernhard constructs a hierarchical typology of characters. From this point of view the characters of *Heldenplatz* do not demonstrate a worthy lifestyle; second, his characters are aware of what they would call their "paranoia." So, despite the fact that some statements of his characters are identical with positions Bernhard articulated in interviews,[6] he "did not say" what he was accused of saying.

It belongs to the contradictions of this man that he really suffered during the controversies he sought and that the counterattacks of the powerful produced deep, irrational anxieties. From a certain point of view, Bernhard was not strong enough for the public affairs he provoked and ultimately died, in February 1989, from the *Heldenplatz* affair,[7] which was, in his personal system of values, a self-determined death in a fight for a good cause.

Politics and History

Bernhard's criticism of Austria has two targets: first, the country's loss of cultural and political greatness. The indictment that today's Austria as a mediocre minor state is ridiculous compared with the past of the Habsburg Empire can also be found in the rare political portion of the early work.[8] In *Heldenplatz* we read:

Jetzt hat alles den Tiefpunkt erreicht
nicht nur politisch gesehen alles

die Menschen die Kultur alles
in ein paar Jahrzehnten ist alles verspielt worden
das ist in Jahrhunderten nicht mehr gutzumachen
wenn man bedenkt was dieses Österreich
einmal gewesen ist.[9]

[Now everything has reached the lowest point
not only in a political sense
people, culture, everything
gambled away in few decades
in centuries one can not make up for it
if one thinks what this Austria has once been.]

The guilty are accused: the government, the intellectuals, even the architects, the megalomaniac republican principle, and Bernhard's special enemies, the Social Democrats, who betrayed their own principles.

The second target is Austria's part in the crimes of the Third Reich, as well as the continuity of elites and attitudes between the Nazi era and the Second Republic. Bernhard uses exaggeration as an art form, and sometimes his criticism is close to traditional Austrian self-hate, which has been named "morbus austriacus," the Austrian disease, by Friedrich Heer.[10] But his comments are part of Austria's intense self-criticism, especially after the Waldheim election, which I think is the central moral event of the Second Republic.[11] The real Heldenplatz is an apt metaphor to combine the two central topics of Bernhard's criticism. The huge square in front of the emperor's palace is part of the Viennese Ringstraße and represents the memory of Austria's lost greatness; Adolf Hitler used the square in 1938 to stage a huge rally and to announce to the screaming audience the annexation of Austria. At one side of the square is the presidential chancellery—Kurt Waldheim's office.

Although Bernhard was part of a greater movement of writers, his strategy in the discussion of Austria's Nazi problem was in a certain way unique. If we observe only the Bernhard of the 1980s, we see a sometimes ruthless critic who finds Nazis and antisemites practically everywhere.[12] We can see this pattern in *Heldenplatz:* "es gibt jetzt mehr Nazis in Wien / als achtunddreißig" (nowadays there are more Nazis in Vienna / than in 1938 [63]); "der Judenhaß ist die reinste die absolut unverfälschte Natur / des Österreichers" (hate against the Jews is the absolute pure nature / of the Austrians [114]); "sie warten alle nur auf das Signal / um ganz offen gegen uns vorgehen zu können" (they are waiting for the signal to attack us openly [63]); "in jedem Wiener steckt ein Massenmörder" (there is a mass-murderer in every Viennese [118]); "[und da] ein Großteil der Österreicher will / daß der Nationalsozialismus herrscht [sei dieser] unter der Oberfläche ... schon längst wieder an der Macht" (as the majority of Austrians want National-Socialism to rule the country ... [the Nazis are] in power under the surface [135]).

So in "Heldenplatz-Austria" everything is, when compared with other countries, the worst. Although this result, which Bernhard shares with some of his followers, has a satirical dimension, it also has an interesting outcome: by demonizing the country, Bernhard is able to restore Austria's lost greatness by default.

Still, uncovering and impeaching were not Bernhard's central concerns. As we can see from a famous sequence of *In der Höhe* (written in 1959),[13] the Holocaust was one of his subjects. But in his great novels up to *Korrektur,* he often portrayed characters absolutely unconnected to Austria's contemporary history. From *Frost* through *Italiener, Ungenach,* and *Verstörung* to *Auslöschung,* a slow process of bringing the characters in contact with a full knowledge of Austria's past was under way, reaching its peak in *Auslöschung.* Bernhard's central topic is not the fact of Austria's past, but the way people handle this fact. I think this is one key to understanding *Heldenplatz.* Bernhard never abandoned his position as a critic of Austria. But ambivalence was a central element of his character and his works. Thus, *Heldenplatz* is both in one: a play that criticizes Austria and at the same time it ridicules Austria's criticism and its exponents.

Is There a Life after Austria's Past?

The manner in which his characters handle Austria's past is an essential part of what Bernhard called their "relation to the world" *(Weltverhältnis).* There is a development of this relationship from the unconscious misery of the painter Strauch in *Frost* to the views on life of Bernhard's characters in his late work, especially in *Alte Meister* and *Auslöschung,* successful despite all their suffering from disease and age. Bernhard's protagonists develop an instrument to master their existential—and also Austrian—problems. They conquer the memory of their early misery resulting from the overlapping of childhood and historical catastrophe; they leave the country and their families and find their "own" place; they write studies about their misery and find the "greatest happiness" in writing; they celebrate a ritual donation of their inheritance *(Abschenkung)* and "choose" an existence as "people of the spirit" *(Geistesmenschen).* Bernhard's world is a hierarchical world: the rank of a figure is established by the degree to which she uses this instrument. This world is manufactured from standardized units: well-known types and social constellations are combined to produce a new result. So the total constellation of *Heldenplatz* is new for us, but the characters are well-known friends from our earlier journeys in the Bernhard world.

In *Heldenplatz* we are confronted with a typical Bernhardesque pathological family system, in which a multifarious hatred is the most visible emotion, relieved by emotional unconnectedness. Professor Josef Schuster, a tyrant who vexes the family and the servants the way the character of the mother usually does in Bernhard's plays, has committed suicide. Schuster was one of Bernhard's "people of the spirit," the kind of person who walks "absolutely alone" through life and accepts the fact that "everybody freezes at his side" ("Ganz allein geht ein Geistesmensch / durch sein Leben / wenn sie auch alle erfrieren an seiner Seite / hat der Professor gesagt" [57]). This could also be said about Glenn Gould, the central character in *Der Untergeher* and Bernhard's incarnation of an "Apollonic hierarch," but unlike the piano virtuoso the professor is married, and the marriages of "people of the spirit" are, with the exception of *Alte Meister,* always ridiculous. So in Bernhard's system of values Schuster is ridiculous, and he has also committed a crime, the "primary crime of reproduction" *(Urverbrechen der Zeugung)* instead of keeping himself in the reproduction-free zone of artificiality *(Künstlichkeit)* that is praised by Murau in *Auslöschung.* According to Bernhard's system of values the sample fact of Schuster's marriage delegitimizes his status as a member of the "people of spirit."

As usual in the Bernhard world, the children are victims of parental terror. Schuster, in his own words the "greatest egocentric," had "abused them all," hated his daughters, and called them "grave-diggers" and his son a "loser" and a "disgusting monster." Even behind the so-called love for his brother Robert there is emotional detachment.

In Bernhard's description, such a family situation is usually the scene for one family member's more or less successful attempt at liberation. Liberation is no theme in the Schuster family: here everybody clamps on to everything, to people and objects. Relations have a compulsive narrowness and last forever: the Schuster couple met at the age of five and is still together at more than seventy years of age. The professor always mistreated his wife, who offered resistance, following Bernhard's rule: "Eheleute bringen sich immer um" (Married couples always kill themselves [68]). Despite the unbearable family life in the large apartment at the Heldenplatz, no one leaves; only the son, an indicated figure of hope, has a "scandalous" affair with an actress, rejects the parental game of "Vienna" or "Cambridge," and is criticized like all Bernhard sons who commit the crime of attempting to live lives of their own.

A total standstill dominates the family. Nothing is given away; even the old, ragged, bloodstained suit of the suicide is preserved. Real estate, the curse over each Bernhard heir, is kept as a place of a pretended happy childhood. The economy of the "people of the spirit" is based upon ridiculous enterprises such as a vinegar factory or even a fez factory. All the family members act as if there were no choice: "bourgeois heir / this burdens us lifelong." This short description shows that Bernhard is more critical than respectful of his characters.

"Weggehen" (going away—the pathos of this word is untranslatable) is in the Bernhard world, where the lost son is the hero, a heroic act and the precondition of a search for selfhood. "Cambridge" is a code word for the high rank of a character in the hierarchy of Bernhard's world, a place of exile for Austrian sons, tormented by their families and the unbearable Austrian situation, but also a place with a high intellectual reputation. It seems that Schuster and his brother went the same way, to Oxford and Cambridge, the place of exile of Roithamer in *Korrektur* (and of Ludwig Wittgenstein). Seen from their position, the two professors are Apollonic hierarchs but one of the comical aspects of the play lies in the disparate relationship between their rank and their helplessness in their family situation. This they share with Roithamer. However, the Schusters are not "Weggeher," but "expelled," and this makes a great difference in the Bernhard world. They did not leave Austria as a subversive act of their own; they were obedient to brutal and unjust laws. In Bernhard's system of values, they did not reach their high rank on their own merits. They are parvenus among the people of spirit, and this also produces a comical effect. The history of the Schuster family provides ample evidence in support of this thesis.

The subsequent behavior of the Schusters, especially after Hitler's defeat, demonstrates that they did not really "go away" in the sense of a "Bernhard-hero." At the first chance they "came back" to Austria, seduced by sentiments, by their possessions, and by empty promises of the Viennese university. There is a consciousness of the mistake in the family, but it does not produce a *Korrektur*, only the question: Who is to blame? The members of the family put the blame on each other. No one is responsible for his own life. Each one thinks in the category of a "whole," which is an illusion. Now they want to go back to Oxford, halfheartedly. Again it is not an act of their choice. Again they blame each other. "I am a Jew," said the professor to a pastry cook with the beautiful name "Handlos," but then: "For my wife's sake I have to go back to Oxford" ("Wissen sie Herr Handlos ich bin nämlich Jude / meiner Frau zuliebe muß ich nach Oxford zurück" [22]).

The professor's suicide ended a paralyzing ambivalence, which is characteristic for Bernhard's "unliberated" characters. As an old man, he does not know which place is good for him: "He did not want to go back to Oxford / he could not stand Vienna" ("Er wollte ganz einfach nicht mehr nach Oxford zurück / in Wien hat er es nicht mehr ausgehalten" [39]). Such a paralyzing ambivalence is in the Bernhard world usually a result of an unresolved conflict from one's childhood. Here, the characters have no consciousness of their early traumas—which means, according to *Korrektur* and *Auslöschung*—that they cannot take control of their own lives.

A Community of Indictments

The play opens in a special Bernhard moment, the moment after the death of the dictator, which could be the moment of liberation. Here liberation is celebrated only in details of no significance: now the apartment can be decorated with flowers and the soup can be spiced with caraway. Death did not end the dictatorship, and the survivors are disturbed by mourning, insecurity about the future, and the sense of guilt. To handle this disturbance—and this is the central point of *Heldenplatz*—the family uses the medium of insulting Austria. There is only one aspect that invites the audience to identify with the Schusters: the indictments against Austria.

These indictments have many functions for the family: they come to an understanding only over the code word "Austria," which is the only thing that gives the deadly environment within the family some drama. "Austria" serves as the common side-enemy that keeps them together. It is the common solution they find for their surplus of aggressive drives. Bernhard liked to describe this type of human relationship. In *Wittgensteins Neffe*, he gave it a name, "community of indictments" *(Bezichtigungsgemeinschaft)*. Collective paranoia constitutes community. The Schuster family is comparable to a sect like that of the Reverend Jim Jones in Guyana. And this is Bernhard's achievement: he brings the public to the point where they can begin to identify with the laments of this extremely problematic family. At the same time, he provokes his opponents to reactions that seem to confirm these indictments.

"Each death leaves only bad consciences behind" ("Jeder Tote läßt nur lauter schlechte Gewissen zurück" [133]). The survivors of a suicide victim are the addressees of his deed, in which they are involved in multiple ways. The Schuster family fights its sense of guilt by indicting Austria. The play knows that these people are tortured by countless unbearable circumstances, but with their indictments they claim their innocence and project their situation onto the whole of society. In this family each member is constantly confronted with hate, but having an outside enemy allows them to have polite and reserved manners.

The indictments against Austria are also the formula for a classical "defense," developed by the late professor: "I am only accurate / but not mad," or "I am not sick, he screamed, I am not sick" ("Ich bin ja nur genau Frau Zittel aber nicht verrückt … ich bin nicht krank ich bin nicht krank schrie er" [27]). All the family members spend their time in a locus classicus of Bernhard's world, the famous asylum "Am Steinhof." The characters of *Heldenplatz* fight against something that Bernhard, a successor of Montaigne, made a duty for all his figures: knowledge of oneself. In fact, they have only a fragmented contact with reality itself; the mystery of Professor Schuster's suicide will be unsolved until the end of the play. These characters are "derealized," like the postwar Germans and Austrians in the famous analysis of Alexander and Margarete Mitscherlich, *The Inability to Mourn*.[14] A pathological family decides that they are healthy and "Austria" is the reason for their suffering: "My biggest misery is / that I am an Austrian" ("Daß ich Österreicher bin / ist mein größtes Unglück" [25]). Children spare themselves the confrontation with the fact that their father was "unhappy for decades / he would have also been so in England" ("Der Vater war schon jahrzehntelang / ein unglücklicher Mensch / das wäre er auch in England geblieben" [108f]).

We, the audience, know after the dialogue of the servants that these characters suffer from something that is not "Austria." So we are confronted with an effect comparable to the puppet theater, the Austrian "Kasperltheater" for children, where Kasperl and his friend Petzi talk very seriously about an imagined danger, but the real danger, the crocodile, is behind them—invisible to them, but visible to the audience. I think this is the central comical effect of *Heldenplatz*. It is a bloody joke that here victims misuse knowledge about Austria's guilt. *Heldenplatz* has been seen as a play "against Austria," but if one reads the play as "against" something, then from a certain point it is also a play against Austria's victims.

The great anxiety that rules this family is the fear of the unpredictable and violent father, a fear that did not stop after his death. Schuster himself was an anxious person who extended his fear to everything and even prohibited his children from sledding. But only one way to name these deep anxieties is allowed: the fear of National Socialism, the fear that "it is now worse in Vienna than it was fifty years ago" ("Jetzt ist es hier in Wien ja schlimmer / als vor fünfzig Jahren Frau Zittel" [43]). This is, I think, a bad sentence, because it plays down the events of 1938. Maybe inside the family, whose dictator calls the others "Untermenschen," everything is worse than in 1938. We should not overlook the repetitions of 1938 in the play: at that time the professor's youngest brother—and many other Jews—committed suicide in the same way that Josef Schuster did. *Heldenplatz* plays with a popular topic of Austria's contemporary literature: that history can repeat itself. It was Hegel's idea that all the great historical events happen twice, but Karl Marx made an addition to this concept that fits *Heldenplatz:* one time as a tragedy, the second time as a "farce." There is also a repetition when a Jewish family has to leave their apartment by the significant date of March 19: in the weeks after the annexation, Jewish property was confiscated (arisiert) and thousands of wealthy Jewish people had to move out of their apartments and were forced to emigrate. Here, however, we have private reasons: the apartment was sold and the new tenant is not a Nazi, but a Persian carpet dealer. The one event offered to us by the characters as a reason for their fear, that Anna was spit at in the city as a Jew, is doubted by the other characters.

The Schuster family also interprets the mother's sickness as a consequence of Austria's political situation. She is believed to be mentally disturbed, but her main symptoms are sounds in her ear, which only she can hear—a typical Bernhard disease, which we know from the "Fürst" in *Verstörung.* The sound she hears, which we also hear at the end of the play, is the screaming of the masses who celebrate "Führer" and "Anschluß" at the Heldenplatz, so the play, which was performed in the "memorial year" 1988, reminds us of Austria's shame. This is a grand idea, effective on stage, which gives Frau Schuster's disease a political dimension and confirms the indictments against Austria. But we amateur doctors know what Frau Schuster really suffers from: it is an organic disease, a disturbance in the blood circulation in the ear, called tinnitus. The disease is used as a metaphor, but the characters treat it as a real diagnosis: "As long as she keeps the apartment / there will be no healing / when she changes the apartment / the disease will leave her" ("Solange Sie die Wohnung nicht aufgeben / wird keine Heilung möglich sein / wenn Sie die Wohnung aufgeben / wird sich die Krankheit zurückziehen" [30]). Ludwig van Beethoven, who often changed his apartments, could confirm that tinnitus will not leave if you leave an apartment. It is an illusion that there will be no tinnitus in Oxford, because there is no Heldenplatz there.[15]

As is often the case in the Bernhard world, the play is open-ended. We do not know if the breakdown of Frau Schuster is the final one—that would mean that Hitler in a strange way found his last victim. Bernhard's favorite question is also raised here: "Is it a comedy? Is it a tragedy?"[16] This play, written by a dying man, contains all the ingredients of a tragedy—suicide, death, disease, misery in the family, sociopathic characters. But the audience laughs; the indictments on stage have a liberating effect, and the folding of the "private" and the "political" sphere is at least funny. So it is a bitter comedy that confirms by its existence the positive balance in the life of Bernhard, who wrote in 1968 in *Ungenach*, "The one who succeeds in writing a comedy on his deathbed is successful in everything" ("Wem es gelingt, auf dem Totenbett eine Komödie oder ein reines Lustspiel zu schreiben, dem ist alles gelungen").[17]

Notes

1. Burgtheater, *Heldenplatz: Eine Dokumentation* (Vienna: Burgtheater, January 1989); Alfred Pfabigan, *Thomas Bernhard—Ein österreichisches Weltexperiment* (Vienna: Zsolnay, 1999).
2. Jens Dittmar, ed., *Thomas Bernhard: Werkgeschichte* (Frankfurt am Main: Suhrkamp, 1990); Jens Dittmar, ed., *Sehr geschätzte Redaktion: Leserbriefe von und über Thomas Bernhard* (Vienna: Edition S, 1991).
3. Hans Haider, "Die Stigmatisierten steigen auf," *Die Presse*, 23 August 1985: "Einen privaten Konflikt hat Thomas Bernhard ausgenützt um für sein letztes Buch sogar die Polizei als Werbehelfer zu benützen."
4. Eva Schindlecker, "Holzfällen: Eine Erregung: Dokumentation eines österreichischen Literaturskandals," in *Statt Bernhard: Über Misanthropie im Werk Thomas Bernhards,* ed. W. Schmidt-Dengler and M. Huber (Vienna: Edition S, 1987).
5. Dittmar, *Thomas Bernhard*, 187–212.
6. Sepp Dreissinger, ed., *Von einer Katastrophe in die andere: 13 Gespräche mit Thomas Bernhard* (Weitra: Bibliothek der Provinz, 1992); Thomas Bernhard, *Eine Begegnung: Gespräche mit Krista Fleischmann* (Vienna: Edition S, 1991); Kurt Hofmann, *Aus Gesprächen mit Thomas Bernhard* (Munich: dtv, 1988).
7. Krista Fleischmann, ed., *Thomas Bernhard—Eine Erinnerung: Interviews zur Person* (Vienna: Edition S, 1992).
8. Thomas Bernhard, "Politische Morgenandacht," *Wort in der Zeit* 1 (1966): 11–13.
9. Thomas Bernhard, *Heldenplatz* (Frankfurt am Main: Suhrkamp, 1988), 96; hereafter cited in the text. All translations are those of the author unless otherwise stated.
10. Friedrich Heer, *Der Kampf um die österreichische Identität* (Vienna: Böhlau, 1981), passim.
11. Alfred Pfabigan, "Breaking Traditions: Fin de Siècle 1896 and 1966," *Partisan Review* 64, no. 2 (1997): 205–10.
12. Thomas Bernhard, "Verfolgungswahn?" *Die Zeit*, 11 January 1982.
13. "… zuerst die schönen Menschen: zu Tausenden, Zehntausenden, Millionen, nackt, blutverschmiert … das Gas hat ihre Köpfe aufgeblasen, ihnen die Gehörgänge verstopft: eine richtige Riesenschaufel schiebt die tote Masse dieser Menschen in einen riesigen Ofen hinein." Thomas Bernhard, *In der Höhe. Rettungsversuch. Unsinn* (Salzburg: Residenz, 1989), 51.
14. Alexander and Margarete Mitscherlich, *Die Unfähigkeit zu trauern* (Munich: Piper, 1967).
15. *Heldenplatz*, 68. The play gives the disease of Frau Schuster some additional meanings; for instance, it is her instrument of power, which she used for two decades against her husband: "such diseases / are real diseases but also theater" ("Die Krankheiten dieser Art / sind wirkliche Krankheiten und doch Theater").
16. Thomas Bernhard, "Ist es eine Komödie? Ist es eine Tragödie?" *Prosa* (Frankfurt am Main: Suhrkamp, 1967).
17. Thomas Bernhard, *Ungenach* (Frankfurt am Main: Suhrkamp 1968), 44.

Chapter 9

PULLING THE PANTS OFF HISTORY

Politics and Postmodernism in
Thomas Bernhard's *Eve of Retirement*

Jeanette R. Malkin

One of Thomas Bernhard's most historically specific plays, *Vor dem Ruhe-stand* (Eve of Retirement, 1979) is also one of his most ritualistic. A play of "doubleness" and unsynthesizable tensions, it is both realistic and metaphoric, structured both causally and cyclically. Steeped in public history, it simultaneously ritualizes history through private memory. This doubleness—the coexistence of historical and ahistorical consciousness, of development and stasis, time and timelessness—is, no doubt, central to Bernhard's work as a whole; and it is knowingly, indeed pointedly used by Bernhard in this play to both reflect and implicate the history and memory of his audience.

The conflation of past and present is a typical ploy of postmodern literature, together with generic self-reflexivity (the play aware of itself as a play), proliferation of perspectives, ironic distancing, fragmentation, lack of synthesis, verbal and visual quotation. All of these characterize *Eve of Retirement*. Postmodernism often involves an explicit (and always "loaded") utilization and reflection of the past, confounded by memory, by a destabilized perspective, or by other deconstructive tactics. Bernhard, like other postmodern dramatists—for example, Heiner Müller or Sam Shepard—depends on the audience's knowledge of the past and how it is conventionally imaged, in order to shock and draw irony through multiple or conflated perspectives. These perspectives are often provocations that challenge the usual representations of that past, or of the present in its light. I would fully accept (and extend to drama) Linda Hutcheon's definition of postmodern fiction as "fundamentally contradictory, resolutely historical, and *inescapably political.*"[1] Hutcheon argues that postmodern fiction is never neutral or detached, but rather contains within it the paradox "of complicity and critique, of reflexivity and historicity, that at once inscribes and subverts ... conventions and ideologies."[2] This temporal and ideological doubleness is, I suggest, of even greater immediacy in the drama, which depends on public performance and group viewing. The audience—and Bernhard always wrote for a *specific* audience—is key to the functioning of such drama. Bernhard's plays, even his least realistic ones, are "locally" inscribed: reflecting (and often parodying) the context of their performance. A prominent example is his infamous ridicule of the important Salzburg Festival—and its "cultured" Austrian audience—in many of the plays officially commissioned by, and specifically written *for*, that festival. Each of the resulting scandals provoked divisive (and profitable) media coverage, and can certainly qualify as a "complicit and critical" relationship with the foremost venue of "official culture" in Austria.[3] *Eve of Retirement* is doubly inscribed: reflecting both a general German-European audience thirty years "after," and the specific Stuttgart audience of 1979 (at the play's premiere performance), which was itself in the midst of a real political scandal involving a prominent political figure who, in the past, had functioned as an active Nazi. The play's contradictions and multiple perspectives assume, perhaps even require, the knowing, "mediating," or oppositional function of an *always complicit and implicated* viewer. Bernhard's plays may begin on the stage, but they always end in the audience.

Setting the Stage

Bernhard had a talent for provocation and outspokenness, especially about the Austrian/German peoples and their history. He mocked them in play after play by unmasking their language, their mentality, and especially their hypocrisy in dense dramatic parables. Most of his eighteen full-length plays tend toward unlocalized metaphor, grounded and politicized through verbal realism. *Eve of Retirement*, however (together with his 1988 play *Heldenplatz* [Hero's Square]), presents us with characters whose ages, activities, objects, and memories are all calibrated to serve as markers for a specific, historically recognizable reality. Judge Rudolf Höller and his sisters Clara and Vera are recognizably situated in Germany of today (the late 1970s, when it was written), possibly in Stuttgart, where the scandalous premiere performance took place and whose (then) minister president, Hans Karl Filbinger, is pointedly referred to in the text. Chief Justice Höller, now in his late sixties and about to retire from the bench, is easily the matured version of "the youngest judge on the entire Eastern front"[4] and substitute commander of a Nazi concentration camp, who, for decades, has secretly practiced the rituals of his loyalty to National Socialism. The play takes place on "October seventh ... everything in him is geared toward the seventh" (125), which is the actual birthdate of SS head Heinrich Himmler and a date Rudolf has been commemorating for over thirty years. The play's minimal plot enacts this yearly ritual in a clear progression: there are Vera's preparations (ironing, cooking); Rudolf's second-act arrival and the annual act of incest between him and Vera; the third-act celebration meal and rituals of remembering; and a final ironic reversal, to which I will return.

The stage Bernhard describes represents a large, old-fashioned, deceptively ordinary living room, unchanged since the days of their childhood. Clara, a paraplegic crippled during a U.S. bomb raid, is first seen reading her leftist newspapers; Vera meanwhile chills the Fürst Von Metternich *sekt*, "the brand Rudolf likes so much" (118). This well-known champagne, with its name recalling the ultraconservative Habsburgian foreign minister who shaped Europe in the nineteenth century, was, we later learn from Rudolf, what "we drank at the camp/ That's something I always paid the greatest attention to/that there was always enough Von Metternich at the camp/otherwise we'd have never been able to take it" (194). The details of Rudolf's past, his membership in the *Hitlerjugend*, volunteering for the army in 1939, the names of the cities where he served during the war, his description of Himmler, of the fate of the Hungarian and Polish Jews, of Auschwitz ("Two and a half million/that's what Eichmann said.... That's what Eichmann said to Gluecks" [202]), the false papers provided by Himmler in 1945 that allowed Rudolf to go underground, his ten years in hiding and subsequent emergence and integration into the legal system in which he has now achieved the "highest position": all these details are historically credible and doubly potent for being both accurate and taboo.

As in the best naturalist tradition, not only is the play locally marked and realistically detailed, the addressee, the audience, is also meant to be specific and marked. *Eve of Retirement* was written for a German audience of 1979, an audience who would understand the nuanced political, historical, and local references (such as the Von Metternich) and who could react to the spare but vital visual stage icons. It was first presented in Stuttgart, capital of Baden-Württemberg, some months after the divisive political scandal involving its powerful conservative minister president, Hans Karl Filbinger, a potential future Christian Democratic Union (CDU) candidate for President of West Germany. Filbinger, like Höller, had long and successfully concealed his active role in the legal system of Nazi Germany as a naval judge famous for his harshness and who, during World War II, zealously inflicted death sentences for trivial offenses. Like Kurt Waldheim in the 1980s, Filbinger reacted to the exposure of his past with vehement denial. He first protested his innocence, then contested the importance of his activities, and only finally, and under severe pressure, resigned his post.[5] This political scandal, which rocked the Baden-Württemberg establishment and required the installation of a new head of state, also led to renewed public anxiety about the "hidden" or repressed Nazi elements in government. It is only the most obvious level of historical signification that runs throughout the play, but it is potent since, as many have noted, "Filbinger served as a symbol for the pernicious continuity between past and present in Germany."[6] The Stuttgart audience certainly understood the references being made in *Eine Komödie von deutscher Seele* (Comedy of the German soul), as the play is subtitled, and re-acted with boos.[7]

Thus, it would seem that localized realism, detailed historical markers, a provocative subject reflecting a hot and current political issue, and a "chosen" audience involved and implicated by the subject set the stage for a political play, an audience-attacking *j'accuse* on lingering fascism, neo-Nazism, the *"unbe-wältigte"* (unmastered) past and such: all not uncommon subjects in German art.

But as soon as we begin reading the play, it becomes obvious that, historical markers and realism notwithstanding, the texture of the play pulls in a quite different direction: the direction of an ahistorical parable, a grotesque and free-floating metaphor. As with all Bernhard's plays, *Eve of Retirement* consists mainly of long repetitive monologues written in open verse lines, unpunctuated and fashioned from a highly idiomatic and musically rhythmic German. Speech is fluid and moves in associative loops from one rumination to the next, circling and repeating private obsessions, aggressions, memories. As Vera says to her crippled sister:

> Say what you like
> It's all right
> I love you and protect you
> but it's hard with a person
> who despises me unnecessarily ...
> What if Rudolf hadn't returned from the war
> What if they had brought him to trial
> Isn't it nice that everything turned out all right
> We are respected people aren't we
> and we are well off ...
> only you are never content
> always plagued by your obsessions ...
> Rudolf often wonders
> if you wouldn't be better off
> in a sanitarium
> Don't worry
> we wouldn't dare
> The three of us are a conspiracy (124)

Alternately cynical and sentimental, these idiomatic voices might belong to that other great Austrian ventriloquist, Ödön von Horváth, except that Bernhard's voices are derealized through the extended monologue form and through the repetitions and contradictions. "Father always knew/how dangerous you were," Clara is told; "Family killer that's what he called you ... you're insane/a fanatic ... Rudolf says so too" (128–29). The characters rummage through gradations of contradictory remembrance, exposing different versions of their relations to each other, their parents, their past. "Rudolf is a good good man," Vera insists; "You are proof of it/What's past doesn't matter/And who's to know how it really was/Now they are digging up the dirt again ... Kindness creates enemies/father used to say/During the war there are no laws/father used to say ... We know/and love our brother/He still is the child/he once was" (152–53). Everything sounds overly familiar, as though all this had been said before, and the sense of unnatural repetition is underscored through repeated quotes: "Poverty is no longer necessary/Poverty is caused/ by the poor themselves/Don't ever help the poor/father used to say" (118). Clara, the crippled leftist, the anti-Nazi enemy, is repeatedly threatened with institutionalization, defamed, and insulted. She rarely reacts and barely speaks, and it soon becomes clear that the threats—and her silence—are built into the relationship, are part of their verbal stock, spoken almost by rote, as are the repeated quotes from Father and the childhood memories, which have surely been remembered before and never manage to sound spontaneous.

What we see is not so much enacted as *re*enacted. As in Strindberg's *Dance of Death*, there is a clear sense that all this has been done before, said before. Thus, already in act 1 Vera can tell us what will, and in fact does, happen at the celebration in act 3: "He will sit here and suddenly not say a word/and that means/he wants me/to bring him the photo album/I have to turn the pages/and I have to look at it with him/picture after picture/the same every year" (141). This intuition of "sameness" is elaborated upon in the text. "Father wouldn't tolerate the slightest change," we are told repeatedly; the furniture, the curtains, are all exactly as their grandparents had left them; even the grime and gray of "this ghastly house/this morgue" (143) is the way it was: "nothing has changed ... nothing has changed" (144). They are forever comparing themselves to their parents, seeing their parents in themselves, quoting and becoming the people they quote. This circularity and repetition invokes a heavy sense of ahistorical stasis, which is countered, problematically, by clear narrative progression and the play's detailed historical realism. Together they produce what Charles Russell, discussing postmodern art, has described as "an art of shifting perspective, of double self-consciousness, of local and extended meaning."[8] This shifting and simultaneity of incommensurable perspectives achieves a typically postmodern political effect. The play's historical grounding is subverted through stasis and return, while the ritual celebration is deeply ironized through its historical grounding. Progression and return, narrative realism and ritual repetition, time and timelessness, entropy and stasis defeat any coherent (or "totalizing") reading either of the narrative of German history or of its ritualization through memory. Past and present cease to function as discrete entities. Rudolf Höller will be read as much through Hans Karl Filbinger as vice versa. I will return to the question of the play's political position, but its shifting stance can already be intimated in the play's multiple, and conflated, time structures.

Staging Time

The plot of *Eve of Retirement* develops causally in a nearly classical three-act structure: the exposition and anticipation of the absent "hero"; his arrival and the subsequent complications among the characters, the "hero" revealing himself in his true colors, threatening and endangering the others; and, finally, the "hero" being "overcome." The narrative progression is clear and realistic; no structural repetitions à la Ionesco or Beckett are apparent. Aside from the nature of the ending, this could be a structural description of Molière's *Tartuffe* with the "hero's" famous third-act entrance, his near destruction of the Orgon family, and the ultimate *deus ex machina,* which leads to a happy reversal. *Eve of Retirement* also ends with an unexpected event, the sudden collapse of the "hero," reversing the plot and bringing an ironic "ending," though certainly no real closure, to the narrative structure.

At the same time, the entire play is structured as one complete and pre-planned action: the preparation for and celebration of an annual ritual whose various parts are fixed and unchanging from year to year. The narrative structure just described, which seemingly moves in time and traces a progress, is thus in fact a repetition, inevitable, with no spontaneity or unique action aside from the ultimate *coup de théâtre.*

These two views of the same plot represent two temporal schemes that parallel Mircea Eliade's description of the differences between "historical and archaic man" in his book *Cosmos and History: The Myth of the Eternal Return.* In Eliade's thesis, historical consciousness is narrative and developmental and assumes "a succession of events that are irreversible, unforeseeable, possessed of autonomous value."[9] Archaic man sets himself in opposition to historical consciousness, and history, through an ideology that is cyclical and refutes change. This ideology is expressed through the faithful reproduction of myths that transmit "paradigmatic models revealed to men in mythical times."[10] Through "the paradox of rite" (hallowed gestures performed *in* time in order to annul time itself), man is projected "into the mythical epoch in which the archetypes were first revealed." This enacts "an implicit abolition of profane time, of duration, of 'history.'"[11]

Thus, what appears to take place over an evening *in* time is simultaneously a rejection *of* time. The celebration of the Höllers' sacred archetype, Himmler, accomplishes a "revolt against concrete, historical time" and effects a "return to the mythical time of the beginning of things, to the 'Great Time'"[12]—which for them is the originary creation of the Nazi universe, its symbols, emotions, ideology, and "hero." For the audience, however, the concrete and detailed references to a common past and the chronological rehearsal of the events of "that time" encourage a simultaneous *historical* evocation of Himmler and the *narrative* of German history. The play thus moves in two different directions or arcs simultaneously: the ritual repetitions of sanctified acts and memories deny change and history, while the narrative structure and historical markers evoke a recognizable past whose plot progression infers change and history.

These two contrary movements do not synthesize; we are neither in the realm of (historical) narrative realism nor in that of (ahistorical) ritual repetition. Eliade claims that mythical ideology "makes it impossible that what we today call a 'historical consciousness' should develop."[13] The two systems are, he argues, mutually exclusive. Yet in *Eve of Retirement* both systems are proposed and offered to the audience; moreover, Bernhard implicitly suggests that both already coexist *in* the audience.

Benjamin Heinrichs, in a review of *Eve of Retirement*, wrote with admiration of Bernhard's capacity to create a text on fascism written simultaneously from within and without, reflecting both "scornful remoteness and despairing proximity."[14] Remoteness and proximity, distance and immediacy characterize an additional perspective, and an additional "time," that further complicates Bernhard's play: the self-reflexive theater metaphors that remove his characters from both narrative time and ritual timelessness and that place them in the *suspended* time of theater. As in many of Bernhard's plays, the characters here are also *players*, acting a role on the double stage of fictive reality and the real theater. "We've been acting our parts for so many years/we can't get out anymore," Vera says; "… we keep acting our parts/to perfection/sometimes we don't understand it ourselves" (139). These "parts" are both the deadly habit and repetition that control their every day and the "parts" written for them by history: "We have rehearsed our play/the parts were cast thirty years ago/each of us got his role" (140). The parts are also, of course, the theater roles rehearsed and being played on stage: "Sometimes I actually see myself/on a stage/and I am not ashamed in front of the audience … We only go on/living/because we keep giving each other the cues" (141). The "loaded" moment of the play's first presentation in Stuttgart, at the peak of the Filbinger scandal, heightened the relevance and implications of this reflexivity. The cooptation of the audience forefronts the present "time" (and context) of performance, asserts links between stage and outside reality, and accentuates the complicit and knowing "role" into which the spectator has been cast.

Objects of Desire

Within the "timeless" bourgeois German salon, act 1 begins in visual innocence. The stage is spare: a wheelchair, an ironing board, chairs, table, a dresser, a piano. Vera stands, ironing Rudolf's judge's robes, the sign of his present rank and profession, while Clara sits, reading her newspapers. Soon, however, Vera begins to bring objects onto the stage that are not "natural" parts of the milieu. In a transparently self-reflexive theatrical gesture, Bernhard sends Vera into the wings to bring out, one by one, objects marked as sites of controversy: a framed picture of Himmler, an SS officer's uniform, the striped jacket of a concentration camp prisoner, SS boots. One by one, Vera irons, brushes, cleans, and polishes these objects. Bernhard gives detailed instructions: during two pages of dialogue, the picture of Himmler is carefully polished by the light of the window, breathed on, polished, breathed on, polished, placed on the windowsill, looked over, and finally taken out backstage. The SS uniform receives much longer care; the jacket is hung on the window where it can be easily seen by the audience while the trousers are slowly ironed, held up against the light and inspected, ironed, held up and inspected, ironed, and so on, until they are finally hung with the SS jacket (onto which Vera pins the Iron Cross of the First Order) and the entire process is slowly repeated for the striped prisoner's jacket—which, we're told, Clara is sometimes forced to wear during the ceremony—and then for the SS officer's boots. The stage fills up with the specific historical symbols of Nazi power, aestheticized and sanctified through Vera's care. The exaggerated attention given these items and the repetition of purifying gestures transform them into fetishized objects, confer upon them an emotional status.

The stretch of these items is expanded in act 2 to include the body of Rudolf himself. Over the entire act he is slowly undressed by Vera, "objectified," turned into a locus of transgression through incestuous desire. Vera massages his neck, his back, removes his shirt, unzips his pants, kneels to massage his feet as the audience watches (participates in?) this taboo eroticism. As with the boots and jacket, the body is sanctified, fetishized. Simultaneously, the real historic body of a murderous Nazi becomes ever more evident through the many things he says: "in our time we simply put the likes of you/under gas" he tells Clara (180). "Whatever I did I was forced to do/and I did nothing/I couldn't justify/on the contrary ... I have no bad conscience" (175).

Finally, the very room they are in, indeed, the entire house, becomes the object of this double coding, historical and mythical, past and present. We learn that Rudolf had a great civic victory today, a victory worthy of October 7 since it parallels an act by Himmler himself forty years ago: "On this day the seventh of October a day of reckoning ... If it weren't for Himmler/this house wouldn't be here/you know what would be here instead/a poison plant/isn't it strange Vera that today/I too could prevent/the construction of a toxic gas plant/right in front of our windows/forty years ago Himmler prevented it/today I prevented it/ There's no such thing as coincidence" (161). Thus, the house saved today by the judge, the house that belonged to his parents and grandparents, is also Himmler's house, and "wouldn't be here" but for him. The view from the window "where nature is still untouched" would have been unbearable had Rudolf, or Himmler, allowed the "profit mongers" to destroy the environment: "cutting down trees/ cutting down those beautiful old trees/for the sake of a chemical plant/which produces nothing but poison" (158). In the end, the house, or rather, the stage, with its timeless German room and windows looking out on the "beautiful old trees" of Germany, becomes a replica and metaphor for "Germany" of then and now, and a conflation of the two.

The choice of a gas factory, a "poison plant," as the object of Rudolf's and Himmler's humane objection is, of course, more than mere (crass) irony; it is blatantly insulting, a refusal by Bernhard to be sensitive toward his audience. The word "gas" is one of the more loaded words for the contemporary German consciousness, one perhaps responsible for the fervent German anxiety of nuclear attack (and retribution?).[15] Another "loaded" subject for the German audience is the Jews. Rudolf, in typical Bernhardian ventriloquism, gives idiomatic voice to the most basic and mythical Jew-hating, using "taboo" words taken from the Nazi vocabulary: "The Jews destroy annihilate [*vernichten*] the surface of the earth/and some day they will have achieved its final destruction/The Jews sell out nature" (163). The audience is further told that Rudolf's view of the Jews is "like ninety-eight percent of the population ... the Germans hate the Jews/even as they claim just the opposite/that's the German nature ... in a thousand years the Jews will still be hated in Germany/in a million years" (138).

Bernhard's "abuse" of the audience led the German critic N. J. Meyerhofer to wonder if Bernhard had not devised *Eve of Retirement* as a "*Rachestück*," a "revenge play" against the German audience in light of the Filbinger controversy.[16] The "abuse" is easily recognizable because it is an embedded text, a suppressed but still active taboo text; Bernhard's strategic evocation and simultaneous destruction of embedded discourse is a typical postmodernist irony. Bernhard practices knowing transgression in his repeated references to gas; in his vitriolic attacks on Jews, America, democracy; and in choosing clearly historied and sensitive objects—an SS uniform, SS boots, a brother's body, Himmler himself—and showing them as ahistorical objects of desire, of ritual idealization. He thus forces his audience to read a historical past and a mythicized past through each other—and through their own historically/mythically formed consciousness.

History and Kitsch

The birthday celebration (act 3) enacts the converging point of public history and ritualized memory, of narrative progression and mythical return. The body we saw "objectified" in act 2 is now fully dressed in the clothes ironed and sanctified in act 1. Like a play within a play, Rudolf, fully costumed in the uniform, boots, and gun of an SS *Obersturmbannführer*—looking "like the very first day you wore it/absolutely perfect" (185)—sits across from Vera, who's in braids and a long brocade gown. Clara in her wheelchair, unchanged in either dress or attitude, silent throughout, sits between them. This *tableau* from the past transports us into the "eternal moment" the ritual is meant to recuperate, and it directs the audience's response. Verbally, history is invoked and ironized via the mawkish device of a "birthday" photo album that "documents" chosen memories. Visually and verbally, this ritual re-creation involves the explicit images, language, details, and dates that, for the audience, function above all as historical markers.

Most of act 3 is given over to the static viewing and discussion of photos (memories) that the audience does not see: "Remembering/once a year/Nothing like memories" (186). Paradoxically, these memories—arranged by Rudolf, "that orderly man"—are chronological, in "perfect order" (141), beginning on "Christmas of thirty-nine," when Rudolf volunteered for the army, and tracing Rudolf, and German history, up to the U.S. bombings of Freiburg in Breisgau and Würzburg. Thus, what at first appears to be a random catalog of personal memories is in fact a thumbnail synopsis of the "plot" and "narrative" of German history from 1939 to 1945. It is here, in the intersection of memory and history, of the personal and the public record, that the play becomes most provocative and most dependent on the audience's knowledge. It is here, in Bernhard's assumption of the spectators' understanding, of their co-evocation of a traumatic past, that the local nature of postmodern politics and the intertextuality of postmodern aesthetics become most evident.

The pictures follow Rudolf, among other places, from a "secret" mission to the Russian front, to the camp where he acted as substitute commander and met Himmler, to Kraków and Litzmannstadt where Rudolf became the "youngest judge on the entire Eastern front"; from Ukraine, where Rudolf shot his first prisoners, to the outskirts of Leningrad in 1942, to Schitomir "when I had bronchitis," to Warsaw and to Auschwitz, where Rudolf did not serve (Rudolf: "It wasn't meant to be"); from Berlin "after the first attack," to Verdun, to Freiburg in Breisgau. Dates are given, cities and rivers named, and a career as varied and complex as the war it parallels, almost incarnates, is evoked in a melange of trivial and horrific fragments—a cold caught here, a circus seen there, "happy" Poles in Kraków, the decayed faces of Jews from Hungary, the Führer on an inspection tour in Kattowitz, a beautiful Polish woman in Warsaw who "was gassed right away," Rudolf and Höss at Auschwitz. It is left to the audience to fill in the gaps, to produce their own versions of Rudolf's pictures, to remember what else had happened in Russia, Ukraine, Schitomir, or Auschwitz.

This is not the only time photos appear in Bernhard's work as an unmasking device. In his novels *Alter Meister* (Old Masters, 1985) and *Auslöschung* (Obliteration, 1986) photographs (which the reader never "sees") again serve as tools for the deconstruction of specific national and cultural myths. And indeed, as Vera predicted in act 1, "for every picture he has a story/a horror story/as if his memory/consisted of nothing but piled-up corpses" (141). The past is recalled and deployed through a mass of explicit details and personal narrative. We get a composite of images, of verbal idioms and historical facts, drawing the audience into the act of memory and implicating them through their own understanding. Bernhard, insensitive as ever, purposely plays on Nazi vocabulary. Vera calls the Poles "ruthless" (*rücksichtslos*); Rudolf tells Clara that she enjoys "the privilege of fools/otherwise we'd have already liquidated you" (187, 191). [17] A high point of "comedy" and Nazi ventriloquism is reached in Rudolf's accusation that Roesch, commander of the concentration camp where he had been substitute commander, was "unscrupulous":

es hat ihm nichts ausgemacht
dass er Tausende und Hunderttausende ins Gas geschickt hat
es hat ihm nichts ausgemacht
ich hab mich überwinden müssen[18]

[it didn't bother him/to send thousands and hundreds of thousands into the gas/
it didn't bother him at all/for *me* it was an effort.][19]

Rudolf's use of escalating numbers—"thousands and hundreds of thousands"—and his "sensitivity" while murdering, obviously recall a number of Himmler's more famous speeches, in which, for example, he describes the "effort" required of the "decent" German soldier "when we had to carry off thousands and tens of thousands and hundreds of thousands"; or Himmler's much-quoted speech to the SS Group Leaders in Posen on 4 October 1943 in which he says, in connection with "the extermination of the Jewish people": "Most of you know what it means to see a hundred corpses lying together, five hundred, or a thousand. To have gone through this and yet ... to have remained decent, this has made us hard. This is a glorious page in our history that has never been written and never shall be written."[20] It is a page that Bernhard evokes, the knowledge of which Bernhard *assumes*. And it is the mixture of kitsch idealism and horrific image that Bernhard—critically, ironically—duplicates here.

While viewing these pictures of the concentration camp with its "lovely countryside/And there you swam in the Weichsel river," and discussing Himmler ("basically a very sensitive human being" [188]), Vera switches on a recording of Beethoven's Fifth Symphony. Act 3 in fact begins with Vera's cliché about life having no meaning without music (Rudolf: "A civilized nation can make its own music" [192]). This becomes a double cliché within the visual context, recalling Heydrich and his violin, the chilling combination of culture and barbarism so well known and overused as to evoke, according to Hellmuth Karasek, uncomfortable, Pavlovian laughter in the Stuttgart audience.[21] It is soon apparent that the semiotic overload—Nazi uniform, picture of Himmler, the photos, the champagne, the specific Nazi vocabulary, together with the heroic strains of Beethoven's Fifth—does not support realism but rather evokes a self-reflexive kitsch, pointedly parodic both of German pathos and of the kitsch elements in Nazism itself.[22] This, when combined with images of war and death camps, of shootings and gassings, produces an aestheticized and critical tableau simultaneously. Bernhard's kitsch, like his discussion of gas and poison plants, is transparent, insulting—Kitsch written large. It does not, as some have claimed, "reproduce" fascist ideology; it is far too ironic and self-conscious for that, though it does, perhaps, force the audience to deconstruct the connections between kitsch emotion and the submission to fascism.[23] The kitsch is further undercut through the double ploy of Clara's silent, critical gaze, her refusal to "play," and the calculated theatrical self-reflexivity.

In this crucial section of the play, with its unsynthesized discourses so typical of postmodern art, self-reflexivity takes the form of metadramatic discussions of memory and history themselves, the objects of that very kitsch. The words "memory," "remembering," and "history" repeat throughout, in varying contexts, and finally climax in a direct attack on, and overt incorporation of, the memory and history of the audience. "The majority thinks just like us," we are told: "It's really absurd/The majority thinks like us and must do so secretly/Even if they insist on the contrary/they still are National Socialists all of them/it's written all over their faces/but they don't admit it" (204). The proof? Insinuation now gives way to present politics, linking a "hidden" past with a current open scandal: "The time will come for us to show it again ... we do have a President now/who was a National Socialist ... this is proof of how far we've already come ... we have a whole bunch/of other leading politicians/who were National Socialists" (204). Thus the Höllers' secret veneration of National Socialism is expanded to include the audience, who have, in fact, just *participated* in the Höllers' ritual of remembrance through their roles as spectators, as coproducers of memory and meaning, and who, in their social roles as citizens of Baden-Württemberg, play a part in the public "controversy" over the Filbinger affair.

As Linda Hutcheon writes, postmodern art challenges the reader "by leaving overt the contradictions between its self-reflexivity and its historical grounding."[24] The historically grounded play within a play, the marked return to "that time," is aware of itself as theater, and aware of the audience as coplayers in the production of both theatrical meaning and the politics of the present. The audience members, it is implied, have played a knowing role in deciphering (and constituting) the play, are integral to the play, are the objects of the Höllers' National Socialism, perhaps even the *condition* for their National Socialism. Like Peter Handke's *Publikumsbeschimpfung* (Insulting the Audience, 1966), this section turns the audience into "actors," challenging them to react, to defend themselves, perhaps to reject the power position implicit in the hold of the stage (in the theater or the political arena) over the passive viewer. Through the extension of the stage, the "site" of Germany's past and present, Bernhard draws direct links between present and past politics, between passivity and complicity, and propels the play toward its conclusion in the audience.[25]

Pulling the Pants Off History

Eve of Retirement draws to an end in a rage of pathos. Rudolf, drunk, inflamed with mythic potency, waves his gun and spits threats, declaring a soon-to-be-reborn National Socialism. Suddenly, with no preamble, he falls over onto the table. The remainder of the play involves the double-speed deconstruction of the stage, the removal of all Nazi objects, the undressing and redressing of Rudolf so that Vera may call their Jewish doctor, Doctor Fromm, for help. In short, the play shifts from pathos to farce.

As in many of his plays (*The Force of Habit*, *Histrionics*), Bernhard has created two temporal processes, conflated them, and now ironizes the entire undertaking in a final self-conscious *coup de théâtre*. Very little dialogue is provided during this section as stage action for the first time overrides speech. While Clara sits unmoving, silent, Vera drags the unconscious Rudolf to the sofa and begins to undo his SS uniform: his jacket, his boots, finally his trousers. Rudolf is now an inert object whose lifeless opposition to Vera's struggle to rid him of his clothing recalls Henri Bergson's definition of comedy as the mechanical or inanimate encrusted upon the living. Moreover, each piece of clothing that Vera struggles to remove is, for the audience, filled with memory and dramatic weight; we watched Vera iron and polish those clothes, we watched her undress Rudolf with erotic slowness and care.

Now, those same clothes are not only torn off his body, they are shorn of their symbolic value as the fetishized objects become a collection of theatrical props. Juxtaposing the figure of the eternal Nazi to the final image of the clown whose pants are pulled off on stage, Bernhard gives us grotesque pantomime.

This speeded-up undressing scene almost reenacts the play in reverse. Vera runs back and forth, carrying out the same objects she had slowly carried on in act 1: Himmler's picture, the uniform, the boots, the pistol, thus accomplishing a comic derigging of the Nazi world. The ironic effect of these final acts is again underlined by their self-reflexive theatricality. Even before Vera begins to undress Rudolf, Bernhard has her "turn Beethoven's Fifth back on exactly where it was interrupted before" (207). Blatantly, tastelessly, this most heroic and overly familiar piece of music accompanies and comments ironically on the transformation of the "heroic" Nazi body into the collapsed remains of a dying old man.

The ending of *Eve of Retirement* removes the play from its mythical "timelessness" and relocates it within narrative progression, a progression toward the simultaneous ending of the ritual, of Rudolf's life, and of Bernhard's play. As Paul Ricoeur wrote on narrative and history: "The form of life to which narrative discourse belongs is our historical condition itself," a condition to which Rudolf is most clearly returned at the moment of his death.[26] But more than this, and contained in this, the ending returns the play to "theater" and to the role of the audience. Throughout the last section, indeed, throughout act 3, Clara has sat stage center, looking on and listening without ever moving or saying a word. She neither responds to her siblings' questions nor reacts to their accusations—reflecting, perhaps, the silent gaze, the voyeuristic immobility of the audience. "It's your fault," Vera says to her in the penultimate words of the play, "you and your silence/you and your endless silence" (207). This is not the first time that Clara's passivity and the audience's have been equated. Toward the end of act 2, following prolonged invective against "what's going on in this country," Rudolf turns to Clara: "Speechless as always … she watches us and waits." To which Vera answers, "It's just a game … we play this comedy" in which Clara, or the silent, watching and waiting audience, "plays the hardest part/We only give her the cues/With her speechlessness/she keeps the comedy in motion" (173). Thus the ending of the play, rather than bringing closure to "this comedy," opens out accusingly to the "endless silence" of the passive, and implicated, spectator.

Two Faces of *Eve*

Is *Eve of Retirement* a political play? Two contradictory readings show the divergence of opinion. Joseph A. Federico claims that "Rudolf and Vera's staunchly defended universe becomes a grotesque symbol for the addiction to National Socialist thinking which, the play suggests, is the secret obsession still lurking within the modern German psyche." The play is thus "a challenge to contemporary society to find an alternative to the historical compulsions which continue to preoccupy it." Federico objects to those critics who try to depoliticize *Eve of Retirement* by making of it a play not about Nazis at all but merely one more misanthropic, postmodern parable, "one more variation woven from Bernhard's central themes: repetition, theatricality, cruelty, obsession, death."[27]

Donna L. Hoffmeister finds no such "meaning" or political essence in *Eve of Retirement*. She complains that Bernhard's postmodern "disruption of time and memory" acts to reduce "all politics to secret caprice, repression and perversion." The memories given "cancel each other out"; they are weightless and lack a counterperspective: "No idea is proposed in earnest and no reality is maintained as a locus of judgment."[28]

For Hoffmeister, the theatrical, reflexive, contradictory gestures in *Eve of Retirement* remain outside history, floating playfully above the audience; for Federico, the politically grounded dramatic *fabula* provides a critique and corrective to the position of the audience. These opposing postures approximate Steven Connor's analysis of the double nature of theories of postmodern cultural politics: theories that offer the "dual prospect, on the one hand of a transformation of history by a sheer act of imaginative will, and on the other, of an absolute weightlessness in which anything is imaginatively possible, because nothing really matters."[29] Both "prospects"—seriousness and weightlessness—are available in Bernhard's play; they coexist in the play's double time scheme, its simultaneous evocation and dissipation of history, its rambling and rectitude of memory, its complex inscription and parodying of the reader, the viewer, within the act of theater itself. Bernhard mirrors "National Socialist thinking," which "still lurk[s] within the modern German psyche," while also acting out the "secret caprice, repression and perversion" of an unfinalized discourse.

In the end, the riddle of conflated cyclical and narrative time, of progression and return, seems to reflect, and seems the *effect*, of the open-ended text of recent German history—as found, among many other places, in the Filbinger affair; and of the memories assumed still active, and still hidden, in the audience. The play can thus be seen as both an unsubtle parody of a continuing "hidden" Nazi mentality and as a serious provocation to remember the past. "Can there be progress without anamnesis [remembrance]?" asks Jean-François Lyotard; "Men and women of my generation in Germany imposed on their children a forty-year silence about the 'Nazi interlude.' This interdiction against anamnesis stands as a symbol for the entire Western world.... Anamnesis constitutes a painful process of working through, a work of mourning for the attachments and conflicting emotions" arising from the past.[30] In *Eve of Retirement*, those "attachments and conflicting emotions" are rendered overt, glaring. Perhaps Bernhard believed, like Ernest Renan, that nations are bound and created not only through shared memories, but also through "a shared amnesia, a collective forgetfulness."[31] Bernhard parodies the shared, official "memory" of a Nazi past through image and icon, while, like Lyotard, forbidding forgetfulness by giving voice to "hidden" taboos, to "unspoken" (yet still active) national texts, by confronting the audience with the conflated facts, memories, taboos, and emotions of a still present past.

Hoffmeister's complaint that "no reality is maintained as a locus of judgment" is valid only if we view the play in isolation from its reception in a specific audience. Bernhard, in typical postmodern fashion, shifts the onus of a "locus of judgment" from the text to the *interaction* between the spectator and the performance, the interaction between text and context. Nor does he assume (as does Hoffmeister) a unified audience with "unifying memories."[32] Bernhard, we might say, works both within and *against* what Hans Robert Jauss has termed a "horizon of expectations."[33] It is the split and fractured viewer, within whom the contrary discourses of the play can resonate, that Bernhard targets, and it is the split and unresolved national history that Bernhard invokes. Audience, author, and characters refract through each other and through the specific "moment" of performance. Thus, Bernhard's conflated temporal structures—history, memory, self-reflexivity—are never finalized. They remain open, encouraging the voices of the past—the characters' past, the audience's past—to engage in what Mikhail Bakhtin termed an "internal dialogue" between an earlier and a later (personal and national) self.[34] Unformalized into univocal meaning, unfinalized into a single locus of judgment, these tensions are lodged in the audience, aimed at provocation and response, at dialogue, at remembrance.

Notes

1. Linda Hutcheon, *A Poetics of Postmodernism: History, Theory, Fiction* (New York: Routledge, 1988), 4; emphasis added.
2. Linda Hutcheon, *The Politics of Postmodernism* (London: Routledge, 1989), 11.
3. His 1975 play *Die Berühmten* (The Famous), for example, ridicules the "famous" names associated with the history of the festival itself. *Die Macht der Gewohnheit* (The Force of Habit; 1974) accuses the festival and its audience of producing and viewing theater merely out of bloodless "habit." In *Der Theatermacher* (Histrionics; 1984), which contains a play within a play, he mimics and attacks the institutions of theater while also parodying an earlier (1972) scandal involving another of his festival plays.
4. Thomas Bernhard, *Eve of Retirement*, in *The President and Eve of Retirement: Plays and Other Writings*, trans. Gitta Honegger (New York: Performing Arts Journal Publications, 1982), 196; hereafter cited in the text. This is the translation I will be using throughout, except where otherwise noted.
5. The political background is well described in Stephen D. Dowden, *Understanding Thomas Bernhard* (Columbia: University of South Carolina Press, 1991), 77.
6. Ibid.
7. Nicholas J. Meyerhofer, *Thomas Bernhard* (Berlin: Colloquium, 1985), 77.
8. Charles Russell, "The Context of the Concept," in *Romanticism, Modernism, Postmodernism*, ed. Harry R. Garvin (Lewisburg, Pa.: Bucknell University Press, 1980), 192.
9. Mircea Eliade, *Cosmos and History: The Myth of the Eternal Return*, trans. William R. Trask (New York: Harper and Row, 1959), 95.
10. Ibid., viii.
11. Ibid., 35. Nazism, of course, claims roots in ancient Germanic myths and symbols; its ideology posits an inevitable return to prominence and power through the renewal of the ancient Reich.

12. Ibid., xi.
13. Ibid., viii.
14. *Die Zeit*, 6 July 1979, my translation; quoted in Helen Chambers, "Thomas Bernhard," in *After the Death of Literature: West German Writing of the 1970s*, ed. Keith Bullivant (Oxford: Berg, 1989), 210.
15. For a discussion of this subject see Dan Diner, "Negative Symbiose: Deutsche und Juden nach Auschwitz," in *Babylon: Beiträge zur jüdische Gegenwart* 1 (1986): 9–20; translated as "Negative Symbiosis: Germans and Jews after Auschwitz," in *Reworking the Past: Hitler, the Holocaust, and the Historians' Debate*, ed. Peter Baldwin (Boston: Beacon Press, 1990), 251–61.
16. Meyerhofer, *Thomas Bernhard*, 74. This view is not shared by all German critics. Bernhard Sorg rejects it outright in *Thomas Bernhard* (Munich: Beck, 1992), 152.
17. I discuss National Socialist vocabulary at greater lengths in my book *Verbal Violence in Contemporary Drama: From Handke to Shepard* (Cambridge: Cambridge University Press, 1992), 49ff.
18. Thomas Bernhard, *Vor dem Ruhestand: Eine Komödie von deutscher Seele* (Frankfurt: Suhrkamp, 1981), 104.
19. My translation; Honegger translates the numbers here as "thousands and thousands into the gas" (195), thus choosing the easy idiom over Bernhard's pointed historical marker and losing some of the irony and history.
20. Quoted in Joachim C. Fest, *The Face of the Third Reich*, trans. Michael Bullock (Harmondsworth: Penguin Books, 1970), 183–84, 177–78.
21. *Der Spiegel*, 1979; the review appears in *Thomas Bernhard Werkgeschichte*, ed. Jens Dittmar (Frankfurt: Suhrkamp, 1981), 216. References to music and concerts appear throughout the play, always in a parodic context. An additional irony for those who know Bernhard's work is the centrality and seriousness with which he treats music, musicians, and especially musical form and technique—repetition and variation—in most of his other writings.
22. For a discussion of kitsch elements in Nazism see Saul Friedländer, *Reflections of Nazism: An Essay on Kitsch and Death*, trans. Thomas Weyr (New York: Harper and Row, 1982).
23. See Vivian M. Patraka, "Fascist Ideology and Theatricalization," in *Critical Theory and Performance*, ed. Janelle G. Reinelt and Joseph R. Roach (Ann Arbor: University of Michigan Press, 1992), 336–49. Patraka applies Friedländer's critique of the "new discourse on Nazism"—a discourse that, while "intending to interrogate and subvert fascism … actually reproduces fascism's aestheticized dualities uncritically" (337)—to (among other texts) Bernhard's *Eve of Retirement*. Friedländer, in *Reflections of Nazism*, claims that part of Nazism's appeal was aesthetic: "a matter of the juxtaposition of opposing images of harmony (kitsch) and death, and of such violently contradictory feelings as harmony and terror" (Friedländer, 50), an appeal replicated in the "new discourse." As examples he cites, among many other texts, R. W. Fassbinder's film *Lili Marleen* and Hans-Jürgen Syberberg's controversial postmodern film *Hitler: A Film from Germany*, films that "allow us to perceive something of the psychological hold Nazism had in its day" (Friedländer, 18) but which also uncritically reproduce that fascination. Friedländer makes clear that texts that employ this "new discourse" create a totalized and hypnotic vision through "a massive use of synonyms, an excess of similar epithets, a play of images sent back, in turn, from one to the other in echoes without end" (Friedländer, 50). Such emotional and textual unity is certainly inapplicable to Bernhard's highly self-conscious and ironic play.
24. Hutcheon, *A Poetics of Postmodernism*, xiii.
25. This same structure, aimed at the same type of memory provocation as well as at political effect, can be found in Bernhard's play *Heldenplatz*, especially in its 1988 production by Claus Peymann at Vienna's Burgtheater, which created a national scandal. Both plays share an interventionist agenda into current politics and into repressions of the past. I discuss this in detail in my article "Thomas Bernhard, Jews, *Heldenplatz*," in *Staging the Holocaust: The Shoah in Drama and Performance*, ed. Claude Schumacher (Cambridge: Cambridge University Press, 1998), 281–97.

26. Paul Ricoeur, "The Narrative Function," in *Paul Ricoeur, Hermeneutics, and the Human Sciences: Essays on Language, Action, and Interpretation*, ed. and trans. John B. Thompson (Cambridge: Cambridge University Press; Paris: Editions de la Maison de Sciences de l'Homme, 1981), 288.

27. Joseph A. Federico, "Millenarianism, Legitimation, and the National Socialist Universe in Thomas Bernhard's *Vor dem Ruhestand*," *Germanic Review* 59, no. 4 (1984): 147.

28. Donna L. Hoffmeister, "Post-Modern Theater: A Contradiction in Terms? Handke, Strauss, Bernhard and the Contemporary Scene," *Monatshefte* 79, no. 4 (1987): 432–33, 436.

29. Steven Connor, *Postmodernist Culture: An Introduction to Theories of the Contemporary* (Oxford: Blackwell, 1989), 227.

30. Jean-François Lyotard, "Ticket to a New Decor," trans. Brian Massumi and W. G. J. Nieslu-chowski, in *Copyright* 1 (1987): 10. See also Lyotard's *The Differend*, trans. Georges Van Den Abbeele (Minneapolis: University of Minnesota Press, 1988), in which he posits the ultimate fracturing of universality and community after Auschwitz.

31. Ernest Gellner, *Culture, Identity, and Politics* (Cambridge: Cambridge University Press, 1987), 6; Gellner discusses this insight with reference to Ernest Renan's *Qu'est-ce qu'une nation?* (1882).

32. Hoffmeister, "Post-Modern Theater," 436.

33. See Hans Robert Jauss, *Toward an Aesthetic of Reception*, trans. T. Bahti (Brighton: Harvester Press, 1982).

34. Mikhail Bakhtin, *The Dialogic Imagination: Four Essays*, ed. Michael Holquist, trans. Caryl Emerson and Michael Holquist (Austin: University of Texas Press, 1981), 427.

MUSICAL THEATER

INTRODUCTION

Conflict and Crosscurrents in Viennese Music

Michael Cherlin

The pre-eminent reference work in English on the history of music, *The New Grove Dictionary of Music and Musicians*, devotes a twenty-nine page article to musical Vienna. In the context of a reference work, a twenty-nine page article is fairly lengthy, yet the article is minuscule in comparison to the numerous separate articles on the musicians and music associated with that city.[1] Even if we were to restrict our comments to Vienna alone, the richness and complexity of that city's contribution to the world of music could fill a library; a book length treatment could hardly do it justice. If we extend that discussion to all of the lands of the Habsburg Empire, and the states that followed its dissolution after World War I, the task becomes necessarily encyclopedic. And so, this introduction and the six chapters devoted to music and dance in this volume make no pretense toward covering anything but a narrow slice of that rich and complex history. The essays offer six separate and individual glimpses into a many faceted and enduring tradition. Their topics are all Viennese, and they concentrate on the eighteenth through the twentieth centuries. For these reasons, my introduction will concentrate on the first great flowering of Viennese music with emergence of the classical style, and then on the second great flowering of Viennese music at the end of the nineteenth century continuing into the first part of the twentieth century. The six chapters on music and dance will be placed into this greater context. But we can begin with a thumbnail sketch of the historical crosscurrents that contributed to the formation of the Viennese musical tradition

One need not be a Hegelian to recognize that creativity is often the result of reconciling opposing ideas or influences. If there is a thread that connects the essays on music and dance in this volume, it is the vital, essential role that the crosscurrents of international and regional influences have played in the musical life of Vienna. Although every culture derives its own personality in part through being affected by the impact of other cultures, the musical life of Vienna is particularly remarkable in this regard. And this is true from its very beginnings.

The international crosscurrents of musical Vienna take root during a period of profound influence by French culture. A convenient place to begin is with the poet-musicians of the *Minnesänger* tradition, who flourished in Vienna during the late twelfth and early thirteenth centuries. This is the same tradition that Richard Wagner evoked some six hundred years later in his opera *Die Meistersinger von Nürnberg*. Although the *Minnesänger* developed their own distinctive style, they first arose out of the earlier French practice of the *troubadours*. French influence continued with the founding of the University of Vienna in 1365; in a short time Vienna became a center for the study of music, but French thought dominated the curriculum.[2] Later in the fifteenth century, the belated importation of polyphony into Viennese practice shows the continued influence of the French compositional practice on the Viennese.[3]

Sixteenth-century Europe finds the music and musicians of the Low Countries in ascendancy, and Vienna is no exception. This was a time during which the imperial *Hofmusikkapelle* dominated the musical life of Vienna, and musicians from the Netherlands held the leading positions.[4] Another stylistic and demographic shift occurs in the early seventeenth century when Italian music began to assert its influence. Italian music remained dominant in Vienna for the next two hundred years, and it is under Italian influence that both instrumental music and opera became central to Viennese musical life.[5]

The tendency toward absorbing and reconciling international differences takes a special turn with the emergence of the "Classical Style" through the works of Haydn and Mozart, and then Beethoven. (Schubert, a Viennese from the next generation, continued aspects of Viennese classicism, and also anticipated aspects of the newly emerging Romanticism.) With the remarkable florescence of the classical style, the music of Vienna fully comes into its own; indeed, during the period beginning around 1775, Vienna is arguably the musical capital for all of Europe. Although Haydn, Mozart, and Beethoven were not native Viennese, Vienna became the center for their compositional activities, and their music has always been associated first and foremost with the city of Vienna.

In many respects, the Viennese classical style is international not only in its origins, but also in its essential aesthetic. Ideals of clarity and grace, derived in large part from the French Enlightenment, intermingle with the conceptualization of music as drama derived in large part from the ascendancy of Italian opera. And both the French and Italian elements of Viennese classicism are conditioned by the reconciliation of the opposing Germanic tendencies of expressivity and formal unity. Charles Rosen argues persuasively for the central significance of this reconciled opposition in his landmark book *The Classical Style: Haydn, Mozart, Beethoven*. Rosen characterizes the classical style as "not so much the achievement of an ideal as the reconciliation of conflicting ideals—the striking of an optimal balance between them."[6] To a remarkable degree, the opposing ideals were best exemplified in the compositions of two of J. S. Bach's sons. "Johann Christian's music was formal, sensitive, charming, undramatic, and a little empty; Carl Phillip Emanuel's was violent, expressive, brilliant, continuously surprising, and often incoherent."[7]

What took place at first (after the Baroque, but before the emergence of the classical style) was nothing coherent: that is why, although every period is one of transition, the years between 1755 and 1775 may be given this title with particular relevance. Briefly and, indeed, over-simply, during these years a composer had to choose between dramatic surprise and formal perfection, between expressivity and elegance; he could rarely have both at once. Not until Haydn and Mozart, separately and together, created a style in which a dramatic effect seemed at once surprising and logically motivated, in which the expressive and the elegant could join hands, did the classical style come into being.[8]

* * * * *

Three of the six chapters on music and dance in this volume are devoted to the period just prior to the emergence of the classical style, and to aspects of the classical style itself. The first of these, chapter 10, is Sibylle Dahms's essay "Vienna as a Center of Ballet Reform in the Late Eighteenth Century." Dahms argues for a reassessment of Franz Anton Hilverding and his student Gasparo Angiolini whose combined efforts brought Viennese ballet to a preeminence during the 1750s and 1760s, preceding the acknowledged innovations of the French choreographer Jean-Georges Noverre. Through the work of Hilverding and Angiolini, Vienna assumed a leading role in the development of ballet in its modern sense: the portrayal of drama through dance alone.

The historical narrative that Dahms develops engages the theme of internationalism—in this case, with the interesting shift from French to Italian domination as ballet developed in the second half of the eighteenth century. (Domination would shift back to France in the nineteenth and early twentieth centuries.) Dahms discusses the developments in the seventeenth and early eighteenth centuries, when ballet developed as an integral part of French opera without yet becoming an autonomous art form capable of expressive story telling in and of itself. The crucial transition into autonomous ballet took place through Italian *opera seria,* where dance used in the *intermezzi* was separated from the rest of the drama, and could evolve as a form of its own. The close relationships between Italian and Viennese music of the period allowed for a fruitful interaction between Italian and Viennese dancers and choreographers. The theme of internationalism continues in the next generation with Vincenzo Galeotti, a student of Angiolini who brought Viennese ballet to the Royal Ballet at Copenhagen.

In chapter 11, Eva Badura-Skoda approaches the topics of internationalism and the reconciliation of opposing styles and aesthetics head-on in "The Viennese Singspiel, Haydn, and Mozart." Badura-Skoda describes the Singspiel tradition, its blending of music, dance and theater, its alternation of comic and contemplative, or even comic and tragic, and its roots in the "'marriage' of Italian opera with the repertoire of German comedies of itinerary troupes." The substantial part of the essay devoted to Haydn is based on careful and insightful archival research, through which Badura-Skoda demonstrates distinctive and compelling traces of Haydn's compositional style, including quotations from his own music, in works firmly grounded in the Singspiel tradition. The hybrid nature of Singspiel is wonderfully exemplified by one aria in particular, "Du könntest ja von allen il mio caro sein," whose text combines German, Italian, and French into a kind of crazy polyglot. In introducing her discussion of Mozart, Badura-Skoda contrasts Leopold Mozart's dislike of Viennese Singspiel comedies with Wolfgang's delight in that same tradition of theater, and then traces the development of the Singspiel influence on younger Mozart's works. Badura-Skoda's discussion makes vivid the continuity between Singspiel and Mozart's operas *Entführung aus dem Serail* and *Die Zauberflöte*, adding another dimension to our understanding of the synthetic nature of Mozart's compositional language.

Chapter 12, Gretchen Wheelock's "Displaying (Out)Rage: The Dilemma of Constancy in Mozart's Operas," deals with eighteenth-century Viennese music. The "constancy" that Wheelock's title refers to is sexual fidelity, and "rage" and "outrage" are among the emotional responses of characters who suspect infidelity. The essay explores the variables of two basic factors in Mozart's portrayals of rage: gender and class or social station. Along the way, we learn much about eighteenth-century perspectives on differences between the sexes as well as differences among social strata. Wheelock's nuanced musical analyses discuss aspects of mode, harmony, rhythm, and orchestration that combine to form Mozart's astounding and wide-ranging characterizations. The integration of conflict and highly expressive content, which we have seen to be basic to Rosen's view of the classical style, thus receives a special focus throughout Wheelock's essay. While not especially central to Wheelock's analyses, the problems of national and international crosscurrents are implicit in the range of Mozart's characters; to name a few examples, Wheelock studies the contrasting emotions of Dorabella and Fiordiligi in *Così fan tutte* (who are seduced by their own lovers disguised as Albanians), Pasha Selim and Osman in *Die Entführung aus dem Serail*, and Susanna and the Countess, as well as Figaro, Bartolo, and the Count in *Le Nozze di Figaro*.

* * * * *

The second great florescence of Viennese music began in the second half of the nineteenth century and continued until the cataclysm of World War II. These are the generations of Brahms and Bruckner, Wolf and Mahler, and then the three great composers of the "Second Viennese School": Schoenberg, Berg, and Webern.

One cannot understand the musical conflicts that were played out in late-nineteenth-century Vienna without taking into consideration the controversy between the supporters of Richard Wagner and those of Johannes Brahms. Wagner, by word and deed, argued that the forms and genres derived from the classical style had been played out, and that "the music of the future" (his music!)

would be based on new modes of expression, hence the Wagnerian concepts of *Musikdrama* and of *Gesamtkunstwerk*. The noted musicologist Carl Dahlhaus nicely summarized this aspect of the Wagnerian polemic and achievement:

> The crucial and significant point about his concept of a *Gesamtkunstwerk* (a pompous synonym for "theater") is not the truism that several different arts join forces and interact, nor the questionable thesis that these arts are equipped with equal rights and privileges, still less the historical myth that the *Gesamtkunstwerk* represents a culmination and sublation of the "special arts." On the contrary, its importance resides in the aesthetic and social demand we raise when we refer to theater as a "total work of art": the notion that theater, although more akin to an event than a work, nevertheless partakes of the ideal of art which was elevated to metaphysical dignity in the classical and romantic age.... And the astonishing thing is that Wagner succeeded in imposing on his age the "revolution of aesthetic values" and in raising for opera the same lofty claims that Beethoven had achieved for the symphony. In doing so, he transformed opera into music drama.[9]

In great contrast, the works of Brahms, not so much by word, but certainly by deed, argued that the genres of symphony, chamber music, and song were far from being exhausted. The influential Viennese music critic Eduard Hanslick famously extolled Brahms as the inheritor of the tradition of "absolute music," music not sullied by extramusical conceits, and promulgated the idea "of absolute music as the quintessence of 'genuine' music."[10] In the late nineteenth century, the music of Brahms became the most celebrated music of Vienna. His symphonic music, concerti, and, most important of all, his extraordinary works of chamber music captured the Viennese imagination. Through the music of Brahms, one sensed a direct lineage through the masters of the classical style—Haydn, Mozart, and Beethoven—brought into the present of late-nineteenth-century Vienna. Brahms through a profound understanding and respect for the achievements of the past, coupled with an equally profound understanding of the expressive and technical aspects of Romanticism, embodied a dialectical tension between conservative and progressive elements. Championed by many in the late nineteenth century as the great musical conservative of his time, Brahms was characterized by Schoenberg as "the progressive."[11] On the other hand, the impact of Wagnerian aesthetics on Viennese music was equally impressive. Anton Bruckner, a deeply conservative Catholic, incorporated radical Wagnerian elements into his looming symphonic forms. Mahler, like Bruckner, brought the influence of Wagnerian techniques into his symphonic forms, but with very different musical results. While holding onto the symphony as his principal musical idiom, Mahler radically transforms just what a symphony might entail. He largely discards the typical four-movement form, explores radical large-scale harmonic designs, greatly expands the orchestral palette, and following the lead of Beethoven's Ninth Symphony, integrates the human voice into his symphonic forms. And while Brahms, through his synthesis of classical and romantic elements in the realm of lieder, continued the tradition of lied composition, which had seen its first great flowering in the songs of Schubert, Hugo Wolf brought the Wagnerian revolution into the realm of art song.

In addition to purely musical and aesthetic issues, there is another component of the controversies swirling around Wagner and Brahms that cannot be overlooked in any discussion of the music of the time: Wagner's explicit and vehement antisemitism. While peripheral to the central aesthetic issues between the supporters of Wagnerian ideals and those of Brahms, the music of Brahms became associated, at least in part, with political liberalism, while the writings of Wagner could be cited in support of the rising tide of German nationalism and antisemitism. And yet, ironic as it may seem, some of Wagner's most influential supporters were Jews evidently willing to overlook the egregious antisemitism of his writings because of the incontestable genius of his musical compositions. Among Viennese musicians, the most influential supporters of Wagner's music included Karl Goldmark, Gustav Mahler, and Arnold Schoenberg.

The issue of Jewish assimilation into German (and hence Austrian) culture takes on special significance in Vienna. By the late nineteenth century, the Jewish presence in Vienna was formidable, especially among its educated classes. At the end of the century, while comprising somewhat less than nine percent of the total Viennese population, Jews constituted about one-third of the student body at the University of Vienna.[12] More importantly, in addition to their extraordinary presence in commerce, Jews were predominant in many of the liberal fields, including law, medicine, journalism, music, and theater.[13] While the social issues and cultural and racial theories that led to antisemitism are diverse and highly complex, that fact remains that with the 1895 election of Karl Lueger as the mayor of Vienna the relatively mild forms of discrimination took a turn for the worse. Steven Beller states the situation succinctly: "In coming to terms with Vienna, Jews after 1895 had to face one salient fact: Vienna was the only European capital at the time to have an elected antisemitic municipal government."[14] While Jews of the generation of Goldmark and Mahler suffered from the diatribes of antisemitic elements of the press, the future held far worse in store for Arnold Schoenberg's generation.

Karl Goldmark, a Hungarian Jew who settled in Vienna, is an example of a Jewish composer who embraced aspects of Wagnerian aesthetics. After a brief heyday in the 1870s, punctuated by the initial success of his opera *The Queen of Sheba* (1875), Goldmark faded into relative obscurity but in his time, he remained a center of critical controversy. Chapter 13, Peter Revers's "Karl Goldmark's Operas during the Directorship of Gustav Mahler," opens with a discussion of Nietzsche's negative assessment of the musical scene during the last part of the nineteenth century. By 1888 Nietzsche, once an ardent supporter of Wagner's music, had turned sour toward Wagner. But his assessments of Brahms and Goldmark were even more severe. Revers cites Nietzsche's caustic comment that Goldmark was one of the "clever apes of Wagner" and that "with the *Queen of Sheba* one belongs in a zoo." The essay goes on to discuss the somewhat equivocal relationship between Goldmark and Mahler, and to recount the views of the contemporary press, both liberal and antisemitic, in its wavering reactions to Goldmark's works. Ironically, Goldmark's light-weight musical eclecticism, berated by members of both the liberal and antisemitic press, can be seen to embody some of the most pervasive characteristics of fin-de-siècle Vienna.

The historic collaborations between Gustav Mahler and Alfred Roller are the topic of Evan Baker's "A Break in the Scenic Traditions of the Vienna Court Opera: Alfred Roller and the Vienna Secession" in chapter 14. Roller was, in 1897, one of the founding members of the Vienna Secession, a loose affiliation of architects, artists and artisans whose motto famously proclaimed: "To the Age its Art, to Art its Freedom."[15] That same year Mahler became director of the Viennese Court Opera and began instituting a series of reforms that, in addition to a greater emphasis on musical rehearsals, sought greater unity in operatic productions to include lighting, costumes, and scenery. After describing the naturalistic set designs of Roller's precursors, Baker describes the more abstract sets designed by Roller for Mahler's productions of *Tristan und Isolde*, *Fidelio*, and *Don Giovanni* during the period from 1903–1905. The most controversial of these productions, the 1905 production of *Don Giovanni*, elicited a wide range of responses from the Viennese press, and this controversy is nicely summarized by Baker through contrasting citations. As important as the earlier productions of *Tristan* and *Fidelio* were in setting precedent, Baker considers *Don Giovanni* to be the true "break" with tradition, one that had ramifications well into the 1930s.

The tension between conserving the past and moving toward the future that had been embodied in the music of Brahms continues with the Second Viennese School. Schoenberg, after an early student period during which he neglected the works of Wagner, and emulated Brahms, embraced both masters. But it was not long before Schoenberg, and his most famous students, Anton Webern and Alban Berg, began to develop their own personal musical languages. The three became known as the Second Viennese School. If we measure the power of an artistic revolution by the impact that it has on future generations, then we find that the music of Schoenberg, Webern, and Berg is in very rare company. Only Debussy, Stravinsky, and Bartók can claim a commensurate impact on the evolution of twentieth-century music.

Perhaps more than any other musician of the twentieth century, Schoenberg is both beloved and hated for the changes he brought to the musical landscape. Schoenberg questioned the very foundations of musical form and expression. He was the first composer to abandon the restrictions of tonality, and he was the first composer to imagine that music might be conceptualized without recourse to melody and accompaniment, or at least without melody and accompaniment in any of their traditional manifestations. Schoenberg is also among the generation of Jewish musicians who left Europe after Hitler rose to power. Although significant musical activity continued in Vienna after the war, and continues to this day, Vienna has never again achieved the supremacy in the world of music that it once had.

My own chapter, chapter 15, "Schoenberg's Music for the Theater," begins by assessing Schoenberg's overall place in musical history. I then go on to discuss aspects of Schoenberg's three principal theatrical works, *Erwartung, Die glück-liche Hand*, and *Moses und Aron*. The first two works are from Schoenberg's Expressionistic period, during which he self-consciously summoned up the creative impulse from his unconscious mind. This is also the time during which Schoenberg perfected what later became known as atonality (a term which he himself never used), a compositional style that abandoned the musical syntax of tonality and that generated its own musical syntax from the internal workings of each unique composition. The specifics of Schoenberg's atonality are peculiar to his own works, but the general principles have continued to inform generations of composers who have followed.

Moses und Aron, Schoenberg's uncompleted opera, was the last major work before his emigration to the United States. Among other things, it is the signal of his return to Judaism, years after his conversion to Christianity. In contrast to the earlier works, *Moses und Aron* is a twelve-tone composition, expansively developing a technique that Schoenberg had first conceived in the years after World War I. While it would be an exaggeration to limit the change from atonality to twelve-tone composition to the replacement of the irrational techniques of the atonal period with the rational techniques of the twelve-tone period, there would certainly be more than a grain of truth to that idea. The development of twelve-tone technique, Schoenberg once proclaimed, would assure the dominance of German music for the next hundred years. The irony of that comment must have haunted Schoenberg in later years. Indeed, twelve-tone composition became the basis of an international style in the decades after World War II. Yet, the real significance of *Moses und Aron*, like that of all great opera, lies in the power of its drama expressed through music. *Moses und Aron* is not merely a great twelve-tone opera, although it is surely that; like all great works, Schoenberg's *Moses* will endure because it addresses fundamental questions of our own humanity.

* * * * *

We close with a paradox: in saying that Schoenberg, or anyone else for that matter, addresses questions fundamental to our own humanity, we run the risk of positing timeless values, which privilege unchanging positions of authority, and hence unchanging canons of art undergirded by unchanging canons of scholarship and criticism. Nothing could be further from the spirit of this volume. Whether we bleakly envision history as Benjamin's storm, with its "one single catastrophe which keeps piling wreckage upon wreckage," or try to imagine a more optimistic narrative where catastrophic setbacks are compensated for by the hope of slow but sure human progress, or choose a third middle ground where nature in process is ultimately indifferent to our historically contingent and locally defined ideas of creation and catastrophe, of glory and ruin, what remains is change. Near the beginning of her introduction, Halina Filipowicz writes, "What emerges most persistently from the debate in this volume is a sense that the situation of the performing arts in Austria and Central Europe does not fit snugly into established theoretical frameworks...." From my perspective, this is necessarily so; the "great tradition," all great traditions, build on their own ruins, hope for their own glories, and always remain resistant to established theoretical frameworks.

Notes

1. Stanley Sadie, ed., *The New Grove Dictionary of Music and Musicians* (London: Macmillan Publishers Limited, 1980), 1713–741.
2. Ibid., 715.
3. Ibid.
4. Ibid., 716.
5. Ibid., 717–18.
6. Charles Rosen, *The Classical Style: Haydn, Mozart, Beethoven,* expanded edition (New York: W.W. Norton, 1997), 43.
7. Ibid., 44.
8. Ibid.
9. Carl Dahlhaus, *Nineteenth-Century Music,* trans. J. Bradford Robinson (Berkeley: University of California Press, 1989), 195.
10. Ibid., 250.
11. See "Brahms the Progressive," in *Style and Idea: Selected Writings of Arnold Schoenberg,* ed. Leonard Stein, trans. Leo Black (Berkeley: University of California Press, 1984), 398–441.
12. See Steven Beller, *Vienna and the Jews: 1867–1938: A Cultural History* (Cambridge: Cambridge University Press, 1989), 34 and 44.
13. Steven Beller provides a thorough statistical analysis of the Jewish presence in various vocations in *Vienna and the Jews,* 52–67.
14. Ibid., 188. See also Carl E. Schorske, *Fin-de-Siècle Vienna: Politics and Culture* (New York: Knopf, 1980, reprint, New York: Vintage Books, 1981), 116–80.
15. See, for example, Schorske, *Fin-de-Siècle Vienna,* 84. Schorske discusses aspects of the Secession movement, *passim.*

Part Three

THE EMERGENCE OF THE
CLASSICAL STYLE

Chapter 10

VIENNA AS A CENTER OF BALLET REFORM IN THE LATE EIGHTEENTH CENTURY

Sibylle Dahms

It is commonly held that France, and in particular Paris, was the leading center in the development of European dance and ballet. To be sure, this is true for most of the Baroque period (the seventeenth and the first half of the eighteenth century). The new intellectual climate of the Enlightenment, however, which brought about a decisive change of social and cultural conceptions and ideas around the middle of the eighteenth century, led among other things to a change of focus in the development of theatrical dance. Because of favorable circumstances in the realm of courtly and public Viennese theater life in the 1750s and 1760s, the Habsburg capital took on a central role in the creation and development of an absolutely new type of dramatic action ballet.

The ballet reform of the second half of the eighteenth century originated in the context of the fundamental change in aesthetic standards effected by Enlightenment ideas. This led to a reorientation of all types of theatrical presentation. For theatrical dance this change of paradigm was of particular and lasting consequence: it brought about the creation of ballet as an autonomous theatrical form, independent from opera, to which it had normally been attached until that time.

In the French opera—the *tragédie lyrique* that was created by Jean-Baptiste Lully and continued as a model until Jean-Philippe Rameau—dance had been an integrated part of the drama. This type of ballet, however, which was based on the canon of Baroque dance, with its more or less strict system of stylized and mechanically standardized gestures, needed a verbal context to convey dramatic action—such means of communication were the sung parts of the opera or the written programs that were handed to the audience.

The new type of ballet, however, arose from the ballet intermezzo that was inserted between the acts of Italian *opera seria*. Here the new dramatic dance style, which aspired to be guided by more spontaneous individual expression as well as taste and common sense, was just at the right place to develop as an autonomous type of theatrical presentation. In this form it gained an ever growing popularity, competing with the opera to which it was attached. It is no wonder that Pietro Metastasio complained in a letter, dated 1771, that his "poor dramma" was in decline and served as an intermezzo for the "ballerini," who, capable of complementing action with real human expression, had rightly gained the full attention of the audience—attention the singers were losing, "contenting themselves with unending boring acrobatics of vocal virtuosity."[1]

In fact this autonomous *ballet en action, ballet pantomime,* or *danza parlante,* which developed out of the intermezzi of the serious Italian opera, proved to be one of the most efficient media for experimentation, particularly since the conception of this new drama type was based on nonverbal communication and necessarily called for the utmost concentration of form and content.

It was therefore not in France—the leading dance nation until the middle of the eighteenth century—that this new type of dance drama took shape, but rather in places with a strong Italian opera tradition. These include Stuttgart, where Niccolo Jommelli worked side by side with Jean-Georges Noverre in the 1760s,[2] and other German cities, Russia, and particularly Vienna, where as early as the 1750s the intellectual climate was most favorable for the unfolding of avant-garde tendencies. The circle around Count Giacomo Durazzo, who in 1753/54 took over direction and management of the court theaters, actively encouraged the new dramatic style.[3]

I would like to outline the Viennese ballet situation of the 1750s and 1760s, particularly concentrating on the two genuinely Viennese ballet masters and choreographers Franz Anton Hilverding and his ingenious disciple Gasparo Angiolini. Usually all credit concerning the ballet reform is given to the Swiss-French Jean-Georges Noverre, but it can clearly be shown that both Hilverding and Angiolini were much more influential than normally acknowledged, particularly during the experimental phase of the new type of ballet, the time before Noverre's arrival in Vienna in 1767. Noverre's ability as a brilliant writer of amusing and cleverly written essays won him Europewide fame, despite their lack in some important points of logic and in substantive information. Noverre's success has distracted historians from the indisputable accomplishments of his Viennese colleagues.

Franz Anton Hilverding (1710–1768), born in a dynastic Austrian theater family, had been trained at the Viennese court ballet. A scholarship granted by Emperor Charles VI enabled him to study for some time during the 1730s in Paris. There he was probably in touch with French avant-garde dancers such as Marie Sallé and François Riccoboni, who at this time began to experiment mostly at the Théâtre Français, aiming for dramatic expression in ballet.

When at the beginning 1750s Hilverding was made *maître de ballet* at the Vienna theaters, he was finally in a position to put into practice his new conceptions (regrettably only in practice and not in written records). He gradually replaced the burlesque acrobatic style, largely based on Italian commedia conventions, with a natural dance style in which emotion was rendered by the entire body in movement. For the contents of these dramatic pantomimes Hilverding presented situations from everyday life, but he also tried to work on literary and historically orientated plots. A series of libretti for Hilverding ballets are contained in diaries known as the Gumpenhuber daybooks. These diaries were provided by Hilverding's assistant ballet master Philipp Gumpenhuber, who scrupulously recorded repertory, cast, plots of ballets, and special events in diaries that were handed down for the years 1758, 1759, and 1763.[4]

The most impressive record of Hilverding's style may be found in the so-called Durazzo Collection. This precious series of about thirty paintings by members of the Quaglio family and by Carlo Galli Bibiena, commissioned by Count Durazzo, document choreographic groups in action, as well as stage designs. Here we can see that during the 1750s, years before Noverre proclaimed asymmetrical group arrangement as his revolutionary novelty, Hilverding had in fact already used this new choreographic technique in many of his ballet productions.[5]

Hilverding's most famous ballet, *Le Turc généreux*,[6] was created in 1758 on the occasion of a visit by Turkish diplomats to Vienna after Sultan Mustafa III's accession of the throne at Constantinople. The ballet was first performed at the Burgtheater on 26 April 1758, presumably with music by Hilverding's favorite composer, Joseph Starzer. An excellent painting by Bernardo Belotto (called *Canaletto*) shows a central scene from this ballet, where the modern expressive style is most clearly demonstrated. There is a remarkable tension between the dynamic movement in diagonal lines on the one hand and the conventional symmetry of the backdrops. Fortunately the music of this ballet was saved. A set of instrumental parts is located today at the precious music and theater archive at Česky Krumlov, in a special collection of music material for nearly 180 ballets, mostly of Viennese provenance and dating from the 1750s to 1770s. In 1765/66 the theater fanatic Prince Josef Adam von Schwarzenberg erected a beautiful theater in his Bohemian residence. Built by the Viennese theater architect Laurentius Makh, it still exists, along with about 250 pieces of wings, backdrops, more than 150 original costumes, machines, and other stage material, mostly created by at least two other Viennese experts in this field, presumed to be Hans Wetschel and Leo Märkl. Thanks to the theatromania of the prince, who wanted to bring Viennese successes to life in his Bohemian castle, particularly among them particularly the new type of ballet, it is possible for us to get an authentic view of the theater and ballet production of this time.[7]

In 1758 Hilverding accepted an invitation of the Russian tsarina Elisabeth II to take the position of *maître de ballet* for her court theater at Saint Petersburg. Some of Hilverding's Viennese star dancers (Jeanne and Louis Mécour, Santina Zanuzzi, and Pierre Aubry) as well as the composer Joseph Starzer, followed him to the Russian court, where he tried to introduce his new ballet style in plots based on Russian topics. As the Russian dance historian Borisoglebski states, the

Austrian Hilverding was the first to show the Russian dancers an "entrechat" with four beats and a pirouette.[8] He also successfully developed native talents, like the Russian dancer and choreographer Timofei Semnovitch Boublikov. When Hilverding in 1764 was forced to give up his engagement because of his declining health, Boublikov followed him with a scholarship granted by Tsarina Catherine II to continue his studies in Vienna. Here Hilverding was charged with the direction of the Viennese court theater at the Kärntnertor. But, along with his ill health, critical financial circumstances, which he was not able to solve and which almost caused the bankruptcy of the theater, brought about Hilverding's early death. He died a poor man in 1768.

When Hilverding had left for Russia in 1758, his position as *maître de ballet* at the Viennese court theaters was taken over by his master pupil, the Florentine-born dancer and choreographer Gaspero Angiolini (1731–1803), who had come to Vienna presumably around 1750 to study with Hilverding.[9] Beginning in 1752 he appeared in Hilverding's ballets, and in 1754 he married the Vienna prima ballerina Maria Teresa Fogliazzi, another pupil of Hilverding, who came from a distinguished Parmese family. In 1757/58 Angiolini returned to Italy, where at the Regio Teatro in Torino he staged the first of his own ballets—among which we find a ballet with the title *La scoperta del' America da Cristoforo Colombo* (1757).[10] But here he also staged a series of ballets by his teacher Hilverding, which is why today we can find musical material for Hilverding's ballets in the Biblioteca Nazionale in Torino. Hilverding's influence is not limited to Torino. In other Italian cities, such as Milano, Venice, and Naples, there was lively exchange among Italian and Viennese dancers and choreographers. Colleagues and students of Hilverding, like the gifted Giuseppe Salomoni or the *grotesco* dancer Gennaro Magri, author of one of the most important Italian dance manuals of the eighteenth century, the *Trattato teorico-prattico di ballo* (Naples, 1779), traveled between Italy and Vienna.[11] All these dancers and choreographers left traces of the Viennese ballet (ballet music, libretti) in various Italian theater archives.

When Angiolini took over Hilverding's position as *maître de ballet* at the Vienna court theaters in 1758, he at first continued in the same style as his teacher. In the early 1760s, obviously encouraged by Durazzo and also by Raniero de Calzabigi, Gluck's ingenious librettist, Angiolini began to work on an even more dramatic and experimental ballet style.[12] Gluck himself might have been stimulated to cooperate with the idealistic and revolutionary-minded young Italian. Angiolini, Gluck, and Calzabigi's first highly dramatic ballet, *Le festin de Pierre*, after Moliere's *Don Juan*, staged for the first time on 17 October 1761 at the Burgtheater, is considered today as a watershed in ballet history. Here Angiolini not only choreographed the ballet but also created the title role. Along with the program for this epoch-making ballet pantomime, Angiolini and Calzabigi published their first "Dissertation," explaining the fundamental changes in the dramaturgical conception of this new type of ballet, changes that aimed for a revival of the ancient Greek and Roman pantomime.[13]

Two programmatic essays were to follow in the next years with Gluck-Angiolini productions for the Vienna court theater. In 1762 Angiolini added an essay about ballet music to the program for Gluck's opera ballet *Citera assediata*, a most interesting essay, since Angiolini also composed the music for a great part of his ballets.[14] In 1765 he finally wrote a more detailed and programmatic dissertation on ballet dramaturgy. It was added to the program of the most extreme experiment of dramatic pantomime of that whole period, the tragic ballet *Semiramis*, after Voltaire's tragedy of the same title.[15] This twenty-five-minute crime and ghost story ballet allows not the slightest relaxation from constant dramatic tension; not a single divertissement can be found. If one looks today at the libretto with its radical reduction of ensemble to the absolute minimum of just four soloists, and also considers the highly dramatic music by Gluck, one can imagine why this production left the audience completely puzzled—unfortunately an audience that consisted of guests celebrating Joseph II's marriage to Princess Maria Josepha of Bavaria. No wonder that Angiolini's extreme experiment was to become a complete failure.

Angiolini's writings—the three dissertations and four (perhaps five) essays with critical arguments against some of Noverre's theories—unfortunately did not achieve the same Europewide attention as Noverre's writings. Nonetheless, the central ideas of the new dramatic ballet pantomime are discussed by Angiolini in a more precise and logical style, combining clear statements with a lot of practical theater experience. For example, Angiolini, in complete contrast to Noverre, expresses the urgent need to develop a new type of dance notation, one capable of documenting the new dynamic ballet style. In fact, it might be that he did try to invent such a notation, as he writes in his "Lettere a M. Noverre";[16] alas, no evidence of such an attempt has yet come to light.

In his further career Angiolini continued to follow Hilverding's footsteps. On an invitation from Tsarina Catherine II he traveled for three successful engagements to the Russian court, from 1766 to 1772, 1776 to 1779, and 1782 to 1786; between these Russian seasons Angiolini worked particularly in Venice, Milan, and Vienna. As a choreographer Angiolini created more than one hundred autonomous ballets, for many of which he wrote his own music; the catalog of his works thus comprises the same number of titles as that of his great competitor Noverre.[17] It may be that traces left by the Viennese ballet reformers Hilverding and Angiolini, particularly in Russia, will be found in the near future in various archives.

However, Viennese ballet reform of the eighteenth century was not restricted to the east, and also influenced the northern countries. In the Royal Library at Copenhagen, we can trace another interesting link to the ballet productions of the Hilverding-Angiolini era. In 1775 Vincenzo Galeotti,[18] a dancer and choreographer born in Florence like Angiolini and in fact a disciple of his was engaged as *maître de ballet* of the Royal Ballet at Copenhagen. When Galeotti traveled to his new destination, his luggage must have contained multiple copies of Angiolini's ballets. In Copenhagen, where, after 1800, he remained for the rest of his career, Galeotti staged a considerable number of ballets by his teacher. These included *Don Juan, Semiramis, Orphelin de la Chine, La chasse d'Henry IV, La Partenza d'Enea*, and so on, and used either the original music by Gluck and Angiolini or newly composed music by the Danish ballet composer Claus Schall. Shortly after his arrival in Copenhagen, Galleotti also performed a ballet with the title *Den großmudige Tyrk*. When I was able to examine the music material and libretto for this ballet pantomime I was surprised to discover that Galeotti had not only completely copied Hilverding's plot of the *Le Turc généreux*, but had also used parts of Starzer's original ballet music.

Considering this interesting connection of Angiolini and Hilverding with the Danish ballet via Vincenzo Galeotti, it would be tempting to speculate whether the famous Bournonville school of the nineteenth century—besides the Russian school, the only one with a long and still lasting tradition—owes some of its characteristics, for instance in the famous pantomime sections, to the Viennese Hilverding-Angiolini school of the eighteenth century.

Another discovery worth mentioning is one that confirmed my speculation that the Viennese ballet style of the late eighteenth century even influenced the court ballet in the western parts of Germany. When I examined the collection of the ballet material contained at the Reiss-Museum in Mannheim I discovered a libretto for a ballet with the title *La Guirlande enchantée*, performed in Mannheim in 1769, which in all detail corresponds with a series of five pictures from the above-mentioned Durazzo Collection. The author of this ballet was a certain Fabiano (no first name given), who during that year was *maître de ballet* at the electoral court in Mannheim. Members of the Fabiano family, in fact, had been part of Hilverding's and Angiolini's Vienna company in 1758/59 and had joined him in Russia in 1764.[19] The music for Fabiano's Mannheim version of Hilverding's *Guirlande enchantée* is lost, but music material for a ballet of this title is to be found in the Schwarzenberg archive at Cesky Krumlow, possibly the original music for Hilverding's *Guirlande enchantée*.

This example should give an idea of how complicated, but also how exciting, research for the dramatic ballet pantomime of the late eighteenth century can be. The more we are able to put together the bits and pieces of this puzzle scattered all over Europe, the more interesting the role of Hilverding's and Angiolini's Vienna ballet seems to be.

The favorable situation for the development of ballet in Vienna came to an end when Emperor Joseph II, whose aversion to this art form was notorious, took over rule from his mother Maria Theresa. He gradually cut short the budget for the ballet at the Burgtheater and Kärntnertortheater, which is particularly regrettable when one considers that by the time Wolfgang Amadeus Mozart settled in Vienna in 1781, where he stayed until his death in 1791, the principle flowering of Viennese ballet had already been over for about five years. We can only just speculate then about the brilliant achievements for ballet and music that might have been the result of a cooperation between Mozart and Noverre or Angiolini.

Notes

1. Pietro Metastasio, *Tutte le opere: A cura di Bruno Brunelli* (Milan: Mondadori, 1954), 5:88f.
2. Sibylle Dahms, "Noverre's Stuttgarter Ballette und ihre Überlieferung: Das Warschauer Manuskript," in *Musik in Baden-Württemberg,* Jahrbuch (Stuttgart: Metzler, 1996), 197–204.
3. Marian Hannah Winter, *The Pre-Romantic Ballet* (London: Pitman and Sons, 1974), 92–99.
4. These diaries are today at the Harvard Theater Collection and at the National Library in Vienna.
5. The collection was sold by members of the Durazzo family in an antiquarian auction during the 1930s and is now scattered in collections all over the world. The Derra de Moroda Collection, Salzburg, holds a complete set of photographs, given to Derra de Moroda by Walter Toscanini.
6. Sibylle Dahms, "Franz Anton Hilverding: *Le Turc généreux,*" in *Pipers Enzyklopädie des Musiktheaters,* vol. 3 (Munich: Piper, 1989), 56–58.
7. Jirí Záloha, "The Chateau Theater in Cesky Krumlov," in *The Baroque Theater in the Chateau of Cesky Krumlov* (miscellany of papers for a special seminar, Cesky Krumlov, 1993), 33–55.
8. Winter, *The Pre-Romantic Ballet,* 97f.
9. Gerhard Croll, "Gaspero Angiolini," in *The New Grove Dictionary of Music and Musicians,* vol. 1 (London: Macmillan, 1980), 425–26.
10. Lorenzo Tozzi, "Musica e balli al Regio di Torino (1748–1762)," *La Danza Italina* 2 (1985): 5–21.
11. Salvatore Bongiovanni, "Gennaro Magri e il *Trattato teorico-prattico di ballo,*" (Thesis, La Sapienza, Roma, 1993), 8–10.
12. Sibylle Dahms, "Gluck und das 'Ballet en action' in Wien," in *Gluck-Studien,* vol. 1 (Kassel: Bärenreiter, 1989), 100–105.
13. For more details, see Christoph Willibald Gluck, "Sämtliche Werke," series 2, vol. 1, in *Tanzdramen: "Don Juan/Semiramis,"* ed. Richard Engländer (Kassel and Basel, 1966).
14. Gerhard Croll, who rediscovered this second dissertation by Angiolini, long believed to be lost, recently published it in *"Traditionen—Neuansätze." Festschrift für Anna Amalie Abert* (Tutzing, 1997), 137–44.
15. For more details, see Gluck, "Sämtliche Werke."
16. Gasparo Angiolini, *Lettere di Gasparo Angiolini a Monsieur Noverre sopra i balli pantomimi* (Milan, 1773), 52–62.
17. Sibylle Dahms, "Das Repertoire des Ballet en Action. Noverre—Angiolini—Lauchery," in *De Editione Musices. Festschrift Gerhard Croll zum 65* (Laaber: Laaber-Verlag, 1992), 125–42.
18. Winter, *The Pre-Romantic Ballet,* 138–40.
19. Sibylle Dahms, "Ballet Reform in the Eighteenth Century and Ballet at the Mannheim Court," in *Ballet Music from the Mannheim Court,* vol. 1 (Madison: A-R Editions, 1996), ix–xxii.

Chapter 11

THE VIENNESE SINGSPIEL, HAYDN, AND MOZART

Eva Badura-Skoda

In Vienna, during the eighteenth century, theater, dance, and music were inter-woven to such a degree that they cannot be separated from each other. Dra-matic performances without any music apparently never existed, at least not prior to 1850. No doubt, for centuries music as well as dance had been an impor-tant integral part of the popular Viennese theater, the *Volkskomödie*.

Therefore, as I will demonstrate, it was not at all exceptional for the comedy or operetta *Der neue krumme Teufel* by Josef Felix von Kurz-Bernardon[1] and Joseph Haydn, performed in the Kärntnertortheater in 1758, to include a pan-tomime with dances as well as Italian arias belonging to an intermezzo. The extant libretto for this operetta indicates that Joseph Haydn had composed the music to the German aria texts and to that of the pantomime. Whether the music of the Italian intermezzo (the composer of which has not yet been identi-fied) was also written by him is not known, and most of Haydn's music for the German play seems to have been lost, presumably forever.[2]

This combination of comic and serious elements was typical of most Viennese popular comedies of the eighteenth century, in which comic and contemplative scenes usually alternated. In contrast, the court opera had banished this old com-bination, adopting the libretto reforms of the great Italian poet Apostolo Zeno, who had introduced some rules of the classic French tragedies into Italian libretti beginning around 1720. In *opera seria*, comic scenes remained banned through-out Zeno's and Metastasio's reign as Viennese court poets, only to return more or less secretly to the Viennese court stage during the late 1770s and the 1780s in the *semi-serie opere* of Mozart's time. However, in the Viennese popular theater, a quick sequence of comic and less comic scenes remained always alive. The *Teutsche Opera burlesca* (the Viennese counterpart to the *commedia dell'arte* and the Venetian *opera burlesca*) of Josef Anton Stranitzky and his immediate successor typified the later Viennese midcentury "comedies with music." These were mainly farces with rather earthy jokes and with improvised dialogues and thus certainly of disputable literary value. They apparently showed no visible serious elements. But the many aria texts and the few complete or nearly complete libretti that survive from this period often reveal an interesting underlying philosophy, portraying human tragedy as well as comic situations, something that can still be found in plays by Raimund and Nestroy, where comic and tragic elements alternate in their depiction of our real life.

It is also worthwhile mentioning that theatrical machinery had attained a special importance not only in the Baroque court opera but also later in the Viennese popular comedies of the late eighteenth and the early nineteenth centuries. Theater historians have included within the category of the "Maschinenkomödie" both the libretto to Kurz-Bernardon's operetta *Der neue krumme Teufel* and Schikaneder's libretto to *Die Zauberflöte*. In the context of theatrical history, Mozart's *Zauberflöte* is not only the grandiose beginning of German opera history but it is—apart from the Masonic element—also a drama embedded in the South German-Viennese Baroque tradition of "Maschinenkomödien."[3]

Relatively little is known about the many flying machines and the complicated stage effects of the older comedies in Stranitzky's time at the Kärntnertortheater. Kurz-Bernardon, however, demanded many machines in his libretti. In one of his advertisements he announced, "Once again I specify nothing about the changes and machines, following the ancient custom, but I can assure you that the invention thereof cost me much trouble,"[4] which makes it quite clear that stage design was an important part of the production and was necessary for achieving success with the Viennese audiences.

An especially great love of music and theater performances characterized the Viennese population in Haydn's and Mozart's time. Unlike any other Austrian or German city, Vienna was able to support popular theaters without regular subsidies for a period longer than a century—this in spite of high rents of by now standing theater houses, which had started to be built in Vienna in the course of the eighteenth century. In Hamburg, Frankfurt, or Leipzig, theaters did not exist for more than a few decades before they were closed for good, mainly because of lack of money or interest or both. Independent operatic theater for the people, as opposed to the performances at court, had been cultivated in Vienna even before the opening of the Kärntnertortheater in 1709. However, the enormous popularity of theater performances continued to increase during the second half of the eighteenth century, as one suburban theater after the other opened its doors in Vienna. There was then not only temporary competition from itinerant troupes but the permanent stimulus of rivalry between the various theater companies.

On the command of the emperor, the Kärntnertortheater was opened in 1709 with performances in Italian. As long as Emperor Charles VI was alive, the official court language remained Italian. More than 10 percent of the city's inhabitants were Italians by birth, and approximately half of the Viennese population spoke or at least understood Italian. But in 1711, the Viennese city fathers allowed the theater principal Stranitzky to play comedies also in German. However, Stranitzky, who was the creator of "Hanswurst" (a kind of harlequin with "Gemüth," i.e., with common-sense mother wit and much more feeling), wanted to offer his audiences not only German comedies but also travesties of those Italian *opere serie* that were performed at the court theater. Against the latter, an Italian impresario who was in the possession of a sole "privilege," a protecting license for Italian operas in makeshift theaters on marked places, loudly protested. Charles VI had solved the ensuing lawsuit between the two rival theater principals with the Solomonic judgment that from that year's date on, Italian opera in the Kärntnertortheater could not be performed unless mixed with German comedies. This imperial command enforced a "marriage" of Italian opera with the repertoire of German comedies of itinerary troupes, and it created the typically Viennese "comedy with music" that could also include Italian arias. It was to be a decisive motivating force in the growth of the later Viennese Singspiel in which an Italian intermezzo got its place and in which music played altogether a much more important role than it ever did in the German Singspiel of the time, which usually included only simple strophic lieder or vaudeville songs instead of full-fledged arias in the Italian style.

* * * * *

We still meet this enforced mixture in Haydn's time in the 1750s: though Haydn's first operetta for Kurz-Bernardon from 1751 or 1752, *Der krumme Teufel,* is completely lost, of the second operetta by Kurz-Bernardon and Haydn, *Der neue krumme Teufel* of 1758, we know at least the libretto. As stated above, it included an Italian intermezzo, which in essence is a short opera with arias and spoken dialogue. That the young Haydn had contact with Kurz and managed to get a well-paid commission ("opera scrittura") is reported by Haydn's interviewer and first biographer, the diplomat G. A. Griesinger: "In the evenings Haydn often went out serenading with his comrades.... Once he went to serenade the wife of Kurz, a comic actor very popular at the time and usually called Bernardon. Kurz came afterward into the street and asked for the composer of the music just played. Hardly had Haydn, who was about nineteen years old, identified himself when Kurz urged him strongly to compose an opera for him. Haydn pleaded his youth in vain; Kurz encouraged him and Haydn composed the opera *Der krumme Teufel....* Haydn received for his opera twenty-four ducats, a sum which at that time he thought made him a very rich man."[5] This event, according to Griesinger, took place in 1751.

Four handwritten volumes preserved in the Vienna Nationalbibliothek contain almost 1700 aria texts from 260 comedies, all performed in the Kärntnertortheater and all from the years prior to 1760. These volumes are entitled *Teutsche*

*Arien welche auf dem Kayserlich privilegierten Wienerischen Teatro in unter-
schiedlich producierten Comoedien, deren Tituln hier jedesmahl bey gedrucket,
gesungen worden* (German arias that have been sung in the imperial privileged
Viennese theater in various comedies, the titles of which are given in each
case). This collection represents probably a large portion of the Kärntnertortheater repertoire from the 1740s and 1750s. Not all texts are by Kurz-
Bernardon, but all go back to the years when he was first a member as an actor
and then the director of the troupe playing at the theater. For the last volume
of this collection of texts a considerable amount of the music for the arias and
ensemble pieces is extant. Robert Haas, when studying and editing this music
in the 1920s, surmised that some, if not all, of these arias were composed by
Joseph Haydn.[6]

In the case of two arias, among those thirty-three arias and duets for which the
music is preserved, I found such a remarkable number of literal quotations of
themes and motifs in other early works of Haydn and so many striking stylistic
similarities that his authorship in these arias is more than probable. The aria
"Wurstl ["Hans Wurst," which literally means John Sausage], mein Schatzerl, wo
wirst Du wohl sein"[7] can certainly be attributed to Haydn, given that the main
melody of the aria is practically identical with the main theme of a movement of
Haydn's Piano Sonata in A Major, Hob. XVI/12, if one disregards the upbeat and
the enlargement of the period in the latter. The aria is in the typical tripartite A
B A form of an Italian opera aria and starts with the usual instrumental prelude
after which the voice comes in with the following words (example 11.1):

Example 11.1 *Wurstl, mein Schatzerl*

The main subject of the piano sonata reads (example 11.2):

Example 11.2 Joseph Haydn, Piano Sonata in A Major, Hob. XVI/12, Finale

while the instrumental prelude with which the aria begins is slightly more ornamented than the original part (example 11.3):

Example 11.3 Instrumental Prelude to *Wurstl, mein Schatzerl*

The second motif starting in bar 4 of the prelude is found as the opening of an early church composition of Haydn, the *Salve Regina* in E Major, Hob. XXIIIb/1, composed in 1756 (example 11.4):

Example 11.4 Joseph Haydn, from the *Salve Regina* in E Major

The aria text is rather characteristic for the Viennese comedy texts of Kurz-Bernardon. Colombina sings:

Wurstl, mein Schatzerl, wo wirst Du wohl seyn?
Auwedl nunmehro ist alles verloren;—Ich seufze ich klage und sterbe vor Pein,
Für was für ein Unglück seynd wir nicht erkoren!
Mein Hansel, Geliebter, nun ist es geschehen,
wir werden einander wohl schwerlich mehr sehen.
Doch soll man im Tode die Treue noch kennen,
Ich will mich die Deine auch sterbend noch nennen.

[Wurstl, my darling, where might you be now!
Oh woe! now everything is lost;
I sigh, I lament, and I die because of pain
For what kind of misfortune are we not born!
My Hansel, beloved, now it has happened,
It's unlikely that we'll see each other again,
but in case one still knows fidelity in death
While dying I still call myself yours.]⁸

The aria of Mirile, "Du könntest ja vor allen il mio caro sein," from Kurz-Bernardon's comedy *Triumph der Freundschaft,* is likewise in all probability a genuine work by Haydn. It apparently was composed for the second wife of the theater principal Joseph Kurz, the well-trained Italian coloratura singer Teresa Morelli (who at short notice was able to take over the part of a prima donna in an Italian opera at Court). The text of this aria is a delightful mixture of three languages:

Du könntest zwar vor allem *il mio caro* sein,
mon prince tut mir gefallen, doch *ciel!* was bittre Pein!
La sorte mia crudele läßt mir das *bonheur* nicht.
Pardonnez schönste Seele, *ne pensez pas* mein Licht,
dass ich Dich kann verschmähen, ach könntest Du doch sehen
dentro il mio cuore mia pena ed' amore.
Perché bin ich jetzt gebunden, *helas,* du mein *marito*
du machst mir viel tiefe Wunden,
perché non sei morto?

[More than anybody, you could be my beloved,
I like my prince, but, heavens, what a bitter pain!
My cruel fate does not let me have the fortune.
Forgive me, most beautiful soul, don't think, my light,
that I can reject you, oh, could you see
in my heart, my pain and my love.
Why am I bound now, alas, my husband,
You give me many deep wounds,
Why are you not dead?]

The instrumental prelude of Mirile's aria (and later also the voice part) start with the following melody (examples 11.5a and 11.5b):

Example 11.5a Instrumental Prelude to *Du könntest zwar vor allen il mio caro sein*

Example 11.5b Joseph Haydn, *Du könntest zwar vor allen il mio caro sein*

The main theme of the Andante from Haydn's Symphony, Hob. I/14 (example 11.6), here transposed from D major to A major, and the C Major Divertimento, Hob. II/11 (a quotation that Georg Feder observed) are similar:

Example 11.6 Joseph Haydn, Principal Theme from Symphony, Hob. I/14
(transposed to A major)

Also, the second theme in Mirile's aria (example 11.7a) resembles a melodic thought found in a movement of a piano sonata (Hob. XVI/6, 3rd movement) (example 11.7b):

Example 11.7a Second Theme of the aria *Du könntest zwar vor allen il mio caro sein*

Example 11.7b Joseph Haydn, Piano Sonata, Hob. XVI/6, excerpt from the third
movement

Melodically as well as harmonically, the next measures of the aria prelude (example 11.8a) resemble the main subject of the Andante from Haydn's Piano Sonata
in G Major, Hob. XVI/6 (example 11.8b):

Example 11.8a From the Instrumental Prelude to *Du könntest zwar vor allen il mio
caro sein*

Example 11.8b Joseph Haydn, Piano Sonata in G Major, Hob. XVI/6, *Andante*

Thus, it is quite clear that Robert Haas's assumption that Haydn should be named as the composer of various arias found in the *Teutsche Comödie Arien* hits the mark indeed. Among the thirty-three arias and ensemble pieces of the *Teutsche Comödie Arien* are some few arias, however, that sound so Italian in style that one of the Italian opera buffa composers living in Vienna in the 1750s, such as Giuseppe Scarlatti (grandson of Alessandro and nephew of Domenico Scarlatti), may have been commissioned to compose them. Kurz could afford to pay all employed composers well.

Many, indeed almost all, of the problems connected with Haydn's first opera *Der krumme Teufel*, performed in 1751 or 1752 or both, still remain unsolved. Kurz, who had written the libretto, presumably knew the original French comedy play *Le diable boiteux*, after a novel by Le Sage, which had been performed in Vienna during 1738. Kurz's version, for which Haydn composed his first operatic music, departed greatly from the original story. That no music survives from this opera is well known, but there seems to be an unnecessary confusion about the fact that we have no libretto for the performances in 1751 or 1752 or (apparently) the two subsequent performances in 1753 of *Der krumme Teufel.* There are several good reasons for believing that *Der krumme Teufel* and *Der neue krumme Teufel* could not have had identical libretto. For the Singspiel *Der krumme Teufel,* there probably never existed a proper libretto; the actors in 1751/52 extemporized the story, adding earthy jokes. However, the libretto of *Der neue krumme Teufel* may have been "cleaned" and also altered to pass the new censorship. One reason for this conviction of mine is that there can be no doubt that early in 1752 Kurz got into serious difficulties in Vienna as a result of Empress Maria Theresa's taking offense at one of his famous extemporized remarks on stage. Without question, her newly introduced censorship in 1752 was directed against Kurz-Bernardon himself, whom she accused of smut.[9] As a consequence, Kurz left Vienna for Prague around Easter 1752. However, his departure was such a financial disaster for the theater that the empress allowed his return in 1753—but under the condition that no extemporized dialogues would be permitted. One might reasonably assume that Kurz considered it necessary to alter the libretto of his successful comedy of 1752 to meet the new demands of the censors, and maybe he had to consider in addition the changed taste of the Viennese audience in 1758. Therefore, in order to emphasize that in 1758 the comedy was not the same play as it had been before, Kurz wisely amended the title to *Der neue krumme Teufel* and submitted the libretto this way to the censor. It was then printed with the following endnote appended: "NB. die Musique sowohl von der Opera comique, als auch der Pantomime ist componiret von Herrn Joseph Heyden" (NB. The Music of the Opera comique as well as of the Pantomime has been composed by Mr. Joseph Heyden).

That Haydn continued to compose arias as late as the 1770s in the style of the *Volkskomödie* and for the popular comic figure "Hanswurst" is proved by the music to the puppet opera or Singspiel *Die Feuersbrunst*, a copy of which long went unrecognized in France under the title *L'incendie*, and which is now preserved in the Yale University Library, where H. C. Robbins Landon identified it twenty years ago.[10] In this little opera, in addition to "Hanswurst," the Viennese version of harlequin, other well-known figures of the *commedia dell'arte*, Colombina and Leander, are members of the cast. The music, which was probably composed in 1777, is as delightful as the text and still typical for popular comedies of the period. Who does not smile when Colombina sings these lines?

Jetzt bin ich was ich war, ein blutig armer Narr, ein blutig armer Narr!
Leander wird vor mir ausspucken, kein süsser Herr wird nach mir gucken,
Ich bin ein arm verächtlich Tier, ach wär doch noch mein Wurstl hier!

[Now one can see what I am: silly fool, a silly fool!
Leander will spit at me, no sweet sir will look at me,
I am a poor despised animal—if only my Wurstl were here!]

But toward the end of the comedy, Colombina can joyfully join in a duet with Hanswurst (example 11.9):

Colombina: Nun ich meinen Wurstl habe, wird mir leicht ums Herz!
Hanswurst: Nun ich Dich, mein Schätzchen habe, wird mir leicht ums Herz!
Both: Komm laß uns verbinden die Herzen und leben in Lachen und Scherzen.

[*Colombina*: Since I now have my Wurstl back, my heart is relieved!
Hanswurst: Since you are back now, beloved one, my heart is relieved!
Both: Come, let us unite our hearts and let us live in laughter and joy.]

Example 11.9 *Nun ich meinen Wurstel habe*

Another kind of Singspiel developed in the Austrian countryside in monastery schools. These were called "Finalskomödien" because such comedies were usually scheduled to be performed by boys at the end of the school year in Benedictine monastery schools. However, around 1760 the tightfisted Empress Maria Theresa, at that time involved in a war with Prussia and in need of money, considered these expensively staged performances a waste of money and started to forbid them in her Crown countries. However, the further away from Vienna a monastery was located the less seriously the monks followed this regulation, and operettas were performed at the end of an academic year despite the empress's ruling.

Such a *Finalskomödie*, or operetta, entitled *Die reisende Ceres*, was discovered some time ago in the Benedictine monastery of Seitenstetten in Lower Austria.[11] A relatively late composition date in the 1770s can be assumed for this "monastery operetta," which originally was also composed most probably by Joseph Haydn. Haydn's name as the composer was mentioned on the old title pages of several musical parts, but the extant manuscript copy of Seitenstetten, though presently it is the only known source of the music of this operetta, is probably a copy of a copy and, unfortunately, a rather second-rate copy. The copyist must have been an inexperienced and rather dilettantish person; he made a lot of writing mistakes that would never have occurred with a good musician. Therefore, it seems likely that Haydn composed—secretly, because he was not permitted to do so—the music for a monastery other than Seitenstetten. In any case, the commission to compose a *Finalskomödie* had to be kept a secret. Evidence that the operetta *Die reisende Ceres* may have originally been intended for the Göttweig monastery is found in a catalog compiled around 1850, which includes an operetta with this title. The author of the libretto was a famous Benedictine monk from Lambach, Pater Maurus Lindemayr, who wrote many plays in the Upper Austrian dialect. The farmer family in the plot speaks in that dialect (e.g., "Wannst zum Stadl dadl firi kimmst …"), while the servant of the goddess Ceres, Phoebe, sings her text in high German (example 11.10):

Example 11.10 *Das hieß nit gefahren, es hieß recht geflogen*

As one can see and hear, the music is delightful, and the attribution to Joseph Haydn as the composer is probably correct. Unfortunately, one voice part is presently missing. Completed and well rehearsed, this Singspiel was successfully performed during a Salzburg Festival in 1977.

* * * * *

Mozart's acquaintance with the comedy performances of the Kärntnertortheater or with those of the other theaters in Vienna can be dated as far back as his second visit with his father to Vienna in 1768, when he was just twelve years old. Leopold Mozart, in a letter to his friend Lorenz Hagenauer in Salzburg from the end of January 1768, criticized the taste of the Viennese audience: "That the Viennese, generally speaking, do not care to see serious and sensible performances, have little or no idea of them, and only want to see foolish stuff, devils, ghosts, magic, Hanswurst, Lipperl, Bernardon, witches and apparitions is well known; and their theaters prove it every day. A gentleman, even a nobleman with decorations, will clap his hands and laugh so much over some ribald or naive joke of Hanswurst as to get short of breath; during the most serious scenes, however,... he will prattle so loudly to his lady that other honest people in the audience cannot understand a word."[12] However, it seems that young Wolfgang Mozart, unlike his father, was quite fond of the Viennese Singspiel comedies. When in the spring of 1781 he decided to live in Vienna for good as an independent artist with the freedom to do what he liked without being under the control of his father, he soon took the opportunity of making himself familiar with Vienna's theater life. In July 1781 he wrote to his sister: "My sole entertainment is the theater.... Generally speaking, I do not know of any [other city's] theater where all kinds of plays are really well performed. But they are here. Every part, even the most unimportant and poorest part, is well cast and understudied."[13] Mozart also spoke of his visits to suburban theaters in later letters to Salzburg, dating from the 1780s.

Naturally, in those years Mozart was most eager to find employment as a theater composer; throughout his life the composing of operas interested him more than anything else. Therefore the commission to compose *Die Entführung aus dem Serail*, received only three months after he had left the archbishop's service, was gratifying for him, indeed. With ardent zeal he started the composition of Johann Gottlieb Stephanie's texts. The extent to which by then he could already gauge the taste of the Viennese audience is evident in his letters to his father: "As the original text began with a monologue, I asked Herr Stephanie to make a little arietta out of it—and then to put in a duet instead of making the two chatter together after Osmin's short song."[14] This duet suggests that Mozart had noticed the important role of duets in the Viennese Singspiel tradition. From the very beginning of the composition of the *Entführung* Mozart was also eager to display the comic features of Osmin, a typically Viennese type of servant, who according to Stephanie's original libretto would have had little to say and sing. The same letter to his father also reveals that Mozart dedicated the drinking duet "Vivat Bacchus" especially "to the gentlemen of Vienna" ("per i signori viennesi")—a dedication apparently well deserved. About the Janissary chorus he commented that "it is, as such, all that can be desired, that is, short, lively and written to please the Viennese." The *Entführung* was commissioned as a German opera or Singspiel with spoken text between musical numbers. Mozart made it very special with a maximum of the allowed music numbers and, what is more, with music of previously unheard quality.

Mozart's inclination for German libretti is documented in his letters. Out of love for the *Volkskomödie*, or Viennese Singspiel, he composed two complete Singspiel aria texts in particell and also parts of the instrumentation for the usual Singspiel orchestra. The aria K435 (416^b) is most likely Mozart's contribution for an unknown Viennese Singspiel (or perhaps already intended for his own planned

Singspiel "Der Diener zweier Herren," as Alfred Einstein suggested). This tenor aria K435 has a typical Singspiel text: "Müßt ich auch durch tausend Drachen ..." (Even if I would have to fight a thousand dragons ...) (example 11.11):

Example 11.11 Wolfgang Amadeus Mozart, *Müßt ich auch durch tausend Drachen*

Likewise the bass aria K. 433 (416ᶜ), "Männer suchen stets zu naschen ..." (Men are always Naschers if left alone with girls), is in the style of a Singspiel aria (example 11.12). It was probably composed for the bass singer Baumann and written during the winter of 1782/83, thus shortly after the *Entführung*.

Example 11.12 Wolfgang Amadeus Mozart, *Männer suchen stets zu naschen*

These two charming arias deserve to be rediscovered by performers and eventually presented in a concert. Mozart also composed music for a Pantomime K. 446 (416ᵈ) in which he mentioned as dancers the quarreling Pantalone and Colombine, perhaps again meant as an insertion in a Singspiel. Unfortunately, this work is only incompletely preserved.

Once, probably in 1786, Mozart had the notion of writing a libretto of his own in the style of the Viennese *Volkskomödie*. The autograph, a fragment of a three-act comedy entitled *Die Liebesprobe* (K. Anh. 28/509c), was at one time in the possession of the publishers Breitkopf und Härtel, from whom it was copied by Mozart's well-informed and reliable biographer Otto Jahn. The cast consisted of Herr von Dummkopf, Rosaura, his daughter, Trautel, her chambermaid, Leander, in love with Rosaura, Wurstl, his servant (Hanswurst), Herr von Knödl (Mr. Dumpling), also in love with Rosaura, Kasperl, valet of Herr von Dummkopf, the witch Slinzkicotinzki, a female dwarf, a female giant. The names of Rosaura, Trautel, Leander, and Wurstl are well known to us from earlier examples of Viennese popular comedies. How seriously Mozart intended to compose his own comic Singspiel text is difficult to say today. One may guess that his ambition was probably little more than to write a "Faschingsschwank," or carnival joke. But it was characteristic for Mozart that in these years of great psychological and physical strain, between compositions such as the C Minor Piano Concerto, K. 491, and the opera *The Marriage of Figaro* on the one hand, and the G Minor Quintet and *Don Giovanni* on the other, he should have found relaxation in writing such a comedy fragment.

In 1790 Mozart composed or helped to compose a duet for soprano and bass (K. 625/592a) as an insertion piece for Schikaneder's Singspiel *Der Stein der Weisen oder Die Zauberinsel* (The Stone of Wisdom; or, The Magic Island). This again shows his true familiarity with the traditions of the Viennese popular comedy. The first performance of this Singspiel took place in September 1790, and the program said that the music was "by Schack and others." The plot is rather simple: Lubana is bewitched when she sings her part and can only answer "Meouw, meouw." The sprite Eytifronte finally helps her to recover, and the operetta finishes happily. The text of this duet reads:

Lubano: Nun liebes Weibchen, ziehst mit mir, mit mir der stillen Hütte zu.
Lubana: Miau, miau, miau, miau.
Lubano: Was redst Du da? Sags nur heraus! Nicht wahr? nun bleibst Du gern zu Haus.
Lubana: Miau, Miau.
Lubano: Der Teufel hol das Miaugeschrei! Sag, bleibst Du mir alleine treu?
Lubana: Miau, Miau …

[*Lubano*: Now, my beloved wife, are you going with me in my hut?
Lubana: Meouw, meouw …
Lubano: What are you saying? Tell me frankly, you'll agree, from now on you will stay at home?
Lubana: Meouw, meouw …
Lubano: To the devil with these meouws! Tell me, will you remain faithful to me?
Lubana: Meouw, meouw, meouw …]

That this duet (example 11.13) is a genuine work by Mozart is suggested by an incomplete autograph manuscript currently held by the Bibliothèque du Conservatoire du Music, Paris. In 1968 my students at the University of Wisconsin at Madison performed this piece in a program during a Conference of the Eighteenth-Century Society. The music of this delightful duet has been available since the nineteenth century in the old complete edition of Breitkopf und Härtel (series 6, vol. 47).

Example 11.13 Wolfgang Amadeus Mozart, *Nun liebes Weibchen, ziehst mit mir*

But did Mozart compose only this duet for Schikaneder's *The Stone of Wisdom?* Recently, David Buch, a colleague from Iowa, found a manuscript copy of this Singspiel in an archive in Hamburg. In this specific manuscript copy, additional pieces and not only the duet were attributed to Mozart. The discovery of supposedly unknown Mozart pieces was publicized immediately, and even the *New York Times* published an article on it in July 1997. However, another manuscript of the Singspiel containing the same additional music pieces exists in a Berlin archive and also in an archive in Frankfurt. According to new research,[15] the handwriting of all copies is of Viennese origin. The Hamburg copy is that of the Viennese copyist Kaspar Weiss, and in this copy the various music numbers are attributed to five composers: Mozart, Henneberg, Schack, Gerl, and Schikaneder. The attributions to Mozart involve not only the duet mentioned but also two other sections from the finale. However, unlike the duet, we have no autograph preserved for these two sections as proof of their authenticity. While the other two sources in Berlin and Frankfurt do not specify composers, the Hamburg score is the only one which gives such a hint.

In Mozart's cat duet, however, we certainly find a kind of genuine relationship to Papageno's arias and duets in *Die Zauberflöte*, in which Mozart also proved that he was completely and effortlessly at home in the language of the Viennese Singspiel. Papageno's two arias "Der Vogelfänger bin ich ja" and "Ein Mädchen oder Weibchen wünscht Papageno sich" and his duets with Papagena are genuine Singspiel pieces. Though in principle similar to comedy arias of other popular Singspiele played in Viennese suburban theaters, Mozart's arias naturally are of a much higher musical quality. Besides, Mozart's score of *Die Zauberflöte* is more than three times as long as the average Singspiel score, which means that instead of six to ten musical numbers as in other comedies of Schikaneder, Mozart composed twenty-one numbers or scenes in *Die Zauberflöte*, adding Italianized bravura arias with most difficult coloraturas for the Queen of the Night; touching dramatic arias for Tamino, Pamina, and Sarastro; choirs and the most beautiful ensemble pieces for the three ladies; incredibly beautiful numbers for the three boys; and so on. With these additions, Mozart broke the boundaries of the Viennese Singspiel and created a full-sized German opera.

Schikaneder must have been a musically gifted man, as versatile as an impresario and a theater director, actor, and singer as Kurz-Bernardon had been. His success in all of these activities was indeed impressive. After all, it was Schikaneder who at the first performance of *Die Zauberflöte* sang the role of Papageno under Mozart's direction. Due to his enthusiasm for Mozart's music, he did not hesitate to spend his last ducats and to borrow additional money to enlarge his troupe, to hire extra singers, including Mozart's sister-in-law, to have extraordinary stage machines built, and to order decorations and costumes for many more performers than usual. Fortunately, the immediate success was so enormous that the investments turned out to be more than worthwhile financially. This speaks for the high level of Schikaneder's musical judgment that he not only commissioned Mozart to compose one of his texts, but that he also dared to spend so much money to stage this new and unusual kind of Singspiel, which became the first great German opera, and was probably at the same time the best German opera ever written. The high quality of popular music in Vienna in the time of Haydn and Mozart, and the affinity of these great composers to folk music, often also present in their instrumental and church music melodies, caused most probably the extraordinary world success of Viennese classical music, unbroken, valid, and alive even today.

Notes

1. Kurz got his double name because of his creation of the comic figure of "Bernardon," whom he impersonated on stage. "Bernardon" acted as the partner of the popular "Hanswurst," a figure his predecessor Stranitzky had created some decades earlier.
2. Various German arias of this Singspiel are (or seem to be) musically identical with some arias found by Robert Haas in a contemporary manuscript; See Haas, "Teutsche Comoedie Arien,"

Zeitschrift für Musikwissenschaft, vol. 3 (Leipzig: Breitkopf und Härtel, 1921), 411f. It was a common practice of theater principals to underlay different texts to the same successful music.

3. See Otto Rommel, "Die Maschinenkomödie," in *Barocktradition im österreichisch-bayrischen Volkstheater*, vol. 1 (Leipzig, 1935), 85f; also Rommel, *Die Alt-Wiener Volkskomödie* (Vienna, 1952).

4. Avertissement zur Komödie *Die glückliche Verbindung des Bernardons*, printed in an eighteenth-century collection of scenarios and aria texts preserved in the Wiener Stadt- und Landesbibliothek (Sign. A 22 200). See also Robert Haas, *Die Musik in der Wiener deutschen Stegreif-Komödie*, in *Studien zur Musikwissenschaft, Beihefte der Denkmäler der Tonkunst*, vol. 12 (Vienna, 1926).

5. G. A. Griesinger, "Biographische Notizen über Joseph Haydn," in Vernon Gotwal's *Joseph Haydn*, which includes a translation of Griesinger's "Biographische Notizen ..." and of "Biographische Nachrichten ..." by A. Dies (Madison: University of Wisconsin Press, 1963). The original books appeared one year after Haydn's death and are based on many interviews with Haydn that took place over a period of years.

6. See Robert Haas, preface to the edition of many of the arias and duets in *Denkmäler der Tonkunst in Österreich*, vol. 64 (XXXIII/1) (Vienna, 1926). Those pieces not published in that volume were subsequently published in vol. 121 of *Denkmäler der Tonkunst*. See also Haas, *Teutsche Comoedie Arien*, op. cit.

7. Printed in *Denkmäler der Tonkunst in Österreich*, ed. C. Schönbaum, vol. 121 (Vienna, 1971). These examples were quoted in my article, "Teutsche Comoedie Arien und Joseph Haydn," in *Der Junge Haydn*, Beiträge zur Aufführungspraxis Bd. 1 (Graz: Akadem. Druck- u. Verlagsanst., 1971), 59f.

8. All translations are those of the author unless otherwise stated.

9. An edict of the Empress Maria Theresia, dated 11 February 1752, reads in translation: "The comedy should play no other compositions than those based on French, Italian or Spanish plays; all compositions of Bernardon and others should not be performed. In case there are some good ones of Weiskern, they should be read before they are allowed to be played; no 'equivoques' [double entendres] or dirty words should be allowed; also, the comedians are not allowed to improvise." See Robert Haas, *Gluck und Durazzo im Burgtheater* (Vienna, 1925), 12.

10. Anthony van Hoboken, the compiler of the *Thematic Catalogue of Haydn's Works*, claimed that he also had seen the manuscript, but apparently he did not recognize Haydn as the author because of the title change. Therefore, the authenticity of the Singspiel sometimes is doubted without any proper foundation.

11. See Eva Badura-Skoda, "An Unknown Singspiel by Joseph Haydn?" in *Report of the Eleventh Congress of the International Musicological Society*, vol. 1 (Copenhagen: n.p., 1972), 236f, and "Zur Salzburger Erstaufführung von Joseph Haydn's Singspiel *Die reisende Ceres*," in *Österreichische Musikzeitschrift* 32 (1977): 317f. A piano reduction of the Singspiel was published by Universal-Edition in 1978; score and parts are also available with this publisher.

12. Letter of 30 January 1768; quoted in *The Letters of Mozart and His Family*, vol. 1, ed. and trans. Emily Anderson (London: Macmillan and Co., 1938), 118. The first sentence only is in Emily Anderson's edition. The complete text is in Wilhelm Bauer and Otto Erich Deutsch, *Mozart: Briefe und Aufzeichnungen: Gesamtausgabe herausgegeben von der Internationalen Stiftung Mozarteum*, vol. 1 (Kassel: Bärenreiter, 1962), 254.

13. Letter of 4 July 1781 quoted in Anderson, ed., *The Letters of Mozart and His Family*, vol. 2, 1117.

14. Letter of 26 September 1781; ibid.

15. See David J. Buch, "*Der Stein der Weissen*, Mozart and Collaborative Singspiels at Emanuel Schikaneder's Theater auf der Weiden," and also Faye Ferguson, "Interpreting the Source Tradition of *Stein der Weisen*," both in *Mozart-Jahrbuch* 2000 (Kassel: Bärenreiter Verlag, 2002), 91–126 and 127–44.

Chapter 12

DISPLAYING (OUT)RAGE

The Dilemma of Constancy
in Mozart's Operas

Gretchen A. Wheelock

A ll men accuse women, but I excuse them even if they do change their affections a thousand times a day. Some call it a vice, others a habit, but to me it seems to be a necessity of the heart.... Repeat with me: Così fan tutte!"[1] Don Alfonso's summary, "Così fan tutte," (all women are like that) has been read by some as simply misogynist and by others as a universalizing statement about the changeable affections of youthful lovers.[2] Even so, it is the young women in this opera who are shown to be unfaithful when put to the test. Indeed, Alfonso's phrase is anticipated and made specific to women by Basilio in the act 1 trio of *Le nozze di Figaro*: "Così fan tutte le belle! Non c'è alcuna novità" (All beautiful women are like that! There's nothing new about it). The theme of woman's fidelity is a central preoccupation not only in *Così fan tutte* but also in many of Mozart's operas, where inconstancy is seemingly taken as a natural condition of female behavior. Far more cynical than Alfonso's conciliatory advice to the young lovers is the dark maxim he recites alone: "Whoever bases his hopes on a woman's heart plows the sea and sows the sand and hopes to catch the wanton wind in a net"—words that do not bode well for the success of Fiordiligi's later affirmation of a constancy that "stands as a rock, immovable against the winds and tempests."[3] In changes rung on this familiar trope, we hear the theme of women's deceptions taken up as common knowledge in Mozart's operas by cheerful servant girls and their grumbling male counterparts—even by pious priests of

---

Music examples are located at the back of the chapter, starting on page 194.

enlightenment. Not surprising, the angry accusers of inconstant women are most often wounded and jealous males, such as Ramiro (*La finta giardiniera*), Count Almaviva and Figaro (*Le nozze di Figaro*), Masetto (*Don Giovanni*), Guglielmo and Ferrando (*Così*), in *opera buffa*, and the rulers Lucio Silla and Mitridate, title characters in the early *opere serie* that bear their names.

Although the young men in *Così* are not called upon to demonstrate their fidelity, but rather to boast of their lovers' faith, they *are* required to display their jealousy. Here it becomes clear not only that wounded pride is at stake, but also that their expectations of constancy are woefully exaggerated: far from condemning his own folly, as Alfonso urges him to do, Guglielmo will hold up the impossibly faithful Penelope as his standard for Fiordiligi. The prospect for jealous suspicions is thus practically assured.

The routine of doubting women's fidelity favors a gendered "economy" of suspicion and conciliation. A familiar scenario in comic genres is one in which women must be suspected of inconstancy and questioned by jealous men. The women become hurt and angry, their indignation in turn reassuring the anxious men, who must now ask forgiveness for doubting their lovers' fidelity. If the men demonstrate that they are truly sorry, they may be forgiven their jealous behavior. And a summarizing moral may be offered, as in the act 2 finale of *Die Entführung aus dem Serail*: "Long live love … let nothing fan the flame of jealousy."[4] At this opera's close the young lovers will celebrate the clemency of the Pasha Selim in a salute to forgiveness: "Revenge disfigures the noble man. To be humane and kind and selflessly to forgive is the mark of a noble soul."[5] (The unforgiving and ignoble Osmin, meanwhile, rushes off in a rage, repeating earlier ineffectual threats of vengeance: "Burn these dogs, they have deceived us miserably … first beheaded, then hanged, then impaled on hot poles," and so on.)[6]

Such moments are reminders that staged performances allowed the public expression of certain passions as more or less "natural" for men or women—and some as simply comic. This seems to me especially telling when looking at Mozart's manners of representing characters in highly charged emotional states. Answering to prevailing values of womanly and manly conduct for aristocratic and bourgeois listeners of the day, such performances provided models of appropriate and inappropriate behavior in staged lessons that eighteenth-century listeners might take in as a kind of conduct literature.

Here the rule of custom plays its part in gendered characterizations of inconstancy. Whereas Don Alfonso intends to expose the fickleness of women, the Countess Almaviva in *Le nozze di Figaro* suggests that men's infidelities are routine, even decreed by nature. Thus, when asked by Susanna, "But how can the Count be jealous of you?" the Countess appeals to received wisdom: "That is the way of modern husbands: on principle they are unfaithful, by nature they are fickle, and by pride all are jealous."[7] On this view, men must be forgiven for being naturally attracted to other women, but just as surely they will not brook inconstancy in their wives. And if it is in a man's nature not only to be unfaithful but also to suspect his wife of infidelity, it is a gentlewoman's role to forgive.

The enraged Count threatens to kill his supposed rival, the love-struck adolescent Cherubino, but the Countess laments and ultimately forgives the repeated indiscretions of her husband. Her servant, Susanna, on the other hand, boxes her Figaro on the ears when roused to the boiling point by jealous suspicions of Marcellina's triumph.[8]

These examples offer further reminders that expressions of rage in Mozart's operas are inflected not only by gender, but also by class and genre. In *opera seria*, larger-than-life characters give voice to exalted passions, displaying rage as emblematic of regal authority and power. In the comic operas, where *seria* and *buffa* character types intermingle, we hear a far greater range of expression among representatives of high, middle, and low classes and styles, variously motivated in voicing anger appropriate to their station and situation. In general the range of effective anger that a character can marshal is proportionate to the status and sphere of influence he or she has in seeking redress.

Among the servant characters in *opera buffa* that sphere is doubly qualified, even though the character's emotion may itself be fully felt. Thus in "Se vuol ballare" (*Le nozze di Figaro*, no. 3), Figaro must self-consciously repress his simmering rage at the Count's designs on Susanna, forcing it down to a mocking challenge delivered as soliloquy to the accompaniment of a "guitar." In this aria Figaro's rising anger is audible in the orchestra's gradual crescendo of volume and motion, in agitated syncopations and dynamic shifts, and in the obsessive repetition of his own words, "Saprò, saprò, saprò ..." (see example 12.1). Harmonically, too, the growing tension of Figaro's repressed rage is heard in the dissonance of protracted dominant pedal points that deflect toward a menacing D minor. A lapse of tonal focus confirms Figaro's loss of control as the sudden shift to F major ushers in a furious momentum of *buffo*-style diction reminiscent of Osmin's ranting in *Die Entführung aus dem Serail*. Here we get the full measure of Figaro's frustration and his impotent fury in the face of the Count's ultimate power.

The Count himself, on the other hand, in venting his more expansive and threatening *furore* in "Vedrò mentre'io sospiro" (*Le nozze di Figaro*, no. 18), commands a full panoply of *opera seria* rhetorical gestures, including an extended accompanied recitative that builds to the aria proper. The range of the Count's fury has been heard earlier, in the opening of the second-act finale, as, with sword drawn, he prepares to confront his "rival," Cherubino. Expressed here in an aria of soliloquy, Almaviva's fulminations are more menacing for their calculated focus on revenge, as frustrated desire rises to murderous fury at his own humiliation. With the backup of imposing orchestral support, the Count is assured of a maestoso display of noise appropriate to his elevated rank and style. Like Figaro, he is given to obsessive repetitions, but he proceeds in sweeping phrases and stabbing accents with the confidence of fully enfranchised passion. The orchestra underscores the threat of his rage in sudden dynamic shifts, menacing chromatic ascents, and agitated syncopations (see example 12.2). This is rage displayed as power to seek retribution for insults, and the Count is jubilant at the thought of his revenge.

Whereas the Count's menacing gestures provide an audible demonstration of the authority he commands to back up his vengeful warnings, Dr. Bartolo's earlier aria, "La vendetta," in this same opera becomes a travesty of the real thing in rage writ too large, as pompous bluster (*Le nozze di Figaro*, no. 4). His music lacks tonal coherence, gets off the track in failing to reach harmonic goals, and degenerates into the sputtering patter that John Platoff has described as a stock feature in *buffo* bass arias[9] (see example 12.3). By the aria's end, Bartolo's repeated threats of vengeance strike us as more sound than fury.[10] In characterizing three such different varieties of rage, Mozart not only locates class distinctions of low, middle, and high, but also registers degrees of irony in treating rage that is self-conscious and cunning though constrained (Figaro's), rage that is ineffectual and blustering bravado (Bartolo's), and rage that is genuinely threatening and ignoble (the Count's).

As noted earlier, much of the rage one hears throughout Mozart's operas, in serious and comic genres alike, is propelled by jealousy, and it falls largely to men to express this passion openly before others, to display jealousy as a condition of pride in the containment of wives and sweethearts—that is, as a kind of inverted constancy. In so doing, they play out a scenario in which women must be suspected of deceitfulness and infidelity, and gentlewomen, especially, must counter with persuasive evidence of their own steadfastness. But if men's angry suspicions were taken to be rightful expressions of pride, women's forgiveness could be read as a natural pliancy in yielding to men's entreaties, a pliancy presumably related to that of which they are accused in the first place. I will return to this conundrum later in this essay, and to consideration of the women in *Così fan tutte* in relation to eighteenth-century views of women's nature. For in this opera, where the expression of women's passions is shaped to exhibit feminine inconstancy, raging sentiments are displayed as hyperbolic performances of excessive sensibility in strangely hybrid versions of constancy. Attention to conventions of antecedent arias in Mozart's *seria* and *buffa* operas and to prevailing views of women's inconstancy can help to locate the effects these displays might have had on listeners of the day and the cultural assignments they represent.

First, I would like to look briefly at some examples of rage and outrage in the arias of women in relation to those of men. (The arias under discussion are listed by opera genre in table 12.1.) Compared with the motivations and expressions of men's ragings—whether in menacing threats or in impotent bravado—the rage of Mozart's women fills a broader spectrum of emotion. In their arias we hear the self-destructive, all-consuming Furies of Electra (*Idomeneo*, nos. 4 and 29) and the Queen of the Night (*Die Zauberflöte*, no. 14); the righteous indignation of Donna Anna's calls for vengeance (*Don Giovanni*, no. 10); the self-dramatizing parodies of *seria* raging in Dorabella's "implacable passions" (*Così fan tutte*, no. 11) and Arminda's eccentric jealousy (*La finta giardiniera*, no. 14); and the defiant outrage of Zaïde (*Zaïde*, no. 9), Konstanze (*Die Entführung aus dem Serail*, no. 11), and Fiordiligi (*Così fan tutte*, no. 14). (One could add to this list the indignant scoldings of Susanna in *Le nozze di Figaro* and Blonde in *Die Entführung*, which

Table 12.1 Rage Arias in Mozart's Operas

Rage arias in Mozart's *opere serie*

	key/tempo
Mitridate, rè di Ponto (Milan, 1770)	
No. 10 (Mitridate), "Quel ribelle"	D Major
obs, hrns, tpts/timp, str	Allegro
rage at disloyalty of first son, Farnace	
No. 17 (Mitridate), "Già di pietà mi spoglio"	C Major
obs, hrns, str	Allegro
rage at betrayal by second son, Sifare, as	
political and amorous rival	
Lucio Silla (Milan, 1772)	
No. 5 (Lucio Silla), "Il desìo di vendetta e di morte"	D Major
obs, hrns, tpts/timp, str	[allegro maestoso]
rage at Giunia's rejection	
No. 9 (Cecilio), "Quest' improvviso tremito"	D Major
obs, hrns, tpts/timp str	Allegro assai
turbulent feelings of hope and fury after dream	
ordering him to kill Silla	
No. 13 (Lucio Silla), "D'ogni pietà mi spoglio"	C Major
obs, hrns, tpts/timp, str	Allegro assai
rage at Giunia's defiant fidelity to Cecilio	
No. 20 (Lucio Cinna) "De più superbi il core"	D Major
obs, hrns, tpts/timp, str	Allegro
philosophical aria about the rages of Jupiter	
Idomeneo (Munich, 1781)	
No. 4 (Electra), "Tutte nel cor vi sento"	d minor
fl, obs, bssns, 4 hrns, str	Allegro assai
"*agitata de gelosia,*" Electra reacts to news of	
Idomeneo's supposed death and his son's attentions	
to her rival, Ilia	
No. 29 (Electra), "D'Oreste, d'Ajace"	c minor
[aria later cut by Mozart]	Allegro assai
fls, obs, bssns, 4 hrns, tpts/timp, str	
tortures of the Furies, madness, suicide	

Rage arias in Mozart's *opere buffe*

La finta giardiniera (Munich, 1775)	
No. 13 (Arminda), "Vorrei punirti indegno"	g minor
obs, bssns, 4 hrns, str	Allegro assai
fury of rejection by Belfiore	
No. 26 (Ramiro-castrato role), "Va pure ad altri in braccio"	c minor
obs, bssns, 4 hrns, str	[allegro]
contrasto d'affetti; jealousy and pain of rejection	

Table 12.1 Rage Arias in Mozart's Operas *(cont.)*

Le nozze di Figaro (Vienna, 1786)

No. 3 (Figaro), "Se vuol ballare, signor contino" — F Major
obs, bssns, hrns, str. — Allegretto-> Presto
rage at the Count's "droit de seigneur"

No. 4 (Bartolo), "La vendetta" — D Major
fls, obs, bssns, hrns, tpts/timp, str — Allegro maestoso
paean to revenge in long-standing grudge against
Figaro for helping Almaviva steal Rosina away

No. 18 (Count Almaviva), "Vedrò mentr'io sospiro" — D Major
fls, obs, bssns, hrns, tpts/timp, str — Allegro maestoso->
rage at Figaro's having the woman he desires, — Allegro assai
jubilant at the prospect of revenge

No. 26 (Figaro), "Aprite un po' quegli occhi" — E-flat Major
cls, bssns, hrns, str — Moderato
jealous diatribe addressed to all men against all
women as "mistresses of deceit"

Don Giovanni (Prague, 1787)

No. 3 (Donna Elvira), "Ah chi mi dice mai" — E-flat Major
cls, bssns, hrns, str — Allegro
rage of the "donna abbandonata"

No. 10 (Donna Anna), "Or sai chi l'onore" — D Major
fls, obs, bssns, hrns, tpts/timp, str — Andante
renewed call for vengeance, now focused on
Don Giovanni

Così fan tutte (Vienna, 1789)

No. 11 (Dorabella), "Smanie implacabili" — E-flat Major
fls, cls, bssns, hrns, str — Allegro agitato
histrionic invocation of the Furies to witness a
"wretched example of fatal love"

No. 14 (Fiordiligi), "Come scoglio immoto resta" — B-flat Major
obs, cls, bssns, tpts, str — Andante maestoso
defiant outrage at the intrusion of would-be suitors

No. 27 (Ferrando), "Tradito, schernito" — c minor->C Major
obs, cls, bssns, hrns, str — Allegro
jealousy, wounded pride at infidelity of lover

Rage arias in Mozart's Singspiele

Zaïde (1780; incomplete)

No. 9 (Soliman), "Der Stolze Löw' lässt sich zwar zähern" — D Major
obs, hrns, tpts/timp, str — Allegro maestoso
rage over the escape of his captive, Zaïde

No. 13 (Zaïde), "Tiger! Wetze nur die Klauen" — g minor
obs, hrns, bssns, str — Allegro assai
martyr-like defiance of captor, Soliman

Table 12.1 Rage Arias in Mozart's Operas *(cont.)*

Die Entführung aus dem Serail (Vienna, 1782)	
No. 3 (Osmin), "Solche hergelauf'ne Laffen"	F Major->a minor
obs, hrns, str + Turkish insts. in coda	Allegro->Allegro
violent, "exotic" rage rendered comic	assai
No. 11 (Konstanze) "Martern aller Arten"	C Major
fl, ob, cls, bssns, hrns, tpts/timp, str	Allegro
defiant fidelity to Belmonte in the face of Pasha	
Selim's threats of torture	
Die Zauberflöte (Vienna, 1791)	
No. 14 (Queen of the Night), "Der Hölle Rache"	d minor
fls, obs, bssns, hrns, tpts/timp, str	Allegro assai
enraged vengeance demanding that Pamina	
murder Sarastro	

Key to abbreviations in Mozart's scoring: fl = flute; ob = oboe; cl = clarinet; bssn = bassoon; hrn = horn; tpt/timp = trumpets and timpani; str = strings

culminate in physical reprimands, although their anger is heard in ensembles rather than arias.) Overall, the voices of angry female characters range more widely in key, mode, orchestration, and variety of musical rhetoric than do those of their male counterparts. One might wonder if they have more reasons to be angry.

Raging passions in men's *seria*-style arias reveal certain distinctions in comparison with those of the women cited above. The aria texts of Mozart's early *seria* characters suggest that the display of rage is an act of free will—an unleashing of the fury that is emblematic of one's power. King Mitridate, for example, on learning that his intended Queen, Aspasia, loves his son, Sifare, plans to slaughter them both as traitors. He narrates the experience of rage as a process of deliberate action: "I now strip my heart of pity.... I give free reign to my fury. An outraged father and lover, I want vengeance."[11] Emperor Lucio Silla, on being rejected by his intended, Giunia, is consumed by blood lust and narrates a physical evolution of passion: "Lust for revenge and death so inflames me that all tender feelings have been transformed into fury now that I have been scorned."[12] In both of these arias, the expression of such overwhelming passions requires an amplitude of fully orchestrated sound and musical gesture, suited to the display of imperial rage.

As shown in table 12.1, most of Mozart's rage arias are scored for full (by eighteenth-century standards) orchestra reinforced by trumpets and drums; four require an extra pair of horns. Of the twenty-four arias, eight are in D major—a good trumpet and drum key—and two in D minor; C major, also a good trumpet and drum key, is chosen for three arias, two of which feature these instruments, as does one of three others in C minor. The trumpet-drum combination in the major-mode arias recalls ceremonial fanfares, signaling the authority of courtly rule and military power, appropriated for comic bombast in the maestoso aria of Bartolo.

Osmin presents the more interesting case of rage defused by Mozart's music, and the only one for which we have the composer's words about his choice of keys and his intentions to make the rage comic. Referring to Osmin's F-major aria, "Solche hergelauf'ne Laffen" (*Die Entführung*, no. 3), in a letter to his father, Mozart explains that his choice of A minor for the unexpected coda was motivated by psychological realism: "A man in such a towering rage oversteps all order, measure, and limit; he does not know himself—so the music, too, must no longer know itself."[13] It goes without saying, apparently, that the uncontrolled rage of Osmin should be expressed in a minor key, whether or not it is the "more distant A minor" that Mozart chooses instead of the normative related key, D minor. Here the coda in the "wrong" key is given a further twist with the addition of "Turkish" instruments that mark Osmin as exotic—and comic—Other (see example 12.4). It is this same passage that returns to usher him off the stage at the end of the opera.

Whereas powerful males in *seria* roles are *en*raged, filled with the heat of their own "natural" human passions, Electra, Zaïde, and the Queen of the Night are literally and supernaturally "furious," their bodies invaded and consumed by the Furies, the goddesses of vengeance. The Queen of the Night will feel "Hell's vengeance boiling up in her heart,"[14] but for jealous rage there is nothing to match Electra, in *Idomeneo*, as she is overcome by the avenging Furies: "I feel you all in my breast, Furies of bitter Hades. Upon her who stole that heart from me, let my fury bring vengeance and cruelty."[15] A distinguishing marker of gender in these arias is the minor mode. Prepared to seek action and bloody revenge, men may rage at insubordination and disloyalty, or in jealousy and wounded pride at the rejection of a lover or intended. But by and large they do so in the stability of major keys, often in the same key as that of the opera as a whole, with clear boundaries of opening and closure, and with the promise of passion brought under control. In contrast, female characters who sing in minor keys are represented as overtaken in spite of themselves by invasive passions, be it jealousy (Arminda, Electra), oaths of murderous retribution (the Queen of the Night), or bold defiance in the face of tyranny (Zaïde). Their arias are less bounded, often slipping from accompanied recitative into aria without cadences to mark beginnings and endings. In this respect they reflect on a larger level the instability of the mutable minor mode itself.

Electra's "Tutte nel cor vi sento" (*Idomeneo*, no. 4) is a telling example. Here the key of the aria, D minor, opens up the dark side of the opera's "ruling" key, D major, and Mozart's unusual scoring for four horns amplifies the tension of an extended orchestral introduction. Thus set up, Electra's rage flows from the agitations of her preceding accompanied recitative, as resolution to the tonic is suspended until the explosive opening words of the aria proper (example 12.5a). Impressive as this storm of passion is, Electra's unstable emotions are betrayed in Mozart's treatment of the mutable minor mode. After unstable vacillations between F major and minor, she "forgets herself" at the critical juncture of thematic and tonal return, seizing upon C minor for an extended recall of opening material before regaining the appropriate tonic key of D minor[16] (example 12.5b). As different as the characters of Electra and Osmin are, Mozart's representation of their "towering rage" in minor-mode music that "forgets itself" marks both as unnatural Others.

Elsewhere I have explored eighteenth-century perceptions of the minor mode as feminine—the *moll* weak, unstable, and unnatural—in comparison with the Major's *dur*—strong, healthy, and built on the firm foundation of Rameau's "chord of nature."[17] Without rehearsing that data here, I might note simply some interesting correlations between mode and gender in Mozart's minor key arias. Not only are these associated with high voices, nearly always female ones, but also one finds that certain affective states tend to cluster around particular minor keys. Grieving, weeping laments are always assigned to women, and nearly always to the key of G minor. C minor is more broadly associated with darkness, fainting, and death; this is the key in which Ramiro (*La finta giardiniera*, no. 26) and Ferrando (*Così fan tutte*, no. 27) express their wounded feelings, vacillating between hate and love in arias of *contrasti d'affetti*. While D minor is here associated with the fury of avenging women, the sample is limited, for the D-minor arias of Electra and the Queen of the Night are the only ones in this key in all of Mozart's operas.

In his study of Mozart's use of D minor, Martin Chusid points out its association with vengeance that is supernatural.[18] *Don Giovanni* comes immediately to mind as an opera dominated by D minor from beginning to (nearly) the end, and by Donna Anna's single-mindedness in bringing her assailant and her father's murderer to justice. Whereas her first oath of revenge is sworn in a D-minor duet with Don Ottavio, she focuses her later call for vengeance in D major (*Don Giovanni*, no. 10), the sole rage aria in this key for a female character. While Chusid does not explore the relationship of mode to gender, he remarks that while divine retribution comes in D minor, in D-major vengeance "human elements alone are involved" (91–92). One might argue that Mozart's use of D major for Donna Anna's "Or sai chi l'onore" signals a future of stability, of order restored to the turbulent D-minor world of Don Giovanni. For she is resolute with righteous anger, "giusto furor," and moves in a broad and steady tempo in gradually rising sequences to demand action and justice (see example 12.6). If Osmin's minor-mode rage suggests some gender confusion, one might wonder if this heroic revenge aria figures Donna Anna as "unnaturally" masculine.

Typically, the minor key arias of Mozart's heroines represent "natural" passions of grieving in laments for their lovers, or fear and anxiety (the damsel in distress in comic genres). Indeed, these are the terms eighteenth-century theorists and composers used to describe the minor mode itself.[19] Such women reveal their constancy and hold up the model of faithful wives and lovers in a more passive role; they do not go out looking for blood. But either way, strong and defiant in arias of rage or tearful and fearful in arias of distress, the minor mode's association with weakness and the unnatural puts it in a position of difference, and presents an unsettling paradox for the constant heroine: in its chromatic mutability the minor mode is unpredictable, functionally *in*constant. Characters who escape the traditional expressive domain of constancy, such as Electra and the Queen of the Night, pay the price of being overtaken by unnatural, even supernatural, passions.

But supernatural fury would not do for a performance of constancy, nor would the minor mode. Let us return to the displays of outrage required of women as proof of their steadfastness. Whereas Mozart's men seethe and explode in jealous anger at perceived betrayals, his women must compose themselves for the performance of righteous indignation. If for Donna Anna this is a single-minded quest for justice and for Donna Elvira a temporary homicidal impulse (*Don Giovanni*, no. 3), for Konstanze it is a public display of resistance to the Pasha Selim's unwanted attentions and threats (*Die Entführung*, no. 10). It might seem a cruel irony that the more resistant she is, the more attractive he finds her. But perhaps it is part of her cultural assignment to promote the desirability of a fiercely faithful woman.[20]

In this company, the two sisters in *Così fan tutte* present a telling contrast. Whereas Dorabella gives way to a frenzy of excessive sensibility, Fiordiligi is required to put on an indignant show of resistance to the intrusion of their "foreign" suitors—their lovers in disguise. In their respective performances of "raging" constancy, Dorabella is surely the easier mark from the beginning. Building up to her aria in stock *seria*-style gestures in accompanied recitative, she insists that Despina and Fiordiligi "respect the madness of a desperate love."[21] Comparison of her aria, in E-flat major, allegro agitato, with Electra's "Tutte nel cor vi sento" is instructive. Like Electra, Dorabella is seized by the agitations of "implacable passions," but she invokes the Furies to "bear witness to a fatal love," not to seek revenge on another. If her passions are as horrible as she claims, approaching madness and supernatural proportions, she might better sing in D minor. Dorabella's aria does resemble Electra's in one respect, however, in that she misses her home key at the appropriate tonic return and continues "off-tonic" for several bars. But in comparison with Electra's surging ascents and upward leaps of a tenth from downward-striding arpeggios, Dorabella's breathless raving sounds a bit square and regular, even dancelike (see example 12.7). The "agitato" arises less from the vocal line of the character herself than from the ostinato figure of syncopated triplets in the accompanying instruments. The too-regular phrasing and resolutely diatonic major mode of her aria subvert the effect of high tragedy and expose the consuming Furies as mere hyperbole, dealing *seria* gestures into the hand of parody.

If Dorabella acts out a histrionic appeal to be left alone to her sorrow, her sister must register indignation at the impertinent advances of the strangers. Here's how Ferrando and Guglielmo set Fiordiligi up for her show of strength: after obligatory references to the God of Love, the two men settle on the metaphor of natural attraction, as of moths to light—represented here by "amorous suffering moths" attracted to the "bright sparks of your shining eyes." Musically the men work on the women's feelings in G minor, "imploring mercy" in a duet recitative that reaches its high note above a chromatic swell, with agitated syncopation, in the strings (see example 12.8). Whereas Fiordiligi seems unmoved, Dorabella turns to her for help: "Sister, what shall we do?" It is up to Fiordiligi, then, to display outrage for Dorabella's benefit and to ward off the taint of scandal. She turns to C major and the French overture topos to order the men out: "Do not let the ill-omened air of scandalous utterances profane our hearts, our ears, and our affections."[22] As Fiordiligi tries to put things back on the grounds of social propriety, the possibility of scandal becomes itself a suggestive natural image, as foul air exerting pressure on organs of sense and feeling. Terry Castle has explored the eighteenth-century vogue of the "female thermometer," which purported to measure the rising passions of women in the presence of men, their reactions being registered in calibrated readings ranging from modesty to lasciviousness.[23] One can imagine the mercury wavering uncertainly as Fiordiligi's harmonic motion hovers in minor harmonies and in vacillating figures of dotted neighbor notes (see example 12.9).

If in her recitative Fiordiligi's putatively "natural" weakness is betrayed in the less than steadfast atmosphere of changeable minor harmonies and unstable rhythmic support, she does work her way to a more confident voice in her B-flat-major aria, which brings the combined arsenal of andante maestoso, French overture style, and fully orchestrated scoring to the task of performing resolute constancy. Against all contemporary estimates of a woman's physiology and ontological status, she compares her besieged constancy to an immovable rock in a storm (example 12.10).

Mozart's listeners might well have regarded this comparison as more hyperbolic than the men's boasting, for Fiordiligi's performance of a constancy as solid as a rock strains credibility from the standpoint of medical expectations and diagnoses of her day. Indeed, a woman's constancy was guaranteed to be soft, by eighteenth-century measures of her physical and moral constitution. Women were judged to have a lower proportion of solids to liquids in their bodies than men; they were also seen as weaker in nerves and fibers, overly sensitive, and volatile in temperament—in short, overdetermined for both melancholy and a surfeit of sexual passion or hysteria.[24] Among received medical opinions of the mid-to-late eighteenth century was the view that hysteria was a concomitant of female sexuality. Philipe Hecquet registers a widespread assumption in his *Le naturalisme des convulsions* of 1733: "A disposition to hysteria is innate, natural and universal among women."[25] The physiological basis of hysteria lay in women's overly sensitive nervous system, which, in reacting to disturbances of the circulatory system, precipitated vapors or the hysterical affections. Lindsay Wilson has noted that hysteria was suspected as a sign of a woman's moral slippage, or, as Hecquet put it, of "the natural penchant of her sex toward seduction."[26] Various treatments were inflicted if it was suspected that an overactive imagination or vanity was the precipitating cause: in such cases Hecquet recommended isolation, intimidation, flagellation, and dunking in cold water until modesty was revived and the vapors dispelled.[27]

In a rather more subtle version of this preoccupation with women's innate predilections, Rousseau's emphasis on modesty and sexual restraint as a woman's natural qualities followed from a social project in which her reproductive imperative was to create desire, while her moral role was to civilize and control that desire[28]—thus the need to reiterate the message of constancy as woman's work. Admitting the potency of woman's sexuality would have additional implications, of course, in men's fears both of pleasure withheld and of women's sexuality beyond their control. Here's where the notion of a "naturally" modest femininity comes in, and that of woman's pliant sweetness as the ultimate civilizer of brutish, savage man. Yet the double bind remained: to prove pliant and yielding would be to enact the very inconstancy that men suspected in women generally: "Così fan tutte."

Irvin Singer, writing on the concept of love in the operas of Mozart and Beethoven, found in Fiordiligi's aria a split personality. Commenting on the extreme registers in "Come scoglio," he observes that it is "as if Fiordiligi contained two female voices within her ... for she is a divided woman, both psychologically and musically," and he locates in her "musical self-presentation a tendency to schizophrenia."[29] To locate a split personality here does not require the analysis of psychopathology, in my view, nor is this a question of vocal registers per se. If there are two voices, they are "split" in gender, and if there is a divide, it lies in Fiordiligi's double assignment. As a model of fidelity to inspire her sister, she must function as the rock-solid embodiment of unwavering love; then too, she must put on a convincing show of high dudgeon to discourage further advances from the amorous strangers. To fortify the impression of power, hers must be a more imposing and extended performance than Dorabella's display of frenzied sensibilities (symptomatic of hysteria, perhaps). Fiordiligi, like Donna Anna and Konstanze before her, must appropriate the imagery and gestures displayed in the maestoso stance of powerful raging men. A distinguishing marker of her gender and class remains, however, in the virtuosic display of her upper register—in which power she is allied not only with Konstanze but also with the Queen of the Night and the heroines of Mozart's *opere serie* before them.

Of course, in a more vulnerable and private moment, Fiordiligi will ultimately yield to Ferrando's ardent protestations of love. And in this she follows contemporary estimates of women as by nature responsive to the men they attract: even if not deliberately unfaithful, women were judged to be—literally—the weaker sex, physiologically less solid, their nervous fibers more pliant than men's. And, by extension or metaphoric implication, they tended to a weakness of moral fiber as a consequence.

In the end, Alfonso's distrust of the young lovers' claims to absolute fidelity is as true to eighteenth-century views of men's and women's natures as was the preoccupation with shoring up women's constancy. As this overview of Mozart's musical characterizations suggests, the performance of rage posed a dilemma of mixed messages in representations of constant women, messages that drew upon a broad range of musical conventions familiar to his listeners. In studying particular representations of rage and outrage, constancy and inconstancy, attention to constructions of gender can help to locate the import of "natural" and "unnatural" passions in the cultural assignments of his characters and the historical context in which they were heard.

Notes

1. *Così fan tutte*, no. 30: "Tutti accusan le donne,/ed io le scuso,/se mille volte al dì cangiano amore,/altri un vizio lo chiama,/ed altri un uso, ed a me par/necessità del core." The librettist, Lorenzo da Ponte, entitled his work simply "La scuola degli amanti," which Mozart adopted as subtitle for his opera. All translations are those of the author unless otherwise stated.
2. Among many studies of the opera, Bruce A. Brown's *W. A. Mozart: Così fan tutte*, Cambridge Opera Handbooks (Cambridge: Cambridge University Press, 1995), is a thoroughly documented treatment of the work's sources, historical context, and reception. Published after this essay was written, Mary Hunter's *The Culture of Opera Buffa in Mozart's Vienna* (Princeton, N.J.: Princeton University Press, 1999) provides a much needed broadening of perspective on Mozart's operas viewed in the context of the prevailing conventions and practices of his contemporaries.
3. *Così fan tutte*, no. 10a: "Nel mare solca,/e nell' arena semina,/e il vago vento/spera in rete accogliere/chi fonda sue speranze/in cor di femmina." Brown (*Mozart*, 69) traces this proverb to Jacopo Sannazaro's *L'Arcadia*, first published in 1504. The original of Fiordiligi's text in aria no. 14, discussed below, reads: "Come scoglio immoto resta/Contra i venti e la tempesta,/Così ognor quest' alma è forte/Nella fede e nell' amor."
4. *Die Entführung aus dem Serail*, act 2, no. 16: "Es lebe die Liebe.... Nichts fache das Feuer der Eifersucht an!" The libretto for this Singspiel was adapted by Gottlieb Stephanie from Christoph Friedrich Bretzner's *Belmont und Constanze, oder Die Entführung aus dem Serail*, published in 1781. In setting Stephanie's adaptation, Mozart himself made many changes, among them a considerably expanded role for Osmin. On the history of the libretto and the correspondence of Mozart with his father during its composition, see Brown, *Mozart*, 12–26.
5. *Die Entführung aus dem Serail*, act 3, no. 21: "Den edlen Mann entstellt die Rache/grossmütig, menschlich, gütig sein,/und ohne Eigennutz verzeih'n,/ist nur der grossen Seelen Sache."
6. Ibid. "Verbrennen sollte man die Hunde,/Die uns so schändlich hintergeh'n.... Erst geköpft, dann gehangen,/Dann gespießt auf heiße Stangen."
7. *Le nozze di Figaro*, act 2, scene 1: "Come lo sono/i moderni mariti: per sistema/infedeli, per genio capricciosi,/e per orgoglio poi tutti gelosi." Lorenzo Da Ponte's libretto, an adaptation of Beaumarchais's *Le mariage de Figaro*, was the first of three collaborations with Mozart, the others being *Don Giovanni* and *Così fan tutte*.
8. *Le nozze di Figaro*, act 3, sextet, no. 18. See also the very different reactions of Konstanze and Blonde to their respective lovers' suspicions in the act 2 quartet, no. 16, of *Die Entführung aus dem Serail*.
9. See John Platoff, "The Buffa Aria in Mozart's Vienna," *Cambridge Opera Journal* 2, no. 2 (July 1990): 99–120.
10. Wye Jamieson Allanbrook, in her *Rhythmic Gesture in Mozart: "Le Nozze di Figaro" and "Don Giovanni"* (Chicago: University of Chicago Press, 1983), 145, suggests that the impact of the Count's rage is undermined by the comedy of Bartolo's earlier misappropriation of *seria* style in the comic "La vendetta." One could argue, however, that the Count's rage becomes truly impressive once Bartolo's call for vengeance is exposed as ineffectual pomposity.
11. *Mitridate, rè di Ponto*, no. 17: "Già di pietà mi spoglio/anime ingrate, il seno:/per voi già sciolgo il freno,/perfidi, al mio furor." Loosely based on Racine's *Mitridate*, by the librettist Vittorio Amedeo Cigna-Santi, Mozart's opera was first performed in Milan in 1770.
12. *Lucio Silla*, no. 5: "Il desìo di vendetta e di morte/sì m'infiamma e sì m'agita il petto/che in quest'alma ogni debole affetto/disprezzato sì cangia in furor." *Lucio* was the second commission from Milan and was first performed there in 1772. The opera's libretto was by Giovanni de Gamberra.
13. From Mozart's letter to Leopold of 26 September 1781, in *Letters of Mozart and His Family*, ed. and trans. Emily Anderson, 2nd ed. (London: Macmillan, 1966), 768–69. Among many who have commented on this passage, see especially Thomas Bauman, *W. A. Mozart, "Die*

Entführung aus dem Serail," Cambridge Opera Handbooks (Cambridge: Cambridge University Press, 1987), 66–68.

14. *Die Zauberflöte*, no. 14: "Der Hölle Rache kocht in meinem Herzen,/Tod und Verzweiflung flammet um mich her!"

15. *Idomeneo*, no. 4: "Tutte nel cor vi sento/furie del crudo averno./… Chi mi rubò quel core,/quel che tradito ha il mio,/provin' dal mio furore,/vendetta e crudeltà." Composed for the electoral court in Munich and first performed there in 1781, the libretto of *Idomeneo*, by Giambattista Varesco, was based upon a French *tragédie lyrique* by Antoine Danchet. See Daniel Heartz, "The Genesis of Idomeneo," in *Mozart's Operas*, ed. Thomas Bauman (Berkeley and Los Angeles: University of California Press, 1990), 15–35.

16. Echoes of Electra's fury haunt the end of the opera as well, as she makes her final exit in D minor, though without benefit of an aria. Mozart originally intended the aria, "D'Oreste, d'Ajace," in C minor, for Electra at this point, but cut it in revisions to shorten the final act. Often sung in modern productions of the opera, this aria is a fitting reminder of Electra's background and of her madness as she embraces the "horned serpents" of Hades.

17. Gretchen A. Wheelock, "*Schwarze Gredel* and the Engendered Minor Mode in Mozart's Operas," in *Musicology and Difference: Gender and Sexuality in Music Scholarship*, ed. Ruth A. Solie (Berkeley and Los Angeles: University of California Press, 1993), 201–21.

18. Martin Chusid, "The Significance of D Minor in Mozart's Dramatic Music," *Mozart-Jahrbuch* 1965/66 (1967): 87–93.

19. See Wheelock, "*Schwarze Gredel*," 205–9. Rita Steblin's *A History of Key Characteristics in the Eighteenth and Early Nineteenth Centuries* (Ann Arbor: University of Michigan Press, 1983; reprint, Rochester, N.Y.: in Eastman Studies in Music, University of Rochester Press, 1996) explores various explanations for the pervasiveness of key associations throughout the eighteenth century, although she does not address the question of gender and mode. Evidence of the construction of a "feminine" minor mode can be found, however, in the extensive appendices to her book that document historical characterizations of major and minor keys, as I show in "*Schwarze Gredel*."

20. I address the cultural scripting of Konstanze's aria, "Martern aller Arten," in "Konstanze Performs Constancy," in *Siren Songs: Representations of Gender and Sexuality in Opera*, ed. Mary Ann Smart (Princeton, N.J.: Princeton University Press, 2000), 50–57.

21. *Così fan tutte*, no. 11: "Ah scostati! paventa il tristo affetto d'un disperato affetto!" Brown (*Mozart*, 65–66) notes Da Ponte's reliance on Ariosto's *Orlando furioso* here and elsewhere in the libretto of *Così*.

22. *Così fan tutte*, recitative before no. 14: "Temerari, sortite fuori di questo loco! e non profani l'alito infausto degli infami detti nostro cor, nostro orecchio, e nostri affetti!"

23. Terry Castle, "The Female Thermometer," in *The Female Thermometer: Eighteenth-Century Culture and the Invention of the Uncanny* (New York: Oxford University Press, 1995), 21–43. Noting that the mercury used in such instruments "established a connection with the theme of human temperament," Castle documents associations of the "mercurial personality" with women, who "were usually considered the primary embodiments of mercuriality—witnessed by their purported fickleness, emotional variability, and susceptibility to hysteria" (25).

24. Among numerous medical treatises of the period that address this subject, see especially P[ierre] Roussel, *Système physique et moral de la femme* … (1st ed. 1775; new ed., Paris 1803), 11–36; Andrew Wilson, *Medical Researches: Being an Enquiry into the Nature and Origin of Hysterics in the Female Constitution, and into the Distinction between that Disease and Hypochondriac or Nervous Disorders* … (London, 1776), 39–58; Bartolomeo Battisti, *Abhandlung von den Krankheiten des schönen Geschlechts* (Vienna, 1784), 1–6, 50–61, and 92–99; Carl Friedrich Pockels, *Versuch einer Charakteristik des weiblichen Geschlechts: Ein Sittengemaehlde des Menschen, des Zeitalters und des geselligen Lebens* …, 4 vols. (Hanover, 1797–1801), 1–57. The relation of medical perceptions of female physiology and temperament to musical representations of

female characters in opera requires a comprehensive and more nuanced study than is possible here; my observations in this essay are preliminary to that larger project.

25. Philippe Hecquet, *Le naturalisme des convulsions dans les maladies de l'épidémie convulsionnaire* (Soleure, 1733), 181; quoted in Lindsay Wilson, *Women and Medicine in the French Enlightenment* (Baltimore, Md.: Johns Hopkins University Press, 1993), 27.

26. Hecquet, *Le naturalisme*, part 2, 28; Wilson, *Women and Medicine*, 29.

27. One wonders about the true origins of the cold shower. Hecquet, 112; Wilson, *Women and Medicine*, 29.

28. For discussion of this point, see Maurice Bloch and Jean H. Bloch, "Women and the Dialectics of Nature in Eighteenth-Century French Thought," in *Nature, Culture, and Gender*, ed. Carol P. MacCormack and Marilyn Strathern (Cambridge: Cambridge University Press, 1980), 25–41. See also Joel Schwartz, *The Sexual Politics of Jean-Jacques Rousseau* (Chicago: University of Chicago Press, 1984).

29. Irvin Singer, *Mozart and Beethoven: The Concept of Love in their Operas* (Baltimore, Md.: Johns Hopkins University Press, 1977), 97. Quoted in Andrew Steptoe, *The Mozart-Da Ponte Operas* (New York: Oxford University Press, 1988), 222.

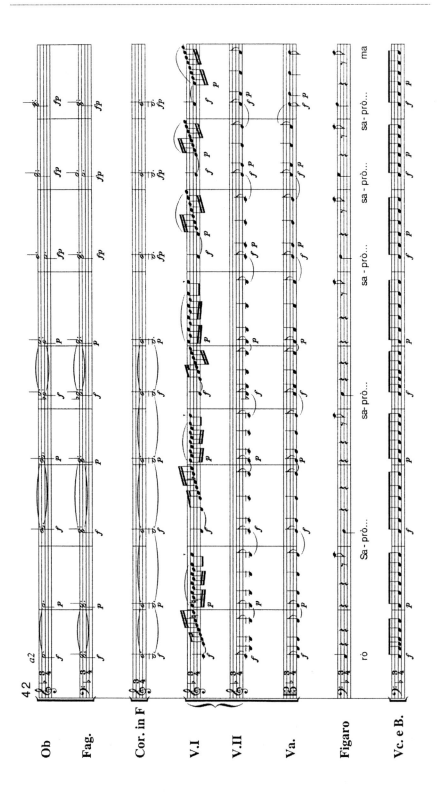

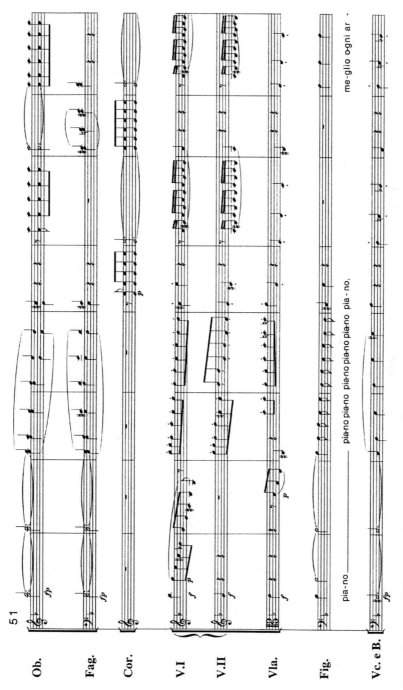

Example 12.1 Wolfgang Amadeus Mozart, *Le nozze di Figaro*, no. 3, mm. 42–71

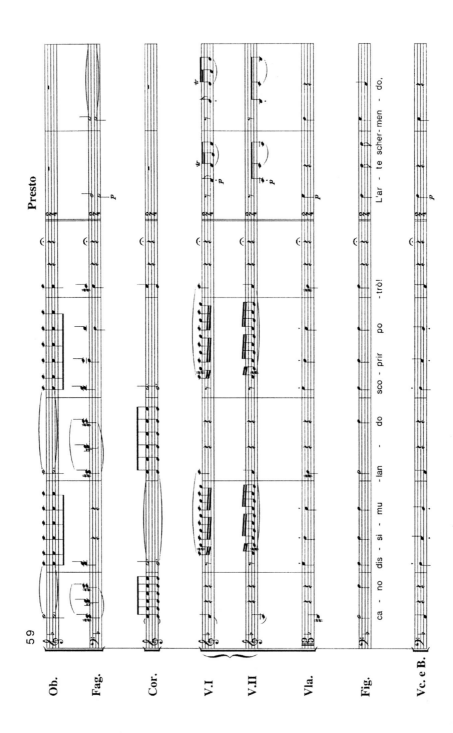

Example 12.1 Wolfgang Amadeus Mozart, *Le nozze di Figaro*, no. 3, mm. 42–71 *(cont.)*

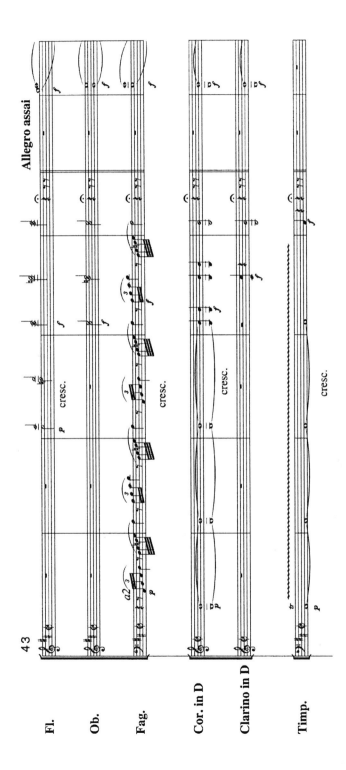

Example 12.2 Wolfgang Amadeus Mozart, *Le nozze di Figaro*, no. 18, mm. 43–66

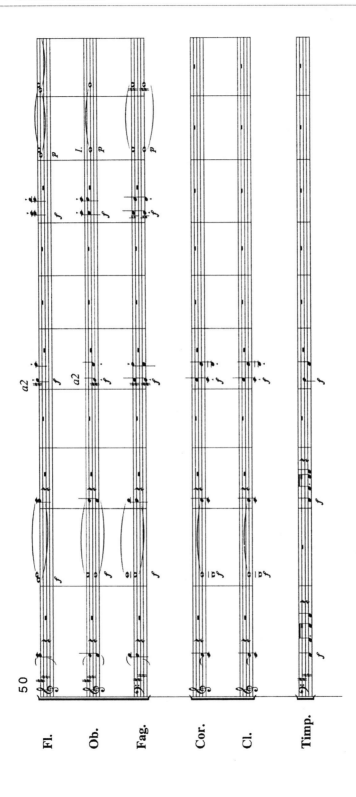

Example 12.2 Wolfgang Amadeus Mozart, *Le nozze di Figaro*, no. 18, mm. 43–66 *(cont.)*

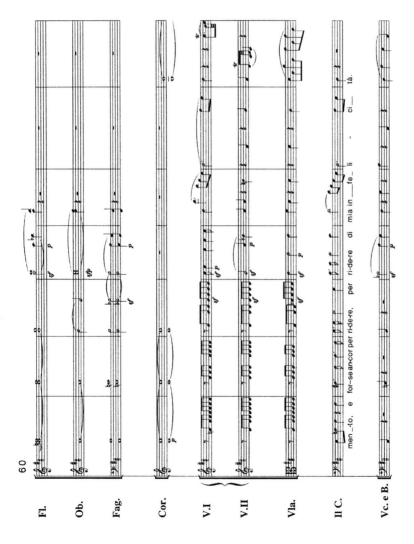

Example 12.2 Wolfgang Amadeus Mozart, *Le nozze di Figaro*, no. 18, mm. 43–66 *(cont.)*

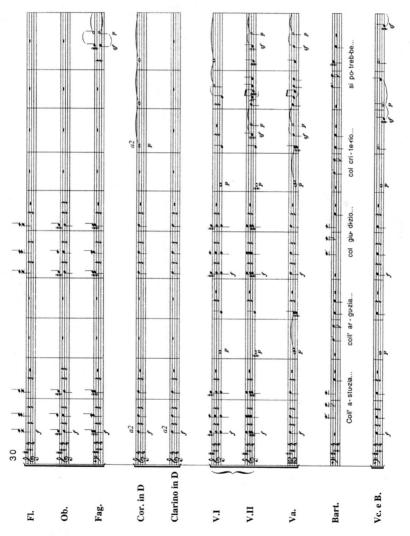

Example 12.3 Wolfgang Amadeus Mozart, *Le nozze di Figaro*, no. 4, mm. 30–50

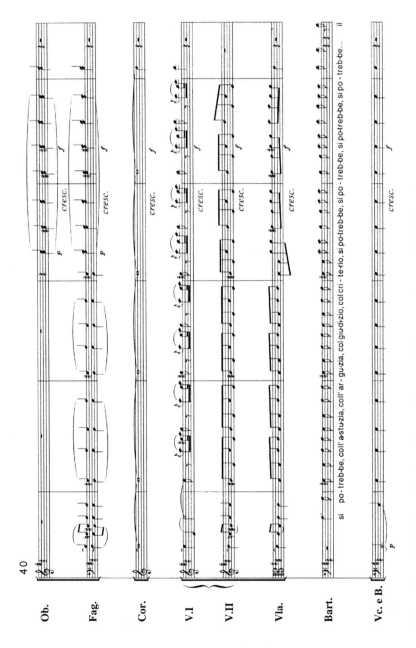

Example 12.3 Wolfgang Amadeus Mozart, *Le nozze di Figaro*, no. 4, mm. 30–50 *(cont.)*

Example 12.3 Wolfgang Amadeus Mozart, *Le nozze di Figaro*, no. 4, mm. 30–50 *(cont.)*

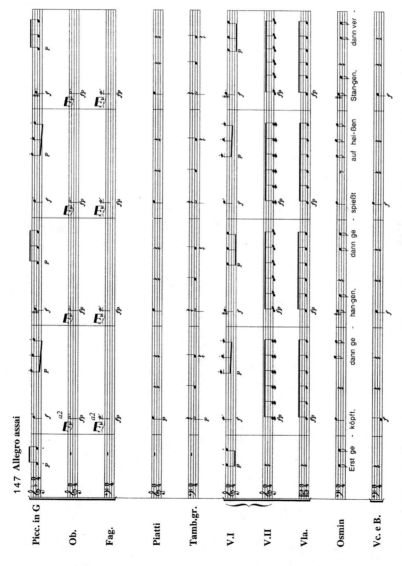

Example 12.4 Wolfgang Amadeus Mozart, *Die Entführung aus dem Serail*, no. 3, mm. 143–151

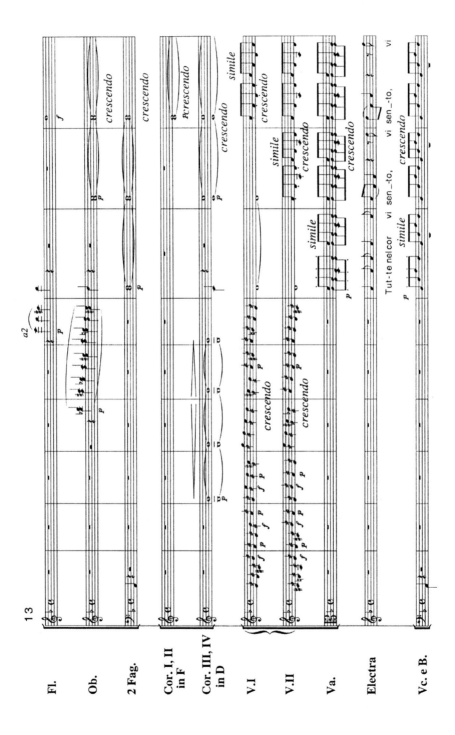

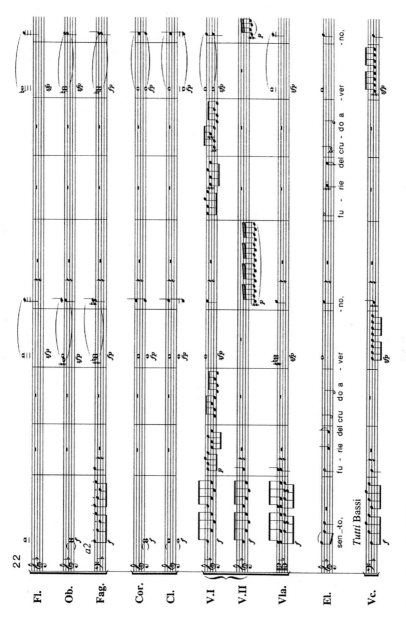

Example 12.5a Wolfgang Amadeus Mozart, *Idomeneo*, no. 4, mm. 13–30

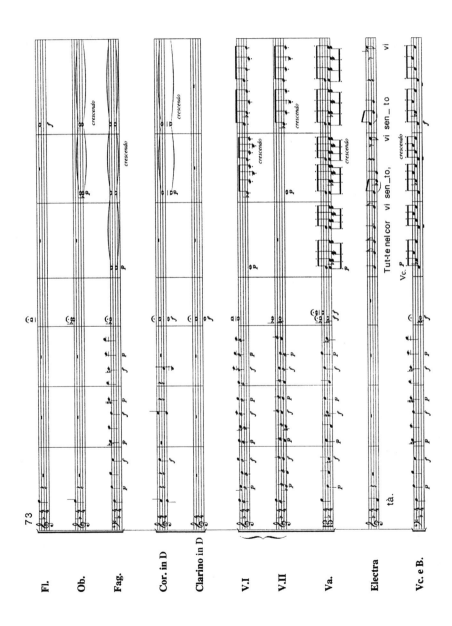

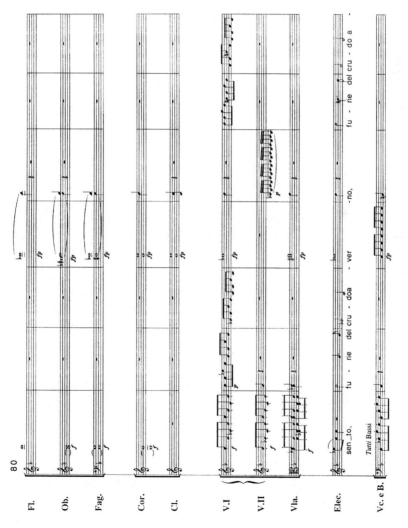

Example 12.5b Wolfgang Amadeus Mozart, *Idomeneo*, no. 4, mm. 73–90

Example 12.5b Wolfgang Amadeus Mozart, *Idomeneo*, no. 4, mm. 73–90 *(cont.)*

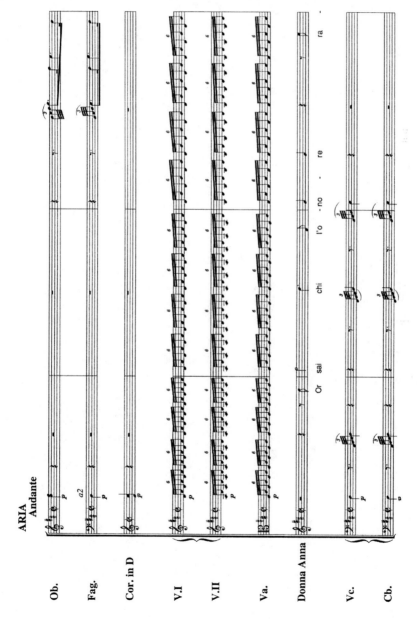

Example 12.6 Wolfgang Amadeus Mozart, *Don Giovanni*, no. 10, mm. 1–6

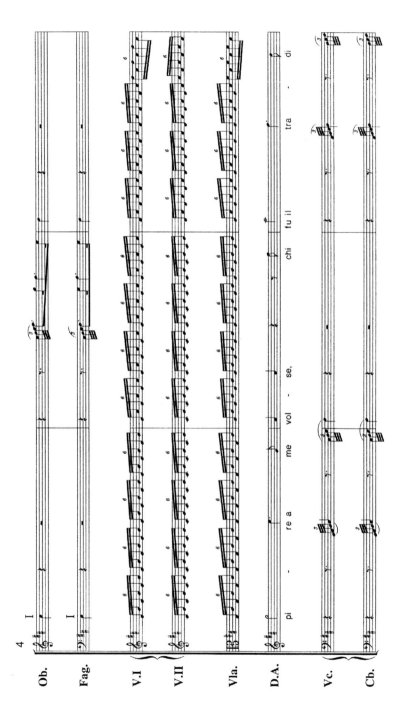

Example 12.6 Wolfgang Amadeus Mozart, *Don Giovanni*, no. 10, mm. 1–6 (*cont.*)

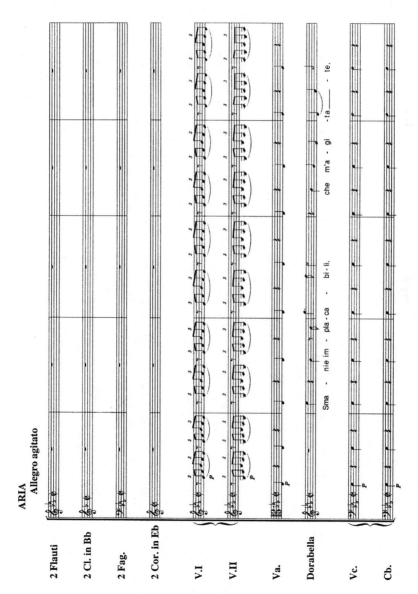

Example 12.7 Wolfgang Amadeus Mozart, *Così fan tutte*, no. 11, mm. 1–15

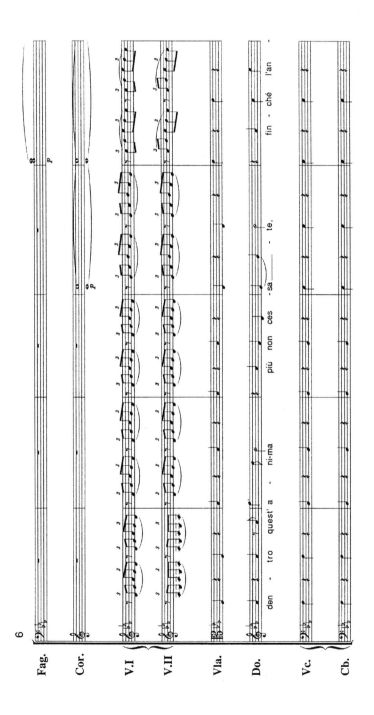

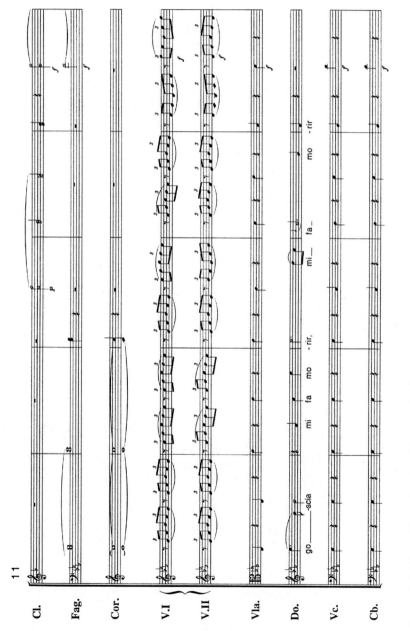

Example 12.7 Wolfgang Amadeus Mozart, *Così fan tutte*, no. 11, mm. 1–15 *(cont.)*

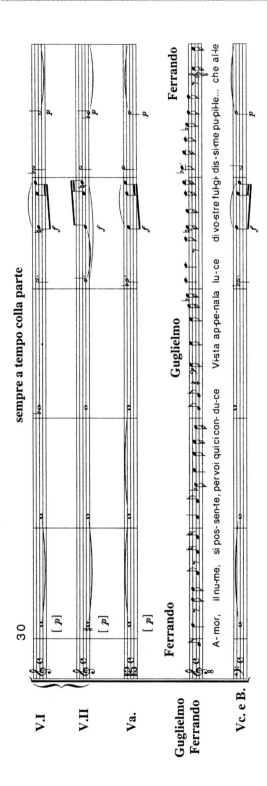

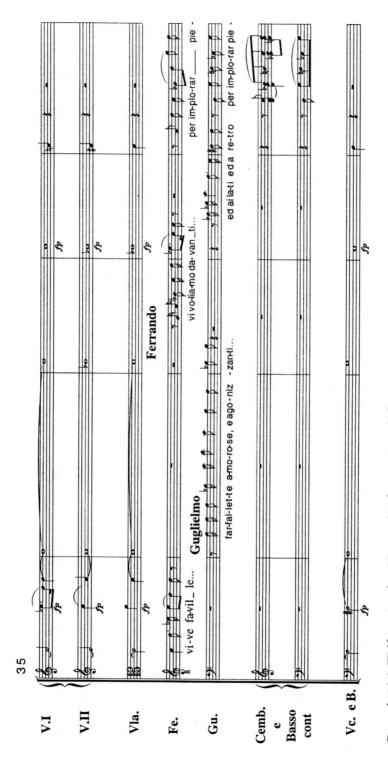

Example 12.8 Wolfgang Amadeus Mozart, *Così fan tutte*, Recit. before no. 14, mm. 30–42

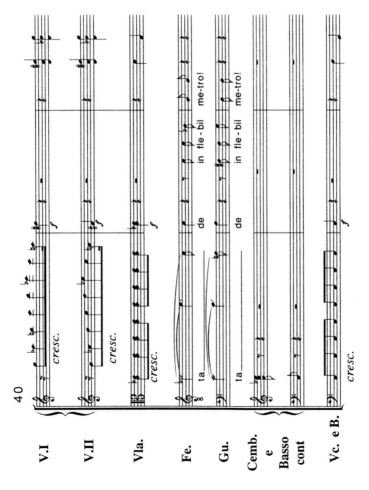

Example 12.8 Wolfgang Amadeus Mozart, *Così fan tutte*, Recit. before no. 14, mm. 30–42 *(cont.)*

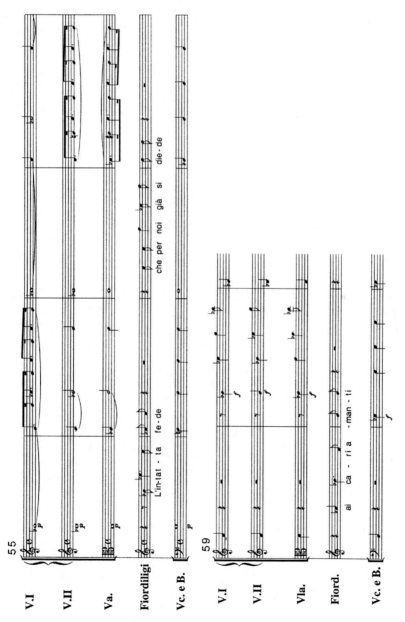

Example 12.9 Wolfgang Amadeus Mozart, *Così fan tutte*, no. 14, mm. 55–60

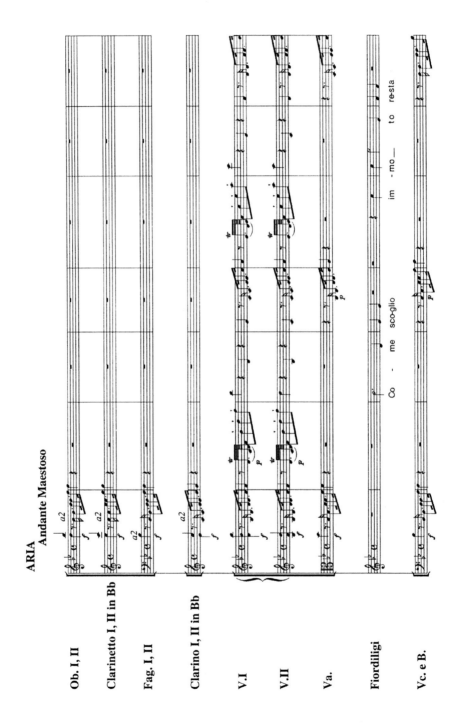

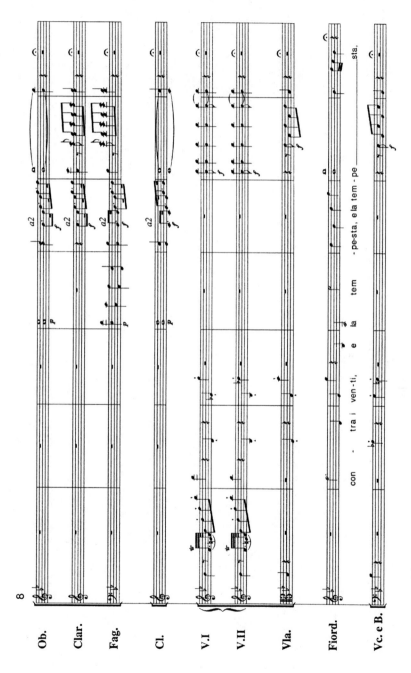

Example 12.10 Wolfgang Amadeus Mozart, *Così fan tutte*, no. 14, mm. 1–14

Part Four

SOME MAJOR TRANSFORMATIONS OF THE NINETEENTH AND TWENTIETH CENTURIES

Chapter 13

KARL GOLDMARK'S OPERAS DURING THE DIRECTORSHIP OF GUSTAV MAHLER

Peter Revers

During the late nineteenth century, Karl Goldmark was among the most internationally celebrated of Viennese composers. Goldmark's opera *The Queen of Sheba* premiered on 10 March 1875, under the baton of Johann Herbeck, Director of the Viennese Hofoper from 1870 to 1875. The work was a huge success, and performances in many European cities followed. Goldmark's centrality as a canonic figure seemed secure. Yet today only a few works by Goldmark are still performed with any regularity—exceptions might include the program symphony *Ländliche Hochzeit* op. 26 (Rural Wedding, 1876), and the Violin Concerto in A, op. 28 (1877).

The Queen of Sheba fit well into the atmosphere of splendid and luxurious settings that was typical of the early *Ringstrassen* period, which was open to lavish eclecticism. Goldmark represented perfectly the glitter and pomp of the late Habsburg monarchy. It was these same attributes that caused a negative reassessment of Goldmark during the early twentieth century. For example, Walther Niemann characterized Goldmark as a "one-sided colorist," denying him any relevance in the development of music after Wagner.[1] Indeed, while Goldmark's music summed up stylistic tendencies of late romanticism, it lacked the innovative tendencies of modernism; as a result, Goldmark's music had gone out of fashion during his own lifetime.

But the early twentieth century was not the first time that Goldmark had received strong negative criticism. In fact, negative criticism begins with Goldmark's contemporaries in the late nineteenth century. The most noteworthy of Goldmark's early critics was the German philosopher Friedrich Nietzsche (1844–1900). In the second postscript to his 1888 essay "The Case of Wagner,"

Nietzsche makes it clear that, although the master of Bayreuth has made a substantial contribution to the downfall of German culture, one could find no better alternative among his contemporaries or followers. As Nietzsche sums it up: "Other musicians don't count compared to Wagner. Things are bad generally. Decay is universal."[2] It is noteworthy that Nietzsche's treatment of other musicians focuses on two composers, Johannes Brahms and Karl Goldmark. He accuses Brahms of suffering from a "melancholy of incapacity," although he at least bothers to formulate some nuanced thoughts about him. With Goldmark, the commentary amounts to little more than a short, thoroughly devastating attack; Nietzsche describes him as one of the "clever apes of Wagner ...: with the *Queen of Sheba* one belongs in a zoo—one can make an exhibit on oneself."[3] As exaggerated as this judgment may sound, it succinctly articulates a component of Goldmark's music that substantially characterized or at least influenced its reception: the accusation of a styleless amalgamation, thoughtless eclecticism, or even the opinion that Goldmark possessed a stupendous ability in orchestral technique, but that he essentially lacked originality. This artistic decadence could hardly be described more pointedly than in a review by Richard Batka of Goldmark's 1896 opera *Das Heimchen am Herd* (after Charles Dickens's 1842 *The Cricket on the Hearth*): "That, then, was the 'Glück und Ende' [auspicious rise and fall] of the celebrated Goldmark. His arrival as a composer and his downfall as an artist in the higher sense of the word ..., fragments of an artist showing signs of a state of peace slowly returning to music after years of pseudo-Wagnerian noises of war, yet no important, lasting achievement,... no solid, organically mature work of art."[4]

Karl Goldmark (1830–1915), the aging composer losing his artistic power, had become world famous twenty years earlier with *The Queen of Sheba* and had been among the internationally recognized artists of the monarchy. Batka's analysis, written a year before Mahler's directorship of the Vienna Opera and certainly not coincidentally echoing Grillparzer's drama *König Ottokars Glück und Ende*, not only documents the downfall of a highly regarded artist; it also points to the crisis that Wagner's followers felt in trying to develop a substantively and qualitatively worthy successor to the Wagnerian model of music drama. It is, in fact, Wagner who largely set the standard for Goldmark's reception. The reactions to the 1896 premiere of *Das Heimchen am Herd* once again point to the degree to which an appreciation of Goldmark in fact represented an evaluation of Wagner. Though Eduard Hanslick does not fail to mention the paucity of melodic invention or the obvious reliance on Albert Lortzing and Carl Ditters von Dittersdorf, he cites the "turning away of modern 'music drama' from... Wagner's supposedly monolithic dramatic system"[5] as something positive about Goldmark's work. Arthur Seidl, in a chapter denigratingly entitled "Fashion and Experiment (Pseudo-Wagnerians)" from his 1902 monograph *Die Wagner-Nachfolge im Musik-Drama* (Wagner's Disciples in Music Drama), refers to this opera as the epitome of typically run-of-the-mill productions and an unscrupulous sellout of the achievements of Wagnerian music drama.[6]

In light of these extremes, ranging from qualified praise (Hanslick) to a devastating aesthetic verdict (Batka, Seidl), Gustav Mahler's reaction to the opera, the first he conducted during his tenure in Hamburg, sounds positively upbeat. Mahler wrote to Goldmark on 12 January 1897, "The performances of *Heimchen* are a veritable oasis in the desert for me in my present position [in Hamburg]; they are of the same high level as ever and continue to be met with acclaim by the audience (the entr'acte always has to be repeated)."[7] At first glance the reasons for Mahler's enthusiasm are obvious; they are closely connected with his requests to Goldmark to intervene on his behalf in his application for the post of conductor at the Vienna Court Opera, a job that would serve as a stepping-stone to an appointment later as director of that house. In the space of three weeks Mahler wrote three urgent letters to the highly renowned Goldmark (letters of 23 December 1896, 4 and 12 January 1897) encouraging him to use his influence.[8] Ludwig Karpath, a relative of Goldmark, summed up the situation in his memoirs:

> Mahler had made a mistake. In the belief that more is better than less, he approached too many people to help him out. Only later did he realize that some of the people he had called upon, though supportive of him and important personalities in their own right, had no influence in the proper circles to intervene on his behalf. One of these men was Carl Goldmark, who, because of performances of his works in Hamburg, was very friendly with Mahler.... Now, the will was certainly there, but Goldmark was a shy, inwardly directed person who underestimated his own influence; it is certain that he undertook nothing substantial in Mahler's cause.[9]

In fact, after learning of Goldmark's passivity in this matter, Mahler took a markedly more distanced position toward him; his judgment of Goldmark's operas, too, underwent a profound transformation: "*Merlin* also deeply disappointed me and I never liked the Ouverture to *Sakuntala*. The only exception is *Die Königin von Saba* [The Queen of Sheba], for I must admit that the first two acts enchant me.... The rest of Goldmark's music is superficial and its witty orchestration and instrumentation do not save it. Brahms was of the same opinion."[10] It would, however, be unfair and inaccurate to attribute Mahler's far more critical attitude toward Goldmark solely to a case of personal disappointment. Rather, it reflects a crisis of German comic opera in the late nineteenth century, for which Goldmark's *Heimchen am Herd* is a paradigmatic example. Mahler articulated the problems associated with this genre quite clearly during preparations for the Viennese production of Emil Nikolaus von Reznicek's *Donna Diana* (which premiered on 9 December 1898). In rehearsing the work (probably at the end of October) he wrote to the composer: "More impulsion and melody! Not recitative, but musical peaks! Dear Reznicek! Do it quickly and send it straight away!"[11]

"Melody—not recitative": this sums up in a few words what was expected of comic opera, meant to be on the compositional level of Wagnerian music drama yet free from all pathos and exaggerated weightiness. The main, admittedly diverse, elements of the genre combined sophisticated melodic shape, progressive harmony, and, above all, a highly developed orchestral technique on the one hand with a Singspiel tradition (especially in the manner of Lortzing) that nevertheless avoided an all-too-obvious simplicity. These qualities, perhaps not surprisingly, proved volatile, vacillating precariously between two risks and doubtlessly constituting one of the decisive reasons that comic opera from this period was not able to retain its place in the repertoire. Even the important function of social integration associated with the comic opera, namely to represent an art form that brought together social classes of differing educations and interests, could be fulfilled only to a diminishing degree. This task was instead increasingly assigned to the operetta, which by now was becoming the main comic genre. *Heimchen am Herd*, while at the end of the nineteenth century "one of the most successful operas in Central Europe,"[12] disappeared almost entirely from the playbill after 1920.

A good example of the idyllic simplicity of this opera (based on a libretto by Alfred Maria Willner after Dickens) is the aria of Dot, happily married and living with the postilion John: in a conversation with herself and the cricket she reveals that she is expecting a child (example 13.1). The predictable and pervasive two-measure groupings coincide with a generally uniform triplet motion that continues uninterrupted until just before the imitation of the cricket with its characteristic recitative singing style (example 13.2). In the exceptionally conventional formal scheme, the B section (the contrasting interjection of the cricket) is followed by the reprise of an almost unchanged musical diction resembling the tone of the "Spielopern" of Lortzing. Indeed, only the harmony, with its chromatic inflections, suspensions, and chains of seventh chords, begins to approach the compositional situation of the late nineteenth century.

The Queen of Sheba was not only Goldmark's most successful opera; it can rightfully be called one of the most beloved musical dramatic works of the last quarter of the nineteenth century. An important precedent set for the work before its long-delayed premiere (due to numerous reworkings and cuts) was a successful concert performance of the close of the first act ("Festlicher Einzugsmarsch der Königin von Saba") under the baton of Otto Dessoff on 11 January 1874, a concert that doubtlessly represented one of the high points of concert life in Vienna at that time as it included appearances by both Franz Liszt and Johannes Brahms. After its sensational premiere on 10 March 1875 at the Vienna Court Opera (with Amalie Materna in the title role), the opera became standard repertory; by 1897 it had received a hundred performances. During Gustav Mahler's reign *The Queen of Sheba* was first produced on 20 April 1901, with Anna Bahr-Mildenburg in the title role and Selma Kurz as Astaroth. Among the changing cast in the following years we find above all Leo Slezak's debut as Assad on 21 May 1904.

The immediate impact of Goldmark's *The Queen of Sheba* was not only due to the opulence of its props, its tendency toward exotic splendor, and the marches and crowd scenes drawn from the tradition of grand opera (especially apparent in the finale of the first act, the "Entrance of the Queen of Sheba"). Equally essential was Goldmark's effort at creating a compositional style that captured an

Example 13.1 Karl Goldmark, *Ein Geheimnis, wundersüss,* from *Das Heimchen am Herd*

atmosphere of exotic charm. Both scenic and musical components are central to the reception history of this opera; both also articulate a social consciousness that come emphatically to the surface for the first time with Mahler's production of the opera. Despite the hugely successful performances, the antisemitic press not only accosted Mahler for the high cost of the production (approximately ten thousand crowns), but also accused him of dedicating too much time and effort to presenting a second-rank work, while not paying sufficient attention to such German composers as Weber, Cornelius, and Wolf.[13] Hans Puchstein of the *Deutsches Volksblatt* censured in unabashedly racist terms Mahler's increasing tendency to "launch new productions of older operas that, of course, must be mainly

Example 13.2 Karl Goldmark, *Ein Geheimnis, wundersüss* (continued), from
Das Heimchen am Herd

written by composers of a certain race."[14] Even if such critiques are isolated and
do not outweigh the largely positive reception of Goldmark's opera, they are
nevertheless symptomatic of a cultural, social, and political attitude that doubt-
less had more than a little to do with the fact that *The Queen of Sheba* disappeared
entirely from the repertoire of the Vienna Opera after 1937 (sadly, never to
appear again). A further striking component of the work's reception history
relates to its musical stylization of the exotic. Hanslick dismissed the "Oriental,
Jewish tunes whose sickly whining to a great extent spoiled for us the undeniable

beauty of this opera," citing these moments as the central weakness of the work.[15] In truth, this critique at best concerns only a few exposed passages. Goldmark was far more concerned with creating a mixed style derived from Oriental *couleur locale* and the conventions of late Romantic opera. He explained his compositional technique with an example from the temple scene (finale) of act 2:

> To musically educated Europeans, oriental music as a whole sounds alike, with only the well-known difference in scales and minor cadences peculiar to it. I had reached the conclusion that the musical style adopted to picture the grove of the Indian penitents in the *Sakuntala* could not be used to portray the magnificent court; that the music appropriate to either scene would not be appropriate to interpret the Arabian *Queen of Sheba*, or for Astharoth's love call. And still all had to have an oriental character, only each one must be different from the others. Then there was another special difficulty: I wanted the temple hymns with their original coloring nevertheless to express a sense of consecration and religious feeling to people familiar only with European music. The problem was to accomplish this without making use of Protestant chorale or any of the Catholic hymns to the Virgin. I had never been in the Orient, but intuition helped me over this lack.[16]

In this final scene a strangely revolving melody emerges along with a harmonic underpinning consisting of parallel triads; the characteristic effect is exotically colored yet fits unproblematically into the conventional aural category of ritual music (example 13.3). Even the most exotic sounding passages (such as Astharoth's seductive vocalises), though new to the Viennese public, demonstrate astounding parallels with a musical work that can be described as a milestone in the effective use of compositional techniques to suggest foreignness, namely Felicien David's symphonic ode *Le désert* which premiered in 1844 (examples 13.4a and 13.4b).

The performances of *The Queen of Sheba* unquestionably constitute the high point of Mahler's efforts on behalf of Goldmark's operas, especially as the opera was taken back into production in 1904 (with the premiere on 25 May) and the previously cut love duet was reinstated at the end of act 4. By comparison, the

Example 13.3 Karl Goldmark, *The Queen of Sheba*, Act II (Scene 5)

Example 13.4a Karl Goldmark, *The Queen of Sheba*

world premiere of *The Captive Maiden* on 17 January 1899 met with no success at all. Mahler's conducting effort was universally hailed as being the best one could find, yet the opera was perceived as an unqualified failure. Hanslick, for instance, noted that *The Captive Maiden* in no way fulfilled its high expectations, and he sharply criticized the "sung declamation over an unrelenting polyphony in the orchestra" and the "monotonous agitation" this produced.[17] In fact, the work was struck from the program after only six performances. Despite sometimes massive interventions on behalf of presenting further Goldmark operas (especially *Götz von Berlichingen*), Mahler's interest in Goldmark ebbed noticeably. The rejection of *Götz*, as well as his advice to Goldmark to pass along the performance of *Merlin* to Frankfurt, documents Mahler's clear-sightedness with regard to the enormous qualitative differences in the level of Goldmark's musical dramatic works. We will have to wait to see whether recent initiatives such as the

Example 13.4b Félicien David, *Le Désert*

production of the opera *Merlin* at the City Theater of Trier in Germany (which premiered on 8 June 1997) and a planned compact disc will lead to an intensified interest in the forgotten operas of Goldmark.

Goldmark's musical dramatic oeuvre is difficult to summarize succinctly. It consists of a diversity of styles and idioms that, though crafted with superb accomplishment, rarely attain a profound richness of musical expression; ultimately, it was this lack of focus that most weakened the value of his works, for they could hardly be integrated into a convincing compositional and dramaturgical whole: Istvan Kecskemeti's search for Goldmark's musical identity might also provide an answer to the increasingly difficult task of clearly localizing the composer's art: "What kind of composer was Goldmark? Austrian? German? Hungarian? Jewish? Goldmark probably regarded himself as all of these in one—an assumption based on his memoirs, and even more convincingly on his oeuvre."[18]

Notes

1. Walter Niemann, *Die Musik seit Wagner* (Berlin, 1913), 70–71.
2. Friedrich Nietzsche, *The Birth of Tragedy* and *The Case of Wagner*, trans. Walter Kaufmann (New York, 1967), 186. "Andere Musiker kommen gegen Wagner nicht in Betracht. Es steht schlimm überhaupt. Der Verfall ist allgemein." Friedrich Nietzsche, *Der Fall Wagner*, ed. Giorgio Colli and Mazzino Montinari, Kritische Studienausgabe, vol. 6 (Munich, 1988), 46.
3. Nietzsche, *The Case of Wagner*, 188.
4. Richard Batka, *Musikalische Streifzüge* (Florence and Leipzig, 1899), 167: "Das also war des gefeierten Goldmark Glück und Ende. Sein Glück als Componist und sein Ende als Künstler in des Wortes höherer Bedeutung …, Fragmente eines Künstlers, Symptome des langsamen Friedens in der Musik nach jahrelangem pseudo-wagnerischen Kriegslärm, aber keine bedeutsame, nachwirkende That,… kein gefügtes, organisch-ausgereiftes Kunstwerk." All translations are those of the author unless otherwise stated.
5. Eduard Hanslick, *Das Heimchen am Herde*, in *Am Ende des Jahrhunderts 1895–1899* (Berlin, 1899), 14: "… die Abkehr vom modernen 'Musikdrama', vom angeblich alleinseligmachenden dramatischen … System Wagners."
6. Arthur Seidl, *Die Wagner-Nachfolge im Musik-Drama* (Berlin and Leipzig, 1902), 207–13.
7. Gustav Mahler, *Briefe*, ed. Herta Blaukopf (Vienna and Hamburg, 1982), 189f.: "Eine wahre Oase in der Wüste meiner hiesigen [Hamburger] Tätigkeit sind für mich die Aufführungen des 'Heimchens', welche sich nach wie vor auf ihrer Höhe halten, und unter der begeisterten Teilnahme des Publikums vor sich gehen (das Zwischenspiel jedesmal da capo)."
8. Ibid.
9. Ludwig Karpath, *Begegnungen mit dem Genius* (Vienna and Leipzig, 1934), 33: "Mahler hatte einen Fehler begangen: in dem Glauben, daß doppelt besser hält, nahm er zuviel Leute in Anspruch, die ihm helfen sollten. Erst später gelangte er zu der Erkenntnis, daß er einige, wenn auch ihm gutgesinnte und bedeutende Persönlichkeiten zu Hilfe gerufen hatte, die an den entscheidenden Stellen einflußlos waren, geeignete Schritte für ihn zu unternehmen. Einer dieser Männer war Carl Goldmark, der gelegentlich der Aufführung seiner Werke in Hamburg mit Mahler sehr befreundet wurde.… Nun, der Wille war ja zweifellos vorhanden, aber Goldmark war eine scheue, in sich gekehrte Natur, er unterschätzte auch seinen Einfluß, sicher ist, daß er zu Gunsten Mahlers kaum etwas Wesentliches unternommen hatte."
10. Natalie Bauer-Lechner, *Mahleriana* (February 1898), cited in Henry-Louis de La Grange, *Gustav Mahler*, vol. 2 (Oxford, 1995), 139f.
11. La Grange, *Gustav Mahler*, 131.
12. Hans Joachim Bauer, "Karl Goldmark: Das Heimchen am Herd," in *Pipers Enzyklopädie des Musiktheaters*, vol. 2 (Munich: Piper, 1987), 486.
13. *Deutsche Zeitung*, 23 April 1901.
14. *Deutsches Volksblatt*, 30 April 1901: "Neueinstudierung von älteren Opern, die natürlich vornehmlich von Componisten der bekannten Race geschrieben sein müssen."
15. Eduard Hanslick, *Merlin: Oper in drei Akten von Karl Goldmark*, in *Musikalisches Skizzenbuch* (Berlin, 1888), 81: "orientalisch-jüdische Weisen, deren krankes Gewimmer uns die unleugbaren Schönheiten dieser Oper stark verleidet hat."
16. Karl Goldmark, *Notes from the Life of a Viennese Composer: Karl Goldmark* (New York, 1927), 210.
17. Eduard Hanslick, *Die Kriegsgefangene*, in *Aus neuer und neuester Zeit* (Berlin, 1900), 8f.: "die gesungene Deklamation über einer unablässig wühlenden Polyphonie im Orchester sowie die daraus resultierende monotone Unruhe."
18. Istvan Kecskemeti, "Liturgical Elements in the Opera *The Queen of Sheba* by Karl Goldmark," in *Essays in Honor of Hanoch Avenary*, Orbis musicae, *Assaph Studies in Arts*, no. 10 (1990/91), 230.

Chapter 14

A BREAK IN THE SCENIC TRADITIONS
OF THE VIENNA COURT OPERA

Alfred Roller and the Vienna Secession

Evan Baker

Through Gustav Mahler's tireless and persistent efforts, by the beginning of the twentieth century the Vienna Court Opera had become the center of operatic production in Europe. Intendants, stage directors, and designers all flocked to Vienna to study the new staging styles and methods of production. However, the progressive aesthetics of the Court Opera did not achieve its full effectiveness until the final years of Mahler's directorship. Three productions stood out as precursors of new scenic styles that would greatly influence future operatic staging. These were *Tristan und Isolde* (1903), *Fidelio* (1904), and, most important, the production of *Don Giovanni* (1905). Each of these productions was staged by Mahler and his colleague Alfred Roller, a founder of the great art movement, the Secession.[1]

When Mahler took charge of the Vienna Court Opera in 1897, the state of the scenic arts and stage direction was stagnant and staunchly bound to pictorial realism. Adherence to the past traditions reigned supreme. Franz Gaul, longtime costume designer and director of production (*Chef der Ausstattungswesens*), attempted to slow Mahler's reforms and was forced into retirement in 1900. Shortly thereafter Heinrich Lefler, a founding member of *Hagenbund*, another and lesser-known Viennese art movement, was named to the post. Anton Brioschi, the third generation in the dynasty of artists and designers at the Court Opera, remained in his position as scenic designer and painter. Mahler himself would stage some of the new productions. He had great expectations, hoping to push the visual styles of the Court Opera into new, different, and exciting directions. But Mahler continued to be frustrated. Although Lefler initiated some scenic reforms and innovations including a large turntable for the stage, he seemed unable to translate Mahler's unique aesthetic ideas of staging into practice. Indeed, Hugo von Hofmannsthal noted in a letter to Alexander von Zemlinsky in 1901: "I fear that what [Mahler] is lacking,... [is] the imagination of the eye. He has a poor understanding of the [visual] genre...."[2] It was not until one year later that Mahler met an artist who understood and shared his views of operatic production. That artist was Alfred Roller, then President of the Secession and a highly respected Professor at the School for the Applied Arts (Kunstgewerbeschule), where he taught the techniques of graphic arts.

* * * * *

How did the Secession affect the scenic arts? Before 1897, the aesthetic values of the Viennese bourgeoisie relating to the visual arts were dominated by the tastes and styles of the Austrian painter Hans Makart and his circle. His paintings espoused historical scenes with the lavish decorative elements, rich and lush colors, muted lighting, and emphasis placed on the sensual. In this, Makart achieved a superficial form of *Gesamtkunstwerk*. No intellectual stimulus was provided or desired. No literary grounding or any kind of theme was present in Makart's works, "for the viewer need not fathom any further than what actually is present in the image."[3] The Viennese were content with these values and rigidly opposed change of any kind. These values carried over in the theater, particularly the Burgtheater and the Court Opera.

At that time, many younger artists were members of the Society of Austrian Visual Artists (Genossenschaft der bildenden Künstler Österreichs), which owned the only publicly available exhibition space, the Künstlerhaus. But many of these artists were restless, for the teaching—chiefly at the Akademie der Bildende Künste—and exhibition authorities were insular, conservative, and locked in the past, and they frowned on change. Nor were they interested in new ideas and movements from other great artistic locales such as Paris, beginning with the Impressionists and continuing with Art Nouveau, in Germany with Jugendstil, and Scotland with the efforts of Rennie Mackintosh.

At about the same time Mahler made his debut at the Court Opera in early 1897, a group of artists including Gustav Klimt, Koloman Moser, Joseph Hoffmann, Carl Moll and Alfred Roller formed an association called the Union of Austrian Visual Artists (Vereinigung bildender Künstlers Österreich). After this group broke away from the Genossenschaft, they were known popularly as the Secession. This term was never an official name of the body, but its use was never discouraged, and it served as the name of their exhibition space. As noted in their journal *Ver Sacrum* for which Roller served as editor, the purpose of the Secession was "to assert its break with the fathers.... The Secession defined itself ... as a new Roman secessio plebis, in which the plebs, defiantly rejecting the misrule of the patricians [read: the current authorities], were withdrawing from the republic [read: current visual styles]."[4]

In that same journal, four points of the Secession were elucidated:

1. To "declare war" on the passive, "same old ruts," rigid sycophants [i.e., authority opposing any kind of change], poor taste, and a break with the past. The break acted as a challenge to the established order, authority, and tradition. The members of the movement were to pledge "themselves to save culture from their elders."
2. To appeal for the vigorous support of those who grasp the idea of art as a high mission of culture and as the educational duty of a civilized nation.
3. To declare that the Secession is not a destructive trend. Neither does it preach for a radical change nor does it dissolve form and color. Works of the old masters are to be studied and cherished, for art does not preach; it creates.
4. To promote not only forms of current Austrian art, but also those from abroad. New forms should be brought to Vienna and made available for examination through regular exhibitions. Through these new works of art, the artistic sensibilities should "awaken the dozing instincts," that lie within every person, instincts toward beauty and freedom of thoughts and feelings.[5]

Further emphasis was given to the ideal of the unity of art. All forms of art should come together to provide an organic whole, or, broadly put, a *Gesamtkunstwerk* (although this word itself was never used). One of the primary intentions of the works of the Secession was to create a condition known in German as *Stimmung*, or "atmosphere," or perhaps even better, "ambience."

The Secession consequently possessed neither a common artistic aesthetic nor a visual or creative "style." It was, rather, an agglomeration of ideas and philosophies. Although there were similarities in the expression of the visual form, such as the "curving styles" comparable to Jugendstil or Art Nouveau, all artists within the Secession had their own concepts, perceptions, and distinct aesthetic identity. They encouraged, nudged, sometimes forced, and often provoked the viewers to think for themselves and "to fill in their own gaps" instead of having everything provided for them.

These ideals were in complete contrast to those governing the scenic arts at the Vienna Court Opera. At that time, the state of the scenic arts was one of stagnation. A series of scenic images provided a locale—sometimes simple, at other times elaborate—for singers who for the most part were content to sing from static positions within the settings on the stage. These settings complemented the effect of the "peep show" created by perspective art amid the confines of painted wings, leg drops, borders, and backdrops. In short, a series of "pretty scenes" were presented, none of which required much intellectual thought on the part of the viewer. Instead, only the senses involving the eyes and ears were engaged, and little was left to the imagination. The idea of a true *Gesamtkunstwerk* in performance at the Vienna Court Opera had not yet arrived.

* * * * *

Before Mahler's arrival, the chief scenic designer and painter at the Court Opera was Anton Brioschi who in 1884 had succeeded his father, Carlo. Although the optical illusion of painted perspective and trompe d'oeil was maintained, the productions rarely reflected the dramatic spirit inherent in the action and the music of opera. Plastic elements such as steps, palatial stairs, and ramps were occasionally used, as in the grandiose second act in the 1875 production of Karl Goldmark's *Königin von Saba*.[6] Properties and set decorations were usually painted directly onto the drops and wings. Scenic decoration continued to be just that; decoration for the stage, a background for the singers.

In this environment, Mahler began to implement his idea of a *Gesamtkunstwerk* into the production of opera. He firmly believed in the organic unity of the arts in the service of the music. Each aspect of operatic production—directing, lighting, acting, costuming, singing, or the playing of the orchestra—had its rightful place within the confines of a performance. Mahler sought to focus the attention of the audience on the overall performance of the opera unfolding on the stage. Merely to view the "pretty settings and costumes" or to hear only the singing of favorite stars was, according to Mahler's intentions, not acceptable.

Early 1902 found Mahler wrestling with proposals for a new production of *Tristan und Isolde*. Sometime before June of that year, Roller drew several sketches and presented them to Mahler at a social encounter. Mahler's reaction was enthusiastic, and he asked Roller to proceed further with more formal designs and stage models. During the summer Mahler decided to use these designs over those presented by Lefler and Brioschi, which did not break with the more standard practices of the time. The previous settings had been designed and painted by Carlo Brioschi in 1883.[7] They were modeled after the original production for the first performances of the opera in 1865 at the Munich Court Theater by Angelo Qualigo. A number of painted sails and hangings created the illusion of a canopy. Another set of decorated curtains upstage served to mask the prow of the ship and to establish a separate space for the great love scene between Tristan and Isolde. Roller's designs, depicting two scenes in act I, emphasized an "acting space," as opposed to the past practice in which scenery functioned merely to decorate the stage.[8] While Brioschi's production of *Tristan und Isolde* created the illusion of the scenic space and its contents through the standard practice of painted scenery (drops and flats), Roller's production never intended a realistic recreation of the deck of a Celtic ship complete with sails, lines, rails. Instead, Roller produced a simple, strong linear setting that suggested the sailing ship. For the first time in the history of staging and scenic practices of the Court Opera, elements of the setting—chiefly colors—were used to create an "atmosphere" (*Stimmung*) that was greatly intensified by stage lighting, which complemented the clearly delineated and plastic settings with massive sails, a sloping deck, and the upstage quarterdeck.

In act I, for example, intense "daylight" was cast upon the massive red-orange sails. A bright, blue horizon could be seen through the gaps of the curtains. At the stipulated moment in the act the sails and curtains were opened, the hidden parts of the ship and the bright sky were revealed. The new production of *Tristan und Isolde* was one of the first attempts to incorporate stage lighting as a vital part of stage picture; that is, to use lighting to create a dramatic mood, rather than merely to illuminate the settings.

In most of the reviews, the production itself was given great emphasis while the singers and the conducting received only passing mention. A number of reviews centered largely on a discussion of the aesthetic effects generated by Roller's work and the influences of the Secession. In a perceptive, detailed review for the *Hamburger Abendblatt*, Max Graf wrote: "This new production was designed by Professor Roller, one of the leaders of the Secession. Every brushstroke, every combination of colors calls out the motto of the Secession from the viewer in the *Parkett* 'to the age its art, to art its freedom.' In the history of the modern scenic art, Roller's endeavors deserve a new chapter, for he actually treads a new path."[9] Another critic, Max Kalbeck, stated that "each of the acts appeared to fit the music, was pictorially right, and the decoration carefully shaded, all of which raised the music—drama to a *Gesamtkunstwerk*, such as Wagner must have had in mind." Kalbeck further declared that "one could see the music with his eyes."[10]

In May 1903, Mahler engaged Roller as Director of Production at the Vienna Court Opera, and the process of scenic renewal accelerated. Mahler was greatly pleased with the results and with Roller's speed in implementing changes and reforms in the scenic and directorial arts. Many of the critics, although at first encouraging, were suspicious of change and of the influences of the Secession. In an interview with the Viennese newspaper, *Illustriertes Wiener Extrablatt* in September 1903, Mahler, seeking to allay the fears of the critics, discussed his opinions regarding the visual aesthetics of operatic production:

> I deliberately avoid the use of the word[s] "lighting effects." We do not need garish effects, but rather lighting, with all its intensities, nuances, and strengths, should be of service to theater. Going only for the crude effect has no artistic value. But lighting alone does not serve its purposes. All modern art must serve the theater, and I say not just the Secession. What matters is the collaborative effort of all arts. It cannot continue with these clichés, for modern art must also extend itself to the costumes, to properties, to everything that can revitalize a work of art.[11]

In 1904, a new production of *Fidelio* replaced the earlier settings created by Carlo Brioschi in 1876. In act I, Brioschi's Prison Courtyard—naturalistic to the extreme—was placed within a castle with a bright city skyline in the background. Roller's production was a complete contrast. He emphasized the use of gray and dark colors, which, together with effective stage lighting, created a dramatic *Stimmung* inherent in the music. The setting was described by Julius Stern in the *Fremdenblatt*:

> Here it is a great surprise, completely different from the previous scene [of Rocco's Stube] and, in any event, far more clever than before. Standing in the background is an immense blue—black wall. At the end of the wall is a low gate and, next to it an even lower basement window. Above the gate, a mighty stone arch rises up and below, parallel to the wall, the gateway for the stairs that leads the condemned prisoners of the state to [their] horrific [fate] below.[12]

Writing in the *Neue Freie Presse*, Julius Korngold referred to Appia's seminal work *Die Musik und die Inszenierung* and noted how important stage lighting had become at the Court Opera:

> [For Appia] the artistic power of light stands at the very top [of the hierarchy of scenic elements]; therefore, he rightfully preferred the plastic and architectural arrangement of the stage before a painted surface, the decoration. Similar tendencies cannot fail to be recognized in the thoughtful endeavors of Professor Roller.... Stage design has been brought forward as an independent artistic participant and appears completely to enter in certain symbolic relationships through the atmospheric elements expressed in the libretto and the music. It was seen in *Tristan*, those scenes were painted through the music. Now one wishes to see similarly painted Beethoven music in the new *Fidelio*.[13]

* * * * *

Roller's next important production was his controversial staging of *Don Giovanni*. This production was the culmination of the Secession's effect upon the scenic arts at the Vienna Court Opera, and represented the first true break in the scenic traditions. While *Tristan und Isolde* and *Fidelio* still used aspects of naturalism—albeit stylized—as the basis for Roller's designs, in *Don Giovanni*, they were not used. Instead of being visually specified, they were suggested through spatial arrangements and colors.[14]

The basic configurations of the stage setting for *Don Giovanni* consisted of four towers (two on each side of the stage) and a checkerboard—patterned groundcloth which covered the stage floor. Roller dispensed with the traditional principle of wings and borders to create scenic illusion. The towers served as part of a frame, and the borders, with their neutral color, functioned to frame the stage space. The two sets of towers were movable only to and from center stage; none moved up- or downstage. Doorways in the towers could be opened or closed. Windows in the upper part of the towers could serve as balconies. Changes of scenery were rapid. Drops could be flown in or out between the towers. For most scene changes, less than a minute was required behind the drop, so interruptions to the flow of the opera remained at a minimum. Consequently, the attention of the viewer was uninterrupted and remained completely focused on the unfolding action in the space between the towers. Thus was developed the basic stage setting in the form of a neutral unit set, the first ever at the Court Opera and the first intended to be used for other operas as a cost-saving measure.[15]

If we now turn to the graveyard scene in the second act of *Don Giovanni*, Roller's design stands in sharp contrast to the naturalistic scene of a church cemetery as designed by Carlo Brioschi in 1869 for the opening of the newly built Court Opera (and renewed by Anton Brioschi in 1887). Roller's dramatic design centered on the Commendatore on horseback amid the gravestones mounted on the stage floor and on the towers, with great emphasis placed on lighting to provide dramatic intensity.[16] Bright moonlight streamed into the scene between the towers from the left. Max Graf described the scene:

The Commendatore: that is in the cemetery, in which walls and gravestones light up in the white moonlight, during which the huge cypresses wave to and fro in the background. There stands [on a pedestal] the mighty statue of a man in armor holding up a field marshal's baton, and seated on the back of an Andalusian horse.[17]

Don Giovanni became the most famous and best known of all of Roller's works during his collaboration with Mahler, for the controversy it sparked had ramifications that continue even today.

To describe this production as controversial is an understatement. It was either praised or damned. Maximillian Muntz gave his first impressions after the premiere in the morning edition of the *Deutsche Zeitung*. It was a terse notice of a distinctly unhappy timbre, calling the production "preposterous," a "sacrilege," and noting that the performance was a "resounding flop" (*eklatanten Durchfall*). Two days later, Muntz expanded his opinions in the feuilleton of the *Deutsche Zeitung*. He called the towers "gray smokestacks," tasteless, and having absolutely nothing to do with Mozart's music. The colors in the lighting were too much: "One minute violet, another orange—yellow light, gray or half—darkness, but never, ever, in natural daylight." He further complained that Mahler had made the musical performance of the opera subservient to the designer.[18]

The most emotional and biased review against Roller's work was filed by Hans Liebstöckl in a sneering tone for the *Illustriertes Wiener Extrablatt*.[19] He denounced the settings in all their forms—the towers, colors, drops, and the lighting: "Scenery! Scenery! Bring forth the high towers with holes! Milkyways! Glaring red trees! Mystifying courtyards! Dark chambers! Yellow castles! Lines, corners, contrasts, clashes of colors! Out with the discordant ingeniousness!" Liebstöckl railed on that one could never be rid of the towers and that "Don Juan would, without a doubt, find them in Hell." He further declared that "these towers have a number of objectives. First, they insult the eyes. Secondly, they are unacoustical, and seventh, no one can explain what they mean." The colors and even the painted groundcloth came under attack: "Everything is extravagant, all thought out as a surprise.... A hateful, clumsy, crude, and horrible thing lies within Roller's glory."

At the opposite end came the positive review from that great chronicler of the Secession, Ludwig Hevesi. He devoted an entire essay of an astounding one and one-half pages in the *Fremdenblatt* to the production alone. Hevesi wrote that the new production was "of greatest interest for the critical observer of the visual theatrical art, [for] conventional realism has been overcome, as every work presses for its own style, its own ambience [*Stimmung*] instead of the purely mediocre waxworks of the past."[20]

And so, the true break in the scenic traditions was the production of *Don Giovanni* with its use of a unit setting complemented by different backdrops to suggest locales. The audience was compelled to think and view the stage picture from a new and different perspective. The principles of the towers were again utilized for productions in the Burgtheater of *Hamlet* (1920) and *Macbeth* (1921).

In 1922, Roller renewed *Don Giovanni* by eliminating the upstage towers and closing up the distance between the left and right towers. In August that year the production traveled to the Salzburg Festival.

The Vienna Court Opera, in the capital of the Austro-Hungarian Empire, was the wealthiest opera company in Europe. Designers, stage directors, and impresarios frequently traveled to Vienna to see these new productions. Consequently, Roller's productions created ripple effects that spread to numerous theaters throughout Europe. The subsequent influences on operatic scenic design provided new impetus for other designers and stage directors, emboldening them to create new styles that would lead to new and exciting productions. Max Reinhardt of the Deutsches Theater in Berlin called on Roller's services. Richard Strauss and Hugo von Hofmannsthal entrusted Roller with the first Viennese production of their *Elektra* in 1909, as well as the premieres of *Der Rosenkavalier* (Dresden, 1911; also staged by Reinhardt) and *Die Frau ohne Schatten* (Vienna, 1919).[21] Artists were inspired to experiment with new styles throughout Germany in the 1920s and 1930s: to name only the most notable, László Moholy-Nagy and Ewald Dülberg at the Kroll Oper in Berlin and the theatrical expressionism of Caspar Neher and Ludwig Sievert. After the war, the designs and productions of Wieland Wagner—that iconoclastic designer and *Regisseur*—and his own subsequent influences upon the operatic arts emanating from the Richard Wagner Festspiele in Bayreuth, would not have been possible without Roller's works.[22] The consequences of the designs and influences of Alfred Roller and the Secession continue to be felt up to the present day.[23]

Notes

1. For further details on Alfred Roller and his works, see Evan Baker, "Alfred Roller's Production of Mozart's *Don Giovanni:* A Break in the Scenic Traditions of the Vienna Court Opera, 1905" (Ph.D. Dissertation, New York University, 1993).
2. Hugo von Hofmannsthal to Alexander Zemlinsky, 18 September 1901; quoted in Ludwig Greve and Werner Volke, *Jugend in Wien: Literatur um 1900* (Marbach am Neckar: Deutsches Literatur Archiv, 1974), 292–93. All translations are those of the author unless otherwise stated.
3. Gerbert Frodl, "Hans Makart," in *Das Zeitalter des Kaiser Franz Joseph: von der Revolution zur Gründerzeit*, vol. 1 (Vienna: Niederösterreichisches Landesregierung, 1984), 476.
4. Max Burckhard, *Ver Sacrum* 1, no. 1 (June, 1898), 1–3; quoted and paraphrased in Carl Schorske, *Fin de siècle Vienna* (New York: Vintage Books, 1981), 214.
5. "Weshalb wir eine Zeitschrift herausgeben?" in *Ver Sacrum* 1, no. 1 (June, 1898), 5–7.
6. Reproduced in Andrea Seebohm, ed., *The Vienna Opera* (New York: Rizzoli, 1987), plate 242.
7. Ibid., plate 81.
8. Reproduced in *Traum und Wirklichkeit: Wien 1870–1930* (Vienna: Historisches Museum der Stadt Wien, 1985), 182.
9. *Hamburger Nachrichten*, 15 March 1903.
10. Max Kalbeck, *Neues Wiener Tagblatt*, 22 February 1903.
11. *Illustriertes Wiener Extrablatt*, 9 September 1903.

12. "Aus der Theaterwelt," *Fremdenblatt*, 25 September 1904.

13. *Neue Freie Presse*, 8 October 1904. Adolphe Appia (1862–1928), a Swiss scene designer and theoretician, advocated a radical change in visual aesthetics of staging opera. His major work *Die Musik und die Inszenierung* (1899) outlines his aesthetics and his ideas for scenery and lighting. He advocates the "clearing" of the stage of superfluous decors and having instead lighting "paint" the stage. At the same time, the audience is called upon to use its imagination to fill in the gaps as necessary. Appia also discusses how the power of the music dictates the action of the opera. Although Wagner's operas are the chief examples used throughout the text, Appia's applications are brought to bear on theatrical production as a whole, for both opera and spoken theater. Movement for the actor as part of the setting is discussed, but it is lighting that is central to his arguments. Roller and Mahler were familiar with Appia's theories. Extracts from Appia's book appeared in the December 1900 issue of the Viennese monthly *Wiener Rundschau*. Roller's correspondence with the artist can be found in his *Nachlass* at the Austrian Theater Museum (see note 23 below).

14. The first scene of the opera is reproduced in Seebohm, *The Vienna Opera*, plate 247.

15. The unit settings were used for one other production, *Die Entführung aus dem Serail*, which premiered 26 January 1906. For further details, see Baker, "Alfred Roller's Production of Mozart's *Don Giovanni*," chapter 6.

16. Reproduced in Richard Specht, *Gustav Mahler* (Berlin: Schuster and Loeffler, 1913), plate 28.

17. *Neues Wiener Journal*, 22 December 1905.

18. *Deutsche Zeitung*, 22 and 24 December 1905.

19. *Illustriertes Wiener Extrablatt*, 22 December 1905.

20. Ludwig Hevesi, *Fremdenblatt*, 22 December 1905. This review was reprinted in toto in a collection of Hevesi's essays, *Alt Kunst—Neu Kunst* (Vienna: Carl Konegen, 1908), 259–64.

21. See Evan Baker, "Rococo Harmony. Alfred Roller: The First Designer of *Der Rosenkavalier*," *Opera News*, 57, no. 11 (13 February 1993): 12–15; translated into German in *Richard Strauss Blätter* 31 (1994): 42–53.

22. Recently, Roller's original designs for *Parsifal* created for the 1934 Festival surfaced. They were published by Oswald Georg Bauer in *Bayreuther Festspiele 1998: Prüfstein "Parsifal." Zur Erstveröffentlichung der Entwürfe von Alfred Roller für den Bayreuther "Parsifal" 1934* (Bayreuth: Bayreuther Festspiele, 1998), 50–77.

23. Most of the drawings, designs, paintings, books, and correspondence of Alfred Roller are preserved in the Austrian Theater Museum in Vienna. For further details, see Evan Baker and Oskar Pausch, "Das Archiv Alfred Rollers (1864–1935): Die Correspondenz," in *Mimundus: Wissenschaftliche Reihe des Österreichischen TheaterMuseums* (Vienna: Böhlau Verlag, 1994).

Chapter 15

SCHOENBERG'S MUSIC FOR THE THEATER

Michael Cherlin

I n several respects, Schoenberg was born in one world and died in another. The time and city of his birth, Vienna 1874, places Schoenberg in the capital of the Austro-Hungarian Empire toward the end of a century celebrated for its achievements in the arts and architecture, science, and commerce. Musically speaking, Vienna in the 1870s, 1880s, and 1890s was the city of the waltz, and of course, it was also a city whose high musical art was dominated by Johannes Brahms. Brahms, more than any other composer, forged the musical values of Schoenberg's youth. The time and place of Schoenberg's death, Brentwood, California, 1951, is unimaginably far removed from the Vienna of his childhood. Two world wars had ravaged Europe, and the Jews, Schoenberg's people, had been especially singled out for suffering during that horrible time. There had been the Einsteinian revolution in physics and a Freudian revolution in human psychology. In the world of music, no one had played a greater role than Schoenberg in initiating the changes that were to be hallmarks of composition in the twentieth century.

With Schoenberg, music enters into new worlds of imaginative possibility. And yet, the musical world remains divided. Along with the legions of musicians and music lovers whose hearts and minds are engaged and rewarded by the works of this profound musician, there are perhaps greater numbers who feel discomfort and even enmity toward Schoenberg. For some, Schoenberg is held responsible for our exile from the Eden of tonality. For others, the density of Schoenbergian counterpoint and the hyperemotionality of Schoenberg's musical language are intolerable. In short, Schoenberg remains an embattled figure in death, just as he was in life. If it is true that his music has become canonical, it is also true that it has resisted total assimilation.

In his book on the Western canon in literature, Harold Bloom writes, "One mark of an originality that can win canonical status for a literary work is a strangeness that we never altogether assimilate, or that becomes such a given that we are blinded to its idiosyncrasies."[1] Bloom's primary example of the first possibility is Dante; the strangeness of his poetic vision imprints itself afresh on every successive generation. Shakespeare is his primary example of the second possibility. Bloom claims that Shakespeare's world of human psychology has so much become our own world that we have become "blinded to its idiosyncrasies." In musical thought we might substitute Bach, Mozart, or Beethoven for Bloom's Shakespeare. The comparison is not perfect, in that no one musician straddles as many worlds in musical thought as Shakespeare does in literature; Mozart perhaps comes closest. Nonetheless, the work of these musical imaginations has become so much a given, so entangled in even the most banal aspects of our musical imaginations, that it takes some effort to hear that work as the utterly strange and idiosyncratic utterance that it is and always will be. Schoenberg, on the other hand, would seem to be like Bloom's Dante; or, closer to Schoenberg's own generation, he is like Bloom's Kafka. His is a strangeness that we "never altogether assimilate." He opened the way to realms of the imagination that had never before been contemplated. He did this by radically transforming his own musical tradition while simultaneously holding on to that tradition as that which provided and always again and again, immanently in the compositions, provides his own point of departure.

* * * * *

In the first years of the century, Schoenberg fashioned a series of masterpieces that synthesized the musical techniques of Brahms and Wagner. Through works such as *Verklärte Nacht, Gurrelieder,* and his tone poem *Palleas und Melisande,* Schoenberg explored and extended the possibilities of chromatic tonality. Prior to Schoenberg, the tonal system of composition, the system shared by a tradition stretching from Bach to Mozart and Beethoven to Brahms, had been thought of, at least by Europeans, as the natural culmination of mankind's musical odyssey. Schoenberg burst that bubble in 1908. His works of the period, largely associated with Expressionism, are the first to abandon tonal cadences, the means by which tonal music achieved coherence, centricity, and closure.[2] No doubt, Schoenberg conceptualized the musical change as being necessitated by emerging needs of *expressivity.* In fact, Schoenberg had invented a musical universe that could express the shifting imagery of dream states, inspired by Freudian psychology, or the lack of centricity of time and space suggested by the emerging Einsteinian physical universe. In tonality, the tonic had functioned as singular center to a world of tones all ultimately subordinated to it. In Schoenberg's post-tonal world, instead of a single pitch center there are multiple and ever shifting perspectives on centricity. And arguably, Schoenberg's music of the same period also shattered the metric time-space that had dominated music for more than two hundred years.

During the same period, Schoenberg imagined something he termed *Klangfarben-melodie*, where shifting timbres and textures would provide alternatives to the hegemony of melody and accompaniment that had become perceived as the "natural" state of music. Less than two decades after Schoenberg had abandoned tonality he initiated a second revolution in the world of music with the development of the twelve-tone technique. In twelve-tone composition Schoenberg had found a new and vastly expandable way to achieve compositional cohesion. In the decades following Schoenberg's death, his twelve-tone technique was to become a major force in shaping the music of Europe and America. And although the direct influence of Schoenberg's twelve-tone technique has waned in the past decades, Schoenbergian ideas continue to inform our thoughts about the open-ended possibilities of musical form and musical expression.

Schoenberg's activities as a composer extended through most of the genres that were available to him. His music ranges through art song, chamber music, symphonic works, concerti, choral music, sacred music, and opera. In addition there was his extensive work in arranging and orchestrating music for the cabaret. He even composed one work for the cinema, *Begleitmusik zu einer Lichtspielscene* (1929/30)—of course, he thought that he could compose the piece first and the film would come later! The only major genre that seems to have held little interest for him was ballet, and even here we have the stunning dance scenes in his largest staged work, *Moses und Aron*.

In addition to the four works that are fully conceptualized as staged music dramas—*Erwartung* (1909), *Die glückliche Hand* (1911/13), *Von heute auf morgen* (1928/29), and *Moses und Aron* (1930/32)—there are two dramatic narratives that are not staged—*Gurrelieder* (1900–1901/1910–11) and *Survivor from Warsaw* (1947)—and there is *Pierrot Lunaire* (1912), which is often done with partial staging, the ensemble behind a scrim and the speaker or singer sometimes in costume. Three of Schoenberg's works specifically for the theater, *Erwartung*, *Die glückliche Hand*, and *Moses und Aron*, remain among his most enduring musical compositions.

* * * * *

Schoenberg's turn to music drama is no doubt first and foremost grounded in his confrontation with the music of Wagner, primarily during the 1890s. For this we must thank Schoenberg's one and only formal teacher of composition, Alexander Zemlinski. At the beginning of his studies with Zemlinski, Schoenberg was a partisan Brahmsian. Zemlinski steered Schoenberg toward a larger musical synthesis. In the years between 1893 and 1899 Schoenberg reportedly saw all of Wagner's major operas, including the Ring cycle, between twenty and thirty times each.[3] And, while we hear the impact of Wagner's musical technique at the surface of only Schoenberg's early tone poems and especially in the orchestral songs of *Gurrelieder*, a deeper impact continues at least all the way through the works of the 1930s.

In a more remote way, it can be argued that Mozart's operas also seem to have had an impact on Schoenberg's music for theater. For example, Schoenberg's treatment of vocal ensembles, especially in *Moses und Aron*, has little relation to the principles and techniques of late Wagner, and may in fact be inspired by the staged works of Mozart. Moreover, the quick psychological shifts that Mozart achieves, most especially in *Le nozze di Figaro*, would seem to be a direct precursor to the quick psychological transformations that one hears, for example, in *Erwartung*.

Taken as a whole, the dramatic works reveal an interesting trajectory, moving first toward a deeper probing of inner psychological space and then toward an engagement with the external world of social and political realities. As is well known, the advent of the Romantic era had brought a remarkable turning inward. This happened first among the poets and eventually affected all of the arts. Writing principally about the realm of literature, Harold Bloom has called this transformation in the arts the "internalization of the quest."[4] In poetry this internalization is exemplified by the Romantic tradition begun in England by Blake, Wordsworth, Shelley, and Keats. In music, self-conscious Romanticism begins with Schumann and extends through the nineteenth century. A generation before Schoenberg, Mahler perfectly exemplifies the internalization that Bloom finds in Romantic literature. Schoenberg inherits and develops this internalization in the realm of music. Although the *Gurrelieder* (1900/02, orchestrated in 1910/11) ostensibly deal with a story line that takes place in the real world, the music and the libretto deal principally with the internal lives of the protagonists. This turn inward is greatly heightened during Schoenberg's expressionistic period, the period to which both *Erwartung* and *Die glückliche Hand* belong. In *Erwartung*, which is essentially a depiction of a psychotic episode, the separation of external reality from hallucinations is purposefully blurred. Schoenberg places his audience in an approximation of the psychological state that the protagonist herself experiences. In *Die glückliche Hand*, Schoenberg avoids external reality altogether and instead portrays a dream state. With *Von Heute auf Morgen*, Schoenberg tries his hand at a domestic comedy, not altogether successfully to my mind, but it is interesting to note that the text has moved from inner space to something happening in the external physical world. Schoenberg's largest staged work, *Moses und Aron*, tries to strike a balance between inner and outer space. Through the music the protagonists (proto-agonists!) reveal their internal lives and struggles, but the clashes among external forces are just as important. *Moses und Aron* is Schoenberg's last major work written in Europe. The rise of antisemitism, specifically the rise of Hitler and the Nazi Party, no doubt provide, at least in large part, the impetus for Schoenberg's shift from portrayals of inner space toward a more fully integrated interaction with the external world. Toward the end of his life, *Survivor from Warsaw* continues this trend, vividly portraying both the psychological states of the survivor and the horrors in the physical world that he survives.

The expressionistic aesthetic of *Erwartung* (and *Die glückliche Hand*) is achieved largely through Schoenberg's dissolution—or repression—of tonality.

Schoenberg's abandonment of tonality, beginning in 1908, is paralleled by his turn toward a more intuitive approach toward composition. For a period of time Schoenberg not only believed that the unconscious mind was the seat of human creativity, he also believed that rational activity beyond a certain point generally interfered with and diminished the creative capabilities of the artist. *Erwartung* is the work that represents the apex of this thought.

* * * * *

The *Erwartung* libretto was written for Schoenberg by the physician and poet Marie Pappenheim at the composer's request. The libretto depicts an episode that might be interpreted as a dream, or as a sequence of events both real and hallucinatory. A woman, never named, is lost in a wood, where she searches for her beloved, who also has no name. She eventually finds his bleeding corpse, or thinks that she has found it. The text suggests that he betrayed her, and it also suggests that she may be his murderer. But nothing is clear. In fact, the only major change that Schoenberg insisted on in the first draft of the libretto concerned a passage where Pappenheim had made it clear that the protagonist had actually killed her beloved and that the corpse that she now sees is very real and not a hallucination.[5] Schoenberg did not want the audience to know for sure what, if anything, in the story had actually happened or was actually happening.

Schoenberg composed the work in a white heat—a seventeen-day period during the summer of 1909. He composed almost totally without sketches.[6] Indeed it would appear that it was not only the woman protagonist of *Erwartung* who had approached the abyss. Schoenberg describes the work's psychological depiction in a letter to Ferruccio Busoni:

> And the musical results I wish for: no stylized and sterile protracted emotion. People are not like that: it is *impossible* for a person to have only one emotion at a time. One has *thousands* simultaneously. And these thousands can no more readily be added together than an apple and a pear. They go their own ways.[7]

Schoenberg's "thousands" of simultaneous emotions is clearly hyperbolic, and yet the idea becomes manifest in the complex polyphonies and quickly shifting musical ideas that one hears throughout the work.

The stage directions tell us that *Erwartung* opens at the edge of a wood. Moonlight illuminates roads and fields, but only the first tree trunks and the beginning of the broad path are lit. A woman enters, dressed in a white garment covered with red roses that are partly shedding their petals. Even the costume is designed to blur the boundary between reality and hallucination.

Pappenheim's libretto consists of a series of short fragments connected to one another by ellipses as the woman darts from perception to perception and from emotion to emotion (example 15.1). The fragmentary and quickly shifting images of the text are paralleled and augmented by the musical setting.

Example 15.1 *Erwartung*, mm. 1–19

(zögernd)	[*(hesitantly)*
Hier hinein?… Man sieht den Weg nicht … Wie silbern die Stämme schimmern … wie Birken …	In here?… The path can't be seen … The tree trunks shimmer like silver … like birches …
(vertieft zu Boden schauend)	*(gazing intently at the ground)*
Oh! Unser Garten … Die Blumen für ihn sind sicher verwelkt … Die Nacht ist so warm …	Oh! Our garden … The flowers for him surely will have withered … The night is so warm …
(in plötzlicher Angst)	*(suddenly anxious)*
Ich fürchte mich …	I am afraid …
(horcht in den Wald, beklommen)	*(listens uneasily toward the wood)*
Was für schwere Luft herausschlägt … wie ein Sturm, der steht …	How heavy the air is that comes out of there … like a looming storm …
(ringt die Hände, sieht zurück)	*(she wrings her hands and looks behind her)*
So grauenvoll ruhig und leer …	So dreadfully silent and empty …]

Despite the radically new kinds of harmonies, phrase rhythms, and contrapuntal textures that Schoenberg develops, there is also an underlying conservatism in Schoenberg's old-fashioned ideas about storytelling through musical depiction. Tone painting, clearly related to the sort that had evolved through the nineteenth century, is an important aspect of *Erwartung*. For example, at the beginning of the third scene (example 15.2) we hear the harps imitating the glimmering of moonlight. The woman's turn toward more wistful memories is paralleled by the accompanying music's bittersweet lyricism, and then the crowding in of overwhelming emotions is powerfully depicted by quick fleeting musical figuration and by the powerful orchestral crescendo. At the end of the scene, the fear of being attacked by some wild beast is portrayed by music that combines the effect of being crowded in or surrounded with a quickening rhythmic ostinato that clearly depicts the accelerated beating of the woman's heart.

The beautiful and powerful conclusion (example 15.3) of *Erwartung* features an uncanny suspension of time portrayed by the regular ostinato of the harp heard against the suspended pedal point in the strings and winds. As in other passages in *Erwartung*, the delicacy and detail of the orchestration forms a wonderful foil against the hushed and then anguished utterances of the voice. The work ends with a masterful layering of ascending and descending chromatic scales moving at various rates throughout the orchestral texture and slowly dissolving into silence.

* * * * *

The intellectual atmosphere in Vienna during the first decade of the century was particularly supercharged with interaction among the arts. *Die glückliche Hand*, Schoenberg's second staged work, is a perfect case in point. Poets such as Stephan

Example 15.2 *Erwartung, Scene 3, mm. 90–125*

Da kommt ein Licht!… Ach! Nur der Mond … Wie gut …	[There's a light … Ah! Only the moon … how good …
(wieder halb ängstlich)	*(again rather anxiously)*
Dort tanzt etwas Schwarzes … hundert Hände …	Something black is dancing there … a hundred hands …
(sofort beherrscht)	*(controlling herself at once)*
Sei nicht dumm … es ist der Schatten …	don't be stupid … it is the shadows …
(zärtlich nachdenkend)	*(musing tenderly)*
Oh! Wie dein Schatten auf die weissen Wände fällt … Aber so bald musst du fort …	Oh! How your shadow falls on the white walls … but you had to leave so soon …
(Rauschen)	*(a rustling)*
(Sie hält an, sieht um sich und lauscht einen Augenblick)	*(She stops, looks around her and listens for a moment)*
Rufst du?…	Are you calling?…
(wieder träumend)	*(dreamily again)*
Und bis zu Abend ist es so lang …	And it's so long until evening …
(leichter Windstoss) (Sie sieht wieder hin)	*(light gust of wind) (she looks around again)*
Aber der Schatten kriecht doch!… Gelbe, breite Augen …	But the shadow is crawling … large yellow eyes …
(Laut des Schauderns)	*(in tones of terror)*
So verquellend … wie an Stielen … Wie es glotzt …	So protruding … as if on stalks … How it glares …
(Knarren im Grass) (entsetzt)	*(a rustle in the grass) (terrified)*
Kein Tier, lieber Gott, kein Tier … Ich habe solche Angst … Liebster, mein Liebster, hilf mir …	Not an animal, dear God, not an animal … I'm so frightened … Darling, my darling, help me …]

Example 15.3 *Erwartung, mm. 416–end*

Wo bist du?… Es ist dunkel … dein Kuss wie ein Flammenzeichen in meiner Nacht … meine Lippen brennen und leuchten … dir entgegen …	[Where are you?… It is so dark … your kiss is like a beacon in my darkness … my lips burn and glow … for you …
(in Entzücken aufschreiend, irgend etwas entgegen)	*(crying out in rapture, addressing something)*
Oh, bist du da … ich suchte …	Oh, there you are … I was looking …
(Vorhang)	*(curtain)*]

George and later Rilke had inspired Schoenberg during this period, as did the architectural work and the general aesthetic of Adolp Loos. Schoenberg was heavily involved with painting; the works of Kokoschka, Kandinsky, and others, as well as his own works as a painter, were central to his life. Moreover, the tragic relation between his wife Mathilde and the painter Richard Girstl, Schoenberg's only painting teacher, was recent history. With specific regard to *Die glückliche Hand,* the work of Max Reinhardt—especially his use of theatrical lighting—was to have a large influence on Schoenberg. Carrying the aesthetic of Richard Wagner into the expressionistic world of his new music, *Die glückliche Hand* was to be Schoenberg's updated version of the *Gesamtkunstwerk.*

The detailed staging directions of the opening scene are typical of the extensive stage directions found throughout the score. The focus and detail of these instructions suggest that Schoenberg may have been influenced in part by that newly emerging art form, film:

> The stage is almost entirely dark. In front lies the man, face down. On his back crouches a catlike, fantastic animal (hyena with enormous, batlike wings) that seems to have sunk its teeth into his neck.
>
> The visible portion of the stage is very small, somewhat round (a shallow curve). The rear stage is hidden by a dark-violet curtain. There are slight gaps in the curtain from which green-lit faces peer: six men and six women.
>
> The light is very weak. Only the eyes are clearly visible. The rest is swathed in soft red veiling, and this too reflects the greenish light.

Although the musical score for *Die glückliche Hand* divides the work into three scenes, a more accurate picture of the dramatic structure would require six scenes. The work opens and closes with interrelated choral sections. Schoenberg composes the choral polyphony, partly sung and partly whispered, so that most of the *words* are not understandable. And though the partly understood text is mostly heard as murmuring, its chastising, anxiety-producing message nonetheless comes across (example 15.4).

In the dramatic form of the work, the opening functions like a dawning of dream consciousness, while the close brings us back into the silence of the unconscious. In between we experience four loosely connected dream sequences. The first dream sequence expresses the unnamed man's longing for an unattainable woman. The grotesque image of the fantastic beast that Schoenberg describes in

Example 15.4 *Die glückliche Hand,* Scene 1, beginning

Still, o schweige; Ruheloser!—Du weisst es ja; du wusstest es ja; und trotzdem bist du blind? Kannst du nicht endlich Ruhe finden? So oft schon! Und immer wieder? Du weisst, es ist immer wieder das Gleiche. Immer wieder das gleiche Ende ...	[Be still and silent restless being!—You know how it always is; you knew how it would be; and yet you remain blind. Will you never be at rest? So many times already! And always again? You know that it is always the same. Always the same end ...]

his libretto sets the tone. In the second sequence the man, fearless and triumphant, now carrying two "Turk's heads" on his belt, creates a diadem with a single blow of his hammer. In the third, fully pantomime, the man undergoes a series of mental transformations, eventually feeling "as though his head is about to burst." This entire dream sequence is depicted by Schoenberg's coordination of color (through theatrical lighting) and sound "crescendo." In the fourth episode, the unattainable woman returns. She eventually crushes the man with a rock that has taken on the shape of the fantastic beast of the first dream.

Example 15.5 shows the libretto for the third scene of *Die glückliche Hand*. The scene opens with the second of our four internal dream sequences. The libretto describes a wild rocky landscape and a group of workmen fashioning a diadem. The image of the workmen fashioning jewels is no doubt Schoenberg's reworking of Wagner's portrayal of the Nibelungen. The man, noticing the workmen, realizes that their work can be done more simply. He approaches their anvil and with one strike of his sword cleaves it in two. He then bends down, reaches into the sundered anvil and pulls out a fully formed diadem. Like the composer who creates through an unhampered flow from his unconscious, the man creates the jewel with one stroke.

Example 15.5 *Die glückliche Hand*, Scene 3

Mann:	[*Man:*
Das kann man einfacher!	That can be done more simply.
So schafft man Schmuck!	Thus one makes jewels!]

* * * * *

The opera *Moses und Aron* is the most ambitious of Schoenberg's twelve-tone works. The libretto, written by Schoenberg and in part inspired by his earlier play *Der biblische Weg*, is loosely based on the biblical account and is largely Schoenberg's own invention. At the core of the work's drama is the impossible task of the prophet Moses: he has been granted a vision that he cannot communicate to the people. His brother Aron will be his spokesperson, but only at the expense of corrupting the message.

Perhaps the most immediately striking characteristic of Schoenberg's portrayal results from the distinctive sonic qualities associated with each of his principal protagonists—the emanations of Divinity, the brothers Moses and Aron, and the collective "Folk Israel." The Divine Voice has two aspects, both polyphonic in nature: there is a disembodied aspect, composed of six solo voices, each of which is doubled by an instrument, and there is a second aspect, visually manifest through the burning bush, musically composed of a speaking choir. Most commentary on the opera refers to these combined forces as the voice of God; however, Schoenberg is careful to avoid naming either the singing choir or the speaking choir as "God" in his libretto. The disembodied solo voices—who are to sit in the orchestra—are simply named "Six Solo Voices." The speaking choir, associated with the burning bush, is called the "Voice from the Thornbush." While the Voice from the Thornbush is heard only in the first scene, the singing choir returns later in the opera, again portraying the Divine, but this time the bush is not present.

With one single exception—a lone twelve-tone row, sung to Aron—Moses speaks and does not sing. In contrast, Aron, cast as a heroic tenor, never speaks and always sings. Thus, the two brothers each articulate one aspect of the Divine Voice, speaking or singing; of course, neither alone is capable of polyphony. The people as a collective, Folk Israel, share the divine aspect of polyphony, and like the Divine Voice, they also combine music that is spoken and sung. But the people are also capable of individuation, and the dynamic flux of individuals emerging from the mass and returning to it is another striking characteristic of the opera. When individuals emerge from the people, they sing, like Aron.[8]

Schoenberg's libretto begins with Moses as he happens upon the burning bush. The Six Solo Voices begin the opera singing the open vowel "O." Only after Moses has uttered the words "Einziger, ewiger, allgegenwärtige, unsichtbarer und unvorstellbarer Gott" (One, eternal, omnipresent, invisible, and inconceivable God) does the Voice shift to spoken and sung *words*, conveyed in a polyphony of multiple, interrelated thought streams that are meant to emanate from the divine presence (example 15.6).

Example 15.6 *Moses und Aron,* mm. 1–28

Moses:
Einziger, ewiger, allgegenwärtige, unsichtbarer und unvorsetellbarer Gott …
Stimme aus dem Dornbusch &
6 Solostimmen:
Lege die Schuhe ab: bist weit genug
gegangen; du stehst auf heiligem Boden;
nun verkunde!
Moses:
Gott meiner Väter, Gott Abrahams, Isaaks
und Jakob, der du ihren Gedanken in mir
wiedererweckt hast, mein Gott, nötige
mich nicht, ihn zu verkünden. Ich bin alt;
lass mich in Ruhe meine Schafe weiden …!
Stimme:
Du hast die Greuel gesehn, die Wahrheit
erkant: so kannst du nicht anders mehr:
Du musst dein Volk daraus befrein!

[*Moses:*
One, eternal, omnipresent, unseeable and
inconceivable God …
Voice from the thornbush &
6 solo voices:
Lay your shoes aside, you have gone far
enough, you stand on holy ground. Now
become my prophet!
Moses:
God, my Father, God of Abraham, Isaac
and Jacob, who has woken again your
thought in me, my God, do not compel
me to be your prophet. I am old; let me
graze my sheep in peace!
Voice:
You have seen the atrocities, and know the
truth: you cannot do otherwise any longer.
You must therefore set your people free.]

The opening of *Moses und Aron* can be related to sources in both the German and Jewish traditions. In the theory of language developed by Richard Wagner, in turn derived from Gottfried Herder, the open vowel expresses the infinite. The consonant bounds the infinite so that it may express the limited apprehensions of human concern and ability.[9] The opening "O" is probably also inspired by the "En-Sof" of Jewish mysticism, what Gershom Scholem characterizes as the "hidden God, the innermost Being of Divinity so to speak, [who] has neither qualities nor attributes."[10] But Moses can only respond with *words*. His list of divine attributes moves through a progression of vowels—"*Ei*nziger, *e*wiger, *a*llgegenwärtige, *u*nsichtbarer *u*nd *u*nvorstellbarer G*o*tt"—that approach but never reach the original "O."

Moses has been given a divine imperative: he must free his people. He resists at first, but finally capitulates in silence, overwhelmed by the many-faceted voice that sings and speaks its polyphony of divine prophecy.

In the second scene Moses meets his brother Aron as their paths cross in the desert. While Aron sings of "Gebilde der höchsten Phantasie" (image of highest fantasy), Moses corrects him: "Kein Bild kann der ein Bild geben vorn Unvorstellbaren" (no image can give you an image of that which cannot be represented). The conflict and the impasse that is central to the opera has been defined. Later, as Moses tries to convey his "unvorstellbarer" message to the people, only Aron's intervention through visible miracles sways the people. Schoenberg's libretto at this point is in stunning conflict with the biblical account. In Exodus 4, God promises to perform the miracles of transformation through Moses—the transformation of the staff into a snake, of the healthy hand into a leprous one, and of water into blood—and so the people will be convinced of Moses' divine imperative. In Exodus 7, we are told that Aron, at Moses' command, is to perform the miracles of transformation that will convince Pharaoh to free the Israelites. Nowhere in the Bible do we find the weakened Moses of Schoenberg's portrayal in act 1.

As the second act begins, Moses has been away for forty days and nights, and the people have grown restless. They confront Aron and demand that the golden calf be fashioned. As Moses had resisted and then capitulated to the divine will in the first act, now Aron capitulates to the overwhelming force of the people. He will give them their image. The golden calf scene that follows is a tour de force of dramatic representation and compositional technique. A massive dance sequence opens into a series of distinctive episodes as the scene intensifies, finally leading to debauchery, murder, and suicide. The drama depicts the extremes of human emotion, and the music matches this with powerful contrasts of mass and energy, achieved through an enormous range of orchestral and vocal colors and textures. By the end of the scene, exhaustion and dissolution are portrayed through a series of stunning flashbacks heard in the orchestral polyphony. At this moment Moses descends from the mountain, and in profound anger commands "Vergeh du Abbild des Unvermögens" (be gone, you image of the unimaginable). The golden calf disappears, and the people exit singing music and text derived from the divine prophecy of the first scene. Once again, Schoenberg's libretto is in strong conflict with the Bible; in the Exodus story, the angry Moses has the golden calf ground into dust and spread upon the water, which the Israelites are made to drink (Exodus 32:20). While Schoenberg had denied magical or miraculous powers to Moses in the first act, assigning the miracles of transformation to Aron, in the second act Schoenberg's Moses has magical powers at odds with the biblical account. Moses has gathered strength, one assumes through his experience at the Mount of Revelation.

And yet, Moses' newfound power remains insufficient to the task. The Israelites leave the stage singing a reprise of the music associated with the divine prophecy of act 1, scene 1, and at the end of the second act, Moses alone confronts Aron (example 15.7). When Aron tells him that the tablets, too, are images, Moses smashes the tablets in anger. This is yet another deviation from the Bible, where Moses destroys the tablets before confronting Aaron and before destroying the golden calf (Exodus 32:19). Alone, at the end of the scene, Moses utters in anguish, "O Wort, du Wort das mir fehlt!" (O word, you word that I lack).

Example 15.7 *Moses und Aron*, conclusion

Unvorstellbarer Gott!	[Inconceivable God!
Unaussprechlicher, vieldeutiger Gedanke!	Inexpressible, many-sided Idea,
Lässt du diese Auslesung zu?	will you let this be so explained?
Darf Aron, mein Mund, dieses Bild	Shall Aron, my mouth, fashion this
machen? So habe ich mir ein Bild gemacht,	image? Then I have made an image, false,
falsch, wie ein Bild nur sein kann!	as an image can only be!
So bin ich geschlagen!	So I am defeated!
So war alles Wahnsinn, was ich gedacht	So was all madness—what I have
habe, und kann und darf nicht gesacht	thought and what can and may not
werden!	be said.
O Wort, du Wort, das mir fehlt!	O word, you word, that fails me!
(Er sinkt verzweifelt zu Boden.)	*(He sinks to the ground in despair.)*]

Schoenberg left Europe with only the first two acts of *Moses und Aron* completed. Although he lived for another nineteen years in America, nineteen very productive years, he was never able to write the music for act 3. And although he wrote the libretto for a single final scene, most students of Schoenberg's music, including myself, feel that the opera has nowhere to go after the end of act 2.

Notes

1. Harold Bloom, *The Western Canon* (New York: Harcourt Brace, 1993), 4.
2. In fact, Simms persuasively argues that Schoenberg's *Erwartung* initiates the entire Expressionist movement. See Bryan R. Simms, "Whose Idea Was *Erwartung?*" in *Constructive Dissonance: Arnold Schoenberg and the Transformations of Twentieth-Century Culture*, ed. Juliane Brand and Christopher Hailey (Berkeley and Los Angeles: University of California Press, 1997), xx.
3. H. H. Stuckenschmidt, *Arnold Schoenberg* (New York: Schirmer Books, 1977), 33.
4. Bloom, *Western Canon*, 17–43.
5. Simms, "Whose Idea was *Erwartung?*" 104–5.
6. Joseph Auner, "'Heart and Brain in Music': The Genesis of Schoenberg's *Die glückliche Hand*," in *Constructive Dissonance*, ed. Brand and Hailey, 115.
7. Quoted in Simms, "Whose Idea was *Erwartung?*" 105.
8. The sonic characteristics of the opera are discussed in David Lewin, "*Moses und Aron*: Some General Remarks, and Analytic Notes for Act I, Scene 1," *Perspectives of New Music* 6, no. 1 (1967): 1–17.
9. Richard Wagner, *Richard Wagner's Prose Works*, trans. William A. Ellis (New York: Broude, 1966), 266ff.
10. Gershem Scholem, *Major Trends in Jewish Mysticism* (New York: Schocken Books, 1941), 207.

REFERENCES

Abert, Anna Amalie. *Traditionen—Neuansätze: Festschrift für Anna Amalie Abert (1906–1996)*. Ed. Klaus Hortschansky. Tutzing: Schneider, 1997.

Adler, Gusti. *Max Reinhardt*. Salzburg: Festungsverlag, 1964.

Ainsztein, Reuben. *Jewish Resistance in Nazi-Occupied Eastern Europe, with a Historical Survey of the Jew as Fighter and Soldier in the Diaspora*. New York: Barnes and Noble, 1974.

Allanbrook, Wye Jamieson. *Rhythmic Gesture in Mozart: "Le Nozze di Figaro" and "Don Giovanni."* Chicago: University of Chicago Press, 1983.

Alms, Barbara, ed. *Blauer Streusand*. Frankfurt am Main: Suhrkamp, 1987.

Altmann, Alexander. *Moses Mendelssohn: A Biographical Study*. London: Routledge and Kegan Paul, 1973.

Altmann, Alexander, with the collaboration of H. Bar-Dayan, E. Engel, S. Lauer, and L. Strauss, eds. *Gesammelte Schriften—Jubiläumsausgabe*. Stuttgart-Bad Canstatt: Frommann-Holzboog, 1977.

Anczyc, Władysław Ludwik. *Kościuszko pod Racławicami*. In *Życie i pisma*. Ed. Marian Szyjkowski. Vol. 3. Kraków, 1908.

Anderson, Emily, ed. and trans. *The Letters of Mozart and His Family*. Vol. 1. London, Macmillan and Co., 1938.

Angiolini, Gaspero. *Lettere di Gasparo Angiolini a Monsieur Noverre sopra i balli pantomimi*. Milano, 1773.

Appia, Adolphe. *Die Musik und die Inszenierung*. Munich: Bruckmann, 1899.

Arens, Katherine. *Functionalism and Fin de Siècle: Fritz Mauthner's Critique of Language*. New York: Lang, 1984.

Asnyk, Adam. *Poezje*. Warszawa: Państwowy Instytut Wydawniczy, 1974.

Auner, Joseph. "'Heart and Brain in Music': The Genesis of Schoenberg's *Die glückliche Hand*." In *Constructive Dissonance: Arnold Schoenberg and the Transformations of Twentieth-Century Culture*, ed. Juliane Brand and Christopher Hailey. Berkeley and Los Angeles: University of California Press, 1997.

"Aus der Theaterwelt." *Fremdenblatt*, 25 September 1904.

Badura-Skoda, Eva. "*Teutsche Comoedie Arien* und Joseph Haydn." In *Der junge Haydn*. Beiträge zur Aufführungspraxis Bd. 1. Graz: Akadem. Druck- u. Verlagsanst., 1971.

———. "An Unknown Singspiel by Joseph Haydn?" In *Report of the Eleventh Congress of the International Musicological Society*. Vol. 1. Copenhagen: [n.p.], 1972.

———. "Zur Salzburger Erstaufführung von Joseph Haydns Singspiel *Die reisende Ceres*." *Österreichische Musikzeitschrift* 32 (1977).

Bahr, Hermann. *Wiener Theater (1892–1898)*. Berlin: Fischer, 1899.

Baker, Evan. "Alfred Roller's Production of Mozart's *Don Giovanni:* A Break in the Scenic Traditions of the Vienna Court Opera, 1905." Ph.D. diss., New York University, 1993.

————. "Roccoco Harmony: Alfred Roller, the First Designer of *Der Rosenkavalier.*" *Opera News* 57 (13 February 1993).

Baker, Evan, and Oskar Pausch. "Das Archiv Alfred Rollers (1864–1935): Die Correspondenz." In *Mimundus: Wissenschafliches Reihe des Österreichischen TheaterMuseums.* Vienna: Böhlau, 1994.

Bakhtin, Mikhail. *The Dialogic Imagination: Four Essays.* Ed. Michael Holquist, trans. Caryl Emerson and Michael Holquist. Austin: University of Texas Press, 1981.

Baniewicz, Elżbieta. "Theatre's Lean Years in Free Poland." Trans. Joanna Dutkiewicz. *Theatre Journal* 48, no. 4 (1996): 461–78.

Bartha, Denes, ed. *Josef Haydn: Gesammelte Briefe und Aufzeichnungen.* Kassel: Bärenreiter, 1965.

Batka, Richard. *Musikalische Streifzüge.* Florence and Leipzig, 1899.

Battisti, Bartolomeo. *Abhandlung von den Krankheiten des schönen Geschlechts.* Vienna, 1784.

Bauer, Hans Joachim. "Karl Goldmark: Das Heimchen am Herd." In *Pipers Enzyklopädie des Musiktheaters.* Vol. 2. Munich: Piper, 1987.

Bauer, Oswald Georg. *Bazreuther Festspiele 1998: Prüfstein "Parsifal." Zur Erstveröffentlichung der Entwürfe von Alfred Roller für den Bayreuther "Parsifal" 1934.* Bayreuth: Bayreuther Festspiele, 1998.

Bauer, Wilhelm and Otto Erich Deutsch. *Mozart: Briefe und Aufzeichnungen: Gesamtausgabe herausgegeben von der Internationalen Stiftung Mozarteum.* Vol. 1. Kassel: Bärenreiter, 1962.

Bauman, Thomas. *W. A. Mozart, "Die Entführung aus dem Serail."* Cambridge Opera Handbooks. Cambridge: Cambridge University Press, 1987.

Bayerdörfer, Hans-Peter, and Jörg Schönert, eds. *Theater gegen das Vergessen: Bühnenarbeit und Drama bei George Tabori.* Tübingen: Niemeyer, 1997.

Becker, Rudolf Zacharias. *Noth- und Hilfsbüchlein für Bauersleute, oder lehrreiche Freude- und Trauergeschichten.* Gotha, 1788.

Beller, Steven. *Vienna and the Jews, 1867–1938: A Cultural History.* Cambridge: Cambridge University Press, 1989.

Ben-Zvi, Linda. "Samuel Beckett, Fritz Mauthner, and the Limits of Language." *PMLA* 95, no. 2 (March 1980): 183–200.

Benjamin, Walter. "Theses on the Philosophy of History." In *Illuminations,* trans. Harry Zohn. New York: Schocken, 1969.

Berlant, Lauren. *The Anatomy of National Fantasy: Hawthorne, Utopia, and Everyday Life.* Chicago: University of Chicago Press, 1991.

Bernhard, Thomas. "Ist es eine Komödie? Ist es eine Tragödie?" *Prosa.* Frankfurt am Main: Suhrkamp, 1967.

————. *Ungenach.* Frankfurt am Main: Suhrkamp, 1968.

————. *Vor dem Ruhestand: Eine Komödie von deutscher Seele.* Frankfurt am Main: Suhrkamp, 1981.

————. *Eve of Retirement.* In *The President and Eve of Retirement: Plays and Other Writings,* trans. Gitta Honegger. New York: Performing Arts Journal Publications, 1982.

————. *Heldenplatz.* Frankfurt am Main: Suhrkamp, 1988.

————. *In der Höhe. Rettungsversuch. Unsinn.* Salzburg: Residenz, 1989.

————. *Eine Begegnung: Gespräche mit Krista Fleischmann.* Vienna: Edition S, 1991.

Bertens, Hans. *The Idea of the Postmodern: A History.* New York: Routledge, 1995.

Bloch, Maurice, and Jean H. Bloch. "Women and the Dialectics of Nature in Eighteenth-Century French Thought." In *Nature, Culture, and Gender,* ed. Carol P. MacCormack and Marilyn Strathern. Cambridge: Cambridge University Press, 1980.

Błoński, Jan. "The Poor Poles Look at the Ghetto." In *Four Decades of Polish Essays*, ed. Jan Kott. Evanston, Ill.: Northwestern University Press, 1990.

Bloom, Harold. *The Western Canon.* New York: Harcourt Brace, 1993.

Bongiovanni, Salvatore. "Gennaro Magri e il *Trattato teorico-prattico di ballo.*" Thesis, La Sapienza, Roma, 1993.

Booth, Wayne. *The Company We Keep: An Ethics of Fiction.* Chicago: University of Chicago Press, 1988.

Bratkowski, Stanisław. *Akademik warszawski.* Warszawa, [1831?].

Bredeck, Elizabeth. *Metaphors of Knowledge: Language and Thought in Mauthner's Critique.* Detroit, Mich.: Wayne State University Press, 1992.

Breuer, Robert. "The Dramatic Value of Space and the Masses." In *Max Reinhardt and His Theatre*, ed. Oliver Sayler. New York: Brentano, 1924.

Brown, Bruce A. *W. A. Mozart: "Così fan tutte."* Cambridge Opera Handbooks. Cambridge: Cambridge University Press, 1995.

Buch, David J. *"Der Stein der Weissen,* Mozart and Collaborative Singspiels at Emanuel Schikaneder's Theater auf der Weiden." In *Mozart-Jahrbuch* 2000. Kassel: Bärenreiter Verlag, 2002.

Castle, Terry. "The Female Thermometer." In *The Female Thermometer: Eighteenth-Century Culture and the Invention of the Uncanny.* New York: Oxford University Press, 1995.

Celan, Paul. "Es war Erde in ihnen und sie gruben." In *Die Niemandsrose.* Frankfurt am Main: Fischer, 1963.

Chambers, Helen. "Thomas Bernhard." In *After the Death of Literature: West German Writing of the 1970s*, ed. Keith Bullivant. Oxford: Berg, 1989.

Chow, Rey. *Ethics after Idealism: Theory, Culture, Ethnicity, Reading.* Bloomington: Indiana University Press, 1998.

Chusid, Martin. "The Significance of D Minor in Mozart's Dramatic Music." *Mozart-Jahrbuch* 1965/66 (1967): 87–93.

Connor, Steven. *Postmodernist Culture: An Introduction to Theories of the Contemporary.* Oxford: Blackwell, 1989.

Cooper, Anthony Ashley, third Earl of Shaftesbury. "The Moralists." In *Shaftesbury: Standard Edition, Complete Works, Selected Letters and Posthumous Writings*, ed. Wolfram Benda et al. Vol. 2, pt. 1. Stuttgart-Bad Canstatt: Frommann-Holzboog, 1987.

Cooper, John Gilbert. "The Power of Harmony: The Design." In *The Works of the English Poets*, ed. A. Chalmers. Vol. 15. London, 1810.

Cremeri, Benedict Dominic Anton. *Eine Bille an Joseph II: Aus der Herzkammer eines ehrlichen Mannes.* Frankfurt and Leipzig, 1780. Reprinted in *Maske und Kothurn* 37 (1991).

Croll, Gerhard. "Gaspero Angiolini." In *The New Grove Dictionary of Music and Musicians.* Vol. 1. London: Macmillan, 1980.

Dahlhaus, Carl. *Nineteenth-Century Music.* Trans. J. Bradford Robinson. Berkeley: University of California Press, 1989.

Dahms, Sibylle. "Franz Anton Hilverding: *Le Turc généreux.*" In *Pipers Enzyklopädie des Musiktheaters.* Vol. 3. Munich: Piper, 1989.

———. "Gluck und das 'Ballet en action' in Wien." *Gluck-Studien.* Vol. 1. Kassel: Bärenreiter, 1989.

———. "Das Repertoire des 'Ballet en Action.' Noverre—Angiolini—Lauchery." In *De Editione Musices. Festschrift Gerhard Croll zum 65.* Laaber: Laaber-Verlag, 1992.

———. "Ballet Reform in the Eighteenth Century and Ballet at the Mannheim Court." In *Ballet Music from the Mannheim Court.* Vol. 1. Madison: A-R Editions, 1996.

———. "Noverre's Stuttgarter Ballette und ihre Überlieferung: Das Warschauer Manuskript." In *Musik in Baden-Württemberg.* Jahrbuch. Stuttgart: Metzler, 1996.

Denkmäler der Tonkunst in Österreich. Vol. 64 (XXXIII/1). Vienna, 1926.

Denkmäler der Tonkunst in Österreich. Ed. C. Schönbaum. Vol. 121. Vienna, 1971.

Derham, William. *Physico-Theology; or, A Demonstration of the Being and Attributes of God from the Works of Creation.* London, 1713.

———. *Des sittlichen Bürgers Abendschule.* Vienna, 1980.

Deutsche Zeitung, 22 and 24 December 1905.

Diner, Dan. "Negative Symbiose: Deutsche und Juden nach Auschwitz." In *Babylon: Beiträge zur jüdische Gegenwart* 1 (1986): 9–20.

———. "Negative Symbiose: Germans and Jews after Auschwitz." In *Reworking the Past: Hitler, the Holocaust, and the Historians' Debate,* ed. Peter Baldwin. Boston: Beacon Press, 1990.

Dittmar, Jens, ed. *Thomas Bernhard: Werkgeschichte.* Frankfurt am Main: Suhrkamp, 1990.

———. *Sehr geschätzte Redaktion: Leserbriefe von und über Thomas Bernhard.* Vienna: Edition S, 1991.

Dowden, Stephen D. *Understanding Thomas Bernhard.* Columbia: University of South Carolina Press, 1991.

Dreissinger, Sepp, ed. *Von einer Katastrophe in die andere: 13 Gespräche mit Thomas Bernhard.* Weitra: Bibliothek der Provinz, 1992.

Dürrenmatt, Friedrich. *Plays and Essays: The German Library.* Vol. 89. New York: Continuum, 1982.

Ekiert, Grzegorz, and Jan Kubik. *Rebellious Civil Society: Popular Protest and Democratic Consolidation in Poland, 1989–1993.* Ann Arbor: University of Michigan Press, 1999.

Eliade, Mircea. *Cosmos and History: The Myth of the Eternal Return.* Trans. William R. Trask. New York: Harper and Row, 1959.

Esslin, Martin. *The Theatre of the Absurd.* London: Eyre and Spottiswoode, 1962.

Federico, Joseph A. "Millenarianism, Legitimation, and the National Socialist Universe in Thomas Bernhard's *Vor dem Ruhestand.*" *Germanic Review* 59, no. 4 (1984): 142–48.

Feinberg, Anat. "Taboris Bremer Theater Labor: Projekte—Erfahrungen—Resultate." In *Theater gegen das Vergessen,* ed. Hans-Peter Bayerdörfer and Jörg Schönert. Tübingen: Niemeyer, 1997.

Ferguson, Faye. "Interpreting the Source Tradition of *Stein der Weisen.*" In *Mozart-Jahrbuch* 2000. Kassel: Bärenreiter Verlag, 2002.

Fest, Joachim C. *The Face of the Third Reich.* Trans. Michael Bullock. Harmondsworth: Penguin Books, 1970.

Fetting, Hugo, ed. *Max Reinhardt: Ich bin nichts als Theatermann.* Berlin: Henschelverlag, 1989.

Fiddler, Allyson. *Reviewing Reality: An Introduction to Elfriede Jelinek.* Oxford: Berg, 1994.

———. "There Goes That Word Again; or, Elfriede Jelinek and Postmodernism." In *Elfriede Jelinek: Framed by Language,* ed. Jorun B. Johns and Katherine Arens. Riverside, Calif.: Ariadne Press, 1994.

Filipowicz, Halina. "The Daughters of Emilia Plater." In *Engendering Slavic Literatures,* ed. Pamela Chester and Sibelan Forrester. Bloomington: Indiana University Press, 1996.

Fleischmann, Krista, ed. *Thomas Bernhard—Eine Erinnerung: Interviews zur Person.* Vienna: Edition S, 1992.

Fortier, Mark. *Theory/Theatre: An Introduction.* London: Routledge, 1997.

Friedländer, Saul. *Reflections of Nazism: An Essay on Kitsch and Death.* Trans. Thomas Weyr. New York: Harper and Row, 1982.

Fritsch, Sibylle. "Vom Scheitern Gottes." In *Die Deutsche Bühne* (1991).

Frodl, Gerbert. "Hans Makart." In *Das Zeitalter des Kaiser Franz Joseph: Von der Revolution zur Gründerzeit.* Vol. 1. Vienna: Niederösterreichische Landesregierung, 1984.

Fuchs, Georg. *Revolution in the Theatre.* Condensed and adapted by Constance Connor Kuhn. Ithaca: Cornell University Press, 1959.

Gall, Joseph Anton. *Liebreiche Anstalten.…* Vienna, 1787.

Galos, Adam. "Tradycje Naczelnika powstania Kościuszkowskiego i Racławic w XIX w." In *Panorama Racławicka: Materiały z sesji popularnonaukowej Wrocław 1984*, ed. Krystyn Matwijowski. Wrocław: Dolnośląskie Towarzystwo Społeczno-Kulturalne, 1987.

Gardner, Monica M. *Kościuszko: A Biography*. London: George Allen and Unwin, 1920.

Geiringer, Karl, in collaboration with Irene Geiringer. *Haydn: A Creative Life in Music*. 3rd rev. and enlarged ed. Berkeley and Los Angeles: University of California Press, 1982.

Gellner, Ernest. *Culture, Identity, and Politics*. Cambridge: Cambridge University Press, 1987.

Gluck, Christoph Willibald. "Sämtliche Werke." In *Tanzdramen: "Don Juan/Semiramis,"* ed. Richard Engländer. Series 2, vol. 1. Kassel and Basel, 1966.

Goldmark, Karl. *Notes from the Life of a Viennese Composer: Karl Goldmark*. New York, 1927.

Gotwal, Vernon. *Joseph Haydn: Eighteenth-Century Gentleman and Genius*. Madison: University of Wisconsin Press, 1963.

Gregor, Joseph. *Das Theater in der Wiener Josefstadt*. Vienna: Wiener Drucke, 1924.

Greve, Ludwig, and Werner Volke. *Jugend in Wien: Literatur um 1900*. Marbach am Neckar: Deutsches Literaturarchiv, 1974.

Grimm, Gunter E. and Hans Peter Bayerdörfer. *Im Zeichen Hiobs*. Königstein: Athenäum, 1985.

Grimminger, Rolf. "Die Utopie der vernünftigen Praxis." In *Hansers Sozialgeschichte der deutschen Literatur*. Vol. 3. Munich: Hanser, 1980.

Gross, Jan Tomasz. *Neighbors: The Destruction of the Jewish Community in Jedwabne, Poland*. Princeton: Princeton University Press, 2001.

Hamburger Abendblatt, 15 March 1903.

Haas, Robert. "*Teutsche Comoedie Arien.*" *Zeitschrift für Musikwissenschaft*. Vol. 3. Leipzig: Breitkopf und Härtel, 1921.

———. *Die Musik in der Wiener deutschen Stegreif-Komödie*. In *Studien zur Musikwissenschaft, Beihefte der Denkmäler der Tonkunst*. Vol. 12. Vienna, 1926.

———. *Gluck und Durazzo im Burgtheater*. Vienna, 1925.

Hadamowsky, Franz. *Reinhardt und Salzburg*. Salzburg: Residenzverlag, 1963.

Hahn, Wiktor. *Kościuszko w polskiej poezji dramatycznej*. Poznań: Księgarnia św. Wojciecha, 1918.

Haider-Pregler, Hilde. *Des sittlichen Bürgers Abendschule*. Vienna, 1980.

———. "Entwicklungen im Wiener Theater zur Zeit Maria Theresias." In *Österreich im Europa der Aufklärung: Internationals Symposion in Wien 20.–3. Oktober 1980*, ed. Richard Plaschka et al. Vol. 2. Vienna: Verlag der Österreichischen Akademie der Wissenschaften, 1985.

Hanslick, Eduard. *Merlin: Oper in drei Akten von Karl Goldmark*. In *Musikalisches Skizzenbuch*. Berlin, 1888.

———. *Am Ende des Jahrhunderts, 1895–1899: Musikalische Kritiken und Schilderungen*. Berlin: Allgemeiner Verein für deutsche Litteratur, 1899.

———. *Die Kriegsgefangene*. In *Aus neuer und neuester Zeit*. Berlin, 1900.

Harrison, R., and K. Wilson. *Three Viennese Comedies by J. N. Nestroy*. Columbia, S.C.: Camden House, 1986.

Heartz, Daniel. "The Genesis of *Idomeneo*." In *Mozart's Operas*, ed. Thomas Bauman. Berkeley and Los Angeles: University of California Press, 1990.

Heer, Friedrich. *Der Kampf um die österreichische Identität*. Vienna: Böhlau, 1981.

Heldenplatz: Eine Dokumentation. Vienna: Burgtheater, 1989.

Hevesi, Ludwig. *Alt Kunst—Neu Kunst*. Vienna: Carl Konegen, 1908.

Hill, Christopher. *Some Intellectual Consequences of the English Revolution*. Madison: University of Wisconsin Press, 1980.

Hoffmeister, Donna L. "Post-Modern Theater: A Contradiction in Terms? Handke, Strauss, Bernhard, and the Contemporary Scene." *Monatshefte* 79, no. 4 (1987): 424–38.

Hofmann, Kurt. *Aus Gesprächen mit Thomas Bernhard.* Munich: dtv, 1988.

Hofmannsthal, Hugo von. "Reinhardt as an International Force." Trans. Sidney Howard. In *Max Reinhardt and His Theatre*, ed. Oliver Sayler. New York: Brentano, 1924.

———. "Dritter Brief aus Wien." In *Aufzeichnungen.* Frankfurt am Main: Suhrkamp, 1959.

———. Jedermann: *Das Spiel vom Sterben des Reichen Mannes und Max Reinhardts Insze-nierungen: Texte, Dokumente, Bilder.* Ed. Edda Leisler and Gisela Prossnitz. Frankfurt am Main: Suhrkamp, 1973.

Holmberg, Arthur. "A Conversation with Robert Wilson and Heiner Müller." *Modern Drama* 31, no. 3 (1988): 454–58.

Holschneider, Andreas. "Die Judas-Macchabäus-Bearbeitung der österreichischen National-bibliothek." *Mozart-Jahrbuch,* 1960/61.

Horowitz, Sara R. "Introduction: The Idea of Fiction." In *Voicing the Void: Muteness and Memory in Holocaust Fiction.* Albany: State University of New York Press, 1997.

Hoyng, Peter. "Austrian: Petit and Haute Bourgeoisie as Obsessive Prisoners of Language: A Comparative Study of Werner Schwab's *Die Praesidentinnen* and Thomas Bernhardt's *Ritter, Dene, Voss.*" Paper presented at the Great Traditions Conference sponsored by the Center for Austrian Studies, Minneapolis, Minn., 1997.

Hunter, Mary. *The Culture of Opera Buffa in Mozart's Vienna.* Princeton: Princeton University Press: 1999.

Hutcheon, Linda. *A Poetics of Postmodernism: History, Theory, Fiction.* New York: Routledge, 1988.

———. *The Politics of Postmodernism.* London: Routledge, 1989.

Ibsen, Henrik. *A Doll's House.* In *Six Plays by Henrik Ibsen*, trans. Eva Le Gallienne. New York: Modern Library, 1951.

———. *Pillars of Society.* In *Henrik Ibsen: Four Plays*, trans. Michael Meyer. London: Methuen, 1990.

Illustriertes Wiener Extrablatt, 9 September 1903 and 22 December 1905.

Jacob, Margaret C. *The Newtonians and the English Revolution, 1689–1720.* Ithaca: Cornell University Press, 1976.

Janson, Stefan. *Hugo von Hofmannsthals* Jedermann *in der Regiebearbeitung durch Max Rein-hardt.* Frankfurt am Main: Lang, 1978.

Jauss, Hans Robert. *Toward an Aesthetic of Reception.* Trans. T. Bahti. Brighton: Harvester Press, 1982.

Jelinek, Elfriede. "Ich schlage sozusagen mit der Axt drein." *Theaterzeitschrift* 7 (1984).

———. "Was geschah, nachdem Nora Ihren Mann verlassen hatte oder Stützen der Gesellschaften." In *Theaterstücke.* Cologne: Prometh Verlag, 1984.

———. "Gespräch mit Elfriede Jelinek." Interview by Riki Winter, in *Dossier über Elfriede Jelinek*, ed. Kurt Bartsch and Günther A. Hofler. Graz: Droschl, 1992.

———. "Wir leben auf einem Berg von Leichen und Schmerz." Interview by Peter von Becker, *Theater heute* 33, no. 9 (1992).

Johnston, William M. *The Austrian Mind: An Intellectual and Social History, 1848–1938.* Berke-ley and Los Angeles: University of California Press, 1971; first paperback printing, 1983.

Kalbeck, Max. *Neues Wiener Tagblatt.* 22 February 1903.

Kann, Robert. *A Study in Austrian Intellectual History: Late Baroque to Romanticism.* London: Thames and Hudson, 1960.

Karpath, Ludwig. *Begegnungen mit dem Genius.* Vienna and Leipzig, 1934.

Kecskemeti, Istvan. "Liturgical Elements in the Opera *The Queen of Sheba* by Karl Gold-mark." In *Essays in Honor of Hanoch Avenary*, Orbis musicae, *Assaph Studies in Arts*, no. 10 (1990/91).

Kiebuzinska, Christine. "The Scandal Maker: Thomas Bernhard and the Reception of *Heldenplatz*." *Modern Drama* 38, no. 3 (1995): 378–88.

Korzon, Tadeusz. *Kościuszko: Życiorys z dokumentów wysnuty*. Kraków: Muzeum Narodowe w Rapperswylu, 1894.

Kowecki, Jerzy. "The Kościuszko Insurrection: Continuation and Radicalization of Change." Trans. Jerzy Kołodziej and Mary Helen Ayres. In *Constitution and Reform in Eighteenth-Century Poland*, ed. Samuel Fiszman. Bloomington: Indiana University Press, 1997.

Kraszewski, Józef Ignacy. *Równy wojewodzie*. Poznań, 1868.

Kraus, Karl. "Nestroy und die Nachwelt: Zum 50. Todestage." *Die Fackel* 349–50. Vienna, 1912.

Krauss, Rosalind. "Poststructuralism and the 'Paraliterary.'" *October* 13 (1980).

Kurzreiter, Martin. *Sprachkritik als Ideologiekritik bei Fritz Mauthner*. Frankfurt am Main: Lang, 1993.

La Grange, Henry-Louis de. *Gustav Mahler*. Vol. 2. Oxford, 1995.

Landes, Brigitte. "Kunst aus Kakanien: Über Elfriede Jelinek." *Theater heute* 27, no. 1 (1968).

Langer, Lawrence L. *The Holocaust and the Literary Imagination*. New Haven: Yale University Press, 1975.

Lederer, Max, ed. *Heinrich Joseph von Collin und sein Kreis: Briefe und Aktenstücke*. Archiv für Österreichische Geschichte 109/1. Vienna, 1921.

Lewin, David. "*Moses und Aron*: Some General Remarks, and Analytic Notes for Act I, Scene 1." *Perspectives of New Music* 6, no. 1 (1967).

Löffler, Sigrid. "Die Gegenwart der Vergangenheit: Das KZ-*Stück Die Kannibalen* und die Fall-Szenen *Schuldig geboren* als Saisonauftakt in George Taboris Wiener 'Kreis'-Theater." *Theater heute* 11 (1987).

———. "Taboris Träume." *Theater heute* 12 (1988): 5–8.

Lubicz-Pachoński, Jan. *Wojciech Bartosz Głowacki: Chłopski bohater spod Racławic i Szczekocin*. Warsaw: Państwowe Wydawnictwo Naukowe, 1987.

Lyotard, Jean-François. "Ticket to a New Décor." Trans. Brian Massumi and W. G. J. Niesluchowski. *Copyright* 1 (1987).

———. *The Differend*. Trans. Georges Van Den Abbeele. Minneapolis: University of Minnesota Press, 1988.

Mahler, Gustav. *Briefe*. Ed. Herta Blaukopf. Vienna and Hamburg, 1982.

Majeranowski, Konstanty. *Pierwsza miłość Kościuszki*. Kraków, 1820.

Makk, Stefan. "Ein politisches Stück übers Kapital." *Kleine Zeitung*, 6 October 1979.

Malkin, Jeanette. *Verbal Violence in Contemporary Drama: From Handke to Shepard*. Cambridge: Cambridge University Press, 1992.

———. "Thomas Bernhard, Jews, *Heldenplatz*." In *Staging the Holocaust: The Shoah in Drama and Performance*, ed. Claude Schumacher. Cambridge: Cambridge University Press, 1998.

Mańkowska, Bogusława. *Tadeusz Kościuszko, czyli cztery chwile życia tego bohatera*. Poznań, 1880.

Manning, Susan. *Ecstasy and the Demon: Feminism and Nationalism in the Dances of Mary Wigman*. Berkeley and Los Angeles: University of California Press, 1993.

Mauthner, Fritz. "Nietzsche und Sprachkritik." In *Beiträge zu einer Kritik der Sprache*. Vol. 1, *Zur Sprache und zur Psychologie*. 2nd ed. Stuttgart and Berlin: Cotta, 1906.

Mautner, Franz H. *Nestroy*. Heidelberg: Stiehm, 1974.

Mendelssohn, Moses. "Abhandlung über die Evidenz in metaphysischen Wissenschaften." In *Gesammelte Schriften—Jubiläumsausgabe*, ed. Alexander Altmann et al. Vol. 2. Stuttgart-Bad Canstatt: Frommann-Holzboog, 1972.

Metastasio, Pietro. *Tutte le opere: A cura di Bruno Brunelli*. Vol. 5. Milan: Mondadori, 1954.

Meyerhofer, Nicholas J. *Thomas Bernhard*. Berlin: Colloquium, 1985.

Miller, J. Hillis. *The Ethics of Reading: Kant, de Man, Eliot, Trollope, James, and Benjamin*. New York: Columbia University Press, 1987.

Mitscherlich, Alexander, and Margarete Mitscherlich. *Die Unfähigkeit zu trauern*. Munich: Piper, 1967.

Mitzner, Piotr. "Epoka Majeranowskiego." *Pamiętnik Teatralny* 39, nos. 3–4 (1990): 337–58.

———. "*Kościuszki pod Racławicami* droga na scenę." In *Dramat i teatr pozytywistyczny*, ed. Dobrochna Ratajczakowa. Wrocław: Wiedza o Kulturze, 1992.

Natoli, Joseph, and Linda Hutcheon. "Introduction: Reading a Postmodern Reader." In *A Postmodern Reader*, ed. Joseph Natoli and Linda Hutcheon. Ithaca: Cornell University Press, 1993.

Neue Freie Presse, 8 October 1904.

Neues Wiener Journal, 22 December 1905.

Newman, Michael. "Revisiting Modernism, Representing Modernism." In *Postmodernism*, ed. Lisa Appignanesi. London: Institute of Contemporary Arts, 1986.

Niemann, Walter. *Die Musik seit Wagner*. Berlin, 1913.

Nietzsche, Friedrich. *Menschliches, Allzumenschliches: Ein Buch für freie Geister*. Stuttgart: Kröner, 1964.

———. *Der Fall Wagner*. Ed. Giorgio Colli and Mazzino Montinari. Kritische Studienausgabe, vol. 6. Munich, 1988.

Nussbaum, Martha. *Love's Knowledge: Essays on Philosophy and Literature*. New York: Oxford University Press, 1990.

———. *Poetic Justice: The Literary Imagination and Public Life*. Boston: Beacon Press, 1995.

Nyssen, Ute. "Afterword to Jelinek." In *Theaterstücke*. Cologne: Prometh Verlag, 1984.

Ong, Walter. *The Presence of the Word: Some Prolegomena for Cultural and Religious History*. New Haven: Yale University Press, 1967.

Österreichische Nationalbibliothek, Handschriftensammlung, Cod. 9717, fol. 538.

Österreichisches Staatsarchiv. Abt. Allgemeines Verwaltungsarchiv. Studienhofkommission (bis 1791).

Palmer, R. R. *The Age of the Democratic Revolution: A Political History of Europe and America, 1760–1800*. Vol. 2. Princeton: Princeton University Press, 1964.

Patraka, Vivian M. "Fascist Ideology and Theatricalization." In *Critical Theory and Performance*, ed. Janelle G. Reinelt and Joseph R. Roach. Ann Arbor: University of Michigan Press, 1992.

———. *Spectacular Suffering: Theatre, Fascism, and the Holocaust*. Bloomington: Indiana University Press, 1999.

Peters, Sibylle. "Die Verwandlung der Schrift in Spiel: George Tabori's Metaphysik des Theaters: Die Goldberg-Variationen." In *Theater gegen das Vergessen: Bühnenarbeit und Drama bei George Tabori*, ed. Hans-Peter Bayerdörfer and Jörg Schönert. Tübingen: Niemeyer, 1997.

Pfabigan, Alfred. "Breaking Traditions: Fin de Siècle 1896 and 1966." *Partisan Review* 64, no. 2 (1997): 205–10.

———. *Thomas Bernhard—Ein österreichisches Weltexperiment*. Vienna: Zsolnay, 1999.

Platoff, John. "The Buffa Aria in Mozart's Vienna." *Cambridge Opera Journal* 2, no. 2 (July 1990): 99–120.

Pockels, Carl Friedrich. *Versuch einer Charakteristik des weiblichen Geschlechts: Ein Sittengemaehlde des Menschen, des Zeitalters und des geselligen Lebens…*. 4 vols. Hannover, 1797–1801.

Porter, Roy. "The Enlightenment in England." In *The Enlightenment in National Context*, ed. Roy Porter and Mikulás Teich. Cambridge: Cambridge University Press, 1981.

Pula, James S. *Thaddeus Kościuszko: The Purest Son of Liberty*. New York: Hippocrene Books, 1999.

Ratajczakowa, Dobrochna. *Obrazy narodowe w dramacie i teatrze*. Wrocław: Wiedza o Kulturze, 1994.

———. "*Kościuszko pod Racławicami* Anczyca—arcydzieło patriotycznej sceny popularnej." In *Kościuszko—powstanie 1794 r.—tradycja: Materiały z sesji naukowej w 200-lecie powstania kościuszkowskiego 15–16 kwietnia 1994 r.*, ed. Jerzy Kowecki. Warsaw: Biblioteka Narodowa, 1997.

Reinhardt, Max. "In Search of a Living Theatre." Trans. Lucie R. Sayler. In *Max Reinhardt and His Theatre*, ed. Oliver Sayler. New York: Brentano, 1924.

Ricoeur, Paul. "The Narrative Function." In *Paul Ricoeur, Hermeneutics, and the Human Sciences: Essays on Language, Action, and Interpretation*, ed. and trans. John B. Thompson. Cambridge: Cambridge University Press; Paris: Editions de la Maison de Sciences de l'Homme, 1981.

Rommel, Otto. "Die Maschinenkomödie." In *Barocktradition im österreichisch-bayrischen Volkstheater*. Vol. 1. Leipzig, 1935.

———. *Die Alt-Wiener Volkskomödie*. Vienna, 1952.

Rosen, Charles. *The Classical Style: Haydn, Mozart, Beethoven*. Expanded ed. New York: Norton, 1997.

Rothschild, Thomas. "Hitler in Wien." *Die Deutsche Bühne* 7 (1987).

Roussel, P[ierre]. *Système physique et moral de la femme....* 1st ed., 1775; new ed., Paris, 1803.

Różewicz, Tadeusz. *The Trap*. Trans. Adam Czerniawski. Amsterdam: Harwood, 1997.

Ruppert, Wolfgang. "Volksaufklärung im späten 18. Jahrhundert." In *Hansers Sozialgeschichte der deutschen Literatur*. Vol. 3. 2nd ed. Munich: Hanser, 1980.

Russell, Charles. "The Context of the Concept." In *Romanticism, Modernism, Postmodernism*, ed. Harry R. Garvin. Lewisburg, Pa.: Bucknell University Press, 1980.

Sadie, Stanley, ed. *The New Grove Dictionary of Music and Musicians*. London: Macmillan, 1980.

Sayler, Oliver M., ed. *Max Reinhardt and His Theatre*. New York: Brentano, 1924.

Schierl, Barbara Maria. *"Tabori-Theater," Shakespeare und Wien/Theater als Therapie: Theater als Lebensform./Zur Rezeption der Wiener Theaterarbeit des George Tabori von 1986 bis 1990: Eine Dokumentation*. Vienna: Diplomarbeit, 1991.

Schillers Werke. Bibliothek Deutscher Klassiker. Berlin and Weimar: Aufbau Verlag, 1974.

Schindlecker, Eva. "Holzfällen: Eine Erregung: Dokumentation eines österreichischen Literaturskandals." In *Statt Bernhard: Über Misanthropie im Werk Thomas Bernhards*, ed. W. Schmidt-Dengler and M. Huber. Vienna: Edition S, 1987.

Schindler, Anton. *Biographie von Ludwig van Beethoven*. Vol. 1. Münster, 1860.

Schlueter, June. *Metafictional Characters in Modern Drama*. New York: Columbia University Press, 1979.

Schmitz, Arnold. "Beethovens Religiosität." In *Bericht über den I. musikwissenschaftlichen Kongreß der deutschen Musikgesellschaft in Leipzig*. Leipzig: Breitkopf und Härtel, 1926.

Schoenberg, Arnold. *Die glückliche Hand*. Universal Edition 13613.

———. *Erwartung*. Universal Edition 13612.

———. *Moses und Aron*. Edition Eulenburg 8004.

Scholem, Gershem. *Major Trends in Jewish Mysticism*. New York: Schocken Books, 1941.

Schorske, Carl E. *Fin-de-Siècle Vienna: Politics and Culture*. New York: Knopf, 1980. Reprint, New York: Vintage Books, 1981.

Schwartz, Joel. *The Sexual Politics of Jean-Jacques Rousseau.* Chicago: University of Chicago Press, 1984.

Seebohm, Andrea, ed. *The Vienna Opera.* New York: Rizzoli, 1987.

Seidl, Arthur. *Die Wagner-Nachfolge im Musik-Drama.* Berlin and Leipzig, 1902.

Sheriff, John K. *The Good-Natured Man: The Evolution of a Moral Ideal, 1660–1800.* University, Ala.: University of Alabama Press, 1982.

Sichrovsky, Heinz. "Heimgekehrt: Voss in einem tiefschwarzen Auschwitz-Drama." In *News* (Vienna) 13 (1996).

Simms, Bryan R. "Whose Idea Was *Erwartung?*" In *Constructive Dissonance: Arnold Schoenberg and the Transformations of Twentieth-Century Culture,* ed. Juliane Brand and Christopher Hailey. Berkeley and Los Angeles: University of California Press, 1997.

Singer, Irvin. *Mozart and Beethoven: The Concept of Love in Their Operas.* Baltimore, Md.: Johns Hopkins University Press, 1977.

Skloot, Robert. "Introduction." In *The Theatre of the Holocaust: Four Plays,* ed. Robert Skloot. Madison: University of Wisconsin Press, 1982.

———. *The Darkness We Carry: The Drama of the Holocaust.* Madison: University of Wisconsin Press, 1988.

———. Review of *Stages of Annihilation: Theatrical Representations of the Holocaust,* by Edward R. Isser. *Shofar: An Interdisciplinary Journal of Jewish Studies* 17, no. 4 (1999): 140–42.

Solomon, Maynard. "Beethoven and Schiller." In *Beethoven Essays.* Cambridge: Harvard University Press, 1988.

———. "The Ninth Symphony." In *Beethoven Essays.* Cambridge: Harvard University Press, 1988.

Sorell, Walter, ed., trans. *The Mary Wigman Book: Her Writings Edited and Translated.* Middletown, Conn.: Wesleyan University Press, 1975.

Sorg, Bernhard. *Thomas Bernhard.* Munich: Beck, 1992.

Spalding, Johann Joachim. *Die Bestimmung des Menschen.* Rev. ed. Leipzig, 1768.

Specht, Richard. *Gustav Mahler.* Berlin: Schuster and Loeffler, 1913.

Steblin, Rita. *A History of Key Characteristics in the Eighteenth and Early Nineteenth Centuries.* Ann Arbor: University of Michigan Press, 1983. Reprint, Rochester, N.Y.: Eastman Studies in Music, University of Rochester Press, 1996.

Stein, Leonard, ed. *Style and Idea: Selected Writings of Arnold Schoenberg.* Trans. Leo Black. Berkeley: University of California Press, 1984.

Steptoe, Andrew. *The Mozart-Da Ponte Operas.* New York: Oxford University Press, 1988.

Stern, Martin. "Haydns 'Schöpfung'. Geist und Herkunft des van Swietenschen Librettos." In *Haydn-Studien* (Cologne) 1, no. 3 (1966).

Stuckenschmidt, H. H. *Arnold Schoenberg.* Schirmer Books, 1977.

Sulzer, Johann Georg. *Allgemeine Theorie der schönen Künste.* 2nd ed. Leipzig, 1792–94.

Tabori, George. *Unterammergau oder Die guten Deutschen.* Frankfurt am Main: Suhrkamp, 1981.

———. *The Cannibals.* In *The Theatre of the Holocaust: Four Plays,* ed. Robert Skloot. Madison: University of Wisconsin Press, 1982.

———. *Interview: Programmbuch,* no. 17 (6 May 1987), Burgtheater, Akademie-Bühne, Vienna.

———. *Theaterstücke.* 2 vols. Frankfurt am Main: Sixcher Tb 12301/2, 1994.

———. *Die Ballade vom Wiener Schnitzler. Theater heute* 5 (1996).

———. *Interview. Tiroler Tageszeitung,* 20 September 1997.

———. "Metaphysik des Theaters: Die Goldberg-Variationen." In *Theater gegen das Vergessen. Bühnenarbeit und Drama bei George Tabori,* ed. Hans-Peter Bayerdörfer and Jörg Schönert. Tübingen: Niemeyer, 1997.

Thompson, James R. Review of *Thaddeus Kościuszko: The Purest Son of Liberty*, by James S. Pula. *The Sarmatian Review* 20, no. 1 (2000): 678–80.

Thomson, James. *Poetical Works I.* Ed. J. Logie Robertson. London: Oxford University Press, 1908.

Thornton, Samuel. *Laban's Theory of Movement: A New Perspective.* Boston: Plays, 1971.

Timofeev, A. G. "M. Kuzmin." In *Teatr IV.* Oakland, Calif.: Berkeley Slavic Specialties, 1994.

Tozzi, Lorenzo. "Musica e balli al Regio di Torino (1748–1762)." *La Danza Italiana* 2 (1985).

Traum und Wirklichkeit: Wien 1870–1930. Vienna: Historisches Museum der Stadt Wien, 1985.

"Vanguard of the Liberated Waltz," *Austria Kultur* 5, no. 6 (November/December 1995).

Voss, Alexander, ed. *Briefe von J. H. Voss nebst erläuternden Beilagen.* Vol. 1. Halberstadt, 1829.

Vossische Zeitung (Berlin), 15 June 1913.

Wagner, Richard. *Richard Wagner's Prose Works.* Trans. William A. Ellis. New York: Broude, 1966.

Walicki, Andrzej. *The Enlightenment and the Birth of Modern Nationhood: Polish Political Thought from Noble Republicanism to Tadeusz Kościuszko.* Trans. Emma Harris. Notre Dame, Ind.: University of Notre Dame Press, 1989.

Wangermann, Ernst. "Maria Theresa: A Reforming Monarchy." In *The Courts of Europe: Politics, Patronage, and Royalty, 1400–1800*, ed. Arthur G. Dickens. London: Thames and Hudson, 1977.

———. *Aufklärung und staatsbürgerliche Erziehung: Gottfried van Swieten als Reformator des österreichischen Unterrichtswesens 1781–1791.* Vienna: Verlag für Geschichte u. Politik, 1978.

———. "Revolution in Music—Music in Revolution." In *Revolution in History*, ed. Roy Porter and Mikulás Teich. Cambridge: Cambridge University Press, 1986.

———. "Gesellschaftliche und moralische Anliegen der österreichischen Aufklärung." In *Europa im Zeitalter Mozarts*, Schriftenreihe der österreichischen Gesellschaft zur Erforschung des 18. Jahrhunderts 5, ed. Moritz Csáky and Walter Pass. Vienna: Böhlau, 1995.

Wedekind, Frank. *Prosa: Erzählungen, Aufsätze, Selbstzeugnisse, Briefe*, ed. Manfred Hahn. Berlin and Weimar: Aufbau, 1969.

Weiler, Gershon. *Mauthner's Critique of Language.* Cambridge: Cambridge University Press, 1970.

Welker, Andrea, and Tina Berger, eds. *Improvisationen über Shakespeares Shylock: Dokumentation einer Theaterarbeit.* Munich: Kammerspiele, 1974.

"Weshalb wir eine Zeitschrift herausgeben?" *Ver Sacrum* 1 (June 1898).

Wheelock, Gretchen A. "*Schwarze Gredel* and the Engendered Minor Mode in Mozart's Operas." In *Musicology and Difference: Gender and Sexuality in Music Scholarship*, ed. Ruth A. Solie. Berkeley and Los Angeles: University of California Press, 1993.

———. "Konstanze Performs Constancy." In *Siren Songs: Representations of Gender and Sexuality in Opera*, ed. Mary Ann Smart. Princeton: Princeton University Press, 2000.

Willey, Basil. *The English Moralists.* London: Chatto and Windus, 1964.

Wilson, Andrew. *Medical Researches: Being an Enquiry into the Nature and Origin of Hysterics in the Female Constitution, and into the Distinction between that Disease and Hypochondriac or Nervous Disorders....* London, 1776.

Wilson, Lindsay. *Women and Medicine in the French Enlightenment.* Baltimore, Md.: Johns Hopkins University Press, 1993.

Winter, Marian Hannah. *The Pre-Romantic Ballet.* London: Pitman and Sons, 1974.

Winther, Fritz. *Körperbildung als Kunst und Pflicht.* Munich: Delphin, n.d.

Witzmann, Reingard, ed. *Die neue Körpersprache: Grete Wiesenthal und ihr Tanz.* Vienna: Eigenverlag der Museen der Stadt Wien, 1986.

Yates, W. E. *Nestroy: Satire and Parody in Viennese Popular Comedy.* Cambridge: Cambridge University Press, 1972.

———. *Nestroy and the Critics.* Columbia, S.C.: Camden House, 1994.

Young, James E. *Writing and Rewriting the Holocaust: Narrative and the Consequences of Interpretation.* Bloomington: Indiana University Press, 1990.

Záloha, Jiří. "The Chateau Theater in Cesky Krumlov." In *The Baroque Theater in the Chateau of Cesky Krumlov.* Miscellany of papers for a special seminar, 1993.

Żeleński, Tadeusz. *Pisma.* Ed. Henryk Markiewicz. Vol. 25. Warsaw: Państwowy Instytut Wydawniczy, 1968.

Zeman, Herbert. "Das Textbuch Gottfried van Swietens zu Joseph Haydns 'Die Schöpfung'." In *Die Österreichische Literatur: Ihr Profil an der Wende vom 18. Zum 19. Jahrhundert (1750– 1830),* ed. Herbert Zeman. Graz: Akademische Verlagsanstalt, 1979.

INDEX